NEEDLEWORK

an illustrated history

Edited by
Harriet Bridgeman and
Elizabeth Drury

NEEDLEWORK

an illustrated history

PADDINGTON PRESS LTD
NEW YORK & LONDON
OPTIMUM PUBLISHING COMPANY LIMITED

Library of Congress Cataloging in Publication Data

Bridgeman, Harriet.
  Needlework: an illustrated history.

  Bibliography: p.
  Includes index.
  1. Needlework–History.   I. Drury, Elizabeth,
joint author.   II. Title.
TT750.B84   746.4'09   78–7238
ISBN 0 7092 0045 5
ISBN 0 448 22066 0 (U.S. only)
ISBN 0 88890 093 7 (Canada only)

Filmset in England by Servis Filmsetting Limited
Printed and bound in Hong Kong
Color separations by Photoprint Plates,

Designed by Richard Johnson and Patricia Pillay,
assisted by Sarisberie Designs
Endpapers: Photographed by Richard Johnson

IN THE UNITED STATES
PADDINGTON PRESS
Distributed by
GROSSET & DUNLAP

IN THE UNITED KINGDOM
PADDINGTON PRESS

IN CANADA
Published simultaneously by
OPTIMUM PUBLISHING COMPANY LIMITED
For information, address:
Optimum Publishing Company Limited
Michael S. Baxendale – Director
245 rue St-Jacques
Montreal, Quebec H2Y 1M6

IN SOUTH AFRICA
Distributed by
ERNEST STANTON (PUBLISHERS) (PTY.) LTD.

Contents

Preface

Needlework: An Illustrated History is a comprehensive survey of needlework in the Western world. It has proved an ambitious undertaking since there exists no precedent and consequently we have been dependent on the scholarship and patient cooperation of the many experts to whom we have turned. Each has supplied us with an essay on the history of needlework in their country, or the country of which they have specialist knowledge, and in a number of cases these comprehensive historical surveys are unique.

The starting point for each essay has been the earliest known ecclesiastical or secular embroidery. The contributors have charted the course and development of the embroiderer's art in each country right up to the present day failing that, the moment at which needlework ceased in the nineteenth or twentieth centuries to play a significant part in a country's professional or leisure activities or contribute anything to its artistic heritage. Contributors have been generous in divulging the results of their most recent research which in some instances has not yet been published in scholarly periodicals.

To avoid duplicating the explanation of words and technical terms that may be unfamiliar to some readers, the definitions have been confined to the comprehensive glossary, compiled by Pamela Clabburn the author of *The Needleworker's Dictionary*. The glossary is illustrated by original artwork and constitutes an invaluable and totally separate section, somewhat similar to a needleworker's *vade mecum* since the major part of the artwork incidentally illustrates how the stitches are executed.

Over 220 black-and-white and 100 color pictures of pieces of needlework from museums and private collections from all over the world illustrate the objects which are described within the chapters, contemporary embroiderers at work, embroidery *in situ* and anything else which is relevant or necessary for an understanding of the subject.

An extensive bibliography for each country lists the major books published throughout the world which will enable interested readers to continue their studies. An index completes this invaluable reference book.

We, as editors of this project, have been enormously helped and encouraged by Mr. Donald King, Keeper of the Department of Textiles and Dress at the Victoria and Albert Museum, London. It is on account of his international reputation as a scholar that experts, already heavily committed to other work, so kindly agreed to write for us since they were aware, as we were, of the value and need for such a book. It is again on account of Mr. King's scholarship and kindness in scrutinizing the book on completion to ensure that no inaccuracies have occurred in the course of translation that we feel confident that the book will be of use and interest; not only to the general reader interested in needlework but also the museum specialist.

Thanks are also due to Miss Pamela Clabburn for her careful reading of texts, enabling her to write precise definitions for the glossary. Miss Santina Levey of the Department of Textiles at the Victoria and Albert Museum for her considerable help and advice; Linda Parry, Pauline Johnstone, Madeleine Ginsburg and Valerie Mendes of the Victoria and Albert Museum; John MacDonald of the Lady Lever Art Gallery; Anne Tucker of Chertsey Museum, Surrey; Deirdre Dandy of the Guildford Museum, Surrey; Mrs. O. M. Matthews for permission to use the illustration of the man's cap; Miss Francesca Barran of the National Trust; National Federation of Women's Institutes for permission to reproduce *The Country Wife*; The Master and Wardens of the Worshipful Company of Merchant Taylors; The Rev. Murray Grant of the church of St. James the Less, Pimlico, for permission to reproduce G. E. Street's altar frontal; Madeleine Jarry of the Mobilier National, Paris; A. Frandenburg of the Musée de Cluny, Paris; Bertrand Jestaz of the Louvre, Paris;

Nadine Gasc and Mariette Sfez of the
Musée des Arts Décoratifs, Paris;
Pierre Lemoine of the Musée de
Versailles; Nicole Hubert of the
Musée de Malmaison; J. M.
Tuschscherer of the Musée Historique
des Tissus, Lyons; Bernard
Tassinari of the firm Tassinari and
Châtel, Lyons; Audrey Walker;
Kathleen Glaskin; Natalia Stucley;
Linda Postan; Elisabet Hidemark; The
Smithsonian Institution, Washington;
Mr. Carl Nodl of the Österreichisches
Museum für Angewandte Kunst; Mr.
Guy Delmarcel of the Musées Royaux
d'Art et d'Histoire, Brussels; Mr. A.
Sioen of the Guild of St. George,
Ghent; Mr. K. Vanderhoeght of the
Kredietbank, Brussels; Drs. Gerard
Th. M. Lemens of the Nijmeegs
Museum, Nijmegen; Mr. Obereigner
of the Historical Museum, Prague;
Razvan Theodorescu of the
Institutul de Istorial Artei, Prague; Dr.
Alena Plessingerova of the Narodni
Museum V. Praze, Prague; The
Director of the Museum Narodwe,
Cracow; Dr. Tamas Hoffmann of the
Ethnographical Museum, Budapest;
Dr. Pal. Miklov of the Iparmuveszeti
Museum, Budapest; Dr. Zeljka
Bjelcic of the Zamaljski Muzej,
Yugoslavia; Dr. Mario Petric of the
Etnografski Muzej, Zagreb; Professor
Hadjinkolor of the Bulgarian Academy
of Sciences, Ethnographical Museum
and Institute Zagreb and Mr. Emilion
Pitta of the Benaki Museum, Athens.
A.D.A.G.P; John Bethell; Gunnlaugur
S.E. Briem; Sally Chappell; Cooper-
Bridgeman Library; Dansk Folke-
museum; Martin Drury; Ray Gardner;
Gisli Gestsson; Michael Holförd
Library; Angelo Hornak; Allan Hurst;
Millar & Harris; John Mills Photog-
raphy Ltd; Myndidn; National Trust;
Professor Pylkkänen; Gordon
Roberton; Statens Historiska Museum,
Stockholm; Studio Helsinki; Victoria
and Albert Museum, London; Vilanova;
Mary Lawrence Wathen.

HARRIET BRIDGEMAN
AND ELIZABETH DRURY
London, 1978

Introduction

NEEDLEWORK IS AN EXTRAORDINARILY versatile art incorporating all work done with a needle – whether embroidery, tapestry, quilting, smocking or patchwork. It is also extremely adaptable. It spans centuries, continents and social classes. It has been practiced by men and women, royalty and ecclesiastics. It has decorated aristocratic costume, peasant dress and even domestic furnishing and has been worked hand in hand with other forms of art – painting, sculpture and engraving.

The enormous range of materials and techniques that needleworkers have employed throughout history shows that needlework can be enjoyed by anyone with enthusiasm, time and patience – rich and poor alike. It has served practical purposes, such as livening up and strengthening inexpensive cloth, but it has also been used for ostentatious displays of wealth and power by the courts and churches of Europe. For modern purposes, the surviving needlework of the past provides a fascinating historical picture of different times – often being a crucial primary source for social historians. Having suffered a decline during the nineteenth century, needlework has since been revived to become an extremely popular pastime today.

Over the years the inhabitants of the Western world, from the Indians of North America to the aristocrats and peasants of Europe and Scandinavia, developed their own distinctive needlework styles so that regional differences became very marked. North American Indians decorated their garments with beadwork, quillwork and fish-skin and fur appliqué; the Swiss acquired an international reputation for their white embroidery on handkerchieves and underclothes; the French used expensive materials such as silk, linen and gold and silver thread; and the Scandinavians employed simple materials, like home-spun woolen yarn either natural in color or tinted with vegetable dyes.

All countries had different customs which gave needleworkers great opportunities to experiment with their skills. In Norway, beautifully embroidered cloths were used to cover the bread which guests traditionally brought with them to feasts; in the Minho region in Portugal, typical peasant needlework was the "sweetheart handkerchief" which young girls embroidered to give to the man of their choice; and in Finland, the embroidery on the bridegroom's shirt was the customary way of demonstrating the sewing skills of the bride.

The social class of needleworkers who have worked as amateurs or professionals over the centuries has ranged from members of European royal families to the humblest peasant woman. Mary, Queen of Scots, worked on numerous embroidery projects during her long captivity, while the milkmaids in eighteenth-century Denmark spent the long winter evenings spinning and producing needlework of outstanding quality.

Perhaps surprisingly, the contribution made by men to the art of needlework has been considerable – though, indeed, their rôle tended to be that of the chief designer rather than of the artisan. During the middle ages, the majority of professional needleworkers were male with women working for them. In Poland, where there was a strong tradition of gold and pearl embroidery, such work was done by men while women worked on finer embroideries and linen. As early as the thirteenth century in France, there was a guild system for embroiderers which included both men and women. Strong family traditions were maintained because sons and sons-in-law of master-broderers were favored.

Needlework has certainly played a significant rôle in politics in the past. The French court, in particular, relied on embroidery to glorify its position. A garment made for Charles of Orléans had sleeves embroidered with the words and music of a popular song with 568 pearls used to represent the musical notes. The Duchess of Burgundy, who was married in 1697 at the age of twelve, was required to wear a wedding dress which is described by contemporary chroniclers as so laden with embroidery that she could scarcely walk.

The Church everywhere employed large numbers of men and women who used gold, silver, precious stones and enamels to embroider elaborate ecclesiastical vestments and hangings for the church. Nuns provided their convents with beautifully worked materials and also taught young girls at school to sew.

By the eighteenth century, and particularly in the United States, private boarding schools existed where young women were taught the skills of the needle.

Needleworkers have rarely worked in isolation. Their debt to painting, sculpture, woodwork and illumination has always been considerable. In the middle ages, the collaboration between artists and embroiderers in Antwerp was so close that they all belonged to the same guild – the guild of St. Luke – and embroiderers were known as *acu pictores*, or painters with the needle. Florentine embroideries depicted figures specifically so that they would resemble frescoes, and in the early fifteenth century, German embroidery took on the character of late Gothic sculptures as figures were created by highly raised embroidery work.

For a long time, engraving was regarded as sufficiently serious an art form to be used as a model by embroiderers, but each engraving obviously had a limited audience. The printed pattern books, which appeared in the sixteenth century, had the radical effect of popularizing and disseminating the art of needlework over a considerably wide area. The different designs and techniques which they illustrated were copied by everybody – particularly the amateur needleworker. This common source of inspiration, together with books containing botanical and bestiary notes and designs, was responsible for a slight reduction in regional differences and the move toward the adoption of an international style.

Samplers too, played a part in propagating designs from embroidery pattern books. The earliest dated English sampler was made in 1598 and is now in London's Victoria and Albert Museum. Until the eighteenth century, when samplers became objects for display and not merely references for stitches and patterns, they were responsible for

passing on old designs from generation to generation and country to country.

By the nineteenth century, embroiderers began to take patterns from single design sheets or journals and periodicals which published them. Of course, in the same way today, women's magazines encourage a considerable number of enthusiastic needleworkers everywhere while many adult education centers are now offering instruction in this age-old art.

Embroiderers did not, however, always use abstract designs in their work; they frequently took simple subjects from contemporary everyday life and developed them. Thus social documentation has always been an important element of needlework. The famous Bradford table carpet, made in England in the sixteenth century, for example, offers an almost complete lesson in Elizabethan social history – showing the manor house with its fashionably dressed inhabitants, the village buildings and the villagers involved in their various occupations. Another example of how invaluable needlework can be to social historians is the wool embroidery created in medieval Germany. There is little information about this period but the surviving needlework of the time throws considerable light on what might otherwise be unknown – depicting such details as the extravagant, parti-colored dresses women wore at the time.

The nineteenth century witnessed a concentration of needlework on peasant clothes in Central and South East Europe. This was partly due to more prosperity among the peasantry at the time, but also to strong nationalist feelings directed toward foreign rulers, whether Habsburgs or Turks. Every single country, district and even valley, produced its own distinctive embroidery pattern which was seen almost as a uniform. A similar localization was so apparent in Russia, that a contemporary observer, Martha Wilmot, commented: "In the villages you may distinguish newcomers from local inhabitants as neither party will alter a single point in conformity to the other."

The volume of needlework produced in a country can also be a reflection on the type of life being led at that time. The early pioneers in North America struggled hard on the land and had little time for leisure activities like needlework. But by the second half of the eighteenth century, the demands of early colonial life had been replaced by a less strenuous existence so more time was available for needlework and experimentation with sophisticated designs and techniques. Even so, the country was still not rich, so the smallest pieces of fabric were saved for quilts, while worn sheets and blankets were used as linings and interlinings. During the economic depression of the 1930s used fabrics were again employed for the utilitarian quilt – quilting being a technique which makes for warmth even when fabrics are thin.

Just as craft people in the other arts have always reacted against increasing conformity and industrialization, so needleworkers have had their own movements and styles. Although the Industrial Revolution, bringing with it its fast machines and synthetic textiles, forced needlework into a decline for several decades, today the number of needleworkers is growing again. New techniques and materials such as paper, glue, stone and ceramics, are being experimented with to make needlework, an art with a rich and lavish history, as exciting and accessible as it has always been.

United States

IN THE EARLY YEARS OF THE COLONIES that were eventually to become the United States, fabric was a precious commodity. The land was abundant with raw materials but manufacture, to turn this material into a usable product, was slow in evolving. The seventeenth century was a time of struggle simply to survive the rigors of a new, unsettled land.

Quilt Making

There are letters in the American Antiquarian Society Collection that were written between the years 1663 and 1684 by John Hall, a London merchant, and Madame Rebekah Symonds, his mother, which give glimpses into life in seventeenth-century New England. To his mother John Hall sent, from England, fashion books, rich articles of dress and accounts of life in London, while she, living in Ipswich, Massachusetts, informed him of the danger of invasion from Indians who inhabited the forests around them. She also remarked on the lack of facilities for comfortable living and the denial of luxuries to many, while those extremes of luxury enjoyed by a privileged few may well have equaled those enjoyed by their English counterparts of the same period.

But the story of America is that of the less-privileged men and women who were rich in land but nonetheless had to struggle for survival. They were not peasants, nor was their work in any true sense "folk art," but living was simple and hard and what time was available for leisure occupations such as needlework reflect this life.

Apart from clothing itself, bedcovers were essential to survive in the cold climate of the New England settlements. The few possessions that the colonists managed to bring with them were jealously safeguarded and carefully used. As these wore away, they were patched, pieced together and used again. The stitching helped to reinforce the aging fabric.

The early American quilt was one of pure utility. No examples of seventeenth-century quilts have survived but tough though worn examples of wool fabrics from the period pieced together in the simplest way would give an idea of what they might have looked like.

By the second half of the eighteenth century, the demands of the early colonial life in clearing the land and generally sustaining existence had been replaced by a less strenuous domestic routine. The consequent increase in their free time meant that housewives could give more consideration to the decorative aspect of such utilitarian concerns as quilt making. At the same time a more plentiful supply of both domestic and imported fabrics was available. Because of this fabrics came to be used more extravagantly. Some quilts were, for example, pieced in a definite pattern, while others were made with the entire top of one fabric which was then decorated with a quilted design. But the old habit of thrift in the use of fabric scraps was not forsaken. The smallest pieces were saved and used, and worn sheets and blankets often served as linings or interlinings.

There are three quilts from one family, the Copps of Stonington, Massachusetts, that reflect the three distinct types, all typical of eighteenth-century North America: the quilted counterpane; the pieced quilt in an overall repeated pattern but of different fabrics; and the pieced quilt in a single motif design using different fabrics.

The quilted counterpane is made of water camblet, a glazed worsted fabric in a beautiful indigo blue, which must have been imported from England. It is quilted in a combination of two popular American colonial patterns, the pineapple and the Tree of Life – which in this quilt trails off into a flowering vine border. The background quilting is in simple diagonal lines. It is dated to the third quarter of the eighteenth century. The quilt is lined with two different worn, wool blankets, one of which shows the initial "C" cross stitched in dark blue. The fabrics are seamed and quilted with two-ply, indigo wool thread, S-twist and the quilt is inter-

Sampler made by Esther Copp, Connecticut, America, 1765. SMITHSONIAN INSTITUTION, WASHINGTON.

lined with carded wool fibers.

The second Copp quilt is a pieced quilt in the Nine-patch pattern. The alternating major pattern squares are made up of nine pieces worked with simple diagonal quilting and stitched together with alternating major squares of the same size in white, worked in shell quilting, to make an overall pattern of intersecting diagonal lines. The top is cotton; the painted fabrics are a variety of brown prints. The quilt is pieced with two-ply linen thread and quilted with both two-ply linen and two-ply cotton thread. The lining, which is linen, appears originally to have been an old sheet marked in cross stitch with the initials "D C." The interlining is again of carded wool. Cotton was rarely used as the interlining in quilts made in the northern parts of the United States until after the machine processing of cotton was introduced to New England in the 1790s.

In the southern, warmer colonies wool is rarely found as an interlining. The cotton was always ginned (separated from the seed), before it was used

as an interlining, either by hand or with the simple roller gin before Eli Whitney's invention of the toothed cotton gin. With machine ginning of cotton, pieces of vegetable matter such as small pieces of leaf and other foreign material, tended to remain in the fiber, all of which had to be "picked" by machine before the fiber was ready for carding and spinning. This unpicked cotton was, however, suitable for interlining a quilt and considerably cheaper; hence it is frequently found in nineteenth-century quilts.

The third of the Copp quilts is a pieced quilt in a variation of the Framed Medallion pattern. The medallion is made up of a group of five- two- and three-quarter-inch (7cm) patches pieced in the Variable Star pattern, surrounded by five rows of patches of the same size, with the initial frame in a two-inch (5cm) Chained Square pattern. The fabrics in this quilt are unusual because of their variety. Although they play an inconspicuous part in the overall effect, at least nine different white fabrics appear on the top – five different dimities and two each of plain cotton and plain linen. There are three different woven silk and linen stripes. The greatest treasure, however, is the variety of printed dress fabrics numbering over one hundred and fifty, dating from the 1770s to the late 1790s. It is difficult to believe that such a variety could represent the fabrics of a single household, even with the help of many friends and perhaps access to the Copp Dry Goods store. The selection was no doubt gathered from a whole community and gives an indication of the large number of printed dress fabrics that would have been available in a single community in eighteenth-century America. In 1784 John, Lord Sheffield, in his *Observations on the Commerce of the American States*, reported that after woolens, linens, and cutlery, "Printed Callicoes and other printed goods" accounted for the largest volume of articles imported into the American states. These printed cottons were to play an important part in quilt making in the following century.

The last Copp quilt contains three major categories of printed fabrics: all linen, cotton and linen and all cotton, with the latter as the dominant fabric. It is stitched with both linen and cotton The smallest piece measures only one-half inch (1·3cm) by one-quarter inch

(0·5cm) by three eighths inch (1cm) and is carefully stitched to create a square. The use of a piece this size is an indication of the value of fabric in late eighteenth-century America.

Quilting was introduced into America by the early settlers and followed the European tradition, particularly in its use of all-white designs. The designs and motifs were adapted and new ones introduced. It was not only used for bedcovers but also for items of clothing, such as petticoats and men's vests and was taught at the few schools that were available for those who could afford them. One advertised in the *Boston News Letter* in 1716: "at the house of Mr. George Bronnell, late School Master in Hanover Street, Boston, all sorts of millinary works done . . . and also young Gentlewomen and Children taught all sorts of fine Works as Quilting, Feather Work. . . ."

Although the all-white quilting tradition continued into the nineteenth century, it is the pieced quilt that represents the true American tradition in needlework. As cotton fabrics became more widely available, and also cheaper with the advent of power weaving and machine printing, the pieced quilts of either patchwork or appliqué became more ornate, varied and plentiful (Plates 5 and 10). Representing many hundreds of hours of painstaking work, they were based on privately-owned patterns which were passed from hand to hand and not commercially exploited as was so often the case.

The golden age of American quilt making was the second quarter of the nineteenth century. Although the large, single-motif design was still used, the repeated pattern, usually in squared multiples, increased in popularity. The advent of the machine, which made repeated-motif design popular in areas other than needlework, may have had an influence, but the greater ease with which smaller design units could be handled while they were being stitched was also a factor. It was not uncommon for the quilt to be finished or quilted by a group of women all working together on one quilt and the quilting bee, or party, was one of the most picturesque of American traditions. It was immortalized in song by Stephen Foster at a date before 1860 when he wrote "Twas from Aunt Dinah's quilting party I was seeing Nellie home."

Another type of quilt which involved

the community was known as the "album quilt." Each woman would make one square of her own in her favorite pattern, sometimes signing her name, and these would be pieced together and quilted and the finished article would be presented as a special or farewell gift to the local pastor and his wife, or to some other community figure. This tradition seems to have been most popular from the 1840s to the 1860s.

Although the machine manufacture of bedcovers by the mid-nineteenth century overtook the production of handmade quilts, the ever-expanding frontier of the United States kept the tradition alive until well past the turn of the century. Unfortunately the quality of the designs deteriorated as patterns became more "picturesque" than artistic, with schoolhouses or town pumps as the main inspiration.

In the late nineteenth century the so-called crazy-patch quilt was at the height of its popularity (Plate 10). Scraps of silk in jewel-like colors and in irregular shapes were pieced together with elaborate feather stitching. Frequently the plain silks would be painted with floral or other designs to demonstrate the artistic skills of the maker.

Pieced quilt with framed medallion, *America*, c.*1800*. SMITHSONIAN INSTITUTION, WASHINGTON.

Quilted counterpane,
*Russelville Fair, Kentucky,
America, nineteenth century.*
SMITHSONIAN INSTITUTION,
WASHINGTON.

These quilts were intended for the
parlor and were frequently called Victorian Slumber Throws. Although some
of the earlier examples may only include
silks saved by the family, by the 1880s
many commercial packages of scraps
and patterns were available to the quilt
maker, although the final choice of
design and the elaborate stitching were
still up to the individual.

A few fine quilt makers continued the
tradition into the twentieth century.
The same geometric patterns continued
to be popular: a variety of repeated
patterns based on pieces cut as triangles, squares, diamonds, rectangles,
arcs, and arranged and rearranged to
form designs of an infinite variety. The
names given to these designs were
sometimes known only locally and
sometimes nationally. The various star
patterns were always popular, such as
Eight-pointed Star, Blazing Star, Le
Moyne Star, Geometric Star, King's
Star, Iowa Star, Star of Bethlehem and
Virginia Star. Many names reflect the
political period in which the quilt was
made, such as Clay's Choice, Union
Square, Old Tippecanoe, Lincoln's
Platform, and others. Then there are
more obscure names such as Robbing
Peter to Pay Paul that were applied to
many different patterns.

The exceptionally fine appliqué
quilts of the early nineteenth century
were made to show the printed designs
of the fabric rearranged to present a
unified design. The later appliqué
quilts lost this quality and frequently
became simply a series of repeated
designs as in the pieced quilt. Appliqué
work did, however, allow for very narrow
pieces such as stems of flowers and
trailing vines that were not possible to
achieve in piecing. Since the same
patterns were frequently used over a
relatively long period of time, it is
important when dating pieces to recog-
nize the period of the individual fabrics
from which the quilt is made. Hand or
machine stitching offers another clue,
though hand stitching continued to be
popular long after the invention of the
sewing-machine. A further guideline as
to date is the thread used to stitch the
quilt.

The great economic depression of
the 1930s in the United States brought
a return to the making of utilitarian
quilts from used fabrics. Unfortunately
the fabrics of the period were not the
beautiful handwoven materials of the
eighteenth century and the end product
was one of utility alone.

American Indian Needlework

A rich supply of decorative needlework
was produced by the aborigines of
North America. Probably the earliest
and most famous is quill embroidery:
the application of porcupine quills to
tanned leathers or birch bark. This form
of decorative art was noted by the early
travelers to North America and one
journal records that "the women manifest much ingenuity and taste in the
work which they execute with porcupine
quills."

Although new materials were introduced as European voyagers began to
trade with the Indians, native materials
such as the quills continued to be used.
The work was not confined to one tribe
or nation but was practiced throughout
the woodland regions of the continent
and among the Plains Indians, the
Menominee tribe in the North, the
Sioux and Chippewa tribes in the region
of the Great Lakes and extending into
Canada with the Indians along the
Mackenzie River. Ceremonial and
ordinary items of clothing and accessories, which included shirts, moccasins,
leggings, knife sheaths, medicine bags
and pouches, were all decorated with
this technique.

There were four general methods of
attaching the quill: by sewing (couch-

ing), weaving, wrapping and by inserting it into holes in birch bark made with an awl. Sewing was the method most commonly used to attach the quills to a flat leather surface. A thin strip of sinew was used for the stitching which was kept moist to make it pliable, apart from the end which was twisted into a stiff, sharp point. This part was kept dry and thus it remained rigid and served as the needle. The sinew did not penetrate the hide but only the upper surface. Holes were made with a small, sharp stone resembling an awl. The sinew thread was worked in small stitches over the quills, which in their turn were bent alternately backward and forward over the stitches to conceal them. While they were working the squaws would hold the quills in their mouths in order to keep them soft and pliable. The reverse side of the completed work showed no signs of the sewing. Most of the early geometrical designs were symbolic. Those that are preserved in museums reflect contact with the white traders and explorers from Europe.

Beads were sometimes added to quillwork and gradually they became the most popular type of decoration. A few late eighteenth-century examples of items which would have been bartered, such as eyeglass cases and card cases of quill on birch bark and black cloth, show the early appreciation for this native work.

Beads have been found on prehistoric sites in the New World, as they have elsewhere. The American Indian had knowledge of, and used, some form of beads before the Europeans introduced trade beads but as early as the time of Christopher Columbus (1451–1506) we have evidence of gifts of "some strings of glass beads" which were offered and accepted. Danish travelers, Russian traders, whalers and others all offered beads in exchange for the furs and other treasures that they were seeking. They were not only more colorful but also easier to use than porcupine quills and gradually replaced them entirely.

The beads, which were stitched to the skins in a similar way and even followed the same patterns as quills, were strung on short threads with a similar number of beads on each, and arranged in evenly spaced rows, thus filling the design area. They could also be embroidered in outline.

Leggings, jackets and other pieces of

TOP:
Girl's dress, *Cheyenne, American-Indian, nineteenth century. Beadwork embroidery.* SMITHSONIAN INSTITUTION, WASHINGTON.

ABOVE AND LEFT (DETAIL):
Cape, *Aleutian, American-Indian, nineteenth century. Fishskin embroidery.* SMITHSONIAN INSTITUTION, WASHINGTON.

clothing and clothing accessories were all finely decorated. However, the moccasin is probably the best-known American Indian artifact, designs for which quickly adapted to European, and particularly Spanish, influence. Realistic "paintings" of figures in beadwork, such as eagles or horses, were combined with abstract motifs representing the elements: triangular lines or semicircles for rain, a disk for the sun, a zigzag for lightning, arched lines for the rainbow. Like other Indian crafts and skills, beadwork continued after the Indians were confined to reservations, but commercialism gradually denuded it of the free spirit so evident in the earlier work.

Eskimos spread across the North American continent from Greenland to the Aleutians and anthropologists claim important cultural differences between them and the Indians. These people have always made widespread use of the animal and vegetable matter native to the Arctic Circle and the decoration of clothing with fishskin appliqué by the Alaskan Eskimo women is distinctive and unique.

When the men go off to the sea to hunt they wear waterproof rain shirts made from seal intestines, which are gaily decorated along the seams with downy feathers appliquéd to the skins, alternating with pieces of fur appliqué. These designs almost certainly came from a number of separate sources. There are evident connections with Asiatic designs of the Far North, attributable, no doubt, to costumes worn by the early continental wanderer, who came to Alaska via the northern Pacific. How they arrived at the particular motifs used in the work can only be a matter for speculation, except in the case of accessories which have been made from first-hand observation. These examples show skill and a high degree of primitive artistry in their simplicity. Seals, whales, salmon, reindeer, birds, bears and other native animals have all been used as decorative motifs on a number of objects in every-day use.

The needlework was executed principally in geometric or conventional forms, but many small objects were sewn into images representing these animals and used as amulets or toys. Seal intestines, dried and inflated, provided a sort of translucent parchment which was cut into strips and stitched, appliquéd and decorated to

Basket quilt *(detail) made by Mary Green Moran, Baltimore, Md., America, 1845. Silk.* SMITHSONIAN INSTITUTION, WASHINGTON.

make men's waterproof clothing. Inland Eskimos substituted the intestines of bears and deer since they lacked the sea animals. The Eskimos of the Lower Yukon used the skins of salmon and losh to make bags, pouches, mittens and a kind of waterproof garment which resembled a dress or shirt and was made to slip over the head. The strips were stitched horizontally and the decoration ran parallel to it. Differing materials such as shell and walrus teeth, in addition to feathers and fur, led to variations in design and color.

Objects etched with figures were sometimes attached to belts and were an important addition to the costume worn by every male Eskimo. A popular symbol was the thunderbird which, as the legend goes, was "A monstrous Eagle-man who flies out over the ocean and kills whales by throwing the Lightning Serpent." This motif was widely adopted along the North Pacific coast and developed in particular in Alaska.

For needlework such as this the Alaskan women depended on implements made from bone. Sewing thread was made from sinew taken from the legs of reindeer, although Lower Yukon women found a substitute in a species of tough grass which, after being beaten and dried, was separated with little ivory combs. Most distinctive of all were the sealskin thimbles which were made from small oval pieces of tough skin. The skin would have had a slit across one end which formed a loop-like strap through which the forefinger was thrust so that the strap rested across the nail and the pad of sealskin on the finger pad. These thimbles were skillfully imitated by carvers in ivory but the women preferred the traditional sealskin thimbles which they would have been taught to use by their forebears.

An isolated group of American Indians, the Seminoles, a tribe of the Muskogean linguistic stock, were formed in the eighteenth century by settlers from the Creek confederacy, primarily speakers of the Creek and Hitchiti languages. Early in the 1800s the Seminoles occupied former Apalachee and Timucua territory in north Florida. As the white settlers moved in after Florida had become a part of the United States, the Seminoles resisted giving up their lands and the Seminole Wars followed. The majority of the tribe agreed to take territory in Oklahoma in exchange for their own land; some refused the offer, however, and moved further south in Florida to the area of the Everglades where they built huts on stilts to safeguard themselves in the alligator-filled waters and where they continue to live to this day.

After the invention of the sewing

OPPOSITE, ABOVE:
Vest, *Cheyenne, American-Indian, nineteenth century. Quillwork embroidery.* SMITHSONIAN INSTITUTION, WASHINGTON.

OPPOSITE, BELOW:
Woman's pieced skirt, *Seminole, American-Indian, nineteenth century.* SMITHSONIAN INSTITUTION, WASHINGTON.

Blue and white eagle quilt,
*America, second quarter of
of the nineteenth century.*
SMITHSONIAN INSTITUTION,
WASHINGTON.

colonial housewife to decorate her household fabrics. She would have learned to sew and embroider at an early age, a skill essential for maintaining the household fabrics and her own and her family's wardrobe.

Each young woman would make her sampler, or "examplar" as they were then called, of designs and stitches that would be needed in marking her linens. The seventeenth- and early eighteenth-century samplers made in North America were like their English counterparts, narrow strips of linen with rows of embroidered border designs, usually including the letters of the alphabet. In many cases the work was marked with the name of the maker, where it was made, the date and even the age of the maker. The narrow samplers could easily be rolled and kept in a workbasket as a convenient source of reference.

With the advent of the eighteenth century the sampler began to take the shape of pictures with one or more border designs acting as a frame and the letters of the alphabet set out in rows in a variety of sizes and designs. Pictorial designs were worked, sometimes with the addition of lines of verse.

Needlework was not popular with all small girls. One of the most endearing lines states that the maker "hated every stitch, she liked to read much more." Each child dutifully worked her sampler whether she liked it or not. One of the earliest examples of an American sampler is in the Pilgrim Museum at Plymouth, Massachusetts; although undated, it is known that it was made by Loana Standish, probably in c.1635. A typical eighteenth-century sampler is embroidered with the words "Esther Copp her sampler made in the eleventh year of her age August 1765"; worked in multicolored silks in tent stitch, eye stitch and cross stitch on a linen ground.

Samplers like this one became treasured family possessions. A descendant of Esther Copp named Phoebe Esther Copp made a sampler in 1822, nearly sixty years later. It is based on the design of its antecedent with the same verse: "Better it is to be of an humble spirit with the lowly than to divide the Spoil with the proud."

In the nineteenth century samplers became increasingly pictorial and were frequently worked on canvas (Plate 4), rather than the linen or fine worsted of the earlier periods. As the machine

machine in the mid-nineteenth century and the enterprising salesmanship shown by Isaac Singer and the company that bore his name, the Singer machine began to appear in many remote parts of the world. Even relatively primitive societies that used few machines were intrigued by, and quickly adapted to, the marvels of a machine that could sew. One such group were the Seminoles, who had moved to the Everglades. These people, who wore simple clothing because of the hot climate of southern Florida, not only used the sewing machine but with, and because of it, changed the style of their tribal dress. The simple skirts and cape-like tops were transformed into row upon row of stitched, colored cottons. As many as forty-four bands of color in one skirt were not unusual. In this one case, the machine inspired creativity rather than decreasing or destroying it.

The Sampler or "Examplar" and other Related Needlework
As soon as time allowed, the desire for beauty and self-expression led the

production of textiles increased, it seemed less important to insist that a little girl should learn to use a needle, particularly after the advent of the sewing machine in the middle of the nineteenth century.

Not all embroidery was learned in the American home. By the eighteenth century private boarding schools and tutors existed where young ladies were taught the skills of the needle. These were usually near the larger cities such as Boston, New York, Philadelphia, Baltimore or Charleston. One of the more far-reaching influences was from the schools supported by the Moravian sect. These people, who were among the first to work with silk, had migrated from Moravia, a part of present-day Czechoslovakia, to the part of the southern colonies now known as the state of Georgia. They started by practicing agriculture. Since the marauding Spanish were close neighbors in Florida and the peace-loving Moravians did not want any conflict with them which would have made them unpopular with some of their Georgian neighbors, they decided it would be preferable to move north and they settled in Bethlehem, near Philadelphia, in Pennsylvania in 1740. Nine years later they founded two schools, one for boys and one for girls.

Silk Embroidery

The Sisters of Bethlehem, who presided over the girls' school, developed the art of fine needlework, especially in silk, which was to become famous throughout the United States. The Moravians soon founded other schools and they established a reputation for culture and learning. Prominent Americans who could afford to do so sought to enrol their daughters since the schools were thought to provide an appropriate and improving environment for the formative years of their lives. As branches of the girls' school were established in other states, so the art and practice of good needlework was extended.

The Moravians are associated with memorial pictures depicting melancholy maidens weeping at memorial urns, dedicated to a loved one or to a national figure such as George Washington. Patriotic and religious subjects were also embroidered in silk in a similar style. The military banners that they produced were both decorative and practical in use. The most closely

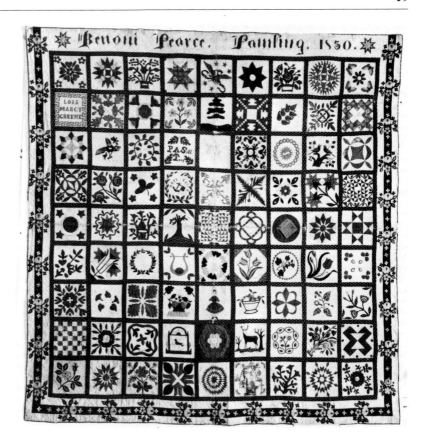

documented example to have survived is the Pulaski Banner which was carried during the American Revolution and was named after the Polish soldier, Count Pulaski, who joined Washington's army in 1777. It was made by the Moravian Sisters and is now in the collection of the Maryland Historical Society, Baltimore.

Sentimental, floral and naval pictures were embroidered in silk, and embroidered maps of individual states or parts of the eastern part of the United States were also popular. Silk embroidery continued to be practiced throughout the nineteenth century and at the beginning of the twentieth century, while late in the nineteenth century the popularity of flowers worked in needle painting was the vogue. This work was usually reserved for table runners, or bureau scarves and other domestic furnishings and the technical skill of the maker generally far outweighed the artistic merit of the finished product.

American Whitework

When colored threads were worked on a white ground, the color could distract the eye from any imperfections in execution, but when the work was white on white, otherwise known as white-

Album quilt *made for Benoni Pearce, Paulling, New York, America, 1850.* SMITHSONIAN INSTITUTION, WASHINGTON.

ABOVE:
Christening dress, *America,*
1880. Cotton embroidered
with broderie anglaise and
pin tucks. SMITHSONIAN
INSTITUTION, WASHINGTON.

BELOW:
Apron, *(detail), America,*
third quarter of the
eighteenth century.
Embroidered linen.
SMITHSONIAN INSTITUTION,
WASHINGTON.

work, the needleworker's skill had to be at its best. A few extant samplers attest to this fact but most whitework is in the finished products. Used sometimes for costume accessories, this type of work can be seen at its most spectacular in embroidered counterpanes. Several references to men designing the patterns for white bedspreads and counterpanes inform us that women did not necessarily design their own, although many probably did.

There is a consistency in the designs even though some are flowing and lightly treated and others are more geometric in style and heavily worked. Two examples from the same Connecticut family are illustrated here. The ground fabric of the first is of corded cotton; the warp of the fabric is linen. Many so-called "cotton" fabrics of the eighteenth century were woven on a linen warp as the cotton yarns produced at that time were not strong enough for fabrics which were heavier in weight. The pineapple design with the running floral pattern and swag border decorated with tassels is in candlewick couched to the ground fabric with two-ply linen thread. This counterpane probably dates from the late eighteenth century.

The second example was probably made a little later as the corded cotton ground has a cotton warp. The geometric and floral design is worked in a firmer candlewick with a knotted stitch. Again there is a swag and tassel border and, in addition, it is seamed and hemmed with two-ply cotton thread: it dates from the early nineteenth century. The fashion for making these elaborate embroidered counterpanes died out in the United States with the invention of Erastus Bigelow's power loom which could weave, at a much lower price, knobbed or knotted counterpanes similar to those made on a hand loom.

The use of the tambour needle, the small crochet-like hook used to make chain stitch, was particularly popular in the United States for the embroidery of sheer muslins from which were made fichus and other whitework costume accessories. Of equal importance was the practice of darning with white thread on machine-made net. Similar patterns were used for both techniques, each offering a less expensive substitute for lace, which was never made in any quantity in North America. Possibly the best examples of fine white needlework are to be seen on wedding handker-chieves and christening dresses; hours of work often went into the embroidery of a single motif on the treasured article.

Other Types of Early North American Needlework

Embroidery in colored silk or wool threads was most rewarding to execute and always popular. The finished article might be purely decorative, representing a picture, or serve to decorate personal clothing or household furnishings, including upholstery. One of the earliest American examples is considered by some to be a form of stumpwork, although none of the figures in the picture is padded out as in the English type. This piece, which is the work of Rebekah Wheeler, is dated "Ye Month May 1664" and illustrates the story of Queen Esther and Ahasuerus. It is in the collection of the Concord Historical Society, Massachusetts.

Examples from the eighteenth century are more numerous. Shops advertized not only fabrics but patterns from London and "all sorts of canvas without drawings." The *Boston News Letter* of April 28, 1743, advertises "Shaded crewels, blue, red, and other colors of Worsteds." A number of these pieces have survived. There is one set of at least eight known as "The Fishing Ladies," on account of its central theme, and one particularly fine example from this group dated *c*.1748 is in the Boston Museum of Fine Arts. All the pieces were in the ownership of New England families and may be the work of a single designer in the Boston district. The central figure is the same in each with variations in the surrounding designs and figures and they are worked in wool on canvas.

Similar work was used for the decoration of pocketbooks, fire screens, tablecloths and furniture upholstery. The latter is probably the same as the crewel recorded in some American inventories as certain pieces of furniture are listed as being covered with crewel upholstery. A wing chair in the collection of the Metropolitan Museum of Art, New York, is still covered in the original upholstery which is decorated with needlepoint, or canvas work, while the back of the chair is worked in crewel embroidery on linen, in the stitches and designs commonly used on bed curtains, which should eliminate all doubt. Unfortunately, in the United

Cushion cover *made by
Martha Washington,
America, late eighteenth
century. Canvas work.*
SMITHSONIAN INSTITUTION,
WASHINGTON.

States, some eighteenth-century wing chairs have been upholstered at a later date in pieces of crewel embroidered bed hangings of the period, which are incorrect for the purpose because of the nature of the stitches. Crewel embroidery has long been popular in the United States and has probably seen more major revivals of interest than any other form of needlework.

American crewel embroidery – colorful Jacobean designs on a linen ground – was obviously a continuing tradition of the English work. Probably the important difference is that the New World designs became less ornate in so much that less of the ground fabric was covered with embroidery. Few dated examples are known, but a 1745 crewel bedcover is in the collection of the Litchfield Historical Society, Connecticut. It is worked principally in browns and gold with a design of pineapples, roses and carnations. A bedcover of 1770 embroidered by Mary Breed in crewel work with flowers and branching trees is in the collection of the Metro-

politan Museum of Art, New York. In the trees there are birds and the entire bedcover is executed in natural coloring. Complete sets of bed hangings consisting of curtains, valances and matching bedcover are rarely found although the individual pieces that survive would most likely have originally formed parts of sets (Plate 2). Many incomplete sets have had substitute pieces embroidered to match at a later date.

Crewel work on petticoats and pockets was also popular in the eighteenth century. A 1749 advertisement in the *Boston Gazette* describes a petticoat of elaborate design: "On the 11th of Nov. last, was stolen out of the yeard of Mr. Joseph Cort, Joiner in Boston, living in Cross Street, a Woman's Fustian Petticoat, with large work'd Embroider'd Border, being Deer, Sheep, Houses, Forrest, etc. so worked. Whoever has taken said Petticoat and will return it to the owner thereof, or to the Printer, shall have 40s. Old Tenor Reward and no Question ask'd." The petticoat in question

Embroidered picture of
George Washington,
*America, mid-nineteenth
century, Berlin wool work.*
SMITHSONIAN INSTITUTION,
WASHINGTON.

was obviously a prized possession of
Mrs. Cort.

Examples of less elaborate petticoats
worked in crewel can be found in many
American museums as well as a variety
of pockets and pocket books. A number
of examples of American crewel work
are worked entirely in shades of indigo;
whether this color limitation was from
choice or necessity is not clear. Delicate
blues and whites were also used, not
only in worsteds on linen but also in
linen embroidery on linen.

Berlin Woolwork
Wool embroidery on linen became less
popular in the nineteenth century
being succeeded in favor by wool on

canvas work both for pictures and
upholstery. This was probably due to
the ease with which this technique
could be worked and also to the availability of patterns.

Needlepoint, as canvas work is
generally called today in the United
States, was done in almost every home.
Small, sentimental pictures of flowers
and animals, bowls of fruit, geometric
and mosaic patterns, biblical scenes
and patriotic figures were all dutifully
re-created stitch by stitch. Few of these
designs were original, most of them
deriving from popular pattern books or
from Berlin woolwork patterns. Both
the brilliant worsted yarns and the
patterns came from Germany and were

extremely popular in the United States following their introduction in the 1850s.

The most popular design subjects included parrots perched on wreaths, herds of deer, sprays or bouquets of roses, birds and animals of various types but in particular dogs: the attractive young girl with her dog Tray was, for example, much in demand. Wools, silks, chenille and beads were used to complete the Berlin patterns. Instructions for embroidering on canvas dating from the 1860s show that some at least of the ideas of the period are still used in needlework today. "One of the best effects of Berlin work," states one such instruction, "can be produced by the Irish or Railroad stitch, as it is called from its rapid execution. It is difficult to describe but simple to work. A beautiful effect is produced by using four or five shades of fawn color, and stripes crossed over the crimson at regular intervals; the stripes formed by the fawn colors running diagonally, and the four shades of crimson the same. The squares formed by the pattern meeting are filled in with black wool. It has the appearance of being raised from the canvas. A set of furniture in this pattern is very handsome. We do not admire the figure and landscape patterns for canvas work, though some are handsome; but the sky is seldom good, or the faces."

Embroidered articles made in the second half of the nineteenth century include note cases, carriage bags, shawl straps, handbags, screens, ottomans, handkerchief cases, braces, cigar cases and lambrequins. Berlin patterns were also produced in raised woolwork. This was described in an 1858 pattern book as follows:

In this, one or more prominent objects in a design, are raised; the remainder being done in cross stitch. Birds, animals, and flowers, look handsome when so worked. Do all the plain parts first. Then thread needles with the various shades you want, and obtain fine flat netting meshes. Begin from the left-hand corner, lowest part, with the proper shade, the wool being "doubled." Bring the needle up "between" the two upright threads of the first cross-stitch. Take a tapestry stitch to the left, bringing the needle out in the same hole. Put the wool round the mesh, and take one to the right, the needle coming out against the same x. Thread round the mesh, and take a tapestry-stitch from the hole of the last down to the right, the wool to the right of it. Thread round. One to the right x. A figure V

is thus constantly formed on the wrong side. When done, wash at the back with gum; cut the loops, and shear them into shape from the pattern, giving proper thickness and form to each part. Sometimes this is done across one thread only.

The lamp mat (Plate 8), in which part of the fruit is free-form and wired to the mat, is an excellent example of this work.

Netting and Crochet

Hand netting was widely fashionable in the American colonies and has been immortalized on canvas by its detailed depiction in a number of American primitive paintings. Netting was used extensively for decorative fringes for bed and table furnishings as well as for complete pieces such as tablecloths. Most of the all-white counterpanes of the late eighteenth and early nineteenth centuries originally had netted fringes but in the majority of cases these have now disintegrated. Many of the pieces that have survived are simple netted fringes varying in width from three to five inches (7cm to 12cm). They are usually finished with knotted tassels or short lengths of cotton tied to give the effect of chenille work. Either plain woven tape served as the edging or, alternatively, the anchor string of the netting.

Also popular in the first half of the nineteenth century was the so-called "darning on net" in which the needle-woman worked with white yarn in silk, linen or cotton on a machine-made net ground to produce a lacy effect. Many fine examples of small shawls, collars and fichus have survived as they were frequently used as wedding veils at this time. In addition to the darning stitch, the tambour hook was used to make the chain stitch on the net ground as it had previously on muslin or silk grounds.

Rugs for Bed and Floor

An early type of American colonial needlework, used in particular for rugs and upholstery, was Turkey work. The style and name both came from England where the technique had become fashionable following the import of Oriental rugs of this description. Although in England the rugs were woven in the same technique as their Eastern counterparts with hand-knotted pile, in America the pattern was copied but the needle was used to form a pile on a prewoven foundation.

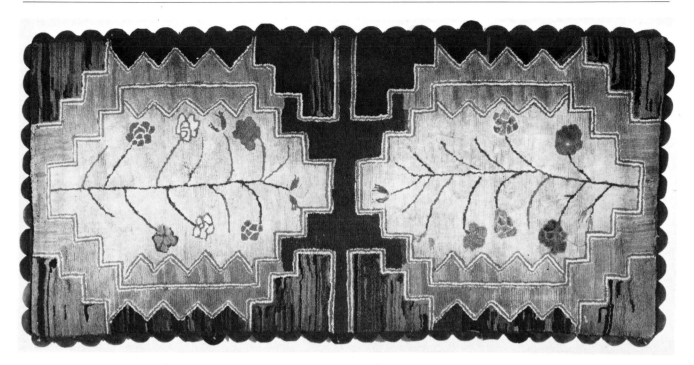

Examples of Turkey work existed as early as 1670, according to household inventories and other records. John Carter of Virginia had several chairs upholstered in Turkey work while several other early records in South Carolina and New England list similar work. It was mainly used for chairs, tablecloths or carpets and bed covers, rarely as a floor covering. Few examples remain and most of these are of a later date, the best being represented by bedcovers or bed rugs (Plate 3). These are frequently worked in pile needlework but they are also found in other embroidery stitches. A few good examples date from the last quarter of the eighteenth century, but the greater number date from the early nineteenth century. It is difficult to date these by the designs since the earlier motifs were retained as the technique developed. A handsome example in the Metropolitan Museum of Art, New York, is worked with large carnations in a small vase that in style suggests a much earlier period than the actual date of 1809.

Although small needlework rugs may indeed have been intended for the floor beside the bed or by the hearth, no known examples survive that can positively be attributed to the eighteenth century. The early nineteenth-century examples probably continued the techniques and traditions at least from the latter part of the previous century. Embroidery stitches, notably tambour and appliqué, were used to make these rugs, some of which were quite small and some room size. The larger versions were frequently made in sections and these were then stitched together.

Needlework rugs with matching stair runners were also popular. One made by Ann and Sophie Moore, daughters of Judge Lliney Moore of Champlain, New York, was started in 1808 and completed in 1812. It was in use on their drawing-room floor until 1825 and is now in the Metropolitan Museum of Art. The entire center of this rug simulates interlaced brocaded ribbons. It was made in pieces while the border, which has a Greek fret pattern, was made separately. Few ambitious rugs of this type survived the nineteenth century without being cut or re-used.

Small rugs were more usual. A number of interesting examples from the first half of the nineteenth century, now in public and private collections, frequently show a naïve and colorful approach to design, but what they lack in sophistication they make up for in primitive charm. This style was however soon replaced by the popularity of the hooked rug.

Early examples of hooked rugs have the same simplicity as other small needlework rugs. The technique is not very different from tambour since it is done on a frame and with a hook, the main difference being that the loops are not interchained and are set closer together. Unfortunately, as with so much

Hooked rug, *Cleveland, Ohio, America, 1876. An original design.*
SMITHSONIAN INSTITUTION, WASHINGTON.

American embroidery, the majority of hooked rugs were not made from original drawings, though the severest lack of originality came when the foundation fabric, burlap, or "sacking" as it is more commonly known in England, could be purchased with the designs stamped in color. The most popular were the Frost patterns that numbered in the hundreds and were available over a long period, first appearing in the 1860s.

Most needlewomen followed the patterns and colors dictated by the designer, few following their own tastes in blending colors or modifying the designs. The hooked rugs made from strips of old fabric and executed in simple designs bear the test of time more effectively than many of the stamped patterns which were rigidly followed and executed in the latest bright woolen yarns of the time.

The hooked rugs of the nineteenth century have for a long time been both treasured and copied. Since the advent of the machine in the United States, textiles made by hand have been more widely appreciated, and the technique needs a relatively small amount of skill but, as with most simple techniques, color and design are of paramount importance.

The American Revival in Needlework

In 1876 a Centennial fair was held in Philadelphia, Pennsylvania, to celebrate the one hundredth anniversary of the independence of the United States of America. One of the most popular exhibits, attracting many American women attending the fair, was the British exhibit of Kensington embroidery. Those who were able to visit England took the opportunity of attending classes at the Royal School of Art Needlework which, in 1875, had moved from Sloane Street to Prince's Gate in London. This schooling served to remind them of the high standard of work that had been practiced in Europe. On their return, the women encouraged magazines to publish designs which they had brought back with them from the Royal School of Art Needlework.

Meanwhile the Boston Museum of Fine Arts had established a school for art needlework to encourage the practice and technical understanding of needlework in its highest artistic form. Both group and private lessons were offered and the program promised two "free days" and that "materials and designs will be furnished at a moderate price."

Few American artists of the late nineteenth and early twentieth century made any direct contribution to needlework. An exception, however, is provided by James McNeill Whistler (1834–1903), whose work was largely responsible for the popularity of the Japanese style in the United States. Whistler's studio was decorated with lacquer and embroideries from Japan and it was through his influential lead that quantities of Japanese motifs began to appear in domestic needlework.

Nevertheless, the most important influence on American embroidery during this period came from across the Atlantic. As in England, an arts and crafts movement in America in the 1880s was prompted by the work of William Morris (1834–96). It was the inspiration for such innovations as Californian mission furniture, the Grand Rapids Morris chairs and the "art embroidery" on rough crash appliqué with bowls of varicolored flowers which were designed to hang in the rooms which were fashionably furnished with oak. More important, however, was the group activity stimulated by Morris and Co. which resulted directly in the formation of the Society of Decorative Arts which was founded in New York City by Louis C. Tiffany (1848–1933), designer of stained glass, Samuel Coleman (1832–1920), textile designer and colorist, and Robert W. De Forest (1848–1931), an authority on carved and ornamental woodwork. Candace Wheeler (1828–1923) was also a member of this group and it was she who as early as the 1880s aspired to the creation of a national and lasting style in American needlework. Large wall hangings were embroidered under the direction of Candace Wheeler in the 1880s and 1890s by the group of Associated Artists. Two examples of her own work are now in the collection of the Metropolitan Museum of Art. Although there is a suggestion of the influence of Whistler in the Japanese style of her flowers, the influence of William Morris is unmistakeable in her general design. While reflecting the influence of two schools, Candace Wheeler also retained an individual style in the understanding she showed of the general fundamentals of design and line.

Grandmother chair *made by Carolyn Vosberg Hall, America, 1976. Soft sculpture.* SMITHSONIAN INSTITUTION, WASHINGTON.

The Society of Decorative Arts was only one of many needlework groups formed at this time. The Society itself encouraged the formation of arts and crafts groups in other cities and the Needlework and Textile Guild of the Art Institute of Chicago worked with the same objective.

Working in close conjunction with both art and industry were two painters from New York City, Margaret C. Whiting (1860–1946) and Ellen Miller (1864–1929), who decided to revive the art of the early blue and white crewel embroidery of New England. They arrived in Deerfield, Massachusetts, in 1896, with the intention of not only staging a revival in needlework but also recapturing the spirit of the previous century. They met with a sympathetic understanding of their objectives and gained the full cooperation of their new neighbors. An identity of interests existed in the town which enabled Miss Whiting and Miss Miller to proceed with the establishment of a group of Deerfield women to work together on the re-creation of this blue and white needlework. Their work became widely known and women came from great distances in order to buy the embroideries designed by Margaret Whiting and executed by her helpers. On each piece that they made they embroidered the insignia of the Deerfield Blue and White Society, an initial "D" in the center of a spinning wheel. The stitches were similar to those used in the early crewel work except that flax was substituted for wool thread and Russian linen for the New England homespun.

Some designs were exact copies of the blue and white work made in New England in the mid-eighteenth century. One such piece is a copy owned by a woman in Buffalo, New York, the original of which has since been lost but the design has been saved because of the work of the Deerfield Society. With the onset of the First World War materials were not available and the women were called to other duties. The work begun by Miss Whiting, however, inspired others in Deerfield to revive the techniques of candlewicking and netting. Old designs were followed but the patterns were simplified and superfluous decoration eliminated. These new compositions showed easy, flowing lines and a competent design sense. Working with twenty helpers, Mrs. Gertrude Cochrane Smith, another Deerfield lady, made thirty-two bedcovers in a year. Her netted canopy for a tester bed was equally noteworthy and she also supplied replacements for many beds of the colonial period.

The needlework revival stimulated interest and guilds were formed to make embroidery for the Church. Unlike most other countries in the world, the United States could boast of no tradition in ecclesiastical embroidery. This was due primarily to the Reformed character of many of the churches but also to the economic conditions and primitive nature of the areas they served. The Spanish missions of what is now California would have been the earliest repositories for any such work but the few church textiles that have survived show little, if any, needlework while vestments have been remade and many pieces altered.

Even after the revival of interest in the late nineteenth century much of the United States's ecclesiastical needlework was imported. There were, and are, exceptions. St. Michael's Cathedral in New York City had pieces made by the St. Hilda's Guild as early as 1894; and the National Cathedral in Washington had needlepoint kneeling cushions made over a period of many years by women in local parish guilds from all over the United States. Although many fine pieces have been made, these are the exception and there still is no strong tradition in guilds or schools, or interest from individuals in creating religious needlework.

There were a number of women in the United States in the 1920s, 30s and 40s whose needlework demonstrates good craftsmanship and a sound design concept. One woman who spanned this period and whose work reflects it is Mrs. Theodore Roosevelt, Jr. (1888–1960). Her works are initialed "E.R." – her given name was Eleanor – but she exhibited under the name of her spouse, whose father had been the twenty-sixth president of the United States. Much of the work that she did was in wool on canvas, but Mrs. Roosevelt also worked in silks. One of her earlier pieces was a miniature screen that was made up of native American birds in a design adapted from an old print. To be certain that the coloring was accurate, she observed the birds in their natural environment and insisted that her children keep watch for the different varieties during the course of their summer holidays in Vermont. The screen was made in 1926 and was awarded first prize at the first *Needlework of Today* exhibition held in New York in 1934. Ancient Chinese embroideries also influenced Mrs. Roosevelt in her choice of design and technique. In a delightful three-fold table screen of blue silk she combined a design from an illustration by Boris Artzybasheff, of two Chinese youths holding fast to a dragon horse, with fantasies of her own design. The entire embroidery, beautifully executed, is in fine chain stitch. In another small screen of the same type, she used a design adapted from an old illuminated manuscript which she had come across in an English church. She embroidered the legend in large old English block letters which reads: "From Ghoules and Ghosties, Long Leggitie Beasties and things that go Bump in the night, Good Lord Deliver us."

Mrs. Roosevelt's delightful humor as well as her excellent needlework are well known. An illustration of both is provided by a panel entitled *Recognition of U.S.S.R. 1933*. The sampler depicts Russian peasants shopping, with houses, walls and the round domes of the Kremlin towering over them. The work

is mainly executed in *petit point* with the sky and one side of a market stall worked in Gobelins stitch. The leaves on the trees are worked in a long, flat, satin-like stitch. When asked the reason for this, Mrs. Roosevelt explained, "I became tired of working continuously with the needlepoint stitch; it seemed to be flat and lifeless, so I made up a stitch that galloped . . ." and it does just that. Questions were raised as to its political overtones when this piece was exhibited in New York, but Mrs. Roosevelt drew attention to the little red devil sitting in a tree ready to pounce on the unwary pedestrians below, a touch of humor characteristic of most of her work.

A truly magnificent floor screen was one of her most ambitious ventures. The three sections were made over a period of three years first in Puerto Rico, where her husband was governor, then in the Philippines and finally, where it was completed, in New York. The screen design was based, in part, on a sketch by a contemporary American artist. Its strength lies in the execution of the design and the superb workmanship. Monkeys colored in black and white swing through the rich jungle foliage and seem to move from panel to panel. These provide a contrast with the tropical plants whose curved leaves soften the straight lines of their stems.

In some of her late work in the 1940s Mrs. Roosevelt tried her hand at elaborate panels in couched and jeweled work of which one is based on the fable of the golden rooster. She kept excellent card records of the work she did with references to the source and to the materials that she used. In the case of her "jeweled" pieces, she stitched small bags of the stones to the back of the piece so that if one were lost it could easily be replaced. Most of Mrs. Roosevelt's work is still with the Roosevelt family; only two pieces are known to have passed out of their possession of which one is now in the permanent collection of the National Museum of History and Technology, Smithsonian Institution, Washington, D.C.

Contemporary American Needlework

Almost every form of needlework is popular as an expression of artistic endeavor in the United States today. Men as well as women enjoy the relaxation of working with a needle, thread and fabric. Most of these amateurs follow pre-sketched designs, designated colors, and even use pre-measured kits of yarns designed specifically for the canvas with which they are bought. Quilt making has also increased in popularity.

At the same time there has been a revival of southern or Appalachian Mountain crafts, where, because of the isolation of the country, earlier traditions of needlework remained for years after they had disappeared from other parts of the United States. Renewed interest in good craftsmanship has encouraged people from this region to create high-quality needlework. Quilts are probably more in demand than any other type of needlework, but articles such as handmade dolls, bonnets, pillows and related items are also made. A similar type of craft survival, or revival, in quilt making can be found among the Mennonites or so-called "Pennsylvania Dutch." Their work is distinctive in that the colors are usually brighter, the patterns bolder and the quilting of good quality.

Among the new forms in needlework, soft sculpture appeared on the scene in the 1960s concurrently with Pop Art. Familiar objects not usually associated with needlework were presented in soft, stitched form. To the viewer they sometimes looked surrealistic but seldom as harsh as Pop Art, possibly because they are "soft." The artists who make soft sculpture like to endear the commonplace and while humor has never been an outstanding feature of the fine arts, soft art refuses to take life seriously. The basic materials are fabric and fibers or yarns although plastics, leathers and other flexible materials can be used; but a basic knowledge of sewing and needlework is essential. The work is three dimensional and stuffing is used. If it pleases the eye, it will withstand the test of time with needlework of the past.

What does the future hold for needlework in the United States? We tire of plastic objects and we like the texture of wood. In fabrics the modern man-made fibers and fast production methods of the machine give us inexpensive, durable textiles that are easy to launder and that withstand hard wear. We would not exchange these for the more troublesome handmade objects of the past, but increasingly we appreciate the time, skill, thought, and artistry required to produce fine pieces of needlework. This appreciation will encourage more and better work.

Great Britain

THE CHARACTER OF BRITISH EMBROIDERY has not remained constant throughout its history and there is no continuous, recognizable style, even though needle-work in Scotland, Wales, Ireland and England has in general developed in a similar way. At various periods external influences, from Europe and the East, have been absorbed to form new styles and, in the case of *opus anglicanum*, elements of design and technique originated in Britain and spread throughout Europe. Embroiderers from medieval times to the present day have a considerable reputation for combining dexterity with originality, for creating works of technical and artistic quality.

Anglo-Saxon and Norman Embroidery

Historical documents provide the first evidence of embroidered cloth in the British Isles. In Wales as early as the sixth century reference is made by the poet Taliesin to "fine raiment," which may have been of embroidered cloth, this being the reward given to the poet at the court of Urien. In England the first specific mention refers to St. Etheldreda, abbess of Ely (died 679), offering a stole and maniple to St. Cuthbert.

Little is known of the appearance of these embroideries for it is not until the ninth and tenth centuries with the examples of work now at the collegiate church of Maeseyck, Belgium (a ninth-century vestment associated with St. Harlinde and St. Relinde), and at Durham Cathedral (a stole, maniple and girdle found in St. Cuthbert's tomb and dated by inscription to between 909 and 916) that it is possible to have any idea of the technique and style of British work before the Norman Conquest (1066). Many further references to early embroidery exist, however, and even to the individuals who were involved in the work.

In the tenth century it is recorded that St. Dunstan worked on designs for embroidery and Aedgytha, queen of Edward the Confessor, is said to have embroidered her husband's coronation mantle. In Scotland Queen Margaret, wife of Malcolm III, was known for her industry with the needle, decorating such objects as copes, chasubles, stoles and altar cloths, and the artistic skills of the maiden Alwid are noted in the Domesday Book as she was given land in Buckinghamshire by the Sheriff Godric providing she taught his daughters the art of embroidery.

Written evidence clearly points to the fact that work done during the Anglo-Saxon period was of a high standard, and that it was admired by foreigners and exported to the Continent. Matilda, wife of William the Conqueror, is known to have given secular objects to the church of the Holy Trinity in Caen, France, for adaptation to church use. At the time of the Battle of Hastings in 1066 the impression made on the Normans by this work is noted by William de Poitiers, William the Conqueror's chronicler, when he describes the splendor of King Harold's banner.

The tenth-century pieces found at Durham provide the richest existing evidence of Anglo-Saxon embroidery. Worked with gold thread and colored silks in stem and split stitches and surface couching, the figures depicted on these vestments represent types rather than individuals and show none of the emotion that was to become characteristic of later work. It seems likely that the embroidery of these items was carried out at Winchester, the capital of Saxon England. A comparison of the pattern used on the Durham embroideries with that on the earlier Maeseyck vestments shows a definite progression in style from the naïve, yet lively, to the more sophisticated formal structures of the Durham work. The latter is derived from Byzantine influences seen in the Carolingian manuscript painting of Tours, in northern France, which in turn influenced the Winchester school of English manuscript painting.

The largest and only complete piece of early Norman embroidery still surviving is the so-called Bayeux Tapestry. It is over 230ft (70m) long and worked in colored wools in laid and couched work and outline stitch on a linen ground. The narrative scenes of the embroidery, which tell the full story of the Norman invasion of England from the Norman viewpoint, have proved an invaluable guide to historians of many disciplines including astronomy, showing as it does the comet (Plate 14) that was to be observed by the English astronomer Edmund Halley in 1680. Although the origin of the embroidery was once in question, it is now thought, on the comparison of architectural details, that the design and manufacture is English and was possibly drawn out by workers of the Canterbury school of manuscript painting. Commissioned by Odo, Bishop of Bayeux, the hanging may have been intended for the cathedral at Bayeux, which was dedicated in 1077 and where it hung for many years. On the other hand the hanging may originally have had a secular purpose and was then presented to the cathedral by Odo at a later date.

The craft of embroidery flourished under the Normans and stylistic changes can be traced throughout this period. Technically the most fundamental change was the introduction of underside couching which provided a means of embroidering in a freer and more expressive way than had previously been possible. Fragments found at Durham Cathedral in the tomb of William of St. Carilef (1060–90) illustrate this technique worked with silver-gilt thread, couched with silk on a silk ground. In these examples the technique is not, however, used to its best advantage as no innovation is attempted, the ornamental motifs being similar to those in the border of the Bayeux Tapestry.

To the simple appearance of Anglo-Saxon design is added, during the Norman period, the more dignified and statuesque characteristics of the romanesque style. Fragments dated to between 1140 and 1170 associated with St. Thomas of Canterbury (now at Sens Cathedral, France, and Erdington Abbey, Birmingham) show a typical

formality in their repeating patterns of interlocking medallions, which are worked in silver-gilt underside couching on a silk ground. Although providing precision of line, the formality of the design is broken up by the surface pattern of the technique, and what must have been a complicated and exacting process is made to look natural. Technical skills displayed in later examples, showing facial expressions, drapery and hand and body movements, surpass British needlework of any other period.

Opus Anglicanum

Opus anglicanum, as early English medieval embroidery was called, provides without doubt some of the finest examples of English needlework. It is thought by many to transcend even the skills of illuminated manuscript painting which, during the same period, was itself reaching new heights of excellence. It became internationally famous and was much sold abroad, a Vatican inventory of 1295 listing more pieces of *opus anglicanum* than of any other embroidery. Bearing in mind the established reputation for fine needlework that England possessed during the period up to the thirteenth century, it is necessary to trace the social and religious climate during the thirteenth and fourteenth century in order to discover why this phenomenon occurred.

It was for the Church that most of these items were worked and although secular pieces were embroidered at this time only a few fragments have survived. The Church was the center of life in medieval England and was as rich and powerful as the sovereign. The people depended on the clergy for guidance and salvation and naturally expected their churches to display the richest artefacts and ornamentation available. To the poor working classes, the greater the riches displayed in churches, the more dramatic and symbolic the effect. Vestments which survive from this period cannot now be fully appreciated as precious metals

Apparel of an amice, England, 1140–70. Silver-gilt and colored silks embroidered in underside couching on crimson silk, 60in × 27in (127cm × 68·6cm). This is part of a set of vestments traditionally thought to have been used by St. Thomas of Canterbury during his exile in France between 1164 and 1170. SENS CATHEDRAL, YONNE, FRANCE.

have worn and tarnished and pearl and jewel decorations have been removed: their beauty is still evident, however.

By the late thirteenth century the manufacture of embroidered vestments had become a highly lucrative industry and many workshops flourished, financed with money from city merchants. Men and women who were put to the trade were expected to serve a seven-year apprenticeship. Some of the established workers are known by name, including Mabel of Bury St. Edmunds, Alexander le Settere and Rose, wife of John de Burford, a merchant of the City of London. It is recorded that in 1263 a gold embroiderer called Gregory left London to become attached to the household of Pope Urban IV. As well as the export of English embroideries, workers trained in England were working on the Continent, thus spreading the influence and production of *opus anglicanum*.

The finest examples of *opus anglicanum* were produced between the mid-thirteenth and mid-fourteenth centuries. It is not only in technique that high standards were achieved but particularly in design, which compares favorably with the fine work being produced by the contemporary school of East Anglian manuscript illuminators. It is probable that both designers and painters were used in the embroidery workshops to draw out the designs in preparation for needlework.

In following the development of design in ecclesiastical vestments through the medieval period, four definite types can be discerned. The most striking difference between these is the outline pattern into which are placed figures of the Holy Family, saints or religious scenes. Copes are the most convenient garments to study because more examples have survived than of any other ecclesiastical vestment. Also, their semicircular shape demonstrates well the ingenuity of the design and the dexterity of the embroiderer.

The earliest geometric arrangement shows interlocking circles and quatrefoils placed across the semicircular shape of the garment in horizontal and vertical lines. This developed into the interlocking barbed quatrefoil shapes as seen on the Syon cope (Victoria and Albert Museum, London), the Steeple Aston cope (on loan to the Victoria and Albert Museum) and the Vatican cope. Little notice is taken of the semicircular limits of the garments in either of these two arrangements as the roundels and quatrefoils are truncated at the circumference.

Another style which developed during this period shows a more fluid design, the radiating lines of the pattern stemming from a Tree of Life or Tree of Jesse motif. This is illustrated in the Salzburg cope in the Abegg-Stiftung, Berne, and the Jesse cope in the Victoria and Albert Museum. The themes and secondary subjects of saints and symbols in these late thirteenth- and early fourteenth-century copes are contained within, and designed specially for, the shape of the vestments.

The most sophisticated design,

BELOW AND DETAIL: Vatican cope, *England, 1280–1300. Silver-gilt thread and colored silks in underside couching, split stitch and laid and couched work on red silk twill, 54½in × 122in (1·38m × 3·09m). In the compartmentalized design are depicted the Coronation of the Virgin, the Crucifixion and the Virgin and Child with saints holding symbols. This cope may be one of the two recorded as having been presented by Edward I to Pope Nicholas IV in 1291 and Pope Boniface VIII in c.1295.* MUSEO SACRO, VATICAN, ROME.

Altar frontal or dossal
(detail), England, 1315–
35. Silver-gilt thread and
colored silks in underside
couching, split stitch and laid
and couched work on linen,
20in × 23¾in (50·8cm ×
60·3cm). The inscription
MCCCXC ROMA on the
embroidery suggests that it
was worked for papal use.
BRITISH MUSEUM, LONDON.

dating from the fourteenth century,
makes use of pointed arcading arranged
in radiating lines around the garment.
The shape of the cope and how it would
be worn were vital considerations in this
style, which is illustrated in examples in
Bologna, in Italy, and Vich, in Spain, as
well as in the Butler-Bowdon cope
dating from between 1330 and 1350
and now in the Victoria and Albert
Museum. Figures stand under the
arcading, which forms a continuous and
unbroken line and provides great scope
for the design of the scenes. The posi-

tion of these scenes falls diagonally with
the garment so that they lie in a natural
position when worn.

It has not been possible to identify
either the embroidery workshops where
individual pieces were worked or the
workers who were responsible. As technical proficiency increased, so the
character of the original design could be
more clearly detected. Two particularly
fine examples of work which are comparable in style date from the first half
of the fourteenth century: the John of
Thanet panel in the Victoria and Albert
Museum and part of an altar frontal or
dossal which depicts Christ Charging
the Apostles and the Betrayal now in
the British Museum, London. The
latter subject shows great skill in composition. Placed within an arch, the
group is positioned in such a way as to
emphasize the emotion of the scene,
from the symbolically placed light
above the head of the utterly submissive
figure of Christ to the grimacing faces
of the soldiers. The surface pattern and
texture of the embroidery, worked in
part in underside couching, are particularly pleasing, with repeating contrasts
of light on dark and curved line on
straight, as in the maypole-striped
stockings of the soldier to the right, and
the twisting, turning edges of Christ's
cloak. The manipulation of silk and
metal thread adds character and drama
to the scene.

From the mid-fourteenth century the
art of English ecclesiastical embroidery
began to decline and from this time the
term opus anglicanum was no longer
used to describe embroidery produced
in England. The Black Death has until
recently been looked upon as the most
serious cause of its decline, but the
effects of the many wars in Europe may
have affected manufacture more
seriously. By the mid-fourteenth century trade was again flourishing, however, and Britain was flooded with
European fashions and textiles.

Late Medieval Embroidery
By 1330 velvet was replacing silk as a
background for embroidery and consequently different techniques were
required. Early examples such as the
Butler-Bowdon cope in the Victoria and
Albert Museum and the Chichester-
Constable chasuble in the Metropolitan
Museum, New York, which date from
the second quarter of the fourteenth
century, show a continuation of the fine

workmanship established during the preceding hundred years; but this did not last. With the demand for more work in less time, speedier techniques were adopted and, as a result, workmanship suffered.

Because of the difficulty of embroidering straight on to the velvet pile, a fine layer of silk or linen was placed over the surface and worked upon and this gradually developed into the quicker technique of working separate motifs on linen and then cutting these out and applying them to the background. Brick, satin and long and short stitches were used for speed; surface couching took over from underside couching; stem stitch tended to replace the finer split stitch.

The crafts guilds began to relax their strict supervision of the workshops and the quality of workmanship, fines were abolished and the practice of destroying work which fell below standard, which had previously guaranteed the maintenance of high standards, was discontinued. In 1423 the House of Commons petitioned Henry VI to protect the interests of the workshops against the self-employed worker but little was achieved even by the establishment of the Broderers' Company in 1430.

The new embroidery techniques, using woven silks and velvets, resulted in coarser work; heavily padded motifs were used in simple imitation of three-dimensional carvings and contemporary European fashions were copied. Embroidery in the "Flanders style" imitated both tapestry weaving and the popular Flemish easel painting, and the technique of or nué was attempted but was not practiced as successfully in Britain as in other parts of Europe. The coarser embroidery became known as façon d'Angleterre and at first proved as popular and as saleable on the Continent as opus anglicanum had been despite showing, as A. F. Kendrick says, "a poverty of artistic impulse."

Information concerning dress from the later medieval period is well documented. The Lutrell Psalter (1340) illustrates earlier forms of decorated clothing while the Duc of Berry's Les très Riches Heures (1416) and other contemporary European chronicles show the importance of richly embroidered costume in the fifteenth century. Dafydd ap Gwilym (1350–80), describing, with poetic license, a woman's headdress as "a hundred pounds worth,

thong, gems and wrought gold," shows the importance of precious metals and gems and it is known that items of costume were given to the Church to be altered to ecclesiastical use, their value being high.

Wardrobe accounts of Edward III mention robe makers by name and many descriptions of clothing exist in wills and inventories. One of the earliest examples of identifiable costume in painting can be seen in the Wilton Diptych in the National Gallery, London, where Richard II is portrayed wearing a robe similar to that described in his own inventories. Extravagance in dress was not encouraged, however, and sumptuary laws were passed to curb this, one forbidding the wearing of embroidered garments by people with less revenue than £200 a year.

Embroidered furnishings in the home were restricted to bed and wall hangings, none of which survive. It seems probable that those used for entertaining were as richly embroidered as the clothing of the day. Everyday woolen hangings would have had little or no decoration.

The tradition of embroidering battle emblems continued. The need to distinguish between friend and foe, between leader and follower – a king's standard was between eight and nine yards (7·3m and 8·2m) long, a duke's seven yards (6·4m) – made the ancient technique of applied decoration popular. The embroidered pennants, banners, badges, shields and streamers used in battle were also utilized for jousting and royal tournaments.

These were not the only ceremonial occasions and, with the setting up of Guilds and Livery Companies, civic pageants were enacted and symbolic dress and decoration (an outward sign of brotherhood) were needed. By the mid-fifteenth century the finest embroideries were being done not only for the Church but also for rich merchants and their Livery Companies.

The most interesting examples of these civic embroideries are the palls, or hearse cloths, kept by the city companies and used at the funerals of members of the guild. Great significance was attached to elaborate public funerals, both for religious and social reasons, with the ceremony lasting up to two days. Each parish also kept such funeral cloths and St. Margaret's, Westminster, charged eight pence for the hire of

theirs. Members of the royal family and individual merchants occasionally commissioned palls for their own use (one associated with Henry VII is now at Cambridge University) and some show the arms of individual families and even portraits of owners or donors of the piece, as in the case of the Fayrey Pall, now owned by Dunstable Priory, Bedfordshire.

Seven city companies still own palls. These are the Worshipful Companies of Brewers, Fishmongers, Ironmongers, Vintners, Saddlers, Parish Clerks and Merchant Taylors. The latter owns two cloths, the earliest of which is dated to between 1490 and 1512. The central panel of cut red velvet and cloth of gold is probably Italian. Applied motifs on the surrounding panels of purple velvet depict scenes from the Life of St. John the Baptist, the patron saint of the Company, together with symbolic badges of scissors and the *Agnus Dei*. The separately worked motifs are of silver gilt, silver thread, colored silks and sequins on a linen ground.

Early Tudor Embroidery

With the accession of Henry VIII in 1509 earlier standards in styles and techniques of embroidery were gradually regained. From this time until the nineteenth century the Church was no longer the principal patron, nor were religious subjects considered the main

source material for embroidered decoration. Many fine early ecclesiastical embroideries were lost during this period although some, fortunately, were smuggled out of churches and put to use in the home. Churchwardens, anticipating royal policy in the early years of Henry's rule, sold off textiles to tradesmen, who refashioned them. References to pursemakers, saddlers, tailors, haberdashers and goldsmiths all appear in contemporary church accounts, and they were probably grateful for the opportunity to buy such high-quality textiles.

One religious embroidery that is worth noting is the Fetternear Banner, now in the National Museum of Antiquities of Scotland in Edinburgh, worked between 1518 and 1522. It is thought that the piece was embroidered in Edinburgh as professionals were working there at the time. Although the banner does not conform to any design or style known to have been employed in embroidery before this date, the technique and linear quality of the design are early examples of what was to become popular in the following four decades. The representation of Christ as the Man of Sorrows with the Instruments of the Passion, the central theme of the banner, bears a strong resemblance to contemporary German woodcuts.

From 1520 onward pattern books for

lacis and needlework, and later for cutwork and lace, were published in Germany and soon the practice was copied in other European countries. In addition to these, books containing botanical and bestiary notes provided invaluable sources of design for the amateur embroideress.

For the first time in an historical survey of the craft it is possible to see from existing samples and paintings the embroidery that was used on clothing and furnishings. Affluent families now required comfort in their homes. Their fashionable, hard seat furniture was covered with cushions, and hangings were placed on walls and beds to exclude draughts. Although embroidery worked by the amateur was becoming a much more common feature, it is nonetheless likely that many domestic items were produced by professional workers.

The style of early Tudor embroideries was influenced by Italian silk patterns, while the linear designs are related to the geometric patterns of the medieval period. In order to represent the sharp contrast between light and dark, as seen in engravings and pattern books, a clean, crisp line was required and so the technique of holbein, or double-running stitch, was adopted. Portraits, by Hans Holbein (1497–1543) and Hans Eworth (active 1549–70) in particular, show the formal embroidered decoration on men's cuffs and collars and women's dresses. This is shown in an early example of a boy's shirt, of *c*.1540, which is of fine linen embroidered in blue silk, the pattern showing formalized columbine flowers arranged in interlocking lines.

Toward the end of the fifteenth century the influence of Turkish and Persian design reached Britain from Europe. Italian trade with the Middle East flourished (Italian artists were employed by the Turkish sultans at Constantinople) and patterns from Persian and Turkish carpets and textiles became popular. The shape most frequently copied was the arabesque, composed of swirling and interlocking forms used on domestic and costume embroidery of the period.

The monochrome of this type of embroidery was often enriched in costume with an abundance of gold thread applied to the outer garments. Such was the sumptuousness of Tudor clothing that it was recorded in 1517 that nearly 450 ounces of fine gold and 850 pearls

were taken off the robes of King Henry VIII in order to be returned to the goldsmith for re-use. Such entries continued to feature in wardrobe accounts throughout the Tudor and early Jacobean periods.

Surviving domestic items from this period are rare although inventories, notably those of an accused murderess, Dame Agnes Hungerford, and Catherine of Aragon, wife of Henry VIII, list embroidered bed hangings, cupboard cloths and table carpets.

Elizabethan Embroidery

Elizabethan embroidery has often been described as "bursting into flower." The frivolity of the age, the preoccupation with gardens and games, are mirrored in the embroidery. Many amateur pieces have survived and in the small domestic items worked in surface and canvas embroidery it is possible to find a parallel purpose and technique with present-day work. It can, therefore, be looked upon as the birth of embroidery as we know and use it today. This is not to say that amateur work eclipsed that of the professional and, indeed, the importance of embroidery as a trade was recognized in 1561 when Queen Elizabeth I granted a charter to the Broderers' Company. The professional concentrated on heraldic and ceremonial embroidery, on armorial trappings and liveries, for example, but also worked on domestic items, drew patterns and instructed the amateur in the home. The fundamental difference between the amateur and the professional was that, for the amateur, embroidery was a pastime or hobby, the work showing a freshness and naïvety of design. At times, however, amateur work reached such heights of excellence in both technique and design that it is difficult to differentiate between the two.

In affluent families young girls were trained to embroider not solely as a practical skill but also as a refined accomplishment and the production of the sampler would appear an important part of this training. The earliest dated British example was made by Jane Bostocke in 1598, and is now in the Victoria and Albert Museum. Worked in silk, silver-gilt thread, seed pearls and black beads, the sampler shows a variety of stitches (back, satin, chain, cross and buttonhole among others) on blocks of formal interlacing patterns reminiscent of work done earlier in the sixteenth

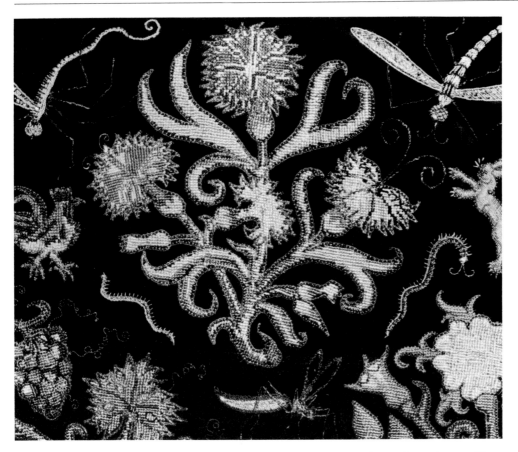

Long cushion cover
(detail), England, late
sixteenth century. Canvas
appliqué embroidery in silver
and silver-gilt thread,
colored silks on a black velvet
ground, 22in × 42in
(55·9cm × 105cm). The
cushion is trimmed with a
tassel at each corner.
VICTORIA AND ALBERT
MUSEUM, LONDON.

century. Naturalistic motifs such as animals and plant forms are attempted at the top of the work.

Techniques developed before this period were continued and, in some cases, improved upon by the Elizabethans. The application of linen and silk embroidered motifs on to velvet remained popular, but the subject matter of the embroidery changed. Floral sprigs, which had crept into designs by the mid-sixteenth century, began to dominate the patterns and insects and animals were also portrayed. These were often out of scale when placed side by side, but all are identifiable with their natural model.

During this period cross- and tent-stitch embroidery, which provided a hard-wearing surface, was used increasingly for domestic items. A late sixteenth-century black velvet cushion cover has applied cross- and tent-stitch embroidered silk flower "slips" (as these separately worked motifs became known), insects and animals. The placing of the design on the background in this way is reminiscent of Flemish *millefleurs* tapestries. The style probably originates, however, from illustrations in one of the many natural history, botanical or herbal books that were

available at that time where the motifs are presented independent of each other. The two most widely used books were Conrad Gesner's *Historia Animalium*, second edition published in Zürich in 1560, and John Gerarde's *Herball or Generall Historie of Plantes* of 1597.

The Elizabethan home was designed with a greater eye to comfort than any of its predecessors. Rooms were smaller and at the same time the emphasis placed on decorating the home for entertainment continued. Beds were luxuriously draped with hangings and valances and they had embroidered coverlets of fine whitework and monochrome embroidery. Oblong cushions were embroidered for chairs, window seats and to support books with richly worked covers. Tables and cupboards were covered with finely worked covers and carpets of canvas embroidery, which also proved suitable for many other purposes in the home.

The Bradford table carpet must have been produced in a professional workshop because of the fineness of the work (about four hundred stitches to the square inch). Worked on linen canvas with colored silks in tent stitch, the center of the carpet shows a design

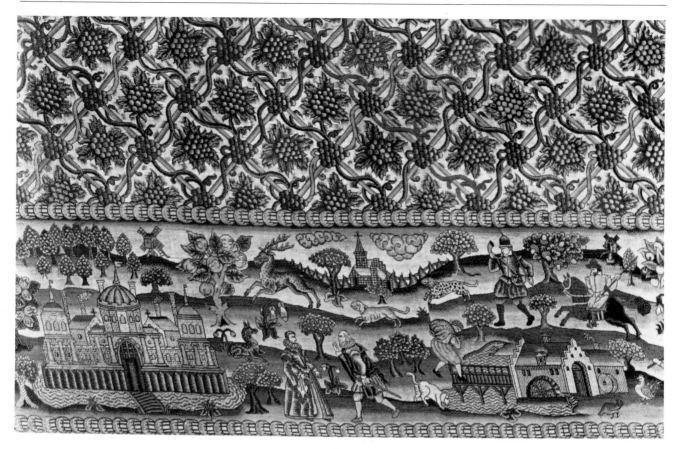

Bradford table carpet
(detail), England, late
sixteenth century. Colored
silks on linen canvas in tent
stitch, 13ft × 5ft 9in
3·96m × 1·75m). The carpet
belonged originally to the
Earl of Bradford. VICTORIA
AND ALBERT MUSEUM,
LONDON.

of interlocking vine leaves and bunches
of grapes. The border offers a lesson in
Elizabethan social history showing the
manor house and its fashionably dressed
inhabitants and the village with its
buildings, people and their occupations.
It has been suggested that the piece
illustrates the development of civilized
man.

Most domestic amateur embroidery
was worked under the supervision of,
and from drawings by, a professional.
It is known that a professional worker
was part of the household in many rich
families for the artist and craftsman
played an important rôle in Elizabethan
life.

The two most celebrated Elizabethan
embroideresses were Mary, Queen of
Scots, and Elizabeth, Countess of
Shrewsbury, better known as Bess of
Hardwick. Many myths surround the
two women and their embroidery and
much of the work ascribed to Mary cannot have been worked by her. Her
nomadic imprisonment in England and
Scotland, during which time most of
her work was produced, would have
made transportation of the large items
such as coverlets and bed hangings very
difficult. Mary's training in embroidery
began in France under Catherine de

Médicis following her marriage in 1558,
at the age of sixteen, to Catherine's
son, the Dauphin (later François II).
She is alleged to have introduced many
French styles of dress and embroidery
to Britain on her return.

While in the custody of George
Talbot, sixth Earl of Shrewsbury, Mary
moved from one to another of his many
houses: Tutbury Castle, Sheffield
Castle, Sheffield Manor, Wingfield
Manor, Worksop Manor, his lodge at
Buxton and his wife Bess's house,
Chatsworth. There is no evidence for
the legend that she was ever at Hardwick Hall in Derbyshire although two
items from the original collection of
the household, now exhibited there, are
marked with her cypher.

One surviving set of hangings is
undoubtedly the work of both Bess and
Mary. Known as the Oxburgh hangings
(they were moved to Oxburgh Hall,
Norfolk, in the eighteenth century), the
panels are of green velvet applied with
canvas embroidered medallions showing animals, plants and flowers,
emblems and devices. Separately embroidered motifs of the same size, from
a dismembered hanging with the same
provenance, are now in the Victoria and
Albert Museum. Although certain

domestic problems were caused by Mary living within the Shrewsbury household, the standard of embroidery done by these two women and their companions, with the help of a professional worker, does not appear to have suffered.

Lists of New Year presents given to Queen Elizabeth I, in most cases worked by the donors, show how highly regarded were embroidered costumes and accessories. Gowns, petticoats, kirtles, doublets, mantles, gloves and purses would all have been the product of the professional tailor and embroiderer. It is possible to see the richness of the techniques and materials used for this embroidery in contemporary portraits, which show that silver gilt, precious gems and pearls were the most desirable decorations. In 1572 sewing gold cost five shillings an ounce so it is difficult to understand how, by 1620, there were seventy-five master wiredrawers and spinners trading in London.

The use of emblems on Elizabethan embroidery is characteristic of a prevailing interest in symbolism. Two of the most widely used books of emblems which became popular for supplying enigmatic motifs for use in embroidery are Claude Paradin's *Devises Héroiques*, published in Lyons in 1557 and translated into English in 1591, and Geoffrey Whitney's *Choice of Emblemes* of 1586. The so-called "Rainbow portrait" of Queen Elizabeth I at Hatfield House, Hertfordshire, shows the Queen wearing a cloak embroidered with eyes and ears and a serpent holding a ruby on the left sleeve symbolizing her vigilance and wisdom. Similarly, the embroidered border of a piece in the Victoria and Albert Museum shows a repeating design of weeping eyes which possibly represents the Passion. The enigmatic emblems that were used by Mary, Queen of Scots, for the Oxburgh hangings have been traced directly to the Claude Paradin pattern book. Other such motifs can be seen on a man's nightcap embroidered with symbolic decorations of swirling serpents and obelisks placed in repeating patterns beneath arches.

Linear embroidery in black silk on a white ground, which became known as blackwork, was a particularly popular technique for the embroidery of costume following, as it did, the monochrome tradition of the early Tudor era. Designs for this embroidery took on a

sophisticated form in Elizabethan work. Speckling, a form of random stitching, was used as shading, while the back and right sleeve of an embroidered jacket, although the iron content of black dye has rotted the silk thread, gives an interesting impression of the technical skill that was employed in blackwork. It also shows the successful adaptation of embroidery motifs from Geoffrey Whitney's *Choice of Emblemes*.

ABOVE:
Man's nightcap, *England, c.1600. Silk embroidery and sequins on linen, the embroidery in chain and buttonhole stitches and French knots, with couched metal purl, circumference 22in (56cm). Nightcaps of this type were used for informal wear and not for sleep. They were embroidered in one horizontal strip and then seamed along the six triangular panels of the crown to make the characteristic domed shape.*
MISS O. M. MATTHEWS COLLECTION, CHERTSEY MUSEUM, SURREY, ENGLAND.

LEFT:
Falkland jacket *(detail), England, early seventeenth century. Silk on linen in stem, back and running stitches and speckling, length at center back 16½in (41·9cm). The designs are taken from Geoffrey Whitney's* Choice of Emblemes, *published in Leyden, Holland, in 1586.*
VICTORIA AND ALBERT MUSEUM, LONDON.

Page from the pattern book "A Schole-house for the Needle," *published by Richard Shorleyker, printed in Shoe Lane, London, England, "at the sign of the Faulcon," 1632. Most of the patterns were taken from earlier pattern books. Dark areas on the page are where chalk has been dusted through holes in the paper to produce a pattern on the fabric to be embroidered.* NATIONAL ART LIBRARY, VICTORIA AND ALBERT MUSEUM, LONDON.

To transfer a design from a pattern book to the fabric, holes were punched in the printed page around the detail. This was then placed on the ground material and dusted with charcoal to produce a dotted impression on the fabric beneath.

Fine book bindings were embroidered throughout the sixteenth century and an excellent example, presented by the printer Christopher Barker to Queen Elizabeth in 1583, is now in the Bodleian Library, Oxford. Worked on crimson velvet, the design shows a symmetrical arrangement of stems and Tudor roses in gold and silver thread and colored silks, decorated with seed pearls. The Bodleian Library also owns a copy of *The Epistles of St. Paul*, the cover of which is similarly embroidered, reputedly by the Queen herself.

Traditional professional work contrasts greatly with the brightly colored floral work of the amateur and it is significant that for the first time there was a division of the sexes in embroidery, men working as professionals (although there were some women in the trade) and women in the home.

Embroidery was used to decorate a greater number of wares than previously and it is true to say that, after the end of the sixteenth century, embroidery rarely attained the same characteristic lightness of heart, natural humor and vigor that it had at this period.

The Early Seventeenth Century

Although the seventeenth century can be divided into three distinct social and

political periods (the early Stuart, the Commonwealth and the Restoration), artistic styles are not so easily defined: the vast range of embroidered work mirrors the many changes that occurred throughout the century.

The accession of James VI of Scotland to the English throne in 1603 saw little immediate difference in the popular styles of costume and furnishings. Blackwork embroidery continued, often becoming heavier and more ornate with the addition of metal thread and spangles. Polychrome silks were also used in floral and animal designs derived from pattern books, particularly Richard Shorleyker's *A Schole-house for the Needle*, published in 1624, and James Boler's *The Needle's Excellency* of 1631, which is prefaced by John Taylor's poem, *The Praise of the Needle*, a statement of the value of embroidery not only for decoration but also for educational purposes.

One of the finest surviving examples of polychrome embroidery is a woman's bodice originally worn by Margaret Laton (Plate 13). A portrait painted between 1615 and 1620 and attributed to Marcus Gheeraerts (active 1590–1630) shows Margaret Laton wearing the bodice. Both the bodice and the painting are presently on loan to the Victoria and Albert Museum.

Clothing worn during the reign of James I (1603–25), although very ornate in its design, is mainly made of plain silk. Embroidered items of clothing do exist, however, which show a predilection for architectural motifs in the designs, such as pyramids and obelisks. In contrast, during Charles I's reign (1625–45) costume became less fussy but more colorful due not to embroidery but to the use of woven silks which were now easier to obtain from abroad. The English woven silk industry had only recently started during this period. Gloves became increasingly ornate with the development of embroidered gauntlets during the first quarter of the century but by 1638, with the setting up of the Glovers' Company under a royal charter, it seems that the trade may have needed support to adapt to the change in fashion. Embroidered costume accessories which did become popular during the first half of the century were heavily embroidered military scarves, now the cherished relics of Civil War battles.

As with costume, so furnishings in

the first half of the century showed little immediate change, with the continued use of blackwork and polychrome embroidery for linen covers and silk canvas embroidery for cushions. Canvas embroidery was also used for the first time for upholstery in the earlier part of the seventeenth century, but this was initially overshadowed by the use of Turkey work, a form of carpet knotting which imitated the so-called "Turkey" carpets imported from the East during the Tudor period.

The seventeenth century saw the climax, and then at the end of the century the decline, of the art of embroidering book bindings, with silk work on satin superseding the heavy metal-embroidered examples of the previous century. Because of the fragility of the bindings, many fine protective covers were made, often as lovingly worked and as admirable as the bindings themselves. Surviving examples of the books and their covers can be seen at the British Museum, the Bodleian Library, Oxford, and the British and Foreign Bible Society, London.

A short-lived revival of church decoration occurred in the 1630s under the influence of Archbishop Laud which resulted in the production of a few pieces of finely worked ecclesiastical embroidery. An altar frontal, dossal and book cushions, commissioned for the Chapel of the Holy Ghost at Basingstoke, Berkshire, and now in the Victoria and Albert Museum, bear the date 1633 and the arms of the Sandys family. The embroidery is in silver and gold with spangles on a purple ground. In direct contrast, due to their lack of decoration, are the few surviving chalice veils embroidered in monochrome which were probably worked domestically for use in Catholic recusant families.

Embroidered Pictures and Samplers
The fashion for embroidered pictures during this period took many forms. Portraits of monarchs, particularly Charles I, were worked in the form of miniatures in silks after engravings by Sir Anthony Van Dyck (1599–1641) and the origin of an example in the Victoria and Albert Museum has been traced to an engraving by Wenceslaus Hollar (1607–77) after Van Dyck. These embroidered pictures were used as presents or, after the King's execution,

as memorials. Worked by both professionals and amateurs, surviving examples show a very high standard of workmanship.

Other types of professionally embroidered pictures show much more clearly the difference between professional and amateur work, however. Religious scenes by the embroiderer Edmund Harrison (1589–1666), identified by comparison with surviving examples of needlework and records at the Broderers' Company, demonstrate great sophistication of design and his most favored technique, a combination of *or nué* and needle painting, shows not only that he was influenced by foreign work but that his training may have been completed on the Continent. He is known to have embroidered heraldic works, court costume and clothes for masques and plays under the patronage of the three kings, James I, Charles I and Charles II, although only three pictures worked by him survive. These are now in the collections of the Fitzwilliam Museum, Cambridge, the Royal Scottish Museum,

Portrait of Margaret Laton, *attributed to Marcus Gheeraerts (active 1590–1630), 1615–20. The jacket worn by Margaret Laton is illustrated as Plate 13.* ON LOAN TO THE VICTORIA AND ALBERT MUSEUM, LONDON.

Sampler, *England, first half
of the seventeenth century.
Silver thread and silks on
linen, 20in × 12½in (50·8cm
× 31·7cm). Tent,
interlacing, plaited braid,
guilloche, Romanian,
Algerian, eye, Florentine,
double-running, cross,
Montenegrin cross, two-
sided Italian cross, crosslet
chain and detached filling
stitches are used in the
execution of this sampler.*
VICTORIA AND ALBERT
MUSEUM, LONDON.

Edinburgh, and the Victoria and
Albert Museum.

Knowledge about the training of the
young embroideress during this century
can be gained both from surviving dated
and inscribed examples and from liter-
ary references. Whereas in the Elizabethan period the teaching of embroidery to the daughters of rich families
was usual but not obligatory, in the
seventeenth century it became a principal part of a young girl's education.
Affluent households would have tutors
in the home and one child records
having "tutors in several qualities,
languages, music, dancing, writing and
needlework."

Specific tasks were set in this training, the first pieces to be completed

being a plain and a colored sampler.
The practice of signing and dating this
type of work developed during the
1630s. Early samplers are long and thin
in format, their shape depending on the
loom width of the ground fabric and
there are no overall patterns as in later
examples: as the name suggests, they
were random trials of many different
stitches and patterns. Toward the end
of the century samplers took on a more
orderly character with rows of stitches
set in horizontal lines across the linen.
These samplers were worked more to
show technical expertise than the
earlier ones, which were made for stitch
and pattern reference.

Raised Work
The next task expected of the young
embroideress was the completion of a
cabinet or workbox in raised stitches,
later to be misnamed "stumpwork."
These cabinets were first worked in flat
sections and then given to the cabinet-
maker to make up in three-dimensional
form. Varied and often complicated in
shape, they had hinged lids and doors,
cupboards and drawers and a great deal
of embroidery was necessary to cover
all these areas. It is not surprising that
an embroidered box, now in the Whit-
worth Art Gallery in Manchester, contains a note to say that the embroideress,
Hannah Smith, had taken two years to
complete the piece.

Raised work in embroidery seems to
have followed the fashion for relief
woodcarving. Small, shaped blocks of
wood or composition were fixed under
the embroidery to give the required
raised appearance and other areas were
stuffed with hair or any other available
material. This use of wood is shown
particularly well in a picture now in the
Lady Lever Art Gallery, Port Sunlight,
Merseyside, where the central subject
of the naked Bathsheba shows a perfectly carved wooden figure without
embellishment of any kind.

Subjects used for these embroideries
came from various classical and religious sources, and Flemish and Dutch
engravings were often copied. Scenes
from Ovid's *Metamorphoses*, first used
in the previous century, retained their
popularity, although the distorting
nature of the raised technique and the
use of contemporary dress and decoration at times make recognition difficult.
A raised-work panel in the Lady Lever
Art Gallery of Pharaoh's Host in the

Red Sea is naïvely and charmingly depicted. Most of the details, especially Moses seen to the left directing the proceedings, are humorously portrayed.

Children were often given another subject to embroider before being considered capable of working on their own, although they might still be very young. It is recorded that one child, Martha Edlin, was only thirteen years of age when she finished her fourth piece, a jewel case. This last exercise would be in one of several techniques. The popular beadwork embroidery was chosen to decorate jewel cases, pictures, trays and purses, for example, and silk embroidery and raised work on satin was adopted for the decorative frames on expensive mirrors.

The Later Seventeenth Century

In domestic and costume embroidery of the second half of the seventeenth century a variety of new and old techniques were employed and the range of items that were so decorated gives a foretaste of what was to follow in the succeeding century. Quilting, which had been used for practical purposes, for bedcoverings and linings for armor since medieval times, was now employed for clothing and worked in decorative floral patterns in silk and cotton. For domestic use a linen ground proved more service-

able, with the quilting in plain linen or yellow silk thread. Much of the re-awakening of interest in quilting was due to the importation of Oriental coverlets by the East India Company. Imported fabrics from China and India provide the largest single influence on embroidery designs and techniques of the late seventeenth century, though the Indian influences have in the past been overemphasized.

Naturalistic flowers had, by the third quarter of the century, become heavier in shape and distorted under the influence of the French and Italian

Raised-work picture, worked by Damaris Pearse (1659–79), Ermington, Devon, England, c.1675. Silks, chenille and metal thread on a white satin ground in padded and raised work, long and short, stem and detached buttonhole stitches with couching and French knots, 13in × 22in (33cm × 55·9cm). The subject is the Overwhelming of Pharoah's Host. LADY LEVER ART GALLERY, PORT SUNLIGHT, BIRKENHEAD, ENGLAND.

Curtain, *England*, c.1696. *Linen and cotton twill embroidered with colored worsted wools in stem, long and short, chain, buttonhole, satin, Romanian, coral and detached chain stitches with French knots and speckling, 70in × 46in (1·77m × 116·8m). Another one in this set of crewelwork hangings is in the Royal Ontario Museum, Canada, and dated 1696.* VICTORIA AND ALBERT MUSEUM, LONDON.

baroque styles, particularly woven silk designs. Mixed with exotic Eastern forms, this resulted in a particularly weird type of design which was used on contemporary embroidered curtains, valances and bed hangings, many of which survive to this day. Worked in worsted or crewel wools on a twill background of cotton or linen, the designs are composed of strange, twisted and gnarled trees and plants growing out of shaded, hilly ground, with exotic birds and animals set either on branches or on the ground. Usually worked in stem, satin, or long and short stitches, the colors of these pieces were at first restricted to various shades of green, blue and brown, although a greater range of colors can be seen in later examples.

Canvas embroidery remained popular for both upholstery and for large wall hangings. A particularly fine set of hangings dating from the second half of the century and found in a house in Hatton Garden, London, is now in the Victoria and Albert Museum. The style of work lacks obvious Eastern influences but shows some of the baroque forms popular in Italy and France, with columns entwined with large distorted leaves and flowerheads.

A third and quite separate technique from those already mentioned became popular at the end of the century. This involved placing knotted and couched cord on linen or silk in complicated, yet formal, cartouches of swirling designs. A set of chairs with red linen knotted cord couched on to yellow silk can be seen at Ham House, Petersham, in Surrey. This technique, which was worked with a shuttle, became a favorite pastime for ladies, particularly Queen Mary II, who was seen knotting wherever she went.

The great mixture of embroidered styles and techniques must have given the late seventeenth-century home an appearance of confusion. This is best illustrated by quoting Celia Fiennes, the noted traveler, when she describes a house in Epsom: "You enter one roome hung with crosstitch in silks . . . window curtaines white satin silk damaske with furbellows of callicoe printed flowers, the chaires crosstitch, the two stooles of yellow mohaire with crosstitch true lovers knotts in straps along and across, an elbow chaire tentstitch . . . many fine pictures under glasses of tentstitch, sattinstitch gumm and straw work also Indian flowers and birds."

The Eighteenth Century

In the eighteenth century the use of embroidery for practical purposes continued while the fashion declined for small cabinets, boxes, mirrors and other objects of no immediate domestic use that had been decorated with embroidery in the late seventeenth century.

The teaching of embroidery became part of a school's syllabus, although little is known of children's work apart from the signed and dated samplers, of which many examples survive. The early part of the century saw a change in the shape of samplers to a squarer format, and the traditional horizontal bands of stitches and varieties of pattern became linked in a single pictorial theme (Plate 18), often with long inscriptions. Thus, by the end of the eighteenth century, with the fashion for embroidering maps and almanac samplers, they became objects for display, not merely visual references for stitches and patterns.

Crewelwork embroidery retained its popularity in the first quarter of the century and the technique was used for decorating costume, especially ladies' jackets and men's waistcoats. For furnishings such as chair seats, wall hangings, carpets and fire screens, however, cross stitch on canvas became the popular technique.

The source of many extant examples of needlework has been traced to specific engravings and book illustrations and the design of as many as thirteen embroideries has been traced to the same illustration. One of the most popular sources was the Ogilvy translation of Virgil's *Aeneid* of 1658, with illustrations by Cleyn, details from which, to mention an important example, were copied in one of the three Stoke Edith hangings now at Montacute House in Somerset (Plate 17). Classical, biblical and pastoral scenes and scenes from fables were chosen to show figures in a landscape and, whereas raised work of the seventeenth century showed apparently alien figures in contemporary dress, in the eighteenth century attempts were made to give the subjects more historical reference. Clearly illustrated is a love of nature that is, however, different from the attitude of the Elizabethans.

The prevalent pastoralism forced false values on nature and it was the superficial trappings of the countryside that were found attractive. Games involving rustic occupations were played and women dressed as milkmaids: Marie Antoinette had her own dairy in the grounds at Fontainebleau. The gardens and parks of country houses were landscaped. Nature was not used as it was found, uncultivated, but was embellished to suit fashionable taste. Unusual, highly colored blooms appear in designs in festoons, garlands, bowers, vases and cornucopiae: very few issue from the ground or other natural surroundings.

The fashion for upholstered chair and settee seats reached its height in the eighteenth century. Those who could afford to ordered French tapestry; those with smaller purses sought professionally embroidered work or, alternatively, had covers that were worked by a mem-

"The Visit to the Boarding School," by George Morland (1763–1804), England, c.1788. Parents inspect the school work of their children which includes a sampler. Trustees of the Wallace Collection, London.

ber of the family. These were sometimes embroidered before the chair was designed or made, showing the fanaticism of the amateur embroideress at this period.

Early designs for chair seats with figures show a marked chinoiserie flavor in keeping with the fashion in interior decoration. Floral subjects, on the other hand, show quite different influences, as in a settee of carved and gilded wood and gesso in the Lady Lever Art Gallery (Plate 16). The seat and back are of cross stitch, the large colorful flowers showing a definite similarity to Dutch still-life paintings and French tapestry panels, which were most sought after in Britain in the mid-eighteenth century.

Few of the large cross-stitch wall hangings worked by amateur embroideresses still exist due to damage by dirt and moth or because they were adapted for use as bed hangings, covers or screens. Many must have been destroyed because of the fashion for plain painted walls and later wallpaper. Those that do exist are in a variety of patterns and provide evidence of admirable patience and good workmanship. The ten hangings worked in wool and silk at Wallington Hall in Northumberland were started in 1717 by Lady Julia Calverley and completed in three and a half years. As each hanging measures nine feet by two feet eleven inches (29cm by 9cm), their completion must be considered a notable feat. Of equal importance is the six-panelled screen worked ten years later by Lady Julia Calverley and her assistants at Wallington with scenes based on Francis Cleyn's illustrations to Virgil's *Eclogues and Georgics*, published in London in 1654 (Plate 19).

The Stoke Edith hangings (Plate 17), already mentioned, which have two panels portraying a formal garden scene in springtime, were at one time thought to have been the work of the five wives of the second Thomas Foley of Stoke Edith, Hertfordshire. In the design of the Mary Holte hangings and carpet at Aston Hall, Birmingham, the embroideress, the daughter of Sir Charles Holte, called on the experience of herself and her family in depicting Aston Hall and Brereton Hall, Staffordshire, which were both family residences, and the Holte coat of arms. The work is inscribed "God be the Guide/And the work will abide/Mary Holte spinster

aged 60 1744." A notable hanging, signed "Anne Grant" and dated 1750, is at Monymusk, Aberdeenshire. Worked in fine tent stitch in wool and silk, the design shows vases of flowers and potted trees placed beneath arches on a yellow background with a black and white tiled floor. This indicates a mixture of influences: Indian flowers, Chinese ceramics and Dutch paintings of interiors.

Costume in the Eighteenth Century

Exotic floral designs were applied to costume as well as furnishings but often in inappropriate arrangements and eccentric sizes. Mrs. Delany, the diarist and a noted needlewoman in her own right, described a petticoat worn by the Duchess of Queensberry to a reception in 1740 as being of a design of brown hills with all sorts of weeds and twining flowers, and with an old tree stump running up to the waist. Another she describes as "much properer for the stucco staircase than the apparel for a lady." The popular form of rococo patterning, which had superseded the heavier, mannered curves of the baroque, adapted more successfully to architecture and other three-dimensional forms than to embroidered fabric. This did not deter the embroideress, however.

After the dominance of woven silks for costume in the late seventeenth century, embroidery gained in popularity even though the eighteenth century was the high point in the manufacture of woven dress silk in England and France. Whereas ladies' dresses were made of woven silk (when it could be afforded), many dress accessories were embroidered. Court dress continued to be professionally embroidered in the traditional way.

Patterns on embroidered costume often show the influence of designs taken from woven silks, which were imported at great expense from Italy and France. Metal thread was used in quantity for both woven and embroidered costume and furnishings. Considering the hazards involved in wearing this, it is surprising that so many items have survived: a new pastime called "*parfilage*" became popular which entailed unraveling gold and silver thread from fabric with the object of selling it. British enthusiasts, or "drizzlers" as they became called, carried scissors in

LEFT: Plate 1
Pocket book, *America,*
dated 1777. This pocket
book which has been worked
in bargello stitch has been
photographed open in order
to reveal the inscription.
CHICAGO HISTORICAL
SOCIETY.

BELOW, LEFT: Plate 3
Bed rug *(detail), made by*
Sara Waterman, Norwich,
New York, America, 1794.
SMITHSONIAN INSTITUTION,
WASHINGTON.

ABOVE: Plate 2
Valance, *America,*
eighteenth century.
Embroidered in crewel work.
SMITHSONIAN INSTITUTION,
WASHINGTON.

Plate 4
Sampler *made by Lucy
Symonds, Boxford,
Massachusetts, America,
1796.* VICTORIA AND ALBERT
MUSEUM, LONDON.

Plate 5
Quilt with single motif of
Rising Sun or Star of
Bethlehem *made by Mary
Totten, New York, America,
early nineteenth century.
Pieced and appliqué work.*
SMITHSONIAN INSTITUTION,
WASHINGTON.

Elizabeth Lawson Sewed This Sampler 1833

LEFT: Plate 7
Quilt, *America, 1840. This quilt top worked in appliqué commemorates the presidential campaign of William Henry Harrison (1773–1841).* SMITHSONIAN INSTITUTION, WASHINGTON.

BELOW, LEFT: Plate 8
Lamp mat, *Kennebunkport, Maine, America, c. 1850. Berlin woolwork with center square worked in cross stitch and with raised woolwork flowers in the corners; the border is worked in raised woolwork with flowers in natural colors.* SMITHSONIAN INSTITUTION, WASHINGTON.

BELOW, RIGHT: Plate 9
Sampler, *America, dated February 1878. A canvas work sampler embroidered as a montage of the popular motifs of the period.* SMITHSONIAN INSTITUTION, WASHINGTON.

OPPOSITE: Plate 6
Sampler *made by Elizabeth Dawson, America, 1833.* JOHN JUDKYN MEMORIAL, FRESHFORD MANOR, BATH.

BELOW: Plate 10
Crazy patchwork quilt,
*America, late nineteenth
century.* SMITHSONIAN
INSTITUTION, WASHINGTON.

ABOVE: Plate 11
Pocket book, *America,
nineteenth century.
Embroidered with needle
weaving.* MR. AND MRS.
ZORACH, NEW YORK.

BELOW: Plate 12
Embroidered picture *by
Ethel Mohamed, America,
exhibited at the Folk Life
Festival of 1976 in
Washington, D.C.*
SMITHSONIAN INSTITUTION,
WASHINGTON.

LEFT: Plate 13
Margaret Laton jacket, England, 1610–30. Linen embroidered with silk and silver-gilt thread in detached buttonhole, stem, plait, braid, chain, long and short, Romanian and speckling stitches with French knots and spangles, length 19in (48cm), chest 31in (79cm). The painting reproduced on page 43 is a portrait of Margaret Laton wearing the jacket. VICTORIA AND ALBERT MUSEUM, LONDON.

BELOW: Plate 14
The Bayeux Tapestry (detail), probably designed and worked in England, possibly Canterbury, third quarter of the eleventh century – second quarter of the twelfth century. Stem and outline stitches with laid and couched work in colored wools on linen, 19½in × 231ft (50cm × 70·4m). The embroidery was made for Odo, Bishop of Bayeux and brother of William the Conqueror, and this detail shows Harold being told of the comet. It consists of six pieces of linen sewn together. The right end of the embroidery is frayed and therefore a section is probably missing. MUSÉE DE LA REINE MATHILDE, BAYEUX.

RIGHT: Plate 15
Pair of gauntlets, *England,
early seventeenth century.
Satin embroidered with
silver-gilt and silver thread,
purl and silk in satin stitch
and couched work with seed
pearls and spangles, trimmed
with silver-gilt and silver
bobbin lace, length 15in
(38·1cm). Traditionally,
these are supposed to be the
gloves given by Henry VIII
to Sir Anthony Denny. The
style of decoration with
crowned thistles and roses
would, however, suggest that
they were made during the
reign of James I and had
some connection with this
monarch.* VICTORIA AND
ALBERT MUSEUM, LONDON.

BELOW: Plate 16
Sofa covered with canvas
embroidery, *England, the
sofa c.1735, on the seat the
embroidery dated 27
September, 1743, and on the
back 17 December, 1748.
Cross stitch in wool on
canvas, depth of seat 21in
(53·4cm), height of back
39in (98·4cm), width of seat
86in (218·4cm). It is likely
that the dates refer to when
the embroidery was begun
and finished.* LADY LEVER
ART GALLERY, PORT
SUNLIGHT, BIRKENHEAD,
MERSEYSIDE.

ABOVE: Plate 17
Panel from the Stoke Edith hangings, *England, second quarter of the eighteenth century. Canvas worked with tent stitch in silk, approx. 10ft × 20ft (3m × 6m). This is one of a set of hangings owned originally by the Foley family of Stoke Edith. Two are garden scenes, in the style of woven tapestry hangings, and the third is scenes from Francis Cleyn's illustrations for Virgil's* Aeneid, *published in 1658.* THE NATIONAL TRUST, MONTACUTE, SOMERSET.

LEFT: Plate 18
Embroidered picture, *worked by Elizabeth Haines, England, c.1720. Woolen canvas embroidered with colored silks in tent and satin stitch, 14in × 12½in (35·6cm × 31·7cm). This piece, which bears the initials EH of the embroideress has 250 stitches to the inch (25·4mm).* VICTORIA AND ALBERT MUSEUM, LONDON.

RIGHT AND BELOW: Plate 21
Three patterns for Berlin
woolwork, *published by
Carl W. Wicht and A. Todt,
Berlin, c.1860. Printed
squared paper, hand colored
with watercolors. It was
from hand-colored patterns
of this type, originally
produced in Germany, that
Berlin woolwork was made.
Each square represents a
stitch on the canvas.*
VICTORIA AND ALBERT
MUSEUM, LONDON.

BOTTOM, RIGHT: Plate 22
Panel of Berlin woolwork,
*England, 1840–50s. Canvas
embroidered in cross stitch
with wools, silks and beads,
25½in × 37¾in (64cm ×
95·1cm). Berlin woolwork
was popular in many of the
countries of Europe and in
the United States in the
mid-nineteenth century,
designs varying from animals
and flowers to reproductions
of famous paintings. This
panel is of high quality and
may have been an exhibition
piece.* VICTORIA AND ALBERT
MUSEUM, LONDON.

OPPOSITE, BELOW: Plate 24
Patchwork quilt, *Wales,
first half of the nineteenth
century. Printed cottons
with a backing of plain white
cotton, quilted in running
stitches, 94in × 83in
(2·4m × 2·1m). A typical
example of domestic quilting,
the mis-matching of patterns
shows that scraps were used
and not enough of each
pattern of printed cotton was
available for strict symmetry.*
VICTORIA AND ALBERT
MUSEUM, LONDON.

LEFT: Plate 23
Smock frock, *England,
c.1860. Heavy white linen
embroidered in linen in
feather and back stitch,
length 48½in (123·1cm),
chest approx. 40in
(100·8cm). This is the most
common type of smock frock,
made and worn in this
instance in east Surrey in
the Mitcham or Farley area.
The embroidery controls the
fullness of the cloth and at
the same time serves as
decoration.* GUILDFORD
MUSEUM, SURREY.

Plate 25
Church banner, *designed by Duncan Grant (1885– 1978), cut out by Vanessa Bell (1879–1961) and embroidered by Mrs. Antrobus, Miss Elwes and Mary Hogarth (1865– 1935), England, 1927. Various fabrics including silk crape, silk damask and blue wool, applied with couching and other embroidery stitches in wool and silk in long and short, satin, chain, fishbone and Oriental stitches and glass beads, 72in × 35in (182·9cm × 88·9cm). Duncan Grant and Vanessa Bell were leading members of the Omega Workshop, founded by Roger Fry shortly before the outbreak of the First World War. The Omega Workshop extended the theories of the Arts and Crafts Movement into the twentieth century.* VICTORIA AND ALBERT MUSEUM, LONDON.

OPPOSITE: Plate 26
"The Magic Garden," *designed and worked by Rebecca Crompton (died 1947), England, c.1937. Appliqué and patterned and colored silks, embroidered with couching, French knots and honeycomb stitches, 20¼in × 14¾in (51·4cm × 37·5cm). Worked to give the greatest contrast in texture and line, the chunkiness of the appliqué stitches gives a three-dimensional quality to the piece.* VICTORIA AND ALBERT MUSEUM, LONDON.

OVERLEAF: Plate 27
"Into the Garden," *designed and embroidered by Audrey Walker, England, 1975. Unprimed artist's canvas, spray dyed and embroidered with French knots, seeding and Cretan stitches, 44in × 32in (111·1cm × 81·3cm). The panel was designed to evoke a small, enclosed garden. The embroideress is a member of the Embroiderers' Guild and the '62 Group.* MR. AND MRS. H. BOWMAN.

Mantua, *England, early
1740s. Red corded silk
embroidered with silver
threads, strip, cord and purl
in laid and couched work,
length at center back 51in
(129cm), width of skirt 66in
(167·6cm). The dress is
signed, as a form of receipt,
in the lining, probably by the
embroideress. A section of
colored silk embroidery under
the train suggests that the
embroideress changed her
mind and reverted to metal-
thread embroidery.* VICTORIA
AND ALBERT MUSEUM,
LONDON.

their purses at all times in order to snip
at whatever they could.

The names of professional dress-
makers and dress embroiderers can be
found in the Royal Accounts in the
Public Record Office. A red mantua in
the collection of the Victoria and Albert
Museum is signed by the embroideress
but in general the names of the embroideresses are not known. Many small
items of costume such as stomachers,
petticoats, pairs of pockets and shoes
took the fancy of the embroiderer and
the fashion for highly ornate aprons is a
reminder of the popularity for dressing
in working clothes. The results, however, are far from practical as may be
seen from an apron in silks, silver gilt,
purl and other metal threads worked on
a silk background.

Whitework was widely used on costume during the early years of the
eighteenth century. White muslin trimming on colorful costume achieved an
effect that contemporary needle laces
were unable to emulate. Later in the
century, when lace was beyond the
pockets of many, a cheaper substitute
was found in embroidered muslin or
"Dresden" muslin (sometimes called
point de Saxe), which rivaled lace in
quality. Amateurs copied this professional work when it was first imported from abroad and early British
examples, often with Chinese motifs,
show great skill. Whitework techniques
can be seen on contemporary samplers
and shirt ruffles, fichus, caps and
lappets. One whitework apron in the
Victoria and Albert Museum is marked
with the age of the fourteen-year-old
embroideress and the same museum also
owns a man's waistcoat of drawn-thread
and white cotton embroidery on a linen
ground, another fine example of whitework.

The fashion for lace trimming led to
an attempt to establish a native linen-
thread industry in Scotland, where
pillow- and bobbin-lace techniques were
also taught in selected schools. This
was not successful and a substitute
technique was found in the embroidery
of fine cotton muslin. Design schools
and manufactories were set up in and
around Edinburgh and this, with the
efforts of Luigi Ruffini, an Italian
emigré who settled in Scotland in 1780
and set up a workroom in Edinburgh
in 1782, are seen as the foundations of
the nineteenth-century Ayrshire whitework industry.

Short apron, *England, first half of the eighteenth century. Silk and metal embroidery on silk, worked in satin, long and short stitches and French knots, 16¾in × 40in (42·6cm × 101·6cm). The embroidery, with the exception of the tendrils and some of the stems, has been applied to the apron and may have been re-used from another, similar apron.* ROYAL ONTARIO MUSEUM, TORONTO.

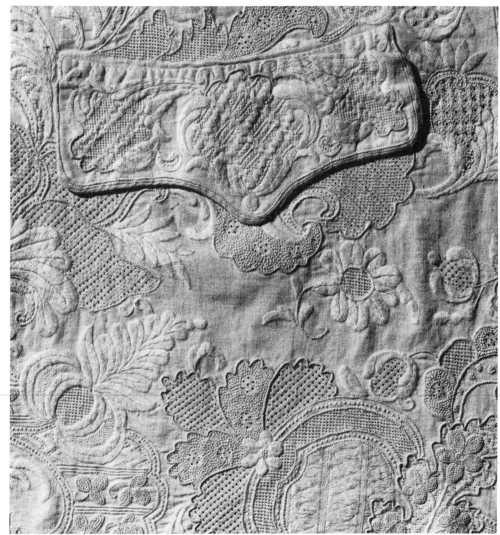

Man's waistcoat *(detail), England, early eighteenth century. Cotton and linen with drawn and pulled work and white linen embroidery, length 33½in (85·1cm). The whitework is executed in satin, coral, buttonhole and Cretan feather stitches with French knots, eyelet holes and punched work.* VICTORIA AND ALBERT MUSEUM, LONDON.

The technique of tambouring provided a new and quicker method of embroidering muslin. Worked with a hook on to fabric stretched across a frame, the effect is of a continuous chain stitch. This became a particularly popular type of costume decoration in the later part of the eighteenth century and was used to embroider dresses, fichus and aprons, the patterns being for the first time available in contemporary magazines.

Embroidered decoration became much lighter during the course of the second half of the eighteenth century. Men's waistcoats, although still heavily embroidered, had diapered backgrounds of small sprigs with front border decorations in embroidered silks, fine metal threads and spangles. Quilting had become popular for costume earlier in the century, both for its decorative qualities and for its warmth, and was used mostly on women's petticoats and men's waistcoats. For domestic use, bedcovers often had a quilted background with silk or crewel-wool surface embroidery. A coverlet in the Victoria and Albert Museum of cord-quilted cotton is embroidered in silk arranged in a conventional Chinese composition, a central circular motif with quadrants filling each corner. With the increasing manufacture of cottons in England they were cheaper to buy and patchwork developed as a technique during the later years of the century. Few examples have survived, however, and it is by examining nineteenth-century pieces that the development of earlier patterns is known.

Neoclassical Embroidery

With the revival of classical design, due to the archaeological finds at Pompeii and Herculaneum in Italy, there was a systematic change in the subject matter of embroidery motifs. The stark, rigid lines of the new style were not suddenly adopted for all British interior design, however, and there were few who were sufficiently rich or progressive to employ an architect of the calibre of Robert Adam (1728–92). There are in fact few existing examples of embroidered furnishings in strict neoclassical style but an exception is a set of wall hangings, originally fourteen in all, that are at Newiston, West Lothian, Scotland, a house that Robert Adam was commissioned to decorate in 1789. Worked in painted felt and stitched in silk thread to a cream woolen ground, the design shows urns of flowers supported by sphinxes with small medallions depicting the muses. This technique, incorporating felt appliqué, is comparable to similar work in the twentieth century.

Classical subjects were used for embroidered pictures and engravings of landscapes after Nicolas Poussin (1594–1665) and Francesco Zuccarelli (1702–88) and figure studies by Angelica Kauffmann (1741–1807), Francesco Bartolozzi (1727–1815) and Francis Wheatley (1747–1801) were frequently copied. The strict classical content of the scene, however, is often weakened by the romantic rendering. Many of these pictures are worked in

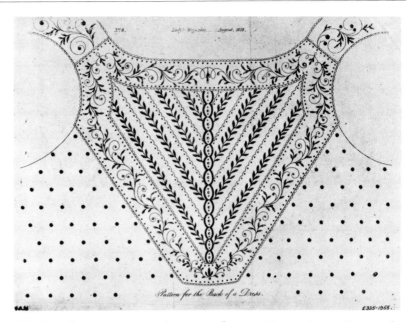

Pattern for tambour work for the back of a dress bodice, *from* The Lady's Magazine, *England, 1813. The neoclassical style of the dress was fashionable from the 1790s to the 1830s, when heavier fabric and wider skirts were adopted.* VICTORIA AND ALBERT MUSEUM, LONDON.

Coverlet *(detail), England, second quarter of the eighteenth century. Fine linen backed with pieces of coarse linen, embroidered with polychrome silks in satin, stem, long and short and fern stitches with French knots, speckling, sheaf, lattice and other filling stitches, the ground quilted in back stitch, 88in × 85in (2·23m × 2·15m). The backing is stamped with the name of William Menzies. The coverlet, which belonged to the Parminster family of Devon, is said to have been made by three sisters as a wedding present for their brother.* VICTORIA AND ALBERT MUSEUM, LONDON.

black silk and called "printwork." A few isolated examples are thought to be worked in human hair. More colorful pictures were worked in various silks and chenilles with details such as faces and hands painted on to the silk ground in watercolor (Plate 20).

In the latter part of the century abstract and geometric patterns became popular for embroidered furnishings, while embroidered pictures were the main vehicles for figure subjects. Individual ladies became famous for their needlework, Mary Knowles (1733–1807) and Mary Linwood (1756–1845) being the two most celebrated. Working from oil paintings, particularly those of Thomas Gainsborough (1727–88), Miss Linwood gained the distinction of having her own permanent London exhibition, first in Oxford Street and later in Leicester Square. She was not credited with technical originality but she was acclaimed for her skill as a copyist. Worked in crewel wools in long and short stitches, her embroidery covers the whole surface of the background fabric and is extremely skillful in execution; but it must, however, be considered as pastiche.

The Nineteenth Century

During the course of the nineteenth century the Industrial Revolution was to have a drastic effect on embroidery, not only because of the development of machinery but also because of the attitude of the embroiderer. New types of objects were chosen to be embroidered and although many traditional techniques, such as whitework, cutwork, canvas and crewelwork embroidery and quilting, were maintained, their appearance changed.

Time became a major factor: machine embroidery was admired commercially for its speed and at the same time the amateur no longer had the patience of her predecessor and chose techniques that could be worked quickly: hence the introduction and success of ready-to-work kits, sold with thick wools which would speedily cover the background canvas. This led to a lowering of amateur standards, but a reaction later in the century produced some of the most imaginative and finely worked British embroideries.

Professional embroidery took on a different form from previously. Many firms employed workers to embroider both in their own homes and in the factories. The status of the professional worker diminished, however, and the harsh conditions and poor pay in similar factories are described in the writings of Charles Dickens and other social commentators.

In the North and the Midlands, with their new found industrial wealth, many more ladies became part of middle-class society with time to spare for needlework. Often untrained in delicate work, they found that counted-thread embroidery on canvas was the most suitable. During the first quarter of the century the delicate tent- and cross-stitch canvas work of the previous century changed dramatically with the sale of patterns printed on squared paper and hand colored to denote where each thread was to go (Plate 21).

First published in Germany in 1804–5, these Berlin woolwork patterns (called after the worsted wools used in them) were by the 1830s being imported and sold by Wilks's Warehouse of Regent Street, London, and by the mid-century Yorkshire factories were producing the characteristically thick wools in all the most popular colors. With the advent of aniline dyestuffs in the late 1850s, English wools, although thicker than the German originals, took over in popularity because of the bright new colors that were available, especially the purples, pinks, greens and dense blacks. Worked in a variety of floral designs, of roses, violets, lilies, convolvuluses (Plate 22) and other favorite blooms, the panels were made into chair seats, cushions, footstools, carpets, bell pulls and lambrequins; and for wear, nightcaps, belts, braces and slippers.

Sentimental scenes were embroidered, deriving either from literature – Sir Walter Scott and Shakespeare in particular – or from paintings of animals or royalty by the socially acceptable artists, Sir Edwin Landseer (1802–73) and Franz Xavier Winterhalter (1805–73). Glass beads and sheared-pile or "plush" techniques were often used to add glitter and texture to the canvas work; beadwork became an independent and popular technique, with "pound" bead (sold by weight not shape) production becoming lucrative.

Even though it was simply a question of copying, the standard of Berlin woolwork varied greatly and some of the pieces exhibited at the International Exhibitions of 1851 and 1862 were well designed and worked.

Whitework in the Nineteenth Century

In marked contrast to most colored canvas work, nineteenth-century whitework, as produced by the Ayrshire sewn-muslin industry, was of a very high quality. The industry had flourished from its birth in 1782, when neoclassical taste demanded softly draped muslin for clothing, and in the 1830s, despite changes in fashion, this form of decoration retained its popularity for costume accessories and babies' dresses. A man's shirt in the Victoria and Albert Museum is decorated with appropriate Scottish motifs.

Much of the earlier Ayrshire work was produced in the workers' own homes but by 1850 firms such as R. & Thomas Brown employed two thousand men and women in their warehouse and between twenty thousand and thirty thousand outworkers both in Scotland and Ireland, to which the craft had now spread. Most of the work produced by the "flowerers," as the workers were called because of the nature of their patterns, was exported.

The development of machine embroidery and the complete change in fashionable clothing in the 1860s gradually led to a deterioration in trade and heavier trimmings on clothing, worked in *broderie anglaise*; and Richelieu and renaissance embroidery superseded the delicate Ayrshire work. Both the latter techniques – cutwork with heavy white cotton embroidery – provided the much more dramatic, yet less subtle, effects that the Victorians required. There were fewer embroidered areas and larger stitches were used so that the work took less time.

A third technique that can loosely be said to have developed from "flowering" was that introduced into the town of Mountmellick in Queen's County, Ireland, in 1825. Heavy, floral patterns were worked on to cotton with white knitting cotton in a variety of stitches. Mountmellick work was particularly suitable for hardwearing domestic items such as bedspreads and other bed linen.

The most traditional whitework technique, it has been argued, is that seen on country smocks. Few examples from earlier than the nineteenth century survive and existing smocks indicate that the period was possibly the high point of their manufacture. First made to protect workers' clothing, smocks are made to two designs: the round frock, where two widths of fabric are joined at the side seams (Plate 23), and the coat frock, which opens down the front. Of simple cut, they were ideally suited to embroidery, which served both as decoration and as a form of cloth control when gathering stitches or "smocking" were used at the wrists and chest.

The garments were usually made of strong cotton twill or homespun linen and embroidered in twisted linen thread or sewing cotton. Stitches such as feather, outline, chain and stem were worked in simple linear patterns over the collar, shoulders and cuffs of the garment, with more detailed pattern motifs in faggot stitch and French knots. Regional differences of patterning exist, although the idea that the wearer's trade can be identified by the pattern has now been disproved. Variations in shape include boat-necked smocks with rolled collars in East Anglia and smocks with additional protective shoulders from the west of England and Wales, so designed to keep off the rain. These

Man's shirt, detail of the front panel, Ayrshire, Scotland, first half of the nineteenth century. Cambric embroidered with cream-colored cotton thread in stem, double darning, satin and brick stitches and speckling, length of front panel 15in (38·1cm). Roses, shamrocks and thistles, the symbols of England, Ireland and Scotland, appear with such characteristic Scottish motifs as a sporan, bagpipes and crossed swords. VICTORIA AND ALBERT MUSEUM, LONDON.

BUCKINGHAM
Shepherd

LANCASHIRE
Gardener

Characteristic regional
patterns on English smocks.

ESSEX
Shepherd

BEDFORD

BERKS

SHROPSHIRE
Butcher

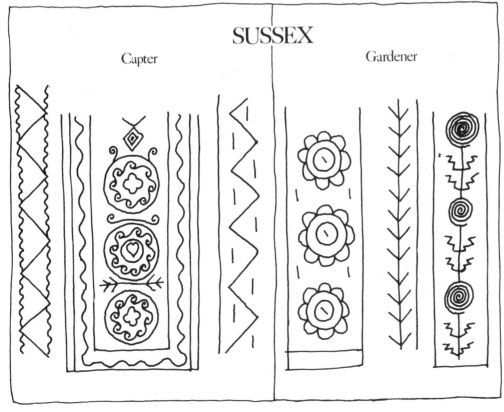

SUSSEX

Capter

Gardener

garments were made in the home but at least one manufactory, in Newark-on-Trent, has been traced, whose smocks were known locally as "Newark frocks." From the 1880s the technique of smocking became popular for fashionable "artistic" dress, with paper patterns facilitating the transfer of the designs on to the printed silks. The use of smocking for children's clothing has remained popular to this day.

Quilting, Patchwork and Samplers

Two other practical techniques put to full decorative use during this century are quilting and patchwork and surviving coverlets show how successfully these were worked. Serviceable patchworks, where scraps of cotton from costume and other household items were re-used, are of conventional designs formed from hexagons or squares, with cotton waste or rag inter-

linings and quilted backings for warmth and extra decoration. Many of the finest examples of this work were sewn in Wales (Plate 24).

More complicated patchwork designs and techniques that were used professionally include forms of appliqué, such as *broderie perse* – where printed motifs are cut out of cotton and applied with buttonhole or overcast stitches – and the fancy techniques of mosaic or pieced patchwork, crazy, box and log-cabin patchwork: all of these illustrate high standards of design and perseverance in pattern and color matching. Pictorial patchworks depicting historical scenes, often made of silk but more usually of felt, were exhibited at the Great Exhibition of 1851 and conform, in endeavor and eccentricity, to the rest of the exhibits. Professional quilters were active during the nineteenth century, touring the countryside and producing new items to order, and also

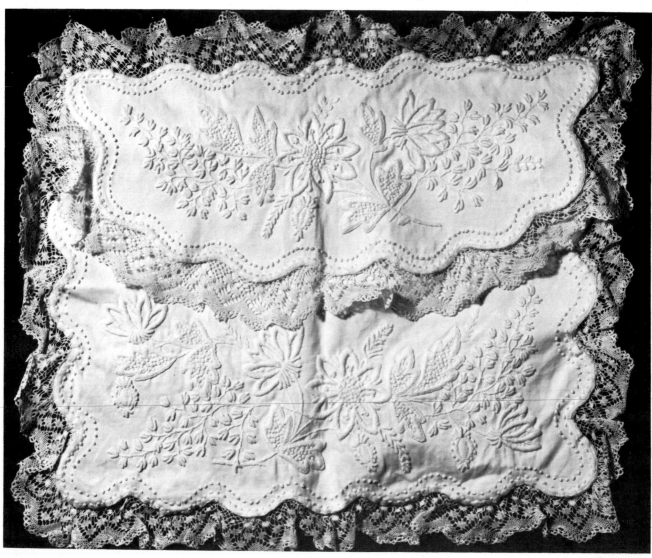

finishing off ready-made patchworks. The quilters of Durham and South Wales have now become legendary.

Young girls continued to embroider samplers at school but the canvas they used became coarser and the restricting techniques of cross and tent stitches gave the pictures and verses a stiff appearance that is characteristic of their work. Samplers worked in darning and plain sewing, made throughout the century, were more practical exercises and show attempts to teach the girls techniques that might be of use to them in their future rôles as wives and mothers.

Ecclesiastical Embroidery

The Catholic Emancipation Act of 1829 led to a renewed interest in church architecture and fittings. The Roman Catholic architect A. W. N. Pugin (1812–52), in his manifesto *Contrasts* of 1836, caused surprise with his advocacy of a return to the Gothic. The same ideas were pursued in the Anglican Church by the Oxford Movement. Like Pugin, the protagonists wished to revive not only the decoration of the Middle Ages but also the ceremony and ritual as practiced in the Roman Catholic Church. In line with this new approach to church decoration, the Cambridge Camden Society started to publish in 1841 a magazine, *The Ecclesiologist*, in which were illustrated, among other items, examples of medieval embroidery.

Contemporary architects adopted the revival styles and one in particular, George Edmund Street (1824–81), followed the example of Pugin in involving himself in details of the interior furnishings – such as embroidered altar frontals – as well as the architecture. Street had an extensive knowledge of medieval embroidery and is known to have given a public lecture on the subject. This interest was clearly felt by Street's sister who, together with Street and her friend Miss Agnes Blencowe, founded in 1854 the Ladies' Ecclesiastical Embroidery Society to embroider copies of medieval works and new designs by G. E. Street and other leading architects of the day, notably G. F. Bodley (1827–1907).

Another group which had its roots in

Sampler, worked by Hannah Featherson, England, 1830. Unbleached linen embroidered in colored silks in cross, herringbone and outline stitches, 16½in × 17¼in (41·9cm × 43·8cm). The embroideress lived close to the Welsh border at Oswestry, Shropshire. WELSH FOLK MUSEUM, CARDIFF.

Three illustrations from "A Manual of Collective Lessons in Needlework," by Helen K. Brietzche and Emily F. Rooper, London, 1885. These show the type of instruction given to children in the Victorian period that at the beginning of the twentieth century Ann Macbeth was anxious to replace. BRITISH LIBRARY, LONDON.

the ecclesiastical revival of the nineteenth century was the Leek Embroidery Society, founded in 1879 by Mrs. Elizabeth Wardle, wife of the fabric dyer and printer Thomas Wardle. This Staffordshire society, which from time to time involved a number of local Leek ladies, was responsible for the embroidery of many finely worked altar frontals, banners and other church pieces in floral and pictorial designs. They are now equally well known for their "Anglo-Indian" work, influenced by – and often worked over the silks imported and printed by – the Wardle firm. The Society is also famous for its copy of the Bayeux Tapestry worked between 1885 and 1886 and now owned by Reading Corporation.

William Morris

The most influential figure in all forms of textile design in the second half of the nineteenth century was William Morris (1834–96), who turned to embroidery early in his career as a designer. As a young man down from Oxford University, Morris was apprenticed to the office of G. E. Street. He cannot have failed to observe the prevailing nostalgic interest in design of those whom he studied and worked with, and it is to the past that he looked for inspiration for all his own designs. He had his own collection of period textiles and in his anxiety to comprehend techniques he event went so far as to unravel pieces.

In 1855 he set up an embroidery frame, dyed some woolen yarns with natural plant and animal dyestuffs and taught himself to embroider in what he considered a suitable and traditional manner. He used mostly worsted wools in darning, long and short, stem and chain stitches, his main influence being seventeenth-century crewelwork,

although some motifs owe more to the design of Italian woven silks and cut velvets of the fourteenth and fifteenth centuries. Their adaptation and the composition of his design, however, is purely individual. Early embroideries, with the figures designed by Sir Edward Burne-Jones (1833–98) and the animals by Philip Webb (1831–1915), were worked by Morris's wife Janey and their friends. They were sold through the firm of Morris, Marshall, Faulkner & Co., which exhibited some works at the International Exhibition of 1862.

With the establishment of Morris & Co. in 1875, embroidery became one of the most popular aspects of their commercial production. Early examples include an unfinished set of panels based on Chaucer's *Legend of Good Women* which was designed for Morris's own home, the Red House at Bexleyheath. The three finished panels have been made into a screen and are currently on loan to the Victoria and Albert Museum. A frieze design by Edward Burne-Jones, the subject again taken from Chaucer, was worked by Lady Margaret Bell and her daughter for their home at Rounton Grange, near Northallerton, in Yorkshire. This is now in the collection of the William Morris Gallery at Walthamstow, Essex.

In 1885 Morris's daughter, May, took over the management of the embroidery workshops at the Merton Abbey works of Morris & Co., and most of the designs from this date are either by her or Morris's chief assistant, John Henry Dearle (1860–1932). Morris had by this time become more interested in the tapestry weaving activities of the firm. By the end of the nineteenth century Morris & Co. were selling embroidery kits consisting of a prepared and marked cotton, linen or flannel ground and naturally dyed wools and

Altar frontal, *designed by G. E. Street (1824–81) and worked by either the ecclesiastical furnishers and outfitters Jones and Willis or the Ladies' Ecclesiastical Embroidery Society, England, 1861. Red velvet decorated with appliqué of cream silk and of canvas embroidered with silver and silver-gilt thread, cream cord and floss silk in long and short stitches with laid and couched work and metal spangles, 36½in × 92in (92·5cm × 233cm).* CHURCH OF ST. JAMES THE LESS, PIMLICO, LONDON.

silks. Many of these anonymously worked "Morris" embroideries survive to this day, and several examples exist of a number of the designs.

Morris's later floral designs of the 1870s and 1880s, used mainly on coverlets and hangings, are similar in composition to his designs for Hammersmith carpets. They seldom repeat and in some cases, like the carpets, show a quartered "mirror" design radiating from a central focal point, with elaborate edgings and borders. The portières designed by Morris show a freshness and love of nature that is characteristic of much of his work.

It was probably Morris's theories on techniques and workmanship, his ideas on the nobleness of toil of the designer/craftsman, more than his own designs, that influenced later embroiderers.

Art Needlework and the Needlework Societies

"Art Needlework," as it became known, was to be as popular as the German woolwork patterns had been earlier in the century, and designs in the fashionable Japanese style were the order of the day. A spate of embroidery groups and societies were set up, the most prestigious being the School of Art Needlework, founded in 1872 under the presidency of H.R.H. Princess Christian of Schleswig-Holstein, daughter of Queen Victoria. It was granted the prefix "Royal" in 1875 and "Art" was dropped from its title at a later date. Its aims were to restore ornamental needlework for secular purposes to the high level it once held among the decorative arts and "to supply suitable employment for poor gentlefolk," and this was followed to some extent for by 1875 over one hundred ladies were employed in restoration work and in the embroidery of designs commissioned from such notable designers as William Morris, Edward Burne-Jones, Walter Crane (1845–1915) and Frederick, Lord Leighton (1830–96). The involvement of practicing artists in the design of embroidery raised the status of the craft and must be looked on as a major achievement by the Royal School of Art Needlework.

Other groups were started, fired by its success, including the Ladies' Work Society, founded in 1875 under the presidency of Princess Louise; the Decorative Work Society, in 1880; the

Portière "The Vine," designed by William Morris (1834–96) in 1878, embroidered by May Morris (1862–1938) at a later date. England. Silk on linen in stem, satin, long and short and chain stitches, 86½in × 62¼in (2·19m × 1·58m). A number of portières in much the same style were designed by J. H. Deale and embroidered by the Misses Battye. VICTORIA AND ALBERT MUSEUM, LONDON.

Wemyss Castle School of East Fifeshire,
which provided work for the local poor;
and the Donegal Industrial Fund,
founded by a Mrs. Ernest Hart in 1883,
which specialized in a form of Irish art
needlework called "Kells embroidery"
based mainly on the illustrations in *The
Book of Kells* and on Celtic manuscripts. Few of the designs worked by
these societies have proved to be worthy
of imitation. The technical training
undergone by those associated with the
societies, however, provided a firm
foundation for later work and for the
teaching of future generations.

In the latter years of the century this
technical ability was often wasted by
the choice of inappropriate designs: the
copying of tapestries, repeating textile

designs and paintings show how the
advice of Morris was disregarded. A
finely worked full-size copy of the oil
painting *The Mill* by Edward Burne-
Jones, worked by ladies of the Royal
School of Art Needlework shows
diligence and skill, however.

The Arts and Crafts Exhibition
Society, formed in 1888, encouraged the
design and display of good embroidery
through its committee, which besides
William Morris comprised Edward
Burne-Jones and Walter Crane, talented
designers such as Lewis F. Day (1856–
1910) and the architect J. D. Sedding
(1838–91). To this society has been
attributed the development of a completely new attitude toward the manufacture of artefacts: the practices of
medieval workshops were revived and
the designer was closely involved with
the production of the work, be it furniture, silver or textiles. Work in the Arts
and Crafts style was produced in workshops in the cities of London and
Birmingham in particular, but in the
case of embroidery much was produced
through cottage industries set up at the
end of the century. The Langdale
Linen Industry of Westmorland and
Mrs. Arthur Newall of Fisherton-de-
la-Mere, Wiltshire, both concentrated
on whitework and cutwork, whereas the
Haslemere Peasant Industry in Surrey,
founded in 1896 by Godfrey Blount,
used appliqué techniques on naturally
dyed and handwoven linen. With
modernistic pictorial and stylized floral
designs, these hangings and portières
give some idea of what was to be the
British Art Nouveau style, a far cry
from the swirling whiplash designs of
their French and Belgian counterparts.

The Glasgow School

It was in Glasgow at the turn of the
century that one of the most individual
British styles was to appear and flourish.
Embroidery worked at the Glasgow
School of Art under the tutorship of
Jessie Newbery (1864–1948) changed
the course of design and technique.

The Glasgow School of Art is now
famed for the stylish design produced
in the late nineteenth and early twentieth century by "the four": the architects Charles Rennie Mackintosh (1868–
1928) and Herbert McNair (active
c.1890–1940) together with their wives,
the two Macdonald sisters, Margaret
(1865–1933) and Frances (1874–1921).
Their revolutionary ideas and new style

were applied to textiles as well as three-dimensional work and in 1894 Jessie Newbery (1864–1948), whose outward-looking husband Francis (1855–1946) had been appointed principal of the School in 1885, started an embroidery class. This was not limited to full-time students and anyone with an interest could join. Working at first in the Morris tradition with crewel wools, Mrs. Newbery had, within a few years, devised an appliqué technique using linens with silk hand embroidery which was, in method if not in style, similar to the work being produced at Haslemere.

The teaching of drawing was a particularly important part of the School of Art course and from their drawings from nature and of the human form their characteristically linear style developed. The overelaborate embroidery of the past was spurned and in its place the women of Glasgow were encouraged to decorate cushions, tray cloths, curtains, tablecloths, casement curtains (the latter became a sign of an artistically liberated household) and even dresses with simple, bold patterns, such as a single curving stemmed rose, carnation or poppy. The aim was to create "beautifully shaped spaces," and suitably worded inscriptions in the "Glasgow script" were also evolved by Mrs. Newbery.

In 1901 Mrs. Newbery enlisted a student, Ann Macbeth (1875–1948), to help with her needlework, embroidery and appliqué class and she continued as her assistant, together with Jessie Marion King (1876–1949) and Frances (Macdonald) McNair, until Mrs. Newbery retired in 1910. Ann Macbeth remained in the post until 1928, when she moved to the Lake District.

BELOW:
Needlework picture, *probably designed by Ann Macbeth (1875–1948), Glasgow, Scotland, c.1905–10. Silk on linen, embroidered in satin, bullion knot, chain and double-running stitches, 13½in × 31in (34·2cm × 78·8cm). Bought by the present owner at a sale at the same time as other, similar works, one of which is marked "Designed by Ann Macbeth. Sewn by Kate Richards."* MRS. KATHLEEN GLASKIN.

The Twentieth Century

It is perhaps too early to evaluate Ann Macbeth's contribution to the history of British embroidery as the effects of her teaching are still felt in schools around Britain. Apart from being a prolific worker herself, she drew designs to be worked by her students and friends as well as for the commercial companies of Liberty's of London, Knox's Linen Thread Company and Donald Brothers of Dundee. With the assistance of Margaret Swanson, her teaching was probably the most advanced and adventurous in Britain and her Saturday classes were attended by hundreds of primary school teachers. The belief that she held that everyone was capable of original work is the basis of needlework teaching in schools today. Her books – *Educational Needlework* (written with Margaret Swanson in 1911) and the *Playwork Book* of 1918 – recommend exercises for children using textured fabrics and basic stitches such as tacking and darning. A new system of embroidery discipline without the use of traditional samplers was evolved: as in the seventeenth century, children progressed from one exercise to another but their tasks were less closely directed and more lively, the aim being to involve the child fully and invoke imaginative responses.

With her teachings in Glasgow and later her lessons to the local Women's Institute in her Lake District home in Patterdale, Ann Macbeth was part of a twentieth-century movement to rejuvenate handicrafts generally and needlework in particular. The Rural Industries Bureau, set up in 1921, with its aim of "maintaining trades ancillary to agriculture" and "fostering rural crafts and reviving those that had declined," was to the cottage tradition of quilting, patchwork, smocking and whitework what the Design and Industries Association, founded in 1915, was to urban commercial designers. The latter "encouraged good workmanship based on excellent design and soundness of materials, which aim could be attained only through the intelligent and friendly co-operation of workers, designers, manufacturers, distributors, educators and the general public."

Art colleges, in particular those at Glasgow, Aberdeen, Dundee and Edinburgh in Scotland and the Royal College of Art and the London County Council Central School of Arts and Crafts in London, took up the baton with encouragement from the Board of Trade and helped many provincial colleges to specialize in the craft associated with their local industries and traditions. The Victoria and Albert Museum, the collections of which had during the second half of the nineteenth century inspired the work of William Morris and his followers, the Royal School of Needlework and the Royal College of Art all assisted the Board of Education by displaying embroidered pieces of merit, some items being retained to form part of permanent collections.

The Rural Industries Bureau was particularly successful in organizing the craft of quilting in the distressed areas of Durham and South Wales during the early 1930s. This redeployment of miners' wives during a period of economic depression, resulted in sales worth £10,000 during the first year of the scheme.

The workmanship of British embroidery has often been considered of a higher standard than its design and it is true to say that, with a few notable exceptions, the leading practicing artists and designers have seldom been particularly interested in it as a medium. The late nineteenth-century tradition of design and workshop practice continued into the twentieth century and the theories of the Arts and Crafts Movement were adopted by a number of groups, a few of which produced items of embroidery. One of the most significant, the Omega Workshop, released design from the tight restrictions which it still retained from the previous century and evolved a free, spontaneous style that was to develop after the First World War. The Workshop was created just before the War, in July 1913. The founder, Roger Fry, and leading members, Duncan Grant (1885–1978) and Vanessa Bell (1879–1961), dabbled in several different media. They recognized the need for good workmanship and, although occasionally producing work themselves, they are better known for their designs carried through by other craftsmen. Mary Hogarth (1865–1935), a distinguished designer and needlewoman, persuaded a number of artists to design for her (Plate 28).

Cubism influenced much of the work done in the 1920s and the technique of appliqué was best suited to this. Texture became all-important, a wide range of surface-patterned textiles being used for contrast. The importance of design was emphasized by Mary Hogarth when she explained that "the technique should be governed by the design." She stressed speed, clarity and ingenuity as the qualities best suited to the new age and its economy and illustrated how appliqué work and hitherto unfashionable materials such as braid and buttons could produce exciting effects. "Historical items should be studied and learned from," she wrote in *Modern Embroidery* in 1933, but "modern embroidery should be the invention of today in design."

Rebecca Crompton (died 1947) revealed a similar approach in her teaching and writings and it is to her that credit must be given for a new feeling for linear design and the harmonious combination of hand and machine embroidery. A teacher of great talent, Rebecca Crompton's own work has a timeless quality and items worked in the 1930s still retain their freshness (Plate 26).

The Needlework Development Scheme was started in 1934 by the firm of J. P. Coats of Glasgow to improve the standard of embroidery in Scotland. Based on the four main Scottish art colleges, the aim was to teach by example, and to this end a collection of fine historical embroideries was formed. This was loaned to interested institutions and clubs and the scheme supplied visiting lecturers and teachers and published booklets covering a wide area of study from the elementary *And so to Begin*, 1953, to the more advanced *Experiment in Embroidery Design*, 1950. The Scheme made a substantial contribution to needlework at this time.

The Scheme's resident expert (in 1937 it was Rebecca Crompton) was not always British and this led to a healthy interaction of foreign and British ideas. By 1939 the collection numbered nine hundred pieces but the Scheme was forced to close during the war years. In 1944 it was restarted and in the 1950s was at its most powerful, holding exhibitions every year from 1950 until 1957 and influencing students not only at schools, adult education centers, technical training and art colleges in Scotland but also at similar institutions in England, Wales and Northern Ireland. In 1961 the Scheme was discontinued and the collections dispersed, not through any lack of interest but because it was felt that it had achieved its fundamental aim.

A great influence on British housewives throughout the twentieth century has been the Women's Institute and many women who have been denied the benefit of art school training have taken the opportunity of attending needlework classes either at their local adult education center, where City and Guild Examinations can be taken, or at their local or county Women's Institute. Working in collaboration at first with the Rural Industries Bureau, which was set up in 1915, and later with such organizations as the Embroiderers' Guild, the Women's Institute offers a system of tuition and examinations ranging from the basic to the instructor level. It supplies instructors to local branches as well as adult education centers and also runs a correspondence course on the more elementary techniques. Much work done by the Women's Institute has a technical bias and in the embroidered panel made for the Festival of Britain individual, technically varied, items were worked by experienced Women's Institute members and then assembled by art college students under the tuition of Constance Howard, one of the most distinguished contemporary needlewomen.

There has been yet another revival in decorative ecclesiastical embroidery in the twentieth century, which has been developed since the end of the Second World War by a number of leading embroideresses such as Beryl Dean. The favored techniques used are those of appliqué and hand and machine work, which give speed and lightness to the work. At the same time other methods such as *or nué* and underside couching are being used in abstract designs, their color and subject matter often having no specific religious significance.

The opportunities for the modern embroideress are limitless. Many polytechnics have Bachelor of Art courses with embroidery as a specialist subject and many leading contemporary designers such as Audrey Walker (Plate 27), head of the Department of Embroidery at St. Martin's College of Art in London, teach in them. For the amateur there are a number of ways to learn the craft: adult education center afternoon or evening classes and at rural and county level, the Women's Institute.

Panel "The Country Wife," *conceived and worked by Constance Howard and her embroidery pupils at Goldsmith's College, London, with individual items designed and made by members of the Women's Institute throughout Britain, 1951. 18ft 6in × 13ft 6in (5·63m × 4·11m). A great variety of materials are used in the appliqué of fabric with embroidery in silks, wools, linens and synthetic yarns. Basketwork, leatherwork, pottery and woodwork are also included in the piece. The panel is three dimensional, the items five-eighths life size.* NATIONAL FEDERATION OF WOMEN'S INSTITUTES, DENMAN COLLEGE, OXFORDSHIRE, ENGLAND.

There are a number of exhibiting societies, of which the Embroiderers' Guild is the most influential. Smaller offshoots such as the '62 Group and The Young Embroiderer's Society afford an opportunity for more experimental work. The profession can also use the facilities of the Crafts Advisory Service which is financed by the Arts Branch of the Department of Education and Science and which acts as a retailer, displaying and selling work.

In professional and amateur work of the present day techniques are changing and a more liberal attitude to the arts in general means that embroidery designers do not restrict themselves exclusively to fabric and thread or to two-dimensional work but experiment with paper and glue, metal, stone and ceramics. All contribute to make exciting pieces of work and help to remove the limitations that once existed in British needlework.

France

THE ART OF EMBROIDERY HAS BEEN practiced in France since remote antiquity. It emerges from the mists of history during the Merovingian period and it still retains a place – though a restricted one – in our modern, mechanized civilization. It is, in fact, an extremely adaptable art. It can be practiced by professionals of dazzling virtuosity and by amateurs who have no qualifications save taste and patience; it lends itself to a variety of uses in dress and furnishing, and to many different styles and techniques; it offers effects of luxury to rich and poor alike.

The Uses of Embroidery

Embroidery has served a multiplicity of uses, both religious and secular; it has been an indispensable ornament of religion, of domestic furnishing and of dress.

In the Christian Church, in France as elsewhere, embroidery was employed from early times to adorn liturgical vestments – miters, chasubles, dalmatics, copes – where it was sometimes confined to narrow bands or orphreys and sometimes covered the whole surface of the garment. In addition church furnishings often included, in the fourteenth and fifteenth centuries, embroidered altar frontals which were virtually paintings made with the needle.

In the secular field, embroidery was as prominent in domestic furnishings as it was in dress. In the vast chilly halls of the Middle Ages, embroidered hangings vied with rich hangings of tapestry. Beds, with their curtains and canopies, their coverlets and numerous pillows, were monuments of embroidery, particularly in the sixteenth and seventeenth centuries. Embroidered table carpets were not rare. In the seventeenth and eighteenth centuries embroidery was used for hangings, curtains, screens and also for ornamental pieces inserted in the paneling of rooms: the walls of the Throne Room at Versailles, in the time of Louis XIV, were entirely covered with a fantastic architecture embroidered in gold and silver thread "after the fashion of marble, representing architectural perspective." *Gros point, petit point* and other types of embroidery were in common use for seat covers from the sixteenth century onward.

In civil and military costume, embroidery played a spectacular rôle from the fourteenth until the nineteenth century. The demands of princely courts and to an even greater extent those of the royal court were insatiable in this respect, and etiquette required courtiers to wear costumes which cost a fortune to produce and were at the same time incredibly cumbersome. For example, the little Dauphine, Duchess of Burgundy, aged twelve, wore for her wedding in 1697 a dress so laden with embroidery that the unfortunate princess was hardly able to walk. Embroidery could adorn every element of dress from headgear to shoes, including personal linen and all the accessories of fashion: fans, ribbons, purses, scarves, shawls, dressing-cases and the like. It was also lavished on horse trappings and harnesses, banners and flags.

In France embroidery long remained a luxury with which princes loved to surround themselves and with which they adorned the house of God, but it was beyond the reach of common mortals. This luxury, however, gradually became accessible to a wider social spectrum until, by the eighteenth century, the craft of embroidery was organized for large-scale commercial production. In the nineteenth century the use of embroidery spread to all classes and it even became an important element in peasant costume.

Embroidery Techniques

The technique of embroidery is infinitely adaptable and varies from extreme simplicity to extreme complexity according to period, according to the function which it is called upon to fulfil and also according to the skills of the men and women who have practiced it, for the art of needlework has always attracted not only professionals, but also amateurs of different degrees of ability.

RIGHT:
Chasuble, *France, c.1275.
Salmon-pink silk
embroidered with gold and
silver threads in underside
couching and polychrome
silks in split stitch and
surface couching, 57in ×
122in (146cm × 310cm).*
SKARA CATHEDRAL, SWEDEN.

A technique which is literally age old is that of *taillure, application,* or applied work; it is both rapid and economical. In the thirteenth century St. Louis sent the Tartar khan a set of vestments and chapel furnishings with scenes from the Gospels in applied work. This technique was in frequent use in the sixteenth and seventeenth centuries. In the eighteenth century and down to the present day patchwork has been a favorite technique of amateur needlewomen. The vestments designed by Matisse for the chapel at Vence in the south of France are applied work of the simplest kind.

Broderie en relief, or raised work, is another technique which was practiced from the Middle Ages onward. Figures, architectural motifs and landscape elements were raised in low or high relief. In the seventeenth century raised work even intruded into the field of costume embroidery, resulting in court dresses and chasubles of inflexible rigidity and monstrous weight. (Indeed it was not until modern times that liturgical vestments were finally liberated from this costly and cumbersome tradition.) Contemporary eye-witness accounts indicate that the famous embroidered wall coverings of the Throne Room at Versailles, with their eighteen enormous pilasters, were worked in astoundingly high relief.

BELOW:
Cope, *France, c.1274. Rose-
colored silk embroidered with
gold and silver threads in
underside couching and pale-
colored silk thread in split
stitch, 57in × 122in
(146cm × 310cm).*
CATHEDRAL TREASURY,
UPPSALA, SWEDEN.

During the Middle Ages the most widely used technique was that of *point couché,* or couched work, executed in wool as in the Bayeux Tapestry (Plate 14), in silk or most frequently in gold thread and silk. From the fifteenth century onward the gold thread was often shaded with silks of various colors to produce the sumptuous effects of *or nué,* or shaded gold. Details of flesh or clothing were executed in *point fendu,* or split stitch (Plate 28). Both secular and liturgical dress was enriched with small pearls, gemstones or little ornaments of precious metal. A garment made for Charles of Orléans in the fifteenth century had sleeves embroidered with a popular song, the musical notes represented by 568 pearls.

From the sixteenth century onward, needlework in *petit point,* or tent stitch, and *gros point,* or cross stitch, was much favored (Plate 32). It is not difficult for amateurs to work and it is very suitable for bed valances and seat coverings. *Point de chaînette,* or chain stitch, which in the eighteenth century was

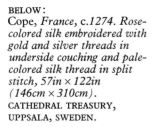

Cope *(detail), France, late thirteenth century. Rose-colored silk embroidered with gold and silver threads in underside couching and colored silks in split stitch, 48in × 120in (122cm × 304cm).* CHURCH OF ST. MAXIMIN, VAR, FRANCE.

sometimes worked with a fine hooked needle (tambour work), *point de boutonnière,* or buttonhole stitch, and *point de tige,* or stem stitch, have long been in use for work on light fabrics and on personal and household linen. Drawn threadwork, cutwork and darned net, or *lacis,* were immensely fashionable in the renaissance period and enjoyed a notable revival in the nineteenth century.

The Embroiderers

The embroiderers must be divided into two categories: professional and amateur. Professional embroiderers generally belonged to the corporation of *brodeurs-chasubliers,* broderers and chasuble-makers, but embroideries were also worked by members of other professional groups: the *tailleurs* for costume embroidery; the *lingères,* or linen-workers, for whitework; the *faiseuses d'aumônières sarrazinoises,* or makers of Saracen purses, for a type of purse popular in the Middle Ages; the *tapissiers,* or upholsterers, for coverlets.

Guild regulations exist for the embroiderers and the makers of Saracen purses in Paris from the thirteenth century onward. Not all embroiderers were subject to such regulations: those working for the court were exempt.

The guild regulations laid down standards of quality both for the materials used and for the workmanship; they established the conditions of the long apprenticeship which the workers served and of the production of the "masterpiece," the indispensable test-piece for those wishing to become master-broderers. It is possible that the superb miniature altarpiece in the Musée des Tissus, Lyons, bearing the name Pierre Vigier and the date 1621, is one of these masterpieces, which, according to the relevant statutes, were supposed to represent four months of work (Plate 31). The guild regulations favored the sons and sons-in-law of master-broderers, thus creating strong family traditions. It seems that from the very beginning there were as many women as men in the profession and

Miter of Archbishop Jean de Marigny, France, first half of the fourteenth century. Green silk embroidered with gold thread in couched work and polychrome silks in split stitch, 9in × 9in (24cm × 24cm). MUSÉE MUNICIPAL, EVREUX.

that they were governed by the same regulations. Each master-broderer was entitled to employ only a very few apprentices, but an unlimited number of workers. There were about two hundred master-broderers in Paris in the thirteenth century and about the same number in the eighteenth century.

No doubt there were embroidery workshops in most parts of the country from the Middle Ages onward and occasional references in contemporary documents provide some evidence of this. But the most active and best-documented workshops, and the most interesting artistically, were those centered around the court. The intense artistic activity in Paris at that time is indicated by the large number of embroiderers named in the records. The second half of the fourteenth century, during the reign of Charles V and the minority of Charles VI, when the "dukes of the fleurs-de-lys" maintained their splendid courts, was clearly a magnificent period for embroidery. Among many other names may be cited Sandrin

le Brodeur, Henriet Gontier, Estienne Bièvre, known as "le Hongre," Robin de Varennes, Arnoul and Hanequin of Utrecht, Marguerite and Guillaume de Leiry, embroiderers who worked for the King, for the Duke of Burgundy, the most lavish of the princely patrons, for the Duke of Orléans and for the King of Navarre.

After 1420 and the fall of Paris, artistic centers began to develop in Touraine, while the dukes of Burgundy transferred their patronage to artists in their own territory, which included Lille, Arras and Dijon. Documents give us the names of embroiderers working at Tours and Blois. The most famous was Pierre du Villant, painter and broderer to Duke René of Anjou, for whom he produced in 1462 a set of embroidered vestments and altar furnishings which were presented to Angers Cathedral, but disappeared at the time of the Revolution. From Colin Jolye, Charles VII commissioned a splendid cope depicting the Life of St. Hilaire for the cathedral of St. Hilaire at Poitiers, where the King was honorary canon.

During the sixteenth century workshops continued to flourish in the Loire Valley and Tours was a particularly lively center. Embroiderers active in Tours included Jean Galle, who was patronized by Queen Anne de Bretagne and the powerful Cardinal d'Amboise; Estienne Bernard, who worked for many years for François I and executed embroideries required for the reception of the Emperor Charles V; and Jean Perrault, who worked for Henri IV. But Paris was gradually reasserting its former importance. The workshop of La Trinité, founded in Paris in 1551 by Henri II to provide apprenticeships for poor children, is chiefly noted for its tapestries, but it also trained embroiderers.

In the reign of Henri IV, the King's broderer, Jean Vallet, was a notable figure. He was concerned with the creation of the Jardin des Plantes, the botanical garden of Paris, which was intended to provide embroiderers with flowers for copying; he also published an embroidery pattern book. Under Louis XIII, Queen Anne of Austria employed an Italian embroiderer, Nicolas de la Fage. She was also noted for her generous gifts of embroidered vestments to monasteries and churches. The French provinces were by no means inactive. One particularly productive workshop was that of the Ursuline convent at Amiens, which flourished from 1627 until the Revolution.

During the reign of the Sun King, Louis XIV, the principal embroiderers were grouped around Paris and Versailles. The landscape-embroiderer Philibert Balland and the figure-embroiderer Simon Fayet were permanently employed at the Gobelins to work on royal commissions, following designs by the painters Jacques ler Bailly (c.1629–79) and François Bon-

nemer (1638–89). Embroiderers at Versailles included Jacques Remy, active c.1665, and Simon Delobel, active c.1685. Delobel's major work was undoubtedly the bed and other embroidered furnishings of the King's Bedchamber on which he worked for twelve years and of which nothing now remains. At Noisy and St. Cyr, the Lherminots, father and son, and De Reynes and his wife added an indispensable professional touch to the work of Madame de Maintenon's young pupils,

ABOVE:
Purse, *France, fourteenth century. Canvas embroidered with gold threads in couched work, silk threads in raised work and split stitch and applied work in green velvet, 14in × 13in (37cm × 32cm).* CATHEDRAL TREASURY, TROYES.

BELOW:
Canopy or tester, *with monogram of Henri II (1547–59) worked in laurel leaves, France, c.1550.* MUSEE DU LOUVRE, PARIS.

Lining of a shield *of
Charles IX (1560–74),
France, c.1570. Red velvet
embroidered with couched
gold and silver threads and
applied work, 27in × 19in
(68cm × 49cm).* MUSÉE DU
LOUVRE, PARIS.

while the orphans of Madame de
Montespan, at the convent of St. Joseph
in Paris, undertook works of a scale and
quality which must likewise imply some
professional assistance.

Under Louis XV and Louis XVI, the
splendor and variety of the patterned
silks woven in Lyons tended to reduce
the demand for furnishing embroidery.
Nevertheless, the court continued to
require work of this kind, sometimes on
a very considerable scale. For example
when, in 1779, it became necessary to
provide a new royal throne for the

chapel of the Order of the Saint Esprit,
three hundred workers were employed
under the supervision of the embroiderer Rocher to adorn it with military
trophies and the symbol of the Holy
Spirit, executed in raised work of gold
thread.

At the same time, the demand for
costume embroidery remained strong
in court circles. From the reign of Louis
XIV onward, the regulations concerning
court dress were almost as strict as
those for church vestments and they
certainly afforded employment for a

considerable number of embroiderers, both men and women, down to the Revolution. The vagaries of Paris fashion likewise produced an incessant demand for embroideries and supported a prosperous group of artisans.

At Lyons embroiderers were active at least as early as the sixteenth century which is hardly surprising in view of the dominant rôle of the town in silk weaving and the silk trade generally. In the eighteenth century the activity of these workshops became very extensive: in 1740, for example, it was Lyons that received the commission for a stupendously lavish set of embroidered vestments ordered for the coronation of the Emperor Karl VII Albrecht (1697–1745) by the Elector Clemens-Augustus, Bishop of Cologne. Indeed, the Lyons workshops enjoyed a near-monopoly in the production of high-quality religious embroidery. In 1780 a traveler reported that, some years earlier, the Lyons silk manufacturers had installed embroidery workshops in their factories and that the city of Lyons was currently employing over six thousand workers on embroidery for costume and vestments which were exported "throughout the world." This work, even that of high quality, was mass produced. For example, parts of garments, especially parts of men's coats and waistcoats, were embroidered and despatched to the fashion houses in the piece, so that they could be cut and made up by the tailors to the exact measurements of individual clients.

Whitework embroidery, which became fashionable in the time of Marie-Antoinette as a consequence of the taste for diaphanous dresses, was made at St. Quentin in northern France (imitating the whitework of Saxony) and at Nancy and elsewhere in Lorraine.

Following the disruption caused by the Revolution, embroidery remained immensely fashionable throughout the nineteenth century. Lyons continued to supply church vestments and embroideries in gold and silver thread. Napoleon, who was anxious to stimulate the industry of the town, commissioned hangings for the palaces of Versailles, St. Cloud, Compiègne and Fontainebleau, including many adorned with embroidered trophies and emblems. The court was instructed to wear Lyons silks, which were enriched with narrow embroidered borders in the classical style.

In the Restoration period, official

ABOVE:
Corporal case *showing the Lamentation over the Dead Christ, France, c.1550. Canvas embroidered with gold and silver threads worked in or nué, 11in × 10in (29cm × 25cm).* MUSÉE DES THERMES ET DE L'HÔTEL DE CLUNY, PARIS.

LEFT:
Chasuble, *France, end of the sixteenth century. Satin ground embroidered with applied work and couched cord, height 49in (125cm).* MUSÉE DES THERMES ET DE L'HÔTEL DE CLUNY, PARIS.

Bed valance, *France, mid-sixteenth century. Yellow silk embroidered with couched gold and silver threads and silk thread in chain and split stitch, 175in × 72in (445cm × 182cm).* THE NATIONAL TRUST, WADDESDON MANOR, BUCKINGHAMSHIRE, ENGLAND.

Wall hanging *showing The reward of Virtue and the dangers of Pleasure, France, mid-sixteenth century. Wool and silk in canvas work, 145in × 197in (368cm × 500cm).* MUSÉE JACQREMART-ANDRE, PARIS.

commissions continued to flow into Lyons. Paris, in the meantime, was producing fashion embroidery and, about the middle of the century, was employing about six thousand needlewomen on such work. When protectionist legislation eliminated competition from Switzerland, *plumetis*, or feather-stitch embroidery, became a prosperous industry in Lorraine, employing upward of forty thousand women and exporting extensively to North America.

More serious than any competition from abroad was that resulting from the introduction of machine embroidery, which was soon to deal an almost fatal blow to hand embroidery, in France as elsewhere. The first mechanical embroidery loom dates from 1828. Perfected from 1834 onward, machine embroidery developed rapidly in Switzerland, France and England. It became very fashionable and in 1883 there were more than eleven hundred embroidery looms in France, of which two hundred and fifty were in Paris and its suburbs, while the rest were grouped around Lyons and, in the north, around St. Quentin. In the twentieth century the industry has suffered a catastrophic decline and the demand for commercially produced embroidery, whether for dress or furnishing, remains at a low level.

Alongside the work of the professionals, amateur embroidery has its own history, equally long and distinguished. Historical records from the Middle Ages onward are full of references to noble ladies who found needlework an apt vehicle for their creative talents. Catherine de Médicis was one of many

enthusiastic embroideresses. She transmitted her enthusiasm to her young daughter-in-law Mary, Queen of Scots, at that time Dauphine of France, who was subsequently to find much solace in needlework during the long years of her captivity. Other queens, Marie-Thérèse and Marie Leczinska, princesses such as the daughters of Louis XV, great ladies such as Madame de Maintenon, Madame de Pompadour and many more were devotees of embroidery which, like cards and music, was one of the recognized court pastimes. In the eighteenth century the taste for embroidery was so widespread that it was practiced even by gentlemen of fashion and Louis XV himself boasted of his prowess with the needle. Amateur embroiderers were everywhere, even in army barracks.

Great ladies also fostered embroidery in the charitable or educational establishments for young girls which they patronized. The most famous of these were the convent of St. Joseph in Paris and, even better known, the educational establishment set up by Madame de Maintenon, initially at Noisy and subsequently removed to St. Cyr, both near Versailles.

These highly privileged amateurs worked under conditions very different from those of more ordinary mortals. In the first place, they were in a position to obtain designs from the best artists. Catherine de Médicis employed a draughtsman specifically for this purpose, while a hanging made at the convent of St. Joseph is based on drawings by Charles Le Brun (1619–90) (Plate 32). Moreover, royal embroideresses and workshops established by great ladies employed professionals to prepare the work, to execute the most difficult parts and to mount the embroidery when completed. Even during her captivity Mary, Queen of Scots, had an embroiderer on her staff – a Frenchman – to provide her with designs and to assist with her innumerable needlework projects. Under such circumstances the embroideries produced in these aristocratic workshops were often of a thoroughly professional quality.

Embroidery was also practiced in religious communities which concentrated chiefly on the production of church vestments. One such community was the convent of the Ursulines at Amiens which, in the early seventeenth century, was favored with various commissions from Anne of Austria; some of its work, naïvely exuberant and by no means unattractive, is preserved in the museum at Amiens.

Finally there were the ordinary amateur embroideresses, who no doubt existed at all periods. The publication of embroidery pattern books from the sixteenth century onward marked the beginning of an enormous expansion in domestic embroidery. Before long, amateur needlewomen could also buy designs in the fashionable styles of the day, drawn out on the embroidery canvas and ready for working. We are told by Charles de St. Aubin (1721–86), in 1770, that some shopkeepers even stocked canvases for armchairs or sofas in which the shaded parts (that is, the most difficult and delicate parts of the design such as the face, flesh and hair) had already been worked: "only the backgrounds remain to be worked, to amuse those who do not care to give themselves too much trouble." The Victoria and Albert Museum in London has such a canvas, which has never been completed. It was with such aids as these that successive generations of women, from the seventeenth to the nineteenth century, spent their leisure hours and adorned their homes, producing vast quantities of cushions and seat covers in *gros point* and *petit point* – or *point de St. Cyr*, as the antique-dealers fancifully describe them.

Figurative Embroidery and Ornamental Embroidery

The designs of embroidery have naturally varied according to period and according to purpose. Embroidery can tell a story, or it can be purely ornamental. During the Middle Ages figurative embroidery reigned supreme: the Bayeux Tapestry (Plate 14) is an outstanding example, which was certainly not the only one of its time. Narrative embroidery, *broderie à "ystoire,"* was also favored for church vestments and altar frontals, on which were represented the customary iconographical themes of the period: scenes from the Old or the New Testament, or from the lives of saints, or simply sacred figures in niches. Purses and caskets depicted graceful scenes from romances. Similar subjects were seen on hangings: in 1420, for example, Philippe le Bon, Duke of Burgundy, owned a set of hangings of crimson silk with the motif of a lady bathing her sparrow-hawk.

Tablecloth, *France*, c.1600.
*Darned net and cut-
work*. MUSÉE DES THERMES
ET DE L'HÔTEL DE CLUNY,
PARIS.

At the same time, medieval embroidery made extensive use of purely ornamental motifs, sometimes as an accom-
paniment to pictorial or narrative subjects and sometimes for their own sake:
heraldic shields, monograms, mottoes,
trees, flowers and animals adorned the
embroidered hangings which, unfortunately, are known to us only through
written records, though some hint of
their style can be gathered from extant
ornamental tapestries of the fourteenth
and fifteenth centuries. As a typical
example we may cite from the records a
set of hangings of blue satin embroidered with trees – date-palms, orange-
trees and others – which was worked by
Henriet Gontier in Paris in c.1390 for
Philippe le Hardi, Duke of Burgundy.

In the renaissance period the importance of ornamental embroidery increased while that of figurative embroidery declined. Floral motifs, foliate
scrolls, interlacings, grotesques and
monograms were to be seen everywhere,
even on church vestments, while sacred
subjects were reduced to symbols or
small pictorial medallions. Nevertheless,
bed valances and canvas-work hangings
were decorated with biblical, mythological or allegorical scenes, as were the
tapestries which they sought to imitate.
By the eighteenth century narrative
embroidery had declined almost to
vanishing point: human figures and
animals were used as elements in a
decorative play of forms which charms
the eye but tells no story. In the nineteenth century efforts were made to
revive figurative embroidery for church
use, inspired by Byzantine or medieval
models.

Styles and Designs
Style in embroidery naturally follows
the same evolution as in other branches

of the arts. In the Middle Ages embroidery was closely allied to manuscript painting, in both style and iconography. The fine embroidery of St. John the Baptist in the museum at Lyons (Plate 28), for example, may be compared with the superb Books of Hours of the period, notably the *Grandes Heures de Rohan*.

In the sixteenth century, the growing importance of the printed book led to a new phenomenon: the publication of an enormous number of pattern books for the use of embroiderers, lace makers and linen workers, providing these artisans with an extensive repertory of motifs, both ornamental and floral. The principal centers of pattern-book publishing in France were Paris and – even more active – Lyons; but foreign publishers also issued editions in French.

Besides the ornamental patterns provided by these specialized publications, embroiderers took designs for their figurative compositions from engravings and book illustrations. Mythological, biblical or allegorical scenes were taken freely from French prints by Bernard Salomon (1508?–61?) and Léonard Gaultier (1561–1641), from German and Swiss prints by Hans Holbein (1497/8–1543) and Tobias Stimmer (1539–84), from Flemish prints by Martin de Vos (1532–1603), from Italian prints by Antonio Tempesta (1555–1630), and so on. Thus a fine needlework hanging in the Musée Jacquemart-André, Paris, is a French work based directly on a print by Holbein, published at Basel in Switzerland.

It was not only pattern books and prints which circulated from one country to another. Catherine de Médicis had in her service a Venetian designer, Frederic de Vinciolo, who supplied the Queen with designs for her own needlework, and also produced the most popular of all the pattern books *Les Singuliers et Nouveaux Pourtraicts pour les Ouvrages de Lingerie*, which appeared in more than ten editions and was first published in Paris in 1587.

At the beginning of the seventeenth century an Englishman, Milour Matthias Mignerak, dedicated to another queen, Marie de Médicis, his book of patterns for *filet*, or *lacis*, *La Pratique de l'Aiguille Industrieuse*, Paris, 1605. Pattern books continued to appear, but it was characteristic of the age that the most productive author was a member of a famous family of

architects, Paul Androuet du Cerceau (*c*.1630–1710). The seventeenth century was marked by a movement toward integration of the arts and their universal subservience to architectural décor. This trend reached its peak in the second half of the century when Charles Le Brun became a veritable dictator of the arts.

In the eighteenth century textile design remained subject to the requirements of interior decoration, but the style was freer and more fanciful, especially in costume, where fantasy ran riot. The art of textile design, whether for embroidery, for weaving or for printing, was in the hands of specialists whose skill and professionalism have never been equaled. The silk industry of Lyons had long taken pains to train designers, who were greatly respected, highly paid and often, indeed, partners in the management of the factories. Accustomed to the special disciplines of designing for pattern weaving, they found no difficulty in designing embroidery for hangings or for dress. An interesting example is the bed of Marie-Antoinette at Fontainebleau which is hung with a patterned silk designed and woven by the manufacturer J. Audin of Lyons and subsequently, in 1791, embroidered in the workshop of the widow Baudouin in Paris; the perfect integration of the embroidery and the woven pattern shows clearly that the use of both techniques was foreseen in the original design. Designers such as Dumas, Jean-Baptiste Pillement (1727–1808), Jean-François Bony (*c*.1760–*c*.1825), Philippe de la Salle (1723–1805) (the most famous of them all), Antoine Artaud (1767–1838) and Pierre Dechazelle (1732–1833) (who specialized in waistcoats and sashes) were highly skilled technicians, *virtuosi* in the art of devising an infinite number of variations on the repertory of floral, exotic, fantastic and pastoral themes. Portfolios containing several hundreds of designs from this period are preserved in the Musée des Arts Décoratifs in Paris.

During the second half of the eighteenth century this art of graceful fantasy was gradually giving way to the severer neoclassical style. Under the Empire, embroidery was almost exclusively devoted to classical ornament: hangings and seat furniture displayed palmettes, crowns, sphinxes and military trophies, while costumes were

Bed *from Château d'Effiat, France, first half of the seventeenth century. Figured velvet embroidered with white and red silk and couched gold cord.* MUSÉE DU LOUVRE, PARIS.

reproduced with dazzling virtuosity motifs of the Directoire period, motifs from China, from Algeria, from Turkey and elsewhere. Church embroidery followed the "Gothic revival" or sought to emulate Byzantine models.

The Destruction of Embroideries

Textiles are frail: they were never intended to last forever and their survival is the exception rather than the rule. In a relatively prosperous and artistically active country such as France respect for faded relics of the past was unusual; palaces and *châteaux* were constantly being refurnished in new and up-to-date styles. Even the garments of royalty were not preserved but distributed to the officials of the court in accordance with strict protocol. The richest embroideries were naturally destroyed as soon as they were outworn or outmoded, in order to recover the precious metals, the pearls and the gems which they contained. *Parfilage*, or drizzling, meaning the unraveling of a fabric to extract the gold and silver threads, was a fashionable pastime in the eighteenth century. Textiles in the care of the Church often benefited from a more conservative attitude; yet even here donations of new vestments often caused the older ones to be consigned to the hazards of dust and rodents.

Moreover, in France more than elsewhere, the accidents of history have dealt harshly with the relics of the past. In the fifteenth century the English occupation of Paris led to the dispersal of the furnishings of the royal palaces. In the sixteenth century, during the wars of religion, the Huguenots systematically destroyed church treasuries wherever they passed, while both factions burned the *châteaux* of their opponents, together with their contents.

The destruction wrought by the Revolution was even more extensive and systematic in all parts of the country. The most valuable vestments were torn to shreds or burned in order to extract their gold, silver and jewels. In this way perished the vestments which had been given to Angers Cathedral by René of Anjou and which were still, even in the eighteenth century, considered to be "the most beautiful vestments in France." What was not destroyed was auctioned. The monasteries suffered the same fate. Not one of the great church treasuries escaped and of all the marvelous vestments described in the records

adorned with Greek key borders, bees and laurel leaves. Nevertheless, the graceful motifs of the preceding age were not entirely forgotten (Plate 35). The elevated style of classical antiquity continued to dominate official embroidery during the Restoration period.

The reaction which then ensued led to an extreme eclecticism of style; nineteenth-century embroidery, whether worked by hand or machine made, was essentially imitative. Furnishing embroideries were made in the Empire or the renaissance style. The Empress Eugénie favored the Marie-Antoinette style. Machine embroidery

Casket *with the monogram of Marie de Médicis, France, first quarter of the seventeenth century. Gold and silk threads worked in tent stitch, 10in × 24in × 17in (25cm × 62cm × 44cm).* MUSÉE DU LOUVRE, PARIS.

of Notre-Dame in Paris, the Ste. Chapelle and St. Denis, of all those in the great cathedrals, the pilgrimage churches, the great monastic houses, scarcely a vestige now remains. It is in Swedish or in Italian cathedrals that we must now seek some of the rare surviving French vestments of the Middle Ages. In France itself the piety of individuals or the isolation of rural communities could save only a few relics of the glories of the past.

The Revolution was only a little more merciful to secular embroidery. The contents of the *châteaux* and town houses of the nobility were either looted or else confiscated and sold. The precious furnishings of Versailles served to pay off the creditors of the Republic.

Under such circumstances the surviving remains can afford us only an imperfect and fragmentary knowledge of French embroidery prior to the Revolution; they suffice, nonetheless, to establish the main lines of its development and to indicate the high quality of its achievements.

The Middle Ages

Since so few examples survive, French medieval embroidery is little known and can hardly be compared on equal terms with the embroidery of England, Germany, Italy or Spain. But even if the reputation of French embroiderers stood less high than that of their English colleagues, there can be no doubt that they produced work of very fine quality. The real difficulty, however, is to determine which pieces are of French workmanship.

The oldest surviving embroidery which is probably French is a fragmentary tunic from the abbey of Chelles, which is now a small community in the Paris area but was formerly one of the residences of the Merovingian kings. It is decorated around the neck opening with embroidery in polychrome silk representing concentric necklaces of cloisonné enamel from which hang medallions and a cross. The tunic dates from the seventh or eighth century and the jewelry is typical of that period.

Mantle *for the image of*
Notre-Dame-du-Pilier
(Our Lady of the Pillar),
France, seventeenth century.
Gold and silver threads in
raised work and couched
work, silk threads in long
and short stitch. CATHEDRAL
TREASURY, CHARTRES.

The second major embroidery associated with France – and the largest
surviving medieval embroidery – is the
Bayeux Tapestry (Plate 14). Though it
is generally attributed to England, this
is far from certain and there are argu-
ments to be advanced on both sides.
The English embroiderers already had
a high reputation, but the hanging was
probably made for the cathedral of
Bayeux, whose bishop was the brother
of William the Conqueror. Even if we
admit that the embroiderers were English, was the artist who traced the
design Norman, or English, or French?
The debate is unproductive. This is in
any case a unique work, not only on
account of its size, but also because it is
the only surviving medieval embroidery
which depicts events from contemporary
history. It is more than likely, however,
that other embroideries of this type
were made. One comparable piece is a
fragment of linen in the treasury of Sens

Cathedral, which shows traces of embroidery depicting a battle scene in a
similarly picturesque and vigorous
narrative style.

The treasury of Sens, the only
church treasury in France which retains
an extensive collection of early textiles,
possesses several vestments said to have
belonged to St. Thomas of Canterbury,
who spent several years in Sens during
the second half of the twelfth century,
and others associated with St. Edmund
of Canterbury, who died at Sens in the
middle of the thirteenth century. There
is also a miter depicting the martyrdom
of St. Thomas of Canterbury and fragments of episcopal footwear, found in
the tombs of thirteenth-century bishops
of Sens, embroidered with elegant
arabesques, resembling those of contemporary wrought ironwork, enlivened
with naïve and expressive human
figures, lions and griffins. All these
embroideries, worked in couched gold

thread, are very similar to fragments preserved at Canterbury and Worcester. They are thought to be English and they form an acceptable intermediate stage between the earlier embroideries at Durham and the masterpieces of *opus anglicanum* made in the thirteenth and fourteenth centuries. In the absence of any work in this style which can be definitely identified as French, it is hard to contest these attributions.

A small purse in the Sens treasury, embroidered in brightly colored silks with an eagle on one side and a horseman on the other, is probably French work and recalls the celebrated twelfth-century wall paintings at St. Savin.

A group of church vestments of some importance, dating from the thirteenth century, may be attributed at least tentatively to France, though they are closely related to English embroidery and have sometimes been regarded as of English origin. The most important of these are a cope at Uppsala and a chasuble at Skara, both in Sweden, a cope and dalmatic now converted into a chasuble at Anagni in Italy and the handsome cope at St. Maximin in the Var, as well as fragmentary pieces at Lyons and the episcopal palace at Troyes.

A variety of circumstances link these vestments with France. The cope preserved in Uppsala Cathedral is probably one which was sent by the Pope to the archbishop of Uppsala at the time of the Council of Lyons in 1274. The bishop of Skara, at about the same period, spent eighteen years of his life in Paris; one may suppose that he brought back with him the cope, now converted into a chasuble, which is preserved at Skara Cathedral. French saints – St. Nicaise of Reims, St. Léger, St. Martin of Tours and the martyrs of Paris, St. Denis, St. Rustique and St. Eleuthère – appear on several of these vestments. Moreover, this group differs from contemporary *opus anglicanum* in its simpler and less sumptuous effects: the backgrounds are either unworked or, if they are embroidered, as at Anagni and St. Maximin, the couched gold shows a simple chevron pattern in place of the rich scrollwork of the English pieces. The composition is also rather simpler. At Skara, saints and angels are scattered over the silk ground fabric, with no framework to enclose them. In the Lyons fragment the figures are enclosed by a spindly arcade; in the Montiéramey cope at Troyes, by

Wall hanging *(detail) of grotesques in the style of Jean Bérain (1649–1711), France, late seventeenth century. Linen and silk material embroidered with wool in long and short stitch and satin stitch, 8ft 9in × 9ft 3in (267cm × 282cm).* VICTORIA AND ALBERT MUSEUM, LONDON.

quatrefoils; at St. Maximin, by simple circles. Between the geometrical frames, angels are almost invariably depicted.

The technique is similar to that of *opus anglicanum*: underside couching for the gold and split stitch in colored silks for flesh, foliage and draperies. The Anagni dalmatic was originally adorned with pearls in gold settings. Certain technical details, however, and the rather less refined execution distinguish these vestments from contemporary English work. But the designs are handsome and vigorous and it is unfortunate that so few examples of ecclesiastical embroidery have survived from the period of St. Louis and his immediate successors.

Medieval church embroidery is also represented by a small group of altar frontals at Château-Thierry, Toulouse and Sens, together with a fine fragment in the museum at Lyons which range in

Bed *of Ambassador Nils Bielke, France, c.1680. Red velvet ground with applied work in white and green silk material.* NATIONAL MUSEUM, STOCKHOLM, SWEDEN.

now dismembered, is conceived in a still more monumental vein (Plate 28). The vigorous, highly individual and masterly character of the design as well as the quality of the execution indicates that it was produced in one of the finest workshops of the early fifteenth century. Another fine work of the same period is an embroidered triptych depicting the Man of Sorrows and two Saints, in the Museum of Chartres.

A small group of miters of very high quality has survived from the fourteenth century. Of the two examples in the Musée de Cluny, Paris, that from the Ste. Chapelle is decorated with large numbers of seed pearls. The miter of Jean de Marigny in the museum at Evreux and that preserved at Sixt in Haute-Savoie (Plate 29) show a strength in design and an assurance of execution which suggest a workshop closely connected with the court.

Church vestments of the later medieval period were generally made of rich Italian silks, while embroidery was limited to narrow bands or orphreys, which almost invariably depict figures of saints in architectural niches. The system proved convenient and very suitable for mass production, but French orphreys of this kind are repetitive in design and unrefined in execution. They were intended to be seen from a distance, like theatrical costume, and they are effective enough in this respect.

Of the secular embroidery of the Middle Ages, practically nothing remains. Only a small group of purses survives, of which some of the best are in the Musée de Cluny, the museum at Lyons and the treasury of Troyes Cathedral. They depict fanciful subjects or subjects drawn from romances, with figures of lovers and graceful monsters among flowering stems; others show heraldry or geometrical patterns. The guild regulations of Paris referred, from the thirteenth century onward, to the "makers of Saracen purses," for the fashion came from the East. The designs are lively and charming and the workmanship highly professional, though less refined than that of ecclesiastical embroidery. The subjects and the technique help us to visualize the sets of embroidered chamber hangings with patterns of birds, trees and figures in gardens which are recorded in the accounts and inventories of royal and princely residences.

date from the early fourteenth to the early fifteenth century. In these, embroidery escapes from the limitations of garments designed to be worn and achieves a freedom comparable with painting, sculpture or goldsmith's work. The frontal in the museum at Toulouse illustrates scenes from the lives of the saints; unfortunately, restoration has destroyed much of the original character of the work, but the technique and the arrangement of the scenes in quatrefoils recall the earlier copes. In the superb altar frontal at Château-Thierry the composition is freer; the figures, whose faces are painted, not embroidered, are applied to a velvet background beneath a graceful arcade. The design shows great refinement; the drapery style and the slender elegance of the figures suggest a date in the first quarter of the fourteenth century. The figure of St. John the Baptist in the museum at Lyons, part of a large altar frontal,

Bed *of the Marquise de Créquy, St.-Cyr, France, 1737–40. Canvas embroidered with silk threads in tent, cross and stem stitch.* PALAIS DE VERSAILLES.

The Sixteenth and Seventeenth Centuries

From the fifteenth century, a period when France was ravaged by war, relatively little embroidery has survived, chiefly orphreys of modest quality. But with the onset of the Renaissance, embroiderers embarked on a period of intense activity. Ecclesiastical embroidery, it is true, did not regain the prestige and quality of the best medieval work, but a new luxury in dress and furnishing called for lavish displays of fine needlework. Pictorial embroidery was still practiced and some small master-

pieces were produced in which the subtleties of drapery, of light and shade, of perspective and foreshortening, are rendered with almost incredible virtuosity by the embroiderer's needle, working from designs of the highest quality. Some of these little pictures are extremely finely executed in *or nué*, others are worked with silk in split stitch, simulating the brushwork of a painting. Some were made for religious purposes, such as the corporal case in the Musée de Cluny depicting the Lamentation over the Dead Christ, after a design from the circle of the painter and

Altar frontal *showing the Virgin of the Apocalypse, France, eighteenth century. Silk ground with gold threads in couched and raised work and silk threads in long and short stitch, 37in × 61in (93cm × 155cm).* MUSÉE DU LOUVRE, PARIS.

engraver Jean Cousin (1490–1560), or the miniature altar-piece inscribed "PIERRE VIGIER – 1621" in the museum at Lyons (Plate 31); others were used in secular furnishings such as the panel showing bear-baiting (Plate 30), which formed part of a hanging depicting scenes from the court of Henri II, inspired by Italian engravings. Pictorial embroidery, however, was gradually falling out of favor. Italian or French velvets and damasks offered all the opulence that was required for church vestments and the "*ystoires*" or pictorial subjects were generally restricted to a modest central medallion in *or nué*.

It was ornamental embroidery, not pictorial embroidery, which reigned supreme from the renaissance period onward, not only in secular and ecclesiastical costume, but also in furnishings. The printed pattern books supplied ornamental motifs in great variety. Floral ornament, highly favored in the sixteenth century, was destined to remain the principal theme of embroidery down to the nineteenth century.

In the sixteenth century, flowers were sometimes used in combination with interlacings and scrollwork patterns executed in applied fabrics outlined with cord, as in a chasuble in the Musée de Cluny, notable for the almost entirely secular character of its ornament. The embroidered lining of the shield of Charles IX is characterized by a simplicity of technique and a vigorous sobriety of design which is reminiscent of book-bindings and goldsmith's

work. A superb casket in the Louvre, Paris, with the monogram of Marie de Médicis, is decorated with symmetrical scrolls of flowers, leaves and fruit worked extremely finely in *petit point* of silk and gold, at least equal in quality to the best English work of the time.

Later in the seventeenth century, robust scrolls, lush foliage and giant sprays of blossom overrun the embroidered surfaces in a riotous display. Couched and raised gold work was extensively used, together with silks in brilliant hues. Court dresses and costly vestments were executed in this way. But their very lavishness was to be the cause of their destruction for raised gold work is fragile and difficult to preserve or store. When the costumes or vestments became outworn or outmoded, the gold was extracted to be used again. At the Revolution vestments that were heavily embroidered or woven with gold were destroyed without mercy. Thus it is that so little remains of the most sumptuous embroideries of the age of Louis XIV.

Embroidery played a major rôle in the decoration of that all-important item of domestic furniture, the bed. A large number of bed hangings were of velvet or satin with applied-work patterns of interlacings and plant scrolls; the lively, vigorous designs of the sixteenth century were succeeded, in the seventeenth, by a more sober and monumental style. These are works of fine quality, obviously executed by professional embroiderers. Another group of sixteenth-century bed hangings is

notable for an extraordinary refinement of style. Embroidered on satin in delicately shaded silks, they show little figures, inscriptions, masks, herms and grotesques. The embroiderers are here interpreting, with admirable skill, the witty and elegant manner of contemporary ornamental engravings. A further large group of bed valances exhibit a more robust and less subtle style. Worked with wool and silk in tent stitch, these are to be found not only in France, but also in England, Scotland and Switzerland. There are also cushions in the same style.

Many of these pieces show courtly scenes, or biblical or mythological subjects, adapted from Flemish or French prints, with the figures dressed in French fashions of the second half of the sixteenth century. They are mannerist in style, dense and rather overladen in composition, and professional in execution. They were clearly produced commercially by workshops which may have been in Flanders, but were at least strongly influenced by French art though it is not possible to establish their location with any certainty. A number of large wall hangings in the same style and technique are worthy of comparison with contemporary tapestries.

This technique of *tapisserie au point*, or canvas work, gave rise to an enormous quantity of work of very varied quality produced by professionals, semi-professionals and amateurs. The designs were derived from pattern books, copied from prints or tapestries, bought ready-traced on the canvas, or, more rarely, they might be original designs by an amateur or a professional artist. The technique, though simple in itself, nevertheless demanded high standards of skill and judgment to achieve satisfactory shading of the colors for the flesh and drapery. Semi-professional workshops such as those of St. Joseph and St. Cyr were capable of producing work of the highest quality in this field (Plate 30), while innumerable beds and chairs were covered with canvas work by needlewomen of more modest attainments.

Filet, or *lacis* was another technique accessible to amateurs. It was very fashionable from the sixteenth century

Sofa cover *(detail)*, France, late eighteenth century. Cream satin ground embroidered with polychrome silks in chain stitch and tambour work in the style of Philippe de La Salle (1723–1805). THE NATIONAL TRUST, WADDESDON MANOR, BUCKINGHAMSHIRE, ENGLAND.

*Waistcoat, France, c.1780.
White silk embroidered with
polychrome silk threads in
satin stitch, stem stitch and
French knots. The original
design for this waistcoat
exists in the Musée
Historique des Tissus, Lyons.*
VICTORIA AND ALBERT
MUSEUM, LONDON.

onward and the printed pattern books
offered a large repertory of designs for
such work.

Although canvas work was especially
suitable for large-scale pieces, wall
hangings were also produced in other
techniques: raised work in gold was
used for the richest pieces, as at Versailles, while others were executed in
long and short stitches, like the
remarkable hangings at Beaugency
(Loiret) or the one in the Victoria and
Albert Museum which rivals the effects
of tapestry.

From 1715–1815
From the Middle Ages until the seventeenth century embroidery had generally been produced in workshops of
small to moderate size, using designs

originated by painters, engravers and
book illustrators. In the eighteenth
century, however, embroidery was profoundly affected by two new factors.
The first was the development of the
large-scale industrial production of
embroidery, especially at Lyons. The
second, a natural consequence of the
first, was the emergence of specialist
textile designers as the principal
originators of embroidery designs.

As a result, embroidery patterns
became more elegant and flowing and,
at the same time, much more intimately
involved with current fashions. The
Lyons manufacturers were in the habit
of changing the designs of their woven
silks every year and they undoubtedly
adopted the same principle for their
embroidered silks. Producers of other

types of embroidery naturally found themselves obliged to follow these changes in fashion. Thus a satin chasuble embroidered with opulent bouquets of flowers and fruit (Plate 32) is comparable in style with the woven silks designed by Jean Revel (1684–1751) in Lyons in c.1735. An elegant silk fabric embroidered with flowers, fruit, birds, ribbons and musical scores at Waddesdon Manor, Buckinghamshire, represents fashionable taste in the time of Marie-Antoinette. The Museum of Malmaison possesses a hanging which was woven and embroidered about 1810 by Bissardon, Bony and Company of Lyons for the small drawing-room of the Empress Marie-Louise at Versailles (Plate 34). It displays flowers, birds, acanthus scrolls, vases and classical columns in a somewhat stiff arrangement characteristic of the designer Jean-François Bony (1760–1825). From the same period are the fine hangings in Vienna in which rural and musical attributes form a happy alliance with acanthus foliage, fasces and classical urns.

The centralization and industrialization of embroidery favored techniques which permitted rapid execution, such as the very adaptable satin stitch, or chain stitch worked on the tambour frame with the aid of a fine hooked needle, a method introduced from China. The embroiderer's work was simplified by ingenious labor-saving ideas, such as the use of chenille thread, of sequins, ribbon and applied work in tulle or muslin which allowed large areas to be embroidered in the minimum time. Most important of all, it was no longer usual for embroidery to cover almost the entire surface of the fabric; instead, it was disposed lightly and sparingly, decorating the fabric but leaving large areas of it untouched – a notable economy of labor.

The concentration of a major branch of embroidery in the hands of the silk manufacturers naturally involved more highly organized methods of production in marketing. This was particularly true of costume embroidery for men. The designers working in this field produced new sets of designs at frequent intervals in accordance with the dictates of fashion; sample swatches were then embroidered and sent out to the fashion houses; finally, complete, uncut lengths of fabric, worked with all the embroidery required for coats or waistcoats,

were despatched to Paris and other fashion centers. These lengths were then handed over to the tailors to be made up into garments. The imagination and variety to be found in this work is astonishing; the motifs include flowers and fruit, both realistic and fantastic, cupids and butterflies, monkeys, birds and rustic figures, in an infinite number of amusing and charming compositions.

While this branch of production was fundamentally transformed in the eighteenth century, others remained strongly attached to earlier traditions. Although many church vestments were now made from the splendid woven silks of Lyons without embroidery, many others continued to be embroidered with raised gold thread, with magnificent and theatrical effect, as in the sumptuous vestments executed at Lyons in 1740 for the coronation of the Emperor Karl VII Albrecht, or in the example preserved at Stonyhurst College, Lancashire. Most church vestments were less ambitious than these, aiming to supply the necessary effect of

Empress Josephine's bedroom, France, designs c.1810, embroidery c.1860. Ceiling embroidered by Maison Picot under the Second Empire after the original designs. MUSÉE DE MALMAISON.

Panel *from the bedroom of Louis XVIII in the Tuileries palace, France, c.1815. Blue figured silk velvet embroidered with couched gold threads.* MUSÉE DU LOUVRE, PARIS.

ecclesiastical splendor at reasonable cost. As in the renaissance period, however, current secular styles made their influence felt on vestments. Woven silks and embroideries with fashionable floral or exotic designs were widely used. In the Empire period, after the Catholic Church had been re-established in France, and even more in the Restoration period, from 1815 onward, vestments were designed in the neoclassical style of the time, and heavily embroidered with gold.

Like church embroidery, embroidery for the court was much influenced by tradition. The "full-dress court robes" of the ladies and "full-dress court suits" of the gentlemen were regulated by strict protocol down to the Revolution and were laden with gold and gems. The young Louis XV, aged eleven, received the ambassador of the Turkish sultan wearing a suit of flame-colored velvet, weighed down with nearly forty pounds in weight of jewels. Although the court and its etiquette perished in the Revolution, the governments of the Directorate and the Consulate (1795–1802) soon felt the need to express their power through splendid

costumes. Eventually the prestige of the Empire demanded new regulations and court dress again became obligatory. Napoleon and his dignitaries appeared on state occasions in sumptuous uniforms bedecked with gold embroidery. At the same time the Lyons manufacturers were working at high pressure to refurnish the Imperial palaces with gold-woven or gold-embroidered hangings under the supervision of the Emperor's architects and designers, Charles Percier (1764–1838) and Pierre François Léonard Fontaine (1762–1853). The grand, classicizing, monumental official style evolved at that time persisted during the Restoration period. It was, in any case, desirable to make use of the imperial furnishings by the simple expedient of replacing the emblems of the empire with those of the monarchy.

Another sector in which taste changed slowly and traditions persisted was that of canvas-work embroidery. Perhaps because this technique, more than any other, belonged to the amateur embroiderer, it never completely rejected the styles of the past and it retained, far into the eighteenth century,

Court train, *made by Gagelin, Paris, c.1855. White silk embroidered with gold thread, 110in × 103in (279cm × 262cm).* VICTORIA AND ALBERT MUSEUM, LONDON.

links with the Renaissance; and this remains true even where the quality of the work indicates a professional hand. A large number of canvas-work seat covers have survived from the eighteenth century, often based on earlier designs; there are also a number of beds or bed valances, besides various panels inspired by engravings of contemporary or earlier date. Nevertheless, fashionable exotic and bizarre motifs are also found, for example in a number of hangings which are of thoroughly professional quality.

From 1815–1914

The historical process which was to transform embroidery from a craft to an industry was begun, as we have seen, in the eighteenth century and was to be completed in the nineteenth. From 1828 onward the embroidery loom was capable of producing most types of embroidery mechanically, although hand embroidery still remained a very active industry for the production of luxury articles. The abundance of the goods produced and their comparatively low cost brought embroidery within the reach of a much wider social class. At the same time the prosperity of the *bourgeoisie* and the ostentatious taste of the time encouraged extravagance in feminine costume. It is true that the embroidery of coats and dresses – apart from ball gowns – was relatively sober. But an abundance of whitework was employed to adorn bonnets, collars, sleeves and flounces, not to mention underwear, night clothes, summer outfits and children's clothes. At the same time every kind and technique of

Dress, *Paris, c.1894.*
Bodice of green velvet with
skirt in beige satin with
bronze and colored beads.
VICTORIA AND ALBERT
MUSEUM, LONDON.

quality of the best pieces is undeniable.

In about 1890, however, a reaction against the rising tide of industrialization made itself felt and artists began to interest themselves in the possibilities of hand craftsmanship. The "Nabis," a group of painters associated with Maurice Denis (1870–1943), showed a special interest in the textile arts; Paul Ranson (1864–1909), Emile Bernard (1868–1941) and Aristide Maillol (1861–1944) (before he took to sculpture) all produced designs for embroidered hangings which were worked for them by wives, sisters, friends or groups of local seamstresses. This kind of interest in embroidery continued during the early years of the present century. Fashion embroideries in the Art Nouveau style, executed by Jeanne Prompt, Jacques and Madeleine Bille, E. Henry ("the master embroiderer of the Faubourg St-Honoré") and Prince Karageorgevitch figured in public exhibitions. Even René Lalique (1860–1945) produced designs for embroidered collars in the style of his famous glassware. But embroidery of this sort was the interest of small groups of intellectuals and was slow to influence the great mass of commercial production.

Amateur needlewomen remained extremely active until the First World War. Whitework embroidery was an indispensable part of feminine education, since underclothes, dresses and blouses in this technique, for both women and children, were often made at home. Other embroidery techniques were employed to furnish the home with canvas-work seat covers, *lacis* curtains and coverlets, and many other accessories. Skill in needlework was probably still the most highly esteemed accomplishment for a young lady in all classes of society. Innumerable pattern books and practical manuals of embroidery were published; those written by Thérèse de Dillmont for the thread manufacturers D.M.C. (Dollfuss-Mieg) of Mulhouse between 1886 and the early years of the twentieth century cover every technique and provide patterns in a great variety of styles.

The nineteenth century witnessed a brief but extraordinary flowering of peasant costume in France. White embroideries and polychrome embroideries, in wool, silk and linen, adorned the waistcoats, shirtfronts and jackets of the men, the coifs, collars, bodices, aprons and shawls of the women in

embroidery was used on purses, gloves, stockings, slippers, shawls, collars, sunshades, fans and other accessories.

The exuberance of the production and the virtuosity of the techniques were matched by the opulence and the endless variety of the designs. Since modern techniques were able to do everything better, more quickly and more cheaply than the craftsmen of the past, the manufacturers vied with each other to copy everything and to imitate everything that had ever been made. Embroidery for fashion or for furnishing was produced in the "Renaissance," "Pompadour," "Trianon," "Directoire," "Chinese," "Algerian," or "Turkish" styles; church embroidery found inspiration in Byzantine or medieval models. The designs are generally very competent, though they often seem excessively derivative and overloaded to our eyes, and the superb

almost every region of the country: in Auvergne, the Pyrenees, Lorraine, Normandy and Savoy. But it was in Brittany, above all, that the effects were most spectacular and long lasting (Plate 39). Most of this embroidery was no doubt produced in local workshops using traditional methods, but there was also some industrial production aimed at this specialized market.

Embroidery since 1914

Following the outbreak of the 1914–18 war, fashions in dress underwent a radical transformation. Opulence and ostentation were succeeded by austerity, by practicality and the triumph of the ready-to-wear garment. By 1930, the rôle of embroidery, both manual and machine made, was drastically reduced and, since then, the growing use of artificial fibers and of nylon underwear has brought about a further decline. Nevertheless, a number of workshops have remained active, both in Paris and in Lyons.

Paris is, above all, the principal center of embroidery for *haute couture*. The fashion houses of Worth, Poiret, Callot sœurs, Madeleine Vionnet, Myrbor, Schiaparelli, Paquin, Jacques Fath, Dior, Givenchy and St. Laurent have all made use of embroidery, produced either in their own workshops, as in the case of Paul Poiret's *atelier Martine*, or in one of the specialized embroidery workshops such as those of Lallemant, Lesage or Rébé. Machine embroidery has also been used for the same purpose. Occasionally, the *couturiers* have called on well-known artists to produce designs.

The rôle assigned to embroidery in *haute couture* is like that of the percussion section in an orchestra: it must dazzle or sparkle, astonish or amuse. The design must be bold and free, and the execution still more so, using shells and sequins, glass beads, metal threads, applied work in a whole range of materials, three-dimensional flowers in tulle or muslin, and so on. Fine detail, refinement and the technical traditions of the past are not to be expected here; any means whatever may be employed, so long as it produces the desired theatrical effect.

The workshops of Carloni-Hamelin and Brocard, also in Paris, specialize in furnishing embroidery. The house of Brocard founded in 1775 produces astonishingly skillful reproductions of old embroidered hangings which are used for refurnishing historic buildings.

In Lyons, machine embroidery of fine quality is produced in the Lyons-Fleury workshops, under the direction of Monsieur Egraz. Hand embroidery is the speciality of the workshops of G. Dutel, Bouvard and Feige, who employ a nucleus of highly qualified embroiderers. These companies, which were chiefly concerned with the production of church vestments, have been obliged in recent years to look for other outlets. The house of Dutel, for example, was responsible for all the decorative hand embroidery commissioned by the Shah of Iran for the celebrations in Persepolis in 1971 of 2,500 years of Persian monarchy. At St. Etienne, the workshop of Julien Faure produces embroidery for *haute couture*, using modern materials.

Maquettes *for a set of red and yellow liturgical vestments designed for the chapel of the Dominican Nuns of Vence, France, by Henri Matisse (1869–1954), c.1950. Gouache on paper, cut and pasted, mount 15ft 1in × 6ft 2½in (4·6m × 1·89m).* MUSEUM OF MODERN ART, NEW YORK.

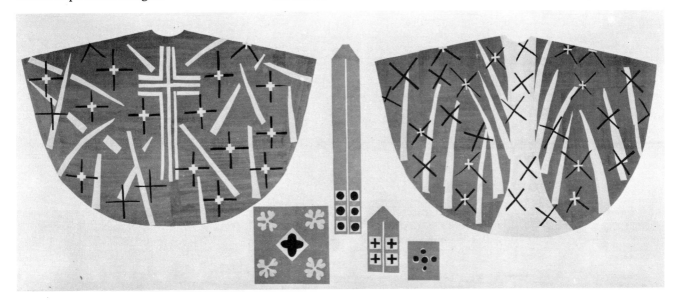

Marie-Antoinette's bedroom, *France. Off-white silk embroidered with gold thread and polychrome silks. Original bedcover delivered in 1787 by Desfarges of Lyons. Wall panels, bed curtains and seats rewoven according to the original designs by the* Syndicat des Fabricants de Soieries de Lyons *and embroidered by the Brocard workshop, Paris, 1975. Palais de Versailles.*

In modern times embroidery is no longer, as it was formerly, the leisure occupation of a high proportion of Frenchwomen. Nevertheless, it retains the allegiance of considerable numbers of enthusiastic practitioners. The firm of D.M.C. and a number of women's magazines encourage amateur needle-women by providing patterns and advice and by organizing competitions, exhibitions and other activities. More-over, the continuing reaction against our industrialized civilization is demon-strated by the increasing number of small craft-workshops operated not only by potters, jewelers, enamelers and the like, but also by weavers and embroid-erers, who create their own designs and very often their own techniques. Their tastes generally favor rustic forms and methods and abstract or naïve designs.

Thus embroidery is by no means dead in France. It has simply adapted itself to our modern conditions. There can be no doubt that, like all basic crafts, it will still be able to meet the needs and the tastes of the future.

Italy

THREE OBSERVATIONS MUST BE MADE about the history of embroidery in Italy. Firstly it is perhaps truer of this than of any other country that embroidery is closely allied to the fine arts, and to a decorative language drawn from the wells of Italy's ancient past. Until the end of the sixteenth century therefore embroidery cannot be regarded as a craft apart, existing independently, but must be studied as part of the whole artistic life of the country.

Secondly by far the greater part of the work that has survived has been made for the Church. If the study of Italian embroidery seems to consist of a procession of altar frontals and chasubles, it must be borne in mind that Italy escaped both the destruction and the rejection of vestments which the Reformation in its various forms brought about in northern Europe, so that large numbers of church embroideries have been preserved. This is in fact a question of the survival of greater numbers and does not mean that embroideries were not made for secular purposes. Where they still exist it can be seen that the style of professional embroidery in any period was very much the same for both secular and ecclesiastical use.

Lastly it has to be remembered that from the Middle Ages Italy has been, and still is, one of the leading producers and weavers of silk in western Europe. Even the rise of the French silk industry in the second half of the seventeenth century, which captured the lead in fashionable design, did nothing to reduce Italian output. Woven silk, which requires great technical skill at all stages of its manufacture, has always been prized above hand embroidery, and this fact must greatly influence the use of embroidery in any country which has a developed silk industry.

The Early Middle Ages

A very few embroideries are known to have been made at this period. A rare surviving example which is worth mentioning can be seen in the Archiepiscopal Museum in Ravenna. It consists of three narrow bands which are thought originally to have decorated an altar frontal and are still known as the *Velo di Classe*, the veil or curtain of Classe, in Ravenna. They are decorated with busts in roundels, worked in colored silks on a gold ground, which represent eighth-century bishops of Verona. This must point to a north Italian origin, possibly Verona itself.

Needlework in Sicily in the Twelfth and Thirteenth Centuries

It is not until three hundred years later that we find evidence of the manufacture of embroideries in Sicily, which was conquered by the Norman barons who had established themselves in the south of Italy during the latter half of the eleventh century. Roger II, who was crowned king of Sicily in 1130 and who was responsible for many of the magnificent mosaics which decorate the churches, was also a great patron of the textile arts. Finding that the weaving and embroidery workrooms of the famous Arab Tiraz in Palermo were still active, he brought in Byzantine weavers to train Sicilians in their superior skills, but continued, it is thought, to use Arab embroiderers. From their hands came one of the most dramatic embroideries of all time, a ceremonial cloak made for Roger II and later used as the coronation mantle of the Holy Roman Emperors. This powerful composition was drawn from Middle Eastern antecedents in animal design. The paired lions attacking camels on either side of a date-palm are rendered with an extraordinary strength and clarity, which is further emphasized by the bold embroidery technique. This is an applied pattern, embroidered in gold thread and colored silks, outlined in pearls and further ornamented with gold and enamel plaques and precious stones. The Arabic inscription in the border contains a eulogy of the wearer and the date 1133. It must be assumed that it was not the only piece of this type and quality produced by the Tiraz workrooms, but no other has survived.

The Sicilian silk industry remained

OVERLEAF, TOP:
The Coronation Mantle of the Holy Roman Emperors *probably made for Roger II of Sicily, Palermo, Sicily, 1133–4. Applied work in red and gold silk, with gold thread and silk embroidery enriched with gold and enamel plaques and pearls, diameter, 135in (342cm). The design, worked by Arab embroiderers, has strong affinities with the animal art of the Middle East.*
WELTLICHE SCHATZKAMMER, VIENNA.

faithful to the traditional patterns of paired birds and animals in roundels which it had inherited from the Middle East through Byzantium. An altar hanging now at Assisi shows that similar patterns were executed in embroidery early in the thirteenth century. It is worked in a continuous pattern of parrots and griffins, in gold thread underside-couched on a background of yellow silk. The decorative network which encircles the paired beasts is strongly influenced by Islamic linear patterns, and its particular form seems to be a hallmark of Sicilian workrooms of the twelfth and thirteenth centuries. It can be seen in other surviving pieces, among them a dalmatic made in the reign of Roger II which also forms part of the coronation vestments of the Holy Roman Empire, a set of vestments given by Pope Boniface VIII to Anagni Cathedral, near Rome, and two roundels with the heads of Christ and the Virgin which decorate a vestment at Speyer in Germany. Both these date to c.1200.

Because of political troubles in Sicily during the late thirteenth century, which increased in the 1280s after the rising and massacre known as the Sicilian Vespers, both weaving and embroidery workrooms ceased to produce work of this quality and many silk weavers emigrated northward and settled in Lucca and Pisa. An embroidery which was evidently made in Sicily at the end of the fourteenth century is in its way unique but is in a more homely style. This is a quilt, of which part is now in the Victoria and Albert Museum in London and part in the Palazzo Davanzati in Florence. It is of extraordinary size, the part in London alone measuring over ten feet (over 3m). In a series of rectangular compartments it tells the story of Tristram after the fourteenth-century *novella*, *La Tavola Rotonda o l'Istoria di Tristano*. The scenes are worked entirely in quilting and are labeled in the same way in Sicilian dialect.

ABOVE AND RIGHT:
Altar hanging *(details)*, *Palermo, Sicily, thirteenth century. Yellow silk ground embroidered in couched gold thread with pairs of griffins and birds in medallions, 237in × 47¾in (600cm × 122cm). The design follows the woven silks of the period but the pattern of the roundels themselves is close to that of other Sicilian embroideries.* TREASURY OF SAN FRANCESCO, ASSISI.

The Fourteenth and Fifteenth Centuries in Italy

By the year 1300 autonomous city states, ruled in many cases with ruthless energy and disposing of increasing wealth, had already emerged from the political chaos of early medieval Italy. The silk industry at Lucca had been greatly strengthened by the influx of workers from Sicily and many were to

move on to other cities in northern
Italy, in particular Venice, founding an
industry which was to dominate Italian
fashion through the centuries to come.

From this time onward embroideries
of high technical skill were produced
which can often be related to the work
of specific artists. An early group from
the years shortly before and after 1300,
which is described in inventories as *de
opere romano* (Roman work), was probably actually made in Rome or at any
rate in central Italy. These embroideries are mainly in split stitch in clear
bright colors with modest gold-thread
backgrounds. The outstanding example
is an altar frontal at Anagni, another
gift of Boniface VIII to the cathedral of
his birthplace, which like many frontals
of the period is arranged to show saints
and scenes framed in architectural
arcading, in this case in two tiers. Artistically the scenes from the lives of St.
Peter and St. Paul in the lower tier have
been compared to the mosaics of the
Life of the Virgin Mary in Sta. Maria
in Trastevere in Rome, by Pietro
Cavallini (active 1273–1308). His work
was influenced by a revival of interest
in Byzantine art which was brought
about when Byzantine masters from
Venice worked on mosaics in Rome
earlier in the century, and traces of the
Byzantine manner can still be seen in
the frontal.

The great maritime city of Venice
had already known several hundred
years of fame and prosperity as a center
of trade with the East. In fact very little

ABOVE:
Coverlet *(detail), Sicily,
c.1400. Linen, quilted, and
padded with wool, another
part of the same quilt is in
the Palazzo Davanzati,
Florence. The scenes relate
the story of Tristram, taken
from a fourteenth-century*
novella, *with inscriptions in
Sicilian dialect.* VICTORIA
AND ALBERT MUSEUM,
LONDON.
BELOW:
Altar frontal, *Rome or
central Italy, c.1300.*

*Worked in polychrome silks
in split stitch with
background and halos in
couched gold thread, whole
frontal 37½in × 77in
(95cm × 195cm). Depicting
the Virgin and Child with
saints and angels, and the
Crucifixion with scenes from
the lives of St. Peter and St.
Paul. The artistic style has
been likened to the mosaics
by Pietro Cavallini in Sta.
Maria in Trastevere, Rome.*
CATHEDRAL TREASURY,
ANAGNI.

Altar frontal (detail), Venice, Italy, c.1330. Gold threads underside couched on red satin with details in polychrome silks, whole frontal 42in × 108¾in (107cm × 276cm). This embroidered version of the Coronation of the Virgin and saints under arcades follows a design by Paolo Veneziano (d. before 1362). The technique of patterned gold on a plain background shows the influence of Venice's close connections with Byzantium. VICTORIA AND ALBERT MUSEUM, LONDON.

Venetian embroidery has survived, but it is not surprising that a major work which has come down to us from this wealthy city should be embroidered almost entirely in gold thread. This is another arcaded altar frontal with the Coronation of the Virgin in the center between two rows of saints, after a design by Paolo Veneziano (died before 1362). Although the artist was Venetian and both the choice of subject and the layout western European, the technique employed, that is the laying and couching of the gold threads in elaborate patterns, which is very different from the colored split stitch of the Roman frontal, has closer affiliations with Byzantine embroidery than with anything made in Italy at this time. Again this cannot surprise us in view of Venice's very close trade and political relationships with that city. The frontal was made about the year 1330 for the cathedral of the island of Krk (Veglia) on the Dalmatian coast, which was formerly a Venetian possession. Two

similar but less elaborate pieces exist in Dalmatia which may also have been made in Venice, but could be locally-made copies of Venetian work.

By the beginning of the fourteenth century Florence was emerging as one of the most important of the city states of north Italy, a thriving, forceful community, adept in commerce, generous in artistic patronage, breeding an independence of mind which nurtured a race of giants from Dante to Michelangelo.

The artists who lived and worked in this intoxicating atmosphere over the next two hundred years were prepared to turn their hands to any facet of their craft. Fresco and panel painting, sculpture and goldsmith's work, for both secular and religious purposes, poured from their workshops, while many of them were equally prepared to turn their attention to the designing of woven silks and subjects for embroidery, and even to the painting of chariots for festive processions.

The style of Florentine embroidery in this period has much more in common with the Roman frontal from Anagni, worked in colored split stitch, than with the Venetian gold work. It has been suggested that a very small altar hanging in the Victoria and Albert Museum in London, which was made in Florence *c.*1300, represents the spread of the central Italian style into Tuscany. By the fourth decade of the century, approximately at the time the Venetian frontal was made, two more major altar frontals, both signed by their embroiderers, show that Florentine workshops had by this time completely mastered their craft. The first, which was made for the church of Sta. Maria Novella in Florence, has, like its Venetian contemporary, a Coronation of the Virgin set in a row of saints framed by arcades (Plate 40). (See also the Bohemian frontal on p. 269 which was almost certainly a copy of an Italian model.) It also has a row of small scenes from the Life of the Virgin which form a superfrontal, much as a series of small panels make up the predella of a painted altarpiece. It is embroidered with a high degree of technical excellence in the clear colors beloved of Florentine painters, and signed Jacopo Cambi with the date 1336.

The companion piece is a frontal with a central Crucifixion and a series of scenes in three tiers on either side, which is now in Manresa in northern

LEFT: Plate 28
Altar frontal, *fragment showing St. John the Baptist, France, early fifteenth century. Canvas embroidered with gold threads in couched work and silk threads in split stitch, 29in × 11in (72cm × 28cm).* MUSÉE HISTORIQUE DES TISSUS, LYONS.

TOP: Plate 29
Miter, *France, second half of the fourteenth century. The Coronation of the Virgin worked in gold and silk embroidery on a silk ground, 12in × 12in (30cm × 30cm).* SIXT PARISH CHURCH, HAUTE-SAVOIE.

ABOVE: Plate 30
Embroidered panel, *France, second half of the sixteenth century. The scene of bear baiting is worked in metal threads and silk.* MUSÉE HISTORIQUE DES TISSUS, LYONS.

ABOVE: Plate 31
Miniature altarpiece,
*France, 1621. Embroidered
with gold and silk in* or nué,
*split stitch, long and short
stitch and worked with the
inscription* Pierre VIGIER
1621, *13in × 26in (32cm ×
64cm).* MUSÉE HISTORIQUE
DES TISSUS, LYONS

RIGHT: Plate 32
Wall hanging *attributed to
the Convent of St. Joseph de
la Providence, Paris,
c.1863–5. The subject of* Le
Feu ou la Guerre *is worked
on a canvas ground with
silver and gilt threads in
couched work and wool and
silk in tent stitch.* MUSÉE DE
VERSAILLES.

LEFT: Plate 33
Wall panel, *France, early
eighteenth century. Canvas
embroidered in wool, silk and
chenille threads, in tent,
satin and Hungarian stitch
and laid and couched work
with couched silver-gilt
threads.* VICTORIA AND
ALBERT MUSEUM, LONDON.

ABOVE: Plate 34
Chasuble *(detail), France,
c.1735. Off-white satin
embroidered with gold and
silver threads in couched
work and polychrome silks in
long and short stitch and
stem stitch, 46in × 25in
(117cm × 73cm).* MUSÉE
DES ARTS DÉCORATIFS, PARIS.

ABOVE, RIGHT: Plate 35
Wall hanging, *France,
c.1800. White silk
background embroidered
with polychrome chenille
threads, 10ft (3m).*
ÖSTERREICHISCHES MUSEUM
FÜR ANGEWANDTE KUNST,
VIENNA.

BELOW, RIGHT: Plate 36
Wall hanging, *Bissardon,
Bony and Co., France,
c.1810. White satin
embroidered in silk and gold
threads, 126in × 85in
(320cm × 215cm).* MUSÉE
NATIONAL DE MALMAISON.

LEFT: Plate 37
Bridal and festival costume
from the district of Pont-
Aven, Brittany, first half of
the nineteenth century.
Jacket, bodice and skirt of
black woolen cloth
embroidered with applied
work in colored silks, tinsels,
spangles and glass beads.
The waistband is embroidered
in silver threads and the coif
and collar are a
reconstruction. VICTORIA
AND ALBERT MUSEUM,
LONDON.

ABOVE AND BELOW, LEFT:
Plate 38
Day dress, *detail of a*
sleeve, Myrbor, Paris,
c.1925. Applied work in silk
material. VICTORIA AND
ALBERT MUSEUM, LONDON.

OPPOSITE, LEFT: Plate 41
Embroidered roundel from
an altar superfrontal, *after
a design by Andrea del
Sarto (1486–1530) of St.
Luke with a bull, Italy,
c.1522. Part of a set of
vestments made in Florence
for Cardinal Silvio
Passerini. Diam. 5¾ins
(15·9cm)*. TREASURY OF SAN
FRANCESCO, CORTONA.

BELOW: Plate 40
Altar frontal *worked by
Jacopo Cambi, Florence,
Italy, dated 1336. Split
stitch on a ground of silver-
gilt threads couched over
string, 14½in × 167¾in
(36cm × 318cm). This
important piece is one of two
major Florentine frontals of
this period to survive.* MUSEO
NAZIONALE, FLORENCE.

RIGHT: Plate 39
Evening dresses by Worth
and Callot, *France. Left:
Evening dress by Worth of
aquamarine chiffon
patterned with sequins,
1928–9. Right: Peach satin
tunic and overdress by Callot
with gold thread, paste and
pearl embroidery, c.1930.*
VICTORIA AND ALBERT
MUSEUM, LONDON.

BELOW: Plate 42
Chasuble, *Florence, Italy, third quarter of the sixteenth century. Couched silver-gilt and silver threads in a renaissance design on violet silk with applied painted figures and the arms of Cardinal Alessandro Farnese, 36½in × 92¾in (92cm × 235cm).* MUSEO DI STA. MARIA DEL FIORE, FLORENCE.

ABOVE, RIGHT: Plate 43
Portrait of Elizabeth,
*daughter of James I of
England by Paul van Somer,
1602. Although the child's
cap and apron are Flemish
work, the lacis bands show
how widespread the use of
Italian patterns was at this
period.* TEMPLE NEWSAM
HOUSE, LEEDS.

BELOW, RIGHT: Plate 44
Embroidered cover, *Italy,
first half of the seventeenth
century. Appliqué in silk
and velvet on dull blue satin,
embroidered with metal
thread and colored silks and
sequins. Grotesque pattern
with strapwork, 21in × 43in
(53·5cm × 109cm).* VICTORIA
AND ALBERT MUSEUM,
LONDON.

ABOVE: Plate 48
Part of a wall hanging,
*Italy, second quarter of the
eighteenth century. Satin
embroidered with long and
short, satin and stem stitches
and laid and couched work,
length 45¾in (115cm). The
pattern which is an
adaptation of a chinoiserie
design, has much in common
with the printed cottons of
the period.* VICTORIA AND
ALBERT MUSEUM, LONDON.

ABOVE, RIGHT: Plate 49
Calabrian girl in peasant
dress, *from E. Pingret,
Costumes Italiens, 1842–8.
Embroidered picture of a
girl from the south of Italy,
mid-nineteenth century.
Canvas embroidered in tent
stitch in wool and silk,
9½in × 8in (24cm × 20·5cm).*
VICTORIA AND ALBERT
MUSEUM, LONDON.

RIGHT: Plate 50
Embroidered picture of a
girl from the south of Italy,
*mid-nineteenth century.
Canvas embroidered in tent
stitch in wool and silk, 9½in
× 8in (24cm × 20·5cm).*
VICTORIA AND ALBERT
MUSEUM, LONDON.

FAR LEFT: Plate 51
Chasuble, *the maker's label
C. Romanini, Roma, Italy,
late nineteenth century. Red
silk embroidered in gold
threads, length 44in
(122cm). Gold embroidery
was a speciality of Roman
workshops during the
eighteenth and nineteenth
centuries.* THE FATHERS OF
THE LONDON ORATORY.

LEFT: Plate 52
Chasuble, *Venice, nineteenth
century. White satin
embroidered in colored silks
and gold-thread. The
refinement of the flower
sprays is typical of church
embroidery design in the
mid-nineteenth century.* STA.
MARIA DELLA SALUTE,
VENICE.

BELOW, LEFT: Plate 53
Valance *(detail), Sicily,
late eighteenth or early
nineteenth century.
Embroidered in linen thread
in cross and long-armed
cross stitch; tablet woven
braid with fringe. Height of
border including fringe,
16½in (42cm). The design is
a simplification of Sicilian
medieval silk patterns where
the animals traditionally
faced each other in pairs.*
VICTORIA AND ALBERT
MUSEUM, LONDON.

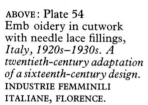

ABOVE: Plate 54
Emb oidery in cutwork
with needle lace fillings,
*Italy, 1920s–1930s. A
twentieth-century adaptation
of a sixteenth-century design.*
INDUSTRIE FEMMINILI
ITALIANE, FLORENCE.

ABOVE AND BELOW: Plate 55
Chasuble, *(front and back)
Venice, between 1929–49.
Green silk with gold
embroidered orphreys.* STA.
MARIA DELLA SALUTE,
VENICE.

MIDDLE:
Chasuble *(detail of front),
Venice, between 1929–49,
7in × 7in (18cm × 18cm).*
STA. MARIA DELLA SALUTE,
VENICE.

FAR LEFT: Plate 56
Dress coat *(detail)*,
*Catalonia, Spain, late
eighteenth century. Brown
velvet embroidered with silk.
This detail of the coat
pocket is embroidered with
multicolored flowers.*
APPAREL MUSEUM-
ROCAMORA COLLECTION,
BARCELONA.

LEFT: Plate 57
Apron, *Salamanca, Spain,
eighteenth century.
Embroidered in gold thread
with gold spangles and
colored sequins and with a
cut-out border edged in blue
silk ribbon and a brocade
frill worked in satin stitch.
Still worn today for festival
days and holidays.*
COLLECTION DOÑA CARMEN
CORTON DE COSSIO.

ABOVE: Plate 58
Towel, *Castile, Spain, late
sixteenth century. Linen
with silk embroidery and
fringe, without fringe, 53in
× 32in (134cm × 81cm) ;
with fringe, 55in × 34in
(140cm × 80cm). Mudéjar
embroidery, as illustrated by
this towel, was worked by
Christians using Hispano-
Moresque embroidery
techniques.* TEXTILE
MUSEUM, BARCELONA.

BELOW: Plate 60
Sampler, *probably from the
province of Toledo, Spain,
dated 1815. The traditional
patterns on this sampler
which was probably made in
Talavera de la Reina where
there was a well-known silk
factory also show an
Oriental influence in the
stylized carnations
embroidered in satin stitch.*
COLLECTION DOÑA NATALIA
COSSIO DE JIMINEZ.

RIGHT: Plate 59
Brocade *(detail), Valencia,
Spain, eighteenth century.
Valencia was famous for her
silks, brocades and damasks.
This brocade which was
probably designed for a
woman's dress, follows the
contemporary Venetian style.*
COLLECTION DOÑA CARMEN
CORTON DE COSSIO.

LEFT: Plate 61
Wedding dress, *designed by Maria Molist, Mataró, Barcelona, 1920. Ivory gauze embroidered with white pearls and paillettes, the embroidery on this dress is typical of that used in twentieth-century fashion design.* APPAREL MUSEUM-ROCAMORA COLLECTION, BARCELONA.

BELOW, LEFT: Plate 62
Empire dress *(detail)*, *Catalonia, Spain, early nineteenth century. Mulberry gauze embroidered with polychrome silks and spangles, this detail of the train is decorated with small flowers and the border with posies.* APPAREL MUSEUM-ROCAMORA COLLECTION, BARCELONA.

TOP, LEFT: Plate 63
Coverlet, *Castelo Branco,
Portugal, eighteenth century.
Embroidered on three strips
of homemade linen in silk
with laidwork, herringbone
and stem stitch, 79in × 91in
(2m × 2·30m)*. MUSEU
NACIONAL DE ARTE ANTIGA
LISBON.

TOP, RIGHT: Plate 64
Rug, *Alentejo, Portugal,
eighteenth century. Pack
cloth embroidered with wool
in plait stitch over counted
threads, 55in × 69in
(1·40m × 1·75m).
Arraiolos is the name given
to these embroidered rugs
made in the town of the*

*same name in the Alentejo
province of Portugal.* MUSEU
NACIONAL DE ARTE ANTIGA,
LISBON.

BOTTOM: Plate 65
Patchwork, *Portugal,
twentieth century.*

Altar frontal, *panel showing the Crucifixion, Florence, Italy, 1380s. Silk split stitch and gold threads (no longer extant) laid over a padding of string, $11\frac{1}{4}in \times 16\frac{1}{2}in$ (28·5cm × 42cm).* MUSEUM OF FINE ARTS, BOSTON.

Spain. It is signed "*Geri Lapi rachamatore me fecit in Florentia*" and must be of approximately the same date as the Jacopo Cambi work. Large and costly pieces of this kind were obviously a regular product of the Florentine workrooms. A frontal which was ordered by the Duke of Berry and given to Chartres Cathedral later in the century must, from its description in the inventories, have closely resembled the Jacopo Cambi work. It was unfortunately destroyed in the eighteenth century. Yet another was ordered by Charles VI of France but never paid for. It had to be sent to Paris in an attempt to find a buyer.

Although only these two major pieces survive, enough smaller works exist – orphreys from copes and chasubles and panels which must have been part of frontals or their superfrontals – to give some idea of the development of embroidery in Florence during the fourteenth and early fifteenth centuries. From the inventories of such great nobles as the Duke of Berry and the Dukes of Burgundy we learn not only that Florence was an important center

for the production of embroidery but that large quantities of this work were exported to France and elsewhere. We know the names of at least two merchants trading in Avignon in the late fourteenth century, when the town was an independent republic; Francesco di Marco Datini, of Prato near Florence, and Michel de Passe, who took orders from the Duke of Burgundy for vestments. Both imported vestments from Florence among many other commodities. Church embroideries were also sold by itinerant traders at the great fairs, and the inventory of the Duke of Berry makes it clear that large embroideries were worked in sections and transported and sold in this way.

All these embroideries were worked in colored-silk split stitch with touches of gold, on gold backgrounds, that is to say in the accepted technique for church embroidery of the Gothic period. One distinguishing feature of the Florentine workrooms from the time of Jacopo Cambi onward was the particularly glossy silk used for broad folds of translucent color in the garments. Here were all the glowing colors from rose and

Orphrey (detail), Florence, Italy, late fourteenth century. Worked with polychrome silk threads in split stitch and laid gold threads, each scene 9in × 6½in (23cm × 16cm). This chasuble orphrey is embroidered with scenes from the Life of the Virgin: the detail illustrated here shows the Meeting at the Golden Gate. VICTORIA AND ALBERT MUSEUM, LONDON.

salmon pinks, through the intense blue of lapis lazuli to the brilliant limes and lemons which make up the palette of the Florentine painters of the Renaissance. Just as the range of color was influenced by the artists, so was the treatment of the embroidered gold backgrounds, which sought to reproduce the gilded gesso of the panel paintings. Where other embroiderers used patterns in the couching stitches to vary their backgrounds, the Florentines achieved their raised designs by first couching a thick string on the linen ground in the required scrolling patterns, and then laying and couching their gold on this foundation. This technique can be clearly seen in the panel illustrated which has now lost the gold threads and shows only the string underlay.

Against this richly patterned gold the small scenes of Jacopo Cambi's superfrontal stand out with jewel-like clarity. They were probably the work of a

follower of Bernardo Daddi (c.1290–1349/51), and the figures fall into the calm statuesque postures of this master's painting.

Another set of small panels, which must have come from a frontal but now exists as separate items, also has scenes posed against the same fine gold work, but it was probably made about fifty years later than the Cambi frontal. Here the figures have been brought to life in response to the ever-increasing desire among artists for naturalism and reality as opposed to idealism in their subjects. This movement, which was the essence of the Italian Renaissance, found a particularly fertile ground among both artists and patrons in the practical and commercial atmosphere of Florence, and was naturally transmitted to embroidery by the painters who supplied the cartoons. The graceful lines of the Gothic tradition may express the anguish of the Crucifixion no less poignantly, but here, the figures at the foot of the Cross (p. 129), have a more telling realism and evoke a more human response. Similarly the Flagellation of Christ from the same set, now in the Metropolitan Museum, New York, which is a remarkably forceful and balanced composition, brings home to us every blow of the lash. These small embroideries from the second half of the fourteenth century reflect clearly the influence of Giotto (c.1266–1337) on Florentine art of the period and were the work of his later followers, in the case of this particular set probably Spinello Aretino.

Although the fashion for gilded backgrounds persisted in panel painting until late in the century, painters had experimented much earlier with arcaded canopies or street scenes as settings for their figures. This does not, as far as we know, occur in embroidery until late in the fourteenth and the earlier part of the fifteenth centuries. Artists had already understood and successfully reproduced something of the illusion of perspective, but the first attempts of the embroiderers in this respect were not wholly successful. Since they were accustomed to work their gold as a flat, ornamented surface, it seems that they did not at first appreciate the effect of light falling at different angles on gold threads laid directionally to follow architectural lines. So it comes about that an embroidered scene preserves its perspective perfectly when seen from one angle, but becomes fragmented and difficult to "read" when the light falls differently. In some instances it seems that the difficulty has been perceived and steps taken to overcome it, such as the shading of the vault of an arch in split stitch, or the covering of a wall in laid and couched silks.

These problems of perspective apply particularly to a number of cope orphreys with scenes from the Life of the Virgin dating from the late fourteenth and first half of the fifteenth centuries. From these also we can learn something of the methods by which the industry worked. Several different orphreys have been worked from the same cartoons. We know from the treatise on artistic techniques written by Cennino Cennini in 1437 and published in 1821 that it was the artist rather than the embroiderer who drew out the design on the linen ground. Cennini gives precise instructions for artists who are called on to do this work for embroiderers, and goes on also to describe what must be done for embroidery that is to be worked on velvet. Owing to the repetition of certain scenes it is a safe assumption that a master's workshop kept iconographical pattern books of such popular subjects as the Life of the Virgin, which could be referred to by the artist who did the work. It can even be seen in these orphreys that the drawing was brought up to date by the introduction of costume and other details. An example of this can be seen in a cope at Sta. Margherita a Montici, Florence.

By the second half of the fifteenth century a new technique in gold embroidery, which probably originated among Flemish workrooms executing commissions for the Dukes of Burgundy, enabled embroiderers to reproduce faithfully every detail of an artist's cartoon. This was *or nué*, or shaded gold, in which gold threads laid horizontally were literally shaded in color by the irregular spacing of colored silk couching stitches. This extremely sophisticated technique resulted in subtle gradations of color shot through with as much or as little gold surface as the embroiderer cared to show, and because the gold lay in one direction only, all possibility of distortion of the angles by reflected light was removed. At the same time the piercingly brilliant silks of the previous century gave way to more conventional colors which were each

shaded through a much wider range of tone.

The outstanding example among many in Italy in the use of this technique is a number of small panels made for the decoration of a set of vestments to the designs of Antonio del Pollaiuolo (1431–98). Twenty-seven pieces survive in all, unfortunately in a poor state of repair. Since the experiments of Masaccio (1401–*c*.1428) with the mathematical principles of perspective in the early years of the century, Florentine painters had mastered the question of depth and turned their

Panel, *one of a set, Florence, Italy, second half of the fifteenth century. Or nué and split stitch, 11¾in × 8¾in (30cm × 22cm). Together with the illustration on page 132 this embroidered panel showing St. John preaching in the wilderness was made for a set of vestments for the baptistery of the Cathedral, Florence, after designs by Antonio del Pollaiuolo (1431/2–98).* MUSEO DI STA. MARIA DEL FIORE, FLORENCE.

Panel, *Florence, Italy, second half of the fifteenth century. Or nué and split stitch, 11¾in × 8¾in (30cm × 22cm). The subject illustrated is Salome presenting the Head of St. John to Herodias.* MUSEO DI STA. MARIA DEL FIORE, FLORENCE.

attention more and more to movement, and this trend is reflected in Pollaiuolo's embroideries. Made for the Baptistery of the Cathedral in Florence, they tell in great detail the story of the Life of St. John the Baptist. The set was ordered by the Merchants' Guild of Florence in 1466 and only finally paid for in 1487, although it may have been completed well before that. The city archives provide a complete record of the payments made and the names of the embroiderers. The chief of these is named as Paolo da Verona, but it is interesting that the team of eleven included two Flemish workers, one of whom, Coppino di Giovanni di Bramante of Malines, is shown to have been the highest paid of all, presumably because he introduced the Flemish technique. Pollaiuolo, who had trained as a goldsmith in his youth, had already worked on the silver altar of the Bap-

tistery, and we may suppose that his interest was awakened by the possibilities of this new method of combining color and gold, which at the same time could be used almost with the freedom of colored pigments to mold highlight and shadow, and produce what Bernard Berenson has called "tactile values."

Many of the small scenes can be directly related to Pollaiuolo's work as a painter. For example the grouping of the figures in St. John Preaching in the Wilderness can be compared to his large altar painting of 1475 of the Martyrdom of St. Sebastian, which must date from about the same time, or perhaps a little later, than the cartoon for the embroidery. The whirlwind movement of Salome's presentation of St. John's head to Herodias is an echo of the same headlong flight in a small, early painting of Apollo and Daphne.

The delightful rural backgrounds which were such a feature of Sienese painting were only gradually adopted by Florentine artists. In the embroideries most of the outdoor scenes have been furnished with no more than a stark setting of jagged rocks and small plants which had been a convention of Florentine painting in the previous century. Only in three panels has some effort been made to create the distant Tuscan valley which can be seen in the Martyrdom of St. Sebastian. They are perhaps the only embroideries of the period in which this has been attempted.

Pollaiuolo's versatility also extended to the designing of silks. He collaborated with the weaver Francesco Mallochi who made the lost silk for the Baptistery vestments. Their work together probably also produced a frontal at Assisi with woven figures of St. Francis and Pope Sixtus IV, and two throne hangings made for Matthias Corvinus, King of Hungary. The remarkable embroidered faces of the figures on the Assisi frontal may have been the work of the same team of embroiderers who made the Baptistery vestments.

Another great artist who supplied cartoons for embroidery, probably mostly in his youth, was Sandro Botticelli (1440–1510). He is credited with a number of orphreys for copes and chasubles with saints framed by arcades and some small scenes for dalmatics. The saints are drawn as patriarchal figures in the naturalistic manner of the High Renaissance, with the swirling folds of their classical dress rendered in *or nué*. The gold and silver arches were evidently added by the embroiderers as a framework for Botticelli's figures, and here we see the working of a fragmentation of labor in a method of production which was becoming increasingly attuned to work on a commercial scale. Although masters like Pollaiuolo, Botticelli and Andrea del Sarto (1486–1530) designed for special commissions, which might be carried out by leading teams of embroiderers, smaller workrooms used and re-used cartoons, as we have seen was the practice a hundred years earlier. Cartoons of popular subjects may in fact have been made for general purposes, being used equally by weavers, embroiderers or engravers.

Embroiderers used scenes by different artists to make up sets of vestments, and even figures from different cartoons to make up composite scenes. Small workshops and convents were employed to produce parts of the whole, such as the arcades.

A piece which is more obviously in Botticelli's mature style is the hood of a cope in the Poldi-Pezzoli Museum in Milan, which shows the Virgin kneeling before the Savior for her Coronation, instead of enthroned beside Him in the traditional medieval manner. It is worked in silks and long and short stitch, and thus becomes literally a painting in silk, losing all the purely decorative element in embroidery which is evident in the early padded gold backgrounds and is to some extent preserved in the glitter of the gold in *or nué*.

Another cope hood worked in the same technique is one embroidered with the Transfiguration which is part of an extremely luxurious set of vestments made for Cardinal Silvio Passerini between 1517 and 1526 and presented to the Cathedral of Cortona. They are made of a superb Florentine velvet brocaded with gold and silver, with embroidered panels from designs by Andrea del Sarto and Raffaellino del Garbo (1466–*c*.1527). (The hood was at one time thought to be by Raphael because of a certain likeness to his Transfiguration in the Vatican.)

Two small points will illustrate the changes which came in with the sixteenth century. The superfrontal of the altar and the orphreys, far from consisting of a whole series of scenes, are merely decorated with small *tondi* or roundels framing half-length portraits

of the Virgin and Child with the Evangelists and saints, worked in *or nué* (Plate 40). The frontal itself relies on the splendor of the brocade but has a large representation of the arms of Passerini embroidered in the center. Not only has the figure embroidery been greatly reduced, but the sketches for the superfrontal by Andrea del Sarto have been identified, and two of them have been pricked for transfer. In this frontal therefore we can see the beginning of the death of the artist/embroiderer relationship, which ended eventually in the virtual extinction of the embroidered story on vestments. The relative sparseness of the decoration (although the portraits are perfectly executed and set in orphreys embroidered with gold decoration) suggests that already artists were less willing, and so perhaps charging more, to do such work. The pricking of the design means of course that it was pounced on to the linen, and the use of this traditional embroiderers' method must also mean that it was the embroidery workshop and not, as previously in Italy, the artist's studio which did it.

Further confirmation of this change of technical procedure at this period is found in a drawing by Raffaellino del Garbo of the Appearance of the Risen

St. Luke with a Bull by Andrea del Sarto (1486–1530), Italy. Chalk, ink and wash, diam. 5¾in (15·9cm). This drawing has been pricked for pouncing and is the original design for the embroidery illustrated as Plate 41. GABINETTO NAZIONALE DELLE STAMPE, ROME.

The Triumph of Minerva
(detail) by Francesco del
Cossa, Italy, mid-fifteenth
century. This detail from del
Cossa's fresco shows women
weaving and embroidering.
PALAZZO SCHIFANOIA,
FERRARA.

type are reproduced in the religious paintings of Cima da Conegliano (c.1460–1518) and other Venetian and north Italian painters. At the same period a description of the famous water fêtes in Venice mentions many embroidered banners, but we do not know what they were like.

Siena is also mentioned as a center for embroidery in records of the period, but no work from that city has been identified. Indeed in 1445–6 the artist Sassetta (c.1400–50) was paid for designs for embroidery which were sent from Siena to Florence to be worked.

Although we have only dealt with professional embroiderers who were organized in guilds, as were most craftsmen of their period, individuals must also have done good work. Vasari, the sixteenth-century biographer of so many artists, records that Parri Spinelli designed an orphrey for his sister to work, although it appears that it was never finished. It is also known that various communities of nuns were producing embroidery in Florence, of a higher standard than that of the mass-produced orphreys, in particular the Convent of the Murate in the Via Ghibellina. These ladies were responsible for a charming altar frontal covered with flying doves made for the cathedral of San Gimignano in 1449, and they apparently also undertook secular commissions. Their work was praised both by the Bishop of Florence and by Savonarola, but by the end of the century the use of rich embroidery in the Church was singled out by this great reforming preacher in a tirade against ecclesiastical luxury.

Christ to the Apostles, which has also been pricked, although the embroidery itself does not appear to have survived. These slight indications from the world of embroidery point to the changing status of the artist from craftsman to the social equal of a gentleman, which the outstanding genius of Michelangelo did so much to promote.

This survey of the church embroideries of the fourteenth and fifteenth centuries has been devoted almost entirely to the professional workrooms of Florence, but it seems that this was in fact by far the most important center in Italy, so that at this period Italian embroidery can only be studied by reference to Florentine embroidery. Venice must also have had many workrooms, but we know very little of their products after the time of the Paolo Veneziano frontal until the end of the fifteenth and beginning of the sixteenth centuries. A group of orphreys has been identified which has saints under arcades with cupolas above which are thought to have been inspired by the domes of St. Mark's. Orphreys of this

Domestic Embroidery in the Sixteenth Century

The fifteenth century had been devoted to embroidery as painting: the sixteenth was to be the era of decorative design. The profound changes in outlook which had been nurtured in the cities of northern Italy for two hundred years reached their climax during the sixteenth century. It was during this period that Italian fashions – in letters, the arts, music, poetry, and perhaps not least in ornament – had their greatest influence among the cultured classes of Europe as a whole.

The search by artists during the fifteenth century for anatomical realism had led them to an ever-deeper study of classical naturalism in art, while at the same time admiration of all things antique aroused an intense interest in every aspect of Roman life. When therefore the excavation toward the end of the fifteenth century of a number of Roman private houses, including Nero's Golden House in Rome, revealed a scheme of decoration totally different from the classical exterior ornament which was all that had hitherto been known, enthusiasm for this newly discovered style was universal. Taken up by renaissance artists everywhere and adapted by them to a more forceful mode of expression in keeping with the spirit of their period, it lasted throughout Europe until well into the seventeenth century. It was revived yet again in a more accurate form, closer to the antique originals, at the end of the eighteenth century. In Italy at least, shadows of this later classical revival affected decorative design throughout the nineteenth century.

Since the excavated houses of ancient Rome, by now buried under the detritus of years, emerged as caves, they became known as grottoes and their wall paintings were described as *grotteschi*, or grotesques. Essentially the style consisted of a light, cool balanced scheme of cartouches set in an airy framework of linear and floral decoration, which was whimsically or even ludicrously interspersed with imaginary beasts, masks and human or anthropoid figures. One of its greatest exponents was Raphael, whose decorations for a loggia in the Vatican inspired many later artists.

At about the same period Islamic decoration, which reached Europe through the trading contacts of Venice and Genoa, was also taken up by renaissance designers. The austere, intricately scrolling stems with their small formal leaf bracts were combined in Italy with Roman acanthus decoration and the graceful curiosities of the *grotteschi*.

This great wave of pattern-making received a still stronger impetus from the appearance early in the sixteenth century of printed pattern books. Those that concern us appear to have been intended mainly for women for use in the home, as their names show, for example *Convivio delle belle donne*, and *Ornamento de le belle et virtudiose doné*. They were probably used mainly for embroidery but they were equally suitable for the weaving of small bands. The patterns they reproduce were part of a much wider application of the same

E auertiffe con el difegno infiemē ti appoſtiamo vn poſilo belliſſi-
mo e vago a locchio coſa non mancho da tenerſe cara che eſſo di
ſegno: laqual coſa da noi ſono ſtata con grandiſſima fatica com-
poſta e ordinata a tua vtilita e pochiſſima ſpeſa.   Uale

ornament. The earliest of the surviving embroidery books was printed in Germany in 1524, to be closely followed by a Venetian example.

Many of these designs were shown on a squared ground, so that they could be used for darning on net or for embroidery on the counted threads of the ground material. Indeed the compiler of one Italian book announced that he would only use counted patterns since women were too lazy to transfer their designs to the material and preferred to count them straight from the book. That this was not always so is shown by the fact that so many pages have been lost from the surviving books precisely because they were torn out for pricking and pouncing. One of the few Italian books which was not published

Woodcut *from the* Libro de Rechami *by Paganino published in Toscolano, Italy, c.1532. This woodcut shows the method of pricking and pouncing a design for embroidery.*

Designs *from* Gli Universali
di tutti e bei dissegni,
raccami e moderno lavori
*by Zoppino, Venice, Italy,
1532. Two pages taken from
a book of embroidery
patterns, the patterns shown
being two renaissance
grotesque designs, a band of
strapwork and one with an
adaptation of an arabesque.*

in Venice, Paganino's *Libro de Rechami,*
published in Toscolano in 1532, illustrates the pouncing method by stages
in a woodcut. Paganino also issued for
use with his pattern books a book of
empty squared pages, simply called
Burato (net), for the worker to draw in
her own designs.

These pattern books brought together the various strands of fashionable
ornament and in effect created for the
embroideress a language of design
which was widely used all over Europe
in the sixteenth century, and continued
to be used in Italy long after that.
The fact that the books were printed in
Venice by no means meant that they
were produced specifically for Venetian
women. The various forms of pattern
which they popularized consisted
of renaissance grotesques, strapwork
patterns deriving from grotesque
ornament (which was another innovation attributed to Raphael), classical
acanthus, scrolling or wave patterns

which were sometimes in the form of
the pure arabesque but were more
often combined with another style,
animal patterns taken from earlier
Middle Eastern design inherited
through Sicily, and flower patterns,
sometimes in a naturalistic scrolling
form but frequently rigidly stylized to
suit the popular counted-thread techniques. There were also some purely
geometric ground-covering patterns. A
characteristic feature of the embroideries themselves, which was not seen in
the pattern books, were borders edged
with a row of small detached slanting
leaves or sprigs.

In addition to the purely ornamental, the language of symbolism,
from the double meaning of an emblem
to a personal sign or *impresa*, which so
fascinated people's minds in the late
sixteenth century but is barely understood today, was frequently employed
in embroidery, together with armorial
bearings and initial letters.

By far the greater part of the embroidery which resulted from all this
activity was made for household purposes. Table and bed linen had been a
source of pride for housewives well
before this date. We know from the
letters of that same Francesco di Marco
Datini, whom we found trading in
Avignon, that his home in Prato, to
which he had returned by 1382, was
provided with plentiful stocks of household linen. Sheets and pillowcases were
embroidered in drawn threadwork and
cross stitch, while others were decorated
with stripes of cotton, which were
probably woven. Headcloths were made
in the same way.

It must not be forgotten that the
Italians were first and foremost weavers.
Towels and tablecloths of cotton,
which were usually woven in blue and
white, were probably first made in
Tuscany, but by the middle of the
fifteenth century were a speciality of
Umbria, particularly associated with
Perugia. Their patterns were frequently
of the confronted animal type which had
perhaps been inherited from the silk
weaving traditions of Lucca. The fountain which so often figures in the
patterns between the paired animals or
birds is said to be the city fountain of
Perugia. A tablecloth with bands of
this kind is reproduced in the fresco of
the Last Supper by Domenico
Ghirlandaio (1449–94) painted in the
church of the Ognissanti in Florence at

the end of the fifteenth century.

In general embroidery is not shown in paintings of domestic scenes, although we can observe the fineness of the table linen. The relief by Donatello (1386–1466) of Herod's Feast, made for the font of S. Giovanni in Siena in 1427, shows a man-at-arms presenting his horrible offering, kneeling before Herod with a wonderfully fine napkin over his arm, as any servant might offer a dish. Another napkin lies on the table, and it seems that both were embroidered round the edge. From the time of the pattern books, however, plenty of examples exist to show how the patterns were used in practice.

In the first place there were the heavy furnishing embroideries made by professional workers. They were used for wall hangings, bed valances and coverlets, covers for chests and tables, horse trappings, and so on, and usually worked on velvet or satin in thick gold threads heavily padded, or in appliqué outlined with braids, with or without silk embroidery. Their patterns often followed the furnishing silks and velvets which were used for the same purposes, that is to say in scrolling designs with acanthus leaves and other large, and largely imaginary, flowers and foliage. Bold strapwork patterns were executed in appliqué, which lent itself particularly to designs of this type.

In this connection Venetian embroiderers are mentioned again. The famous Genoese admiral, Andrea Doria, had workers brought from Venice and also from Milan to carry out embroideries for his new palace near Genoa. The work was done between 1545 and 1565 to designs by Perin del Vaga (1501–47). The leading embroiderer was one Nicolo Veneziano who was described by Vasari as a "rare and unique master of embroidery." At this period a French abbot visiting Italy also maintained that the embroiderers working at the court of the Sforza's at Milan were more skillful than any of their contemporaries.

The lighter household embroideries were probably carried out at home, although many fine examples, particularly those with gold thread, must have been professional or convent work. Numerous techniques were used to work patterns from the range already outlined. Cross stitch was especially popular. It was used in some cases to create the pattern, and in others to fill

in the ground so that the pattern was left in reserve on the white linen.

Many of the more sophisticated renaissance designs were carried out in this way, and both ground linen and stitchery are usually very fine. Various types of cross stitch were used to fill the grounds, such as long armed, and Italian which covered the surface on both sides of the material. Another method of covering the back as well as the right side was to run parallel threads through the straight stitches which are the normal "wrong side" of ordinary cross stitches. Lines of fine double darning were also used, and simple drawn work with the remaining threads of the ground whipped in both directions to make a strong squared net. The patterns themselves were often worked in double running or holbein stitch (*punto scritto*), which was either intended as a preliminary outlining when pattern or background was to be filled, or sometimes left in its own right. Satin stitch was also used, often for delicate strapwork borders. By far the most usual color for these embroideries was red, but they are also found in blue and green and various attractive shades of golden yellow.

Another technique which was particularly favored in Italy was *lacis*, or darning on net in soft thick threads to produce solid patterns. In other words

BELOW:
Band, *Italy, late sixteenth/ early seventeenth century. Linen ground embroidered in yellow and blue silk threads with foliage and grotesques in tent and back stitch, 8¾in × 8½in (22cm × 21cm).* COOPER HEWITT MUSEUM, NEW YORK. GIFT OF RICHARD CRANCH GREENLEAF.

BELOW MIDDLE:
Band, *Italy, late sixteenth/ early seventeenth century. Linen ground embroidered with green silk thread in long-armed cross and back stitch with bobbin lace edge, 8½in × 29in (20cm × 74cm). This band illustrates the the story of The Garden of Eden.* COOPER HEWITT MUSEUM, NEW YORK. GIFT OF RICHARD CRANCH GREENLEAF.

BOTTOM:
Band, *Italy, late sixteenth/ early seventeenth century. Linen ground embroidered in red silk thread with a pattern of tree trunks in tent and back stitch, 8½in × 33in (21cm × 84cm).* COOPER HEWITT MUSEUM, NEW YORK. GIFT OF RICHARD CRANCH GREENLEAF.

Underdress *(detail), Italy, seventeenth century. Linen embroidered in polychrome silk and metal thread and trimmed with bobbin lace, length 41in (104cm).* VICTORIA AND ALBERT MUSEUM, LONDON.

the patterns in the books which were shown on squared paper were reproduced exactly. Many patterns in the earlier books were intended for this technique, but after about 1560 cutwork became more and more popular and pattern books with new designs were almost entirely devoted to this type of work. At first these were scrolling patterns worked by the *punto in aria* method, that is, embroidery made on threads laid by the worker over a linen ground, which is later cut away so that the embroidered threads are literally left "in the air." By the end of the century an equally popular technique was cutwork, or *reticella*, in which squares were cut out of the ground linen and filled in by over-embroidered threads. *Reticella* tends to lead to geometric designs with lacy insets, whereas *punto in aria* usually gives freer patterns.

Both these types of work can still be regarded as embroidery, but as the techniques were elaborated further they led to the creation of needlemade lace in which no linen ground was used. A flourishing lace industry existed in Venice from the second half of the sixteenth century which was in fact the beginning of lace making in Italy.

All these patterns and stitches were practiced or recorded on samplers. Earlier examples were haphazard in their arrangement, in other words they were simply pieces of material on which experiments were made. During the seventeenth century patterns were more often aligned in orderly rows, and this method, as well as many of the Italian stitches, was copied in various parts of Europe.

No mention has been made so far of embroidery on dress, of which there is in fact less evidence in Italy than in the northern countries of Europe. This was obviously another result of Italy's position as the leading producer of high fashion woven silks. The aristocratic classes, that is to say the classes which commissioned portraits, were those most likely to wear these magnificent materials. At the same time, in view of the popularity of embroidered table linen among the bourgeois classes, it seems likely that they also wore embroidered shifts and shirts, but there are relatively few indications that this was so. Toward the end of the fifteenth century, embroidered underdresses appear in paintings by Botticelli, for example, in his frescoes of the Life of

Moses in the Vatican, and Cima da Conegliano, who obviously appreciated embroidery, gives his paintings of the Virgin pretty white headscarves with embroidered borders, which frame the face under the traditional blue veil. In these instances both painters would have been thinking of their subjects as coming from the well-to-do middle class.

Full-gathered women's underdresses with fine black embroidery seem to have originated in Germany at the end of the fifteenth century, and by the first half of the sixteenth, embroidery at neck and wrists was high fashion everywhere for both men and women, as portraits by Dürer (1471–1528) and Holbein (1497/8–1543) show. Examples from Italy are less common, but the portrait of a woman by Paolo Cavazzola (1486–1522) of *c*.1515 shows her underdress embroidered in red *punto scritto* at the neck. In general portraits in Italy are less helpful because the low décolleté which was fashionable there meant that the shift could hardly be seen at the neckline, whereas embroidery on the high-necked underdresses of more northern countries shows above the gown. Here again it is likely that more embroidery was worn by ladies who were well-to-do but of less than aristocratic status. For example the portrait by Parmigianino (1503–40) of the courtesan Antea, painted in Rome in the 1520s, shows her embroidered cuffs and delicate apron (Plate 47). Closely studied, the bands on the apron consist of a light pattern of strapwork which was probably worked in satin stitch.

Men can occasionally be seen to wear narrow collars and cuffs embroidered in black, or black and gold, with the typical scrolling designs of the pattern books, but the Italian gentleman of the sixteenth century appears to have preferred plain dark clothes, leaving elaborately embroidered shirts to his northern neighbors. He did however wear the fashionable gloves with embroidered gauntlets of the late sixteenth and early seventeenth centuries, although these were not particularly elaborate, and at the same period he could be seen in doublet and hose of satin or velvet embroidered all over in small patterns of gold thread.

The Seventeenth Century and Later

The first half of the seventeenth century may be regarded virtually as a continu-ation of the sixteenth. It was only in the second half of this century that changes took place which profoundly affected the course of embroidery design. Many of the domestic styles which we have considered were continued through the seventeenth century and even beyond, but the tendency was for the more sophisticated renaissance designs to die out and, as time went on, for the less elaborate patterns to survive at lower levels in the social scale where they became the basis of the traditional peasant embroideries and laces. Designs gradually became more colorful and less formal, embracing richer and more naturalistic flower patterns. This tendency can be seen especially in *lacis*, and in professional embroideries in colored silks, such as the christening set of the baby Duke of Urbino, whose portrait was painted by Barroccio in 1605.

Appliqué continued to be used for heavy professional work, and the type known as "incised" was popular. By this method two colors are reversed in complementary panels, leading to a

Portrait of a Woman *by Paolo Cavazzola (1486–1522), Italy, c.1515. The woman is wearing a blouse embroidered in red* punto scritto *(holbein stitch).* GALLERIA DELL' ACCADEMIA CARRARA, BERGAMO.

Portrait of Federico, Prince
of Urbino *by Federico
Barocci, Italy, 1605.*
PALAZZO PITTI, FLORENCE.

great saving in expensive material. A
still richer version, where the cut-out
flower shapes are embellished with
inner detail shaded in colored split
stitch and couched work, appears to
have been a speciality of Roman workshops.

Although little costume embroidery
now exists from the sixteenth century,
underdresses survive from the early
seventeenth. They can be embroidered
in white or with sprigs in colored silks
and metal thread. Portraits of ladies
from Padua from the early seventeenth
century show shifts of this type, with
their full flowered sleeves showing
under the open cape-like sleeves of their
brocade dresses. The small embroidered
sprays, slanted alternately to left and
right, echo the fashionable silk designs
of the period.

Italian examples of the type of
embroidery often called in English
"Florentine" are found during this
period, when the stitch was internationally popular. They are for the
most part worked in wool in shades of
dark blue and green, reminiscent of the
contemporary "*verdure*" tapestries, and
were used for hangings and furnishings.
By the eighteenth century the stitch was
used in Italy and elsewhere in brighter
colors and more often worked in silk.
The Italian names for it are *punto a*

fiamma (flame stitch) and *punt' unghero*
(Hungarian stitch).

Throughout the seventeenth century
and later embroideries in a pictorial
style were made, both large and small,
religious and secular. Large examples
were obviously professional work, made
in emulation of woven tapestry. A number of these pieces now in the royal
collections in England are surrounded
by elaborate renaissance borders in the
manner of those employed by the
tapestry weavers, and are of comparable
size to tapestries. The subjects are taken
from religious paintings by Tintoretto
(1518–94) and others.

Smaller pictures are more likely to
have been the work of individuals. The
name of one Caterina Cantona of Milan
has come down to us. She was evidently
known as an embroideress about the
year 1580 but none of her work has
been identified. From the seventeenth
century a Ludovica Pellegrini (or
Liduina Peregrina) is said to have
embroidered portraits of saints for
Milan Cathedral, although it is possible
that she has been confused with Anto-
nina Peregrina, who worked pictures
of the Adoration of the Shepherds and
other religious subjects. A small picture
of this kind, by an unknown embroideress, was made for (or perhaps by) a
member of the Farnese family early in

the seventeenth century (Plate 46). The subject, St. Francis in Ecstasy, after a painting by Paolo Piazza (1557?–1621), is typical of the Counter-Reformation, when a revived cult of St. Francis devised a new iconography of this saint, emphasizing the mystical aspects of his story. The charming flowers in the border are in the style of herbals of the period and were probably intended to have some symbolic significance.

The second half of the century, however, saw the eclipse of the long Italian supremacy in the world of culture and fashion by the golden aura of the Sun King. The panache of the French court in the time of Louis XIV drew the emulation of fashionable Europe, while at the same time the commercial vigor of his minister Colbert ensured the rapid expansion of the French luxury industries, not least among them the silk weaving at Lyons. From the end of the 1660s French silk designers and weavers took the initiative in the production of dress silks, and their patterns were copied throughout the eighteenth century by newly established looms all over Europe. Italy was no exception, and while she continued to weave her magnificent furnishing silks and velvets in the formal patterns of the Renaissance (which are still produced and widely copied today), Italian dress silks became fashionably French in design.

Embroidery took second place and seems to have been used as a substitute for the more difficult skills of silk and tapestry weaving, following the changing styles of international decoration as they were reflected in these arts. We find, for example, a set of wall hangings, which may have been made in Naples, illustrating scenes taken from Tasso's epic poem on the First Crusade, *Gerusalemme Liberata*. They date to the last years of the seventeenth century. The perceptible influence of Chinese painting in the interpretation reflects the fashionable preoccupation with the arts of the Far East. Other embroideries were more obviously influenced by chinoiserie fantasies in silk weaving or cotton printing (Plate 48).

By the eighteenth century embroiderers were again following tapestry weaving in producing cartouches for room settings enclosing pastoral scenes in the manner of Boucher (1703–70) and Watteau (1684–1721). Most floral embroidery for bed furnishings and the upholstery of chairs followed the changing

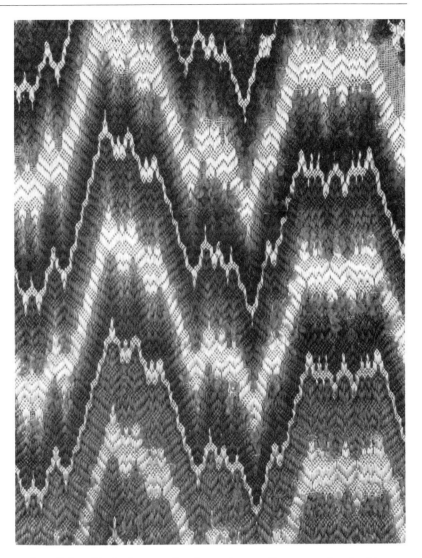

styles of the silk designers. By the end of the century Piedmont was producing a type of furnishing embroidery in floral patterns strongly influenced by French design which were worked in wool on a thick cotton material called *bandèra*.

Inevitably silk played an all-important part in dress fashions, and the large number of small embroidered accessories which were so popular in more northerly countries at this period, stomachers, aprons, bags, firescreens and so on, are very much less in evidence in Italy. Men's coats and waistcoats embroidered with pretty floral borders on the front edges, which were internationally fashionable during the second half of the eighteenth century, were based on French examples, following French changes in cut and decoration, and are only distinguishable by the slightly greater size and exuberance of the flower sprays.

Even on peasant dress little embroidery was worn on the outer garments, as

Fragment of embroidery, *Italy, seventeenth/eighteenth century. Linen canvas embroidered in flame or Florentine stitch with wool and silk in shades of brown, pink, yellow, cream and green.* VICTORIA AND ALBERT MUSEUM, LONDON.

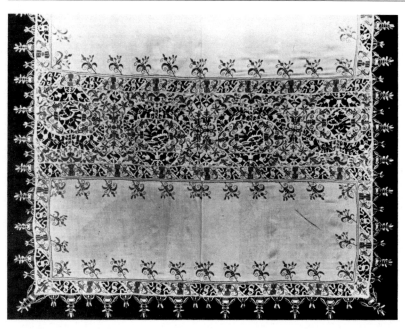

End of a cover or altar cloth, *Italy, seventeenth century. Cutwork with silk and metal thread embroidery trimmed with needle lace, 66in × 36in (168cm × 91cm)*. VICTORIA AND ALBERT MUSEUM, LONDON.

Church Embroidery from the Sixteenth to the Nineteenth Century

We have already seen that the figure embroideries of the fifteenth century were dying out by the beginning of the sixteenth. By the end of this century ornament had taken their place, occasionally surrounding an individual figure which was as likely to be painted as embroidered. The embroidered decoration was normally worked in gold threads, in much the same styles as professional goldwork on household embroideries. In the latter part of the sixteenth century the patterns were often of a rather flamboyant type of arabesque and acanthus.

It has already been mentioned that one reason for the dramatic change from narrative embroidery to the ornamental was the improving social status of the artist and his growing tendency to specialize rather than involve himself in a whole range of the minor arts. Probably the mass production and over-hasty workmanship which began to be noticeable at the end of the fifteenth century contributed to the change, while yet another, and more important, reason was the Church's final abandonment of the medieval concept of religious instruction through illustration. Religious scenes or pictures of saints on vestments from the late-sixteenth century onward were regarded as traditional decoration, rather than literal storytelling.

By the end of the sixteenth and throughout the seventeenth century the production of vestments received a fresh impetus from the thrust of the Counter-Reformation, spearheaded from Rome by the newly founded Society of Jesus. In those northern countries where the Reformation had had its greatest effect, vestments and all the ceremonial and splendors of which they were part had been set aside. The Roman Catholic Church, on the other hand, in mounting its counter-offensive, used exactly the opposite tactic to win people back to the faith.

The interiors of the new churches in the baroque style were dazzling in white and gold, deliberately designed to reject the stern face of reform and appeal to the senses with a lavish display of wealth. Vestments obviously played their part here, and those designed to suit the formal glories of the early baroque were often embroidered

the sketches of Tiepolo (1696–1770) and many others testify, although the dress of the well-to-do countrywoman was rich and colorful. In the important silk-producing districts the rough silk spun from damaged cocoons was used by the peasant women for their own festive clothes. In one or two districts, notably the Abruzzi and Calabria, aprons and other small items were decorated with floral embroidery worked in wool or silk and taken from upper-class eighteenth-century patterns, (Plate 49).

In spite of the predominance of French influence in the sphere of fashion, it must not be forgotten that it was the Italian renaissance revival of classical ornament which provided a seemingly bottomless well from which the inspiration for new ornamental ideas could constantly be drawn. The *rocaille*, or rock and shell creations of Italian garden ornament, which gave its name to the rococo period, were yet another version of the grotto theme, the shell motif in particular lending itself to the gaiety of design in the early eighteenth century. Embroidery in colored silks and gold proved an excellent medium for the reproduction of the shell and strapwork patterns intermingled with flowers which were the latest expression of the grotesque. In the same way the return to international favor of the classical taste at the end of the eighteenth and the beginning of the nineteenth century had the effect of refining and formalizing embroidery design in Italy as elsewhere.

almost entirely in gold and silver in severely elegant patterns, which nevertheless seem to derive from the perpendicular lines of Raphael's interpretation of the grotesque. A very fine chasuble at Trento is a good example of many vestments made in this style in the first quarter of the seventeenth century. Once the effects of the Counter-Reformation began to make themselves felt across Catholic Europe, Italian vestments were not only widely exported but also widely copied. Gold embroidered chasubles of this type, although not always of this superb quality, may be seen in church treasuries all over the southern half of Europe.

As baroque architecture and interior decoration in churches grew increasingly flamboyant, vestments were required which could hold their own in color and impact. By the end of the century many were of brocaded silks in the new French floral patterns. The new embroidery was also floral, at this period arranged in striking, formally balanced compositions, designed to fill the whole surface of the vestment. The flowers employed were sometimes exotic, but more often in themselves naturalistic, and their arrangement on a central axis still recalls echoes of the traditional grotesque pattern-building. The vestments themselves were for the most part made of cream satin, with embroidery in brilliantly shaded colors in long and short stitch, in the glossy floss silk which was characteristic of Italian work. The applied orphrey disappeared, but the orphreys of a chasuble were always indicated, either by lines of gold braid or in the design of the embroidery itself. An alternative technique was laid and couched work in colored silks, crossed and held down by spaced lines of gold thread. In general very much less gold was used in this type of embroidery than in earlier periods, but some examples are found with complete backgrounds of couched gold, on which the colored flowers glow warmly.

Many vestments of this type are attributed to Naples, where the Kings of Naples and the Two Sicilies held a wealthy and luxurious court (Plate 45). The style may have originated in the south – Catanzaro in Calabria was another center for embroidery – but it spread rapidly, both inside and outside Italy, and like the gold-thread chasubles of the earlier part of the century, set an

ecclesiastical fashion throughout the Roman Catholic Church, which lasted right through the eighteenth and much of the nineteenth centuries. Only the arrangement of the flowers changed slightly in the early eighteenth century, becoming lighter and less formal as the baroque gave way to the frivolities of the rococo style.

A slightly different version of the style developed in the north of Italy, where the floral compositions were combined with volute patterns in raised gold embroidery, which gave the whole a more architectural appearance.

As might be expected Rome was also a leading center for church embroidery. The speciality of the Roman workshops was gold embroidery which showed great inventiveness and technical skill.

Chasuble of Bishop of Madruzzo of Trento, *Italy, first quarter of the seventeenth century. Blue silk ground embroidered with couched gold and silver threads, length 42in (107cm).* CATHEDRAL TREASURY, TRENTO.

Apron *(detail), Italy,*
seventeenth/eighteenth
century. Linen ground
embroidered with green silk
thread in cross stitch and
trimmed with green and
white needlelace, 42in × 33in
(107cm × 84cm). Peasant
work from the Abruzzi.
VICTORIA AND ALBERT
MUSEUM, LONDON.

grapes and ears of wheat which were favorite symbols of nineteenth-century ecclesiastical designers everywhere.

The Embroidery Revival in the Late Nineteenth Century

The nineteenth century was not a period of great activity in embroidery in Italy. Silk continued to be used for clothing and house decoration and at a domestic level even Berlin woolwork was not taken up with the enthusiasm which it was accorded elsewhere. Small pictures and cushion covers do exist (Plate 50), but it seems that the Berlin floral patterns were used as much for the church as for the home.

We have seen that peasant embroidery was directly descended from the upper-class domestic embroideries of the sixteenth century. The work was done on stronger materials and as far as embroidery was concerned, as opposed to lace, there was a tendency to simplify the patterns and reject the more sophisticated renaissance designs. By far the greater proportion of Italian peasant embroidery was whitework, made for underdresses, shirts and household linen, and also as gifts for the parish churches, usually in the form of borders for altar cloths. Much of this work was cutwork and *reticella* and was sufficiently elaborate to come under the heading of lace rather than embroidery. Indeed needle laces were quite as much a part of the peasant tradition in Italy as stitched embroidery. As time went on certain types of pattern began to be repeated in certain areas and eventually became traditional in these places. For example, aprons with wide cross-stitch borders were worn in Pesco-constanzo in the Abruzzi, and animal patterns left in reserve against backgrounds of drawn threadwork were a speciality of Sicily and Sardinia (Plate 53). Both cross-stitch patterns and drawn-thread backgrounds were sometimes worked in color, red being the most popular. In the Romagna colored embroidered cloths were made to cover the oxen for festive occasions.

The standard of these crafts had remained high throughout the seventeenth and eighteenth centuries but by the end of the nineteenth the practice of fine needlework and lace making was dying out. At this time a movement started among aristocratic ladies which was intended both to help the poor by encouraging women to take up lucra-

Designs during the eighteenth century were luxuriant, following the fashionable floral trends but worked entirely in laid and raised gold, employing a variety of different threads and techniques. The entire furnishings of the chapel of San Rocco in Lisbon were designed and made in Rome in the 1740s, and included complete sets of vestments in white, red, rose and violet, all embroidered in gold by professional workers whose names have survived.

Later in the century, in the 1780s, an English Roman Catholic family, still at this period living under religious restrictions, had a set of vestments for their private chapel designed by one of Queen Charlotte's embroideresses, but sent it to a convent in Rome to be worked. The floral style is that of the English silk industry, but the technique, in this case in colored silks and gold, recalls many Italian vestments. The Roman gold work, however, maintained its high technical standards throughout the nineteenth century (Plate 51).

Trends during the nineteenth century were for lighter but more formal designs in keeping with the neoclassical fashions of the early years of the century. Floral patterns never lost their popularity, but new flowers such as the lily of the valley began to appear among the tulips and peonies, as well as the

tive work, and also as a patriotic exercise to save and revive the crafts of the newly founded state of Italy which had only been united in one kingdom since 1861. The idea began in Burano (an island in the Venetian lagoon), where the craft of lace making was revived in the late 1870s. Workrooms in other areas quickly followed until most parts of the country were involved. In nearly every case the initiative was taken by an educated woman who recruited workers and undertook the organization and sale of the finished products. The women of the villages were encouraged to remember their old skills in embroidery and lace making, and at first the work produced had a strong regional character. Gradually research into the old pattern books resulted in a wider spread of the simpler sixteenth-century patterns, adapted to suit the tablecloths and cushion covers which would sell successfully.

Special mention must be made of the society formed in Bologna under the name of Aemilia Ars which was one of the earliest to encourage a revival in the decorative arts. Among the chief promoters of the movement was the artist Alfonso Rubbiani, who was responsible for many of the designs. The society fostered the crafts of book binding, enamel work and jewelery as well as an embroidery workroom under the Countess Lina Cavazza Bianconchini. All the needlework carried out was whitework. Two embroidered tablecloths in the Art Nouveau idiom were exhibited at the international exhibition in Turin in 1902, but most of the designs created for the workroom were for particularly rich cutwork and *reticella* which is lace rather than embroidery. This type of work is still made from the Society's early designs, either in the Art Nouveau style or as adaptations of traditional patterns.

Another workroom which was started in Assisi at about the same time specialized in early designs of the type left in reserve on backgrounds of long-armed cross stitch. From this they started to make their own designs based on motifs from the mosaic floor and other decoration in the church of St. Francis at Assisi. So well known did their work become that the technique has come to be called Assisi work.

In 1903 a cooperative society was

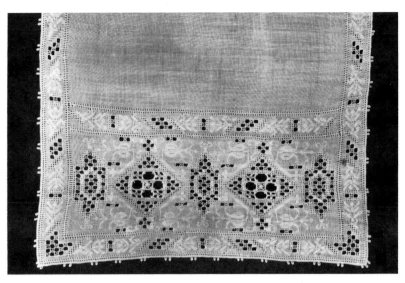

formed in Rome under the name Industrie Femminili Italiane, to bring together the various workrooms, to maintain standards and undertake publicity for their work. An exhibition of work by affiliated firms was held in Milan in 1906. While many pieces continued to be made in traditional styles, the workers had by this time been able to interest artists in their craft and had gained sufficient confidence to produce embroideries in the Art Nouveau fashions of the time. Good pieces were still being produced in the 1920s, for example, by the Laboratorio di Vittorio Zecchin in Murano, working in the Art Deco idiom, by Matilde Piacentini Festa of Rome, who designed and worked a large curtain for the Teatro Savoia in Florence, and by many others.

The Industrie Femminili has ceased to exist today (a shop of that name in Florence is a private business and not a cooperative). The craft of embroidery is for the most part carried on by outworkers making table linen for sale, but while the technical standards are high the designs are not adventurous. Good work is still done in reproducing old patterns adapted for modern use. Otherwise patterns tend to be in a "lingerie" style from the 1920s and 1930s. Appliqué and shadow work are much used on fine cotton lawn.

A certain amount of more up-to-date work is produced for the Church, but this is often carried out in machine embroidery, probably for reasons of economy. A good modern chasuble worked in laid gold and probably made in the 1930s, is illustrated in Plate 55.

ABOVE, TOP:
Embroidery in drawn threadwork *(detail)*, *Florence, Italy, twentieth-century adaptation of sixteenth-century design, 1920s/30s.* INDUSTRIE FEMMINILI ITALIANE, FLORENCE.

ABOVE:
Tablecloth *(detail)*, *Italian 1970s. Embroidered in cream and green in satin stitch, shadow stitch and drawn thread work, 60in × 48in. (152cm × 122cm).* MERLETTI GERLI, VENICE.

Spain

TWO DIFFERENT TYPES OF EMBROIDERY were produced in the various regions of the Iberian peninsula: first, costly embroidery for the aristocracy and the Church and, second, peasant embroidery. The Church rather than the aristocracy was the most important client of the former for even if secular clothes were not plain, they never equaled ecclesiastical robes in their magnificence.

Gothic Embroidery

Gothic embroidery, produced from the beginning of the thirteenth to the end of the fourteenth century, was strongly influenced stylistically by the North and also, although to a lesser extent, by Moorish embroidery. This period was very prosperous for all the kingdoms of Spain, and the prosperity resulted in higher living standards and more opulent garments. Embroidery reacted to this new wealth by shedding the simplicity which had characterized it during the romanesque period and becoming both more detailed and more naturalistic as a result of the influence from gothic painting.

On the magnificent chasubles produced in the thirteenth century the images were usually concentrated in the orphreys and represented specific scenes. It was not until the middle of the thirteenth century that orphreys depicted a narrative, a practice which was to continue throughout the renaissance and baroque periods. The most noteworthy piece, produced toward the end of the thirteenth century, is the altar hanging of the Life of Our Lord (Gerona Cathedral, Catalonia) which is simply worked on a gold ground.

The classic period of gothic embroidery spanned the latter part of the thirteenth and the early part of the fourteenth centuries, and it is from then until the fifteenth century that we find early examples of individual figures embroidered within quatrefoil medallions. One example from this time is the miter of Santa Maria de l'Estany (Episcopal Museum, Vich), the raised pattern worked in gold thread and, to represent the flesh tints, various silks.

In the fourteenth century several embroiderers are known by name for the first time. At the court in Barcelona there were Jewish embroiderers such as Jussef and Salamó Surí and Mosé Abenabes, but the most famous royal embroiderer was Jaume Copí (active 1360–94), who created the canopy for the annual procession of Corpus Christi. Other embroiderers in royal service included Jaume Casals de Ros, Jaume Soler and Ramon Dessoler.

The fifteenth century saw the foundation of the great workshops, each with a characteristic style, and these were to continue in production until the baroque period. The most important centers were Barcelona, Toledo and Seville, followed by Valencia and Majorca. Barcelona had achieved fame in the previous century but its reputation was now enhanced by such masters as Llorenç Erbol, Joan Tell, Arnau Cellent and Salvador Guerau. The greatest of all, however, was Antoni Sadurní who, in 1458, began to work for the *Generalitat*, as the Government of Catalonia is called, and was commissioned to decorate the Chapel of St. George. Italian artists came to work in his studio and from quite an early stage the influence of the Italian Renaissance was apparent, indicating that Catalonia was the first region to adopt the new style.

The Toledo school had its origin in the cathedral workshop and here, among the most important craftsmen, should be mentioned Gil Sánchez, Rui González, Juan Rodríguez and Juan de la Torre. The master Alfonso founded his own workshop, where Juan de las Fuentes, Juan de Paiso and later, Sancho García were the most important names. It was in this workshop that the first lay embroiderers of the monastery of Guadalupe learned their trade and this formed the basis for the monastery's own workshop, which was founded in the middle of the century and was to become one of the most important in the peninsula.

The Seville workshop was active

from the beginning of the century and boasted such important artists as Juan González, García Alcocer, Pedro González, Fernán Sánchez, the Fernán brothers, Gonzalo and Juan Rúiz, Antonio Gil, Juan Rodríguez and Juan de Sosa. Although women were not uncommon as embroiderers of peasant work, they rarely worked on luxury embroidery until the middle of the century, when several women became attached to the Seville workshop, notably Juana González, Isabel Fernández and Isabel Valdés.

In the fifteenth century, gold formed the ground for all embroidery but it was worked using different techniques. One was stretched gold in which single gold threads followed the design, giving the embroidery a raised effect; another was drawn gold in which the gold thread was interlaced in four directions forming a cross with two intersecting diagonals, and in this way they achieved a completely covered surface. The combination of these two techniques was known as "galloon." Gold thread was also padded and couched and it was used in a variation of the form known as *or nué*, where it was partially covered with different colored silks. Later this developed into shading and traversing, which set the thread horizontally. While gold continued to be used as a ground for embroidery throughout the century, in the latter years it was almost always covered with silk to give a polychrome impression.

Foreign Influences on Spanish Needlework

During the fifteenth century Spanish embroidery became increasingly divorced from Moorish styles through the arrival of various European influences. In chronological order these were English, French, Flemish and Italian. The English influence was of short duration but the French, which was first evident in the fourteenth century in Catalonia and can be seen in the altar hanging of San Juan de las Abadesas (Museum of San Juan de las Abadesas), had a more powerful effect. Two important pieces dating from the first half of the fifteenth century also illustrate this point, namely the chasuble in the Textile Museum of Barcelona, which is from a local workshop and has figures of saints in quatrefoil medallions, and also, some twenty years later, the green velvet chasuble from the mona-

Chasuble, *Barcelona, Spain, fifteenth century. Velvet with central embroidered band with figures of saints in quadrefoil medallions, 492in × 264in (1250cm × 670cm). An example of French influence in the fifteenth century.* TEXTILE MUSEUM, BARCELONA.

stery of Guadalupe, which is a work by Brother Jerome using a tapestry technique.

The Flemish influence was strong and lasting, and it was through this influence that perspective – a recent subject for study and experiment in Flemish painting – was introduced into pictorial embroidery. Other typical features were gold backgrounds and the employment of Gothic frames, as in altarpieces, thus making embroidery into a type of painting in threads.

The Flemish introduced the *or nué* or shaded gold technique which persisted during the following century; this new style was brought by the numerous Flemish embroiders who migrated to the peninsula and it was also copied from imported Flemish works. Some of these immigrants founded workshops that continued to be active in the following century, as was the case in Barcelona, a city through which flowed strong Flemish influences which affected both painting (witness the works of Lluis Dalmau) and embroidery. Two of

the most important pieces of this period
in the Flemish style are the chasuble of
the High Constable (Museum of Sacred
Vestments of the Monastery of Guadalupe) from the workshop at Guadalupe
in which, to represent the wings of the
angels, feather stitching is used for the
first time; and, dating from *c.*1391, the
chasuble with scenes from the Life of
the Virgin Mary (Episcopal Museum,
Vich). Another important work in this
style is the altar frontal of Henry II of
Castile (Museum of Sacred Vestments
of the Monastery of Guadalupe) with
three pictorial scenes from the Lives of
the Virgin Mary and of Jesus. The background is of gold and the figures in the
foreground are embroidered in raised
appliqué while flat appliqué is used for
the flesh tints. This is thought to be the
work of Flemish artists who had come
to Guadalupe. Another piece from this
period is the Rich Altar Frontal in
Guadalupe (Museum of Sacred Vest-

ments of the Monastery of Guadalupe).
Attributed to Fray Diego de Toledo, it
consists of seven panels representing
scenes from the Life of the Virgin Mary
and Jesus, and it has a frontlet above
embroidered with heads of angels and
the hieratic head of Christ in the center.
It was extensively restored during the
sixteenth and seventeenth centuries.

By the turn of the century Italian
embroidery was becoming increasingly
influential, and works imported from
Florence were quite common. This influence is seen in the depiction of more
vivacious and naturalistic figures and
also the use of urns as a decorative
motif. Gothic frames did not disappear
completely, however.

Another technique that came from
Italy was silver embroidery in which
parts of the design were first worked in
raised embroidery; tiny rings of silver,
each one held with minute stitching and
worked one on top of the other to form
a mesh, were then applied to these
raised parts. The applied technique was
used for the first time with different
pieces of cloth applied to the ground to
create the motifs and figures; the pieces
were applied flat, since the impression
of folds on the costumes of the figures
was achieved by means of chain stitch.
One of the most notable works from
this period is the altar cloth in the
Chapel of St. George in the Palace of
the *Generalitat*, a work by Antoni
Sadurni of *c.*1460. This typically *quatt-
rocento* work consists of a central panel
showing St. George, the dragon and the
princess, and two symmetrical side
panels, each with an urn in the center,
from which arise coils and two full-face
gryphons supporting the coat of arms of
St. George. The side panels appear to
be more stylistically sophisticated than
the central one, a proof of the persist-
ence of medieval modes alongside those
of the Renaissance.

Another outstanding work from this
period is the altar frontal of the Passion
(Museum of Sacred Vestments of the
Monastery of Guadalupe). In its five
scenes, which depict the Passion, the
composition is supremely Italianate and
the distribution of the figures is superb.
It is embroidered with pearls and
precious stones and the highly colored
effect is produced by applied work in
silk. The stitching of faces and hands
on counted threads give an impression
of modeling, and shiny silk is used to
produce metallic effects.

Renaissance embroidery, which falls into two periods roughly corresponding to the first and second halves of the sixteenth century, was now at its height and it was one of the most magnificent periods for Spanish embroidery. Excellence was achieved in various techniques, in particular with gold threads: these, in couching, padding or shading, spread to larger areas of the work to depict not only the costumes of the figures but also the landscape and the background.

This century also saw the perfection of the technique of shading in long and short stitch which was known at that time as "flesh stitch." Raised work was richer in silks and gold, and paper was often used as padding material. Applied work was widely employed for the renaissance decorative motifs, such as urns, scrolls and grotesques. The themes were clearly Italian, with a strong admixture of classical elements, such as niches with vaults and classical columns. The figures were realistic and the medallions that contained them were round or oval, connected by decorative borders.

During the Renaissance there was an enormous increase in ecclesiastical, but not in secular, work, the latter becoming increasingly somber. Vestments had a central design with a decorated border. Among the ecclesiastical pieces feature the appearance of *mangas*, or drapes, hanging from crosses and held by a truncated cone support so that the whole surface of the embroidery was visible; the ground materials employed were usually velvet or satin.

The most important pieces from the first period of renaissance embroidery are the two sets of ecclesiastical vestments known as the "Vestments of

ABOVE:
Altar cloth of St. George *by Antoni Sadurni, Barcelona, Spain, c.1460. Embroidered with silver and gold thread, silk and precious stones,* *126in × 71in (320cm × 180cm). A typically renaissance example of fifteenth-century Catalan embroidery.* CHAPEL OF ST. GEORGE OF THE GENERALITAT, BARCELONA.

Empress Isabella," a work from the Guadalupe workshop, and the rich vestments of Cardinal Cisneros; and also the pontifical set of Fonseca. The last two were made in Toledo. The second set of vestments served as a model for one of the most important works of the second period of renaissance embroidery, namely the Vestments of the Rich Set (Museum of Sacred Vestments of the Monastery of Guadalupe), a work by the brocade worker Pedro López. According to some authorities the two tunicles in the set are by different hands, though Antonio Floriano Cumbreño maintains that they are by the same craftsman. A silver brocade ground was used, over which the decoration was worked.

Another significant piece is the so-called "Old Cloth," from the Monastery of Guadalupe which is a *manga* for the base of a cross, but it is now unfortunately in poor condition. This has been inconclusively attributed to Pedro López. It consists of two parts, an upper section and a pendent main part supported on a truncated cone base. The background to the scenes are renaissance landscapes, and in the Circumcision there is a baptistery with a round cupola in the pure classical style of the Florentine architect Bramante. The whole composition is full of life and elegance, especially in the movement of the figures in the Assumption, and the scenes are linked by architectural and decorative elements. The technique employed is of two superimposed stages. First the figures and scenes are embroidered on a linen ground, and then the buildings are worked in gold chain stitch and pearls.

Needlework in the Baroque and Rococo Styles

The complicated and sumptuous features that typify the baroque style were employed to create some magnificent works of embroidery. However, the imagery gradually disappeared under a wealth of decoration which covered the whole surface, and although at first chasubles retained their orphreys, these were superseded by extensive plant decoration. Altar frontals were the works produced most frequently, and they were decorated with friezes of stylized flowers. An element of decadence is apparent in that the treatment of the images is neither beautiful nor perfectly executed. Hemp

was used to achieve a higher relief, and couched gold was worked over the padding. String, chamois and paper were all used as a base for raised work, and these were then covered with silks.

Appliqué work reached a high standard in the baroque period, its *chiaroscuro* effects being achieved in part with silks, but more especially by the use of the paint-brush. The greatest success, however, was in metallic embroidery, in which gold thread was sometimes used and sometimes tinsel which is gold wound round a silk thread. In metallic embroidery there was an increasing use of sequins of gold or silver left plain or painted in different colors. At first these were applied one at a time, but soon the entire piece of needlework was covered with raised work.

The set of tunicles from Fuentonovillos are notable examples of seventeenth-century baroque embroidery. They consist of pieces of velvet worked in appliqué. The figures are out of proportion and badly drawn, which is clear proof of the deterioration of pictorial embroidery. The best work from the seventeenth century is the altar frontal of St. Jerome (Museum of Sacred Vestments of the Monastery of Guadalupe), in which narrative scenes and decorative motifs were used in combination. The former, which are in the upper section, represent scenes from the Life of the Virgin Mary, while in the center an angel appears to St. Jerome. In the pictorial scenes the technique is couched gold, but in the decoration of the border the gold thread follows the design in the stitch which contemporary documents call "*punto retirado*," or concealed stitching.

With the advent of the Bourbon dynasty at the beginning of the eighteenth century, French influence permeated all the decorative arts, including embroidery, and there was a great freedom in design. Rococo and chinoiserie styles were adopted and there was a widespread use of raised work and silk, the latter often being employed as the ground for raised work. It was also an important period for shaded embroidery since the delicacy and variations in tone of the silks of this time were ideally suited to achieving the effect of subtle gradations of light and color. The material for the ground – usually silk – was white or a pale color, in contrast to the dark velvets of previous centuries.

One of the main works from the eighteenth century is the tunic, worked by Antonio Gómez de los Ríos, which formed part of the robes of state of Ferdinand VI. It is of white silk, decorated with the emblems of Castile and León as well as the Bourbon fleur-de-lis, with pictorial scenes worked in chain stitch set within medallions. Also from this century is the altar frontal of St. Catherine now in the Museum of the History of the City, Barcelona, but originally in the old Barcelona convent of St. Catherine; but this is not a particularly sumptuous piece by eighteenth-century standards. It was during this same period that whitework became widespread – in particular on waistcoats and coats – and secular garments were now richly embroidered.

Secular Needlework

From the end of the eighteenth century secular garments succeeded ecclesiastical embroidery in importance. During the First Empire (1804–15) ladies' garments were simple in form but they were decorated with high-quality embroidery, usually worked in *passementerie* and in shading. Later, when it became less fashionable on clothes, embroidery entered a period of partial decline, and this was exacerbated after the seizure of church property in 1836, directed by the Minister, Mendizábal. The Church lost a great part of its riches and could no longer remain the embroiderers' principal client. The male workers now abandoned the trade, leaving embroidery to the women, and many convents became workshops, providing young women with a training, albeit not a wholly professional one. In about the middle of the nineteenth century, workshops were set up in Andalucia for the production of embroidered shawls which until then had been imported from Manila; the shawls were decorated with flowers of a purely western variety and they were highly colored. At the same time embroidery on a white ground and a type known as Laussin or lithographic embroidery, both enjoyed a certain vogue, in particular in the last three decades of the century. Bullfighters' costumes and work on the hangings for the Easter procession floats were also important and these were the only items still worked by men.

In the twentieth century, embroidery has become extremely sober. Only a few designers have given rein to their

Altar cloth of St. Catherine *(detail) from the convent of St. Catherine, Barcelona, Spain, eighteenth century. Scarlet linen embroidered with gold thread, 122in × 43in (310cm × 110cm). The coat of arms of the Convent of St. Catherine are depicted in the center of this altar cloth.* MUSEUM OF THE HISTORY OF THE CITY, BARCELONA.

fantasies, and in these cases the work has been executed by men.

Peasant Embroidery

The best peasant embroidery was produced in the seventeenth century or earlier, and it declined throughout the eighteenth and nineteenth centuries. In the twentieth century, owing largely to ethnological studies, the interest in it has revived.

A few pieces are signed and dated from the sixteenth century onward, but this is by no means the rule; consequently it is difficult to determine the age and origin of most work, especially since many of the subjects were repeated often over the centuries. The only feasible survey is by areas, since peasant embroidery can be classified according to artistic regions, the equivalent of the more sophisticated schools of embroidery. For each region there is an indigenous style; border areas between regions show a cross fertilization of ideas and these are known as "zones of transition" producing, as they do, work showing several influences. The principal areas where peasant embroidery was produced are Toledo, Salamanca, Zamora, León, Segovia, Avila, Cáceres, Valencia and Majorca.

Most peasant embroidery shares certain common characteristics: the cloth, the threads, the colors, the techniques, the subject matter and also the purposes for which the pieces were intended. In general, the ground is homemade, evenly woven white linen which makes techniques based on the counting of threads easy to work. From the eighteenth century onward cotton replaced linen, but its quality was never as good.

The most widely used thread was wool, although later linen, silk, cotton and a combination of gold and silk known as Cyprus gold were all employed. There is a predominance of bright and primary colors, particularly black and red, while pale colors were seldom used.

Four principal types of stitch or technique were employed: interlacing, simple, appliqué, and spirals and cross stitch, all of which have variations. The interlacing technique includes interlacing proper, meshing and quilting. The simple technique has the following variations: back stitch, double-back stitch, buttonhole, chain stitch, faggot stitch, fern stitch, long stitch, and overcast stitch. The variations of cross stitch are Algiers stitch, braiding, cross stitch proper and herringbone, all of which are known as shading stitches because they are used to cover large areas of cloth.

As regards subject matter, the favorite themes were a lady with a gentleman and a dancing lady. Of the animals that were depicted the most popular were lions, followed by horses, dogs, doves and small birds. Eagles, falcons, fish, lambs, deer and pelicans were also depicted. Bouquets of various flowers such as carnations, rosettes, tulips, lotus flowers, palms, pines, the Tree of Life (from Persia), various nuts and pomegranates were among the plant forms that were used. Symbolic objects include some of pagan origin, such as urns and baskets, while others are of Christian inspiration: the cross, the monstrance, the attributes of the Passion, the Lamb of God and fonts decorated with birds of early Christian provenance. Many of these motifs take on geometrical forms, as do those of Moorish influence, although the latter are notably abstract. Graphic motifs are derived from highly decorated letters similar in style to those used in Arabic and Gothic calligraphy. As to its uses, peasant embroidery was intended for clothing or for decorating the home and church.

Hispano-Moresque Embroidery

Pure Moorish embroidery was produced in Morocco and Granada. It grew in Morocco under Coptic influences. The ground cloth was usually white linen and the thread employed was generally monochrome silk, with a predominance of red, worked in reverse embroidery with motifs and background both fully worked in regular darning and lacing stitches. Few examples of this work have survived since it was never well received in the peninsula.

Granada embroidery was made by people living in the desert. It uses linen as its ground and silk threads of bright colors are employed mainly in the characteristic cross stitch, to cover the entire surface with forms worked in lozenge shapes.

The third variety is Hispano-Moresque embroidery proper which was produced for as long as Moslems lived in the peninsula. Moslem elements are mixed with Visigothic, pre-romanesque, romanesque and gothic details. The ground employed was linen cloth and the silk threads were at first brightly colored, although later paler colors were favored. The design generally covers the whole area and the stitching is restricted to the cross stitch known as Algiers stitch. In the later periods the motifs were worked in chain stitch, producing effects similar to pottery. The decorative motifs which were geometrical were repeated to form an overall pattern of chains of bows and effects similar to Moorish stucco work; subsequently certain highly stylized animal and plant motifs were introduced.

True Moorish embroidery is from a later period, developing between the fifteenth and the seventeenth centuries. A fine linen cloth was used as the base and it was worked with pale, monochrome thread. The technique involved counting the threads of the cloth, which was then embroidered with herringbone stitch and a variety of Italian braiding stitch. Geometrical designs were employed to decorate the borders, and the finished product was embroidered on both sides to resemble lace work. This type of embroidery, worked in a variation of Italian braiding stitch, is still produced in certain villages in New Castile, in particular Caleruela de Oropesa.

Peasant Embroidery in Toledo

Toledo is the region where embroidery has had the longest continuous tradition and its products are still highly regarded. There are four centers in the region, each with its own characteristics: Navalcán, Lagartera, Oropesa and Talavera.

The embroidery of Navalcán, worked with meshing or quilting, is of Coptic

Underbodice of Lagartera
peasant costume, *Lagartera,*
Spain, nineteenth century.
Off-white cotton
embroidered in black thread
with geometrical motifs.
TEXTILE MUSEUM OF
BARCELONA.

origin and was introduced by the Egyptians who accompanied the Moors in their conquest of the peninsula. The ground is of linen and the thread of wool or cotton. The technique is one of the interlacing varieties and the cloth is worked on the reverse side. The designs are geometrical, and they are arranged as borders at the extremities of the pieces. These are still made today and are used in particular for undergarments and offertory cloths.

Lagartera produces the most famous embroidery of Toledo and it had a strong influence over the whole region.

The ground is homemade linen and the thread is wool, cotton or silk of mixed colors. Early works were made in black, but more recently red has been introduced. One of the two techniques employed starts from a design based on counting the threads and this is then worked in a combination of cross stitch, back stitch, faggot stitch, chain stitch and fern stitch, which together are known as royal stitching. The other technique starts from a drawing and uses only chain stitch and satin stitch. The decorative themes include geometrical elements such as stylized

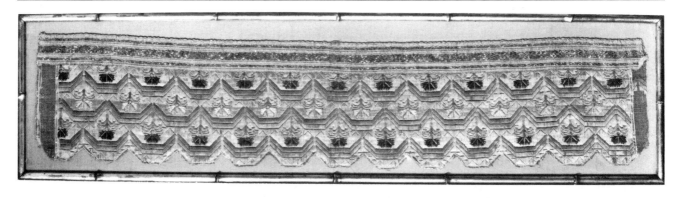

Altar frontal *(detail)*,
Talavera de la Reina,
Toledo, Spain. Hand-
woven linen embroidered
with polychrome silks and
silver thread in satin stitch.
COLLECTION DOÑA CARMEN
CORTON DE COSSIO.

flowers, coats of arms and the Tree of
Life. These themes form wide borders
surrounding the pieces or are arranged
in decorative squares covering the whole
of the surface. This work was often
combined with openwork which surrounded the embroidered geometrical
and floral motifs. The style based on
counted threadwork is used for offertory
cloths, while the drawn variety is used
for garments.

The embroidery of Oropesa, which
was restricted to pieces for domestic
use, was greatly influenced by Lagartera
and also French luxury embroidery of
the eighteenth century. Both styles
make use of a linen ground with wool
thread for monochrome work and cotton
for the polychrome pieces. In early
work bright colors predominated although nowadays the colors are softer;
counted threadwork and satin stitch
were employed in both styles.

There are two types of Talavera embroidery: one influenced by that of

Lagartera, using the same materials,
colors, techniques and cloth; the other,
a more indigenous style in which the
colors and themes are similar to those
used in the production of Talavera
ceramics.

Peasant Embroidery in
Salamanca, Zamora and Léon

The embroidery of Salamanca (known
as *serrano*) has certain characteristics of
its own. The ground is linen cloth,
which was homemade until the end of
the seventeenth century, and the thread
was at first wool or worsted, and later
silk, all these materials being twisted
together into one thread. The favorite
colors are red and yellow, green and
blue, and black, with the first four
worked in pairs and the last used to outline the motifs.

As regards technique, this embroidery uses a combination of preparatory
drawing and counted threadwork for the
interior of the motifs, and chain stitch

Offertory cloth *(detail)*,
Salamanca, Spain,
seventeenth century. Linen
embroidered with silk,
47in × 27in (120cm ×
70cm). INSTITUTE OF
VALENCIA DE DON JUAN,
MADRID.

is used for the outline. The decoration is limited to animals and plants. Lions rampant or passant, suckling lionesses, doves with a twig in the beak, one and two-headed eagles as well as trout, which are regarded as lucky in the Salamanca region, are the animals most frequently depicted. Among the plant themes which are usually set in squares are bouquets, lotus and papyrus flowers, carnations, rosettes, palms and pomegranates.

Salamanca embroidery was mainly employed on clothing, in particular for the sleeves of the dress shirts used for weddings, for offertory cloths, hangings and for decorative use in the home.

The region of Zamora and León covers specific areas, such as the towns of Toro, Zamora and Benavente and the rural districts of Los Carvajales. Because of the important wool industry in the area, both the highly colored grounds and the threads are of wool. The work is used for clothes, both outer garments and underwear, for the drapes that are hung from balconies during processions and for offertory cloths. The colors of the threads are bright like the ground materials and are used in contrasting combinations. Two techniques are worked together: appliqué and satin stitch. Flannel is used as the material for the appliqué work, the motifs being worked in satin stitch and applied to the ground material with back stitch or overcast stitch. The ornamental motifs are geometrical or large flowers, such as tulips, palms and roses; also symbols such as castles, crosses, monstrances and nails of Moorish inspiration. These elements are distributed closely but symmetrically over the entire surface, with the larger motifs worked in the center.

Peasant Embroidery in Segovia, Avila, Cáceres

Segovia produces peasant embroidery that is closest in character to ecclesiastical embroidery, for the Segovians not only imitate the works of Toledo, Salamanca and Avila, but their own style is a product of the influence of various luxury styles. Segovia's heyday lasted from the fourteenth century until the seventeenth century and nowadays very little is produced. The ground is homemade cloth of which the warp is finer than the weft. The thread is black or pale-colored linen, or wool, which in the case of worsted was dyed.

Two techniques were employed: that of counted threadwork which entailed cross stitch, herringbone, back stitch, chain stitch, fern stitch, faggot stitch, braiding stitch, chevron and quilting, and that based on a pattern, on the basis of which embroidery is worked in chain stitch and buttonhole stitch and surrounded by a narrow band of lace work. The decoration is geometrical or based on plant forms. The Segovian school offers a greater variety of geometrical designs than any other, the principal motifs being chains of concentric circles and bands of zigzags, as well as human, animal and symbolic elements, all composed of geometrical shapes. These decorative elements are arranged in large, separate compositions or along transversal borders. Segovian embroidery is used in particular for offertory cloths for weddings and burials, for bedspreads and for table sets.

Avila embroidery which was used for ladies' garments, in particular for the necks of blouses, for altar and funeral cloths and for general decorative purposes in the house, was at its best in the sixteenth century and is characterized by the reverse style. This originated in Persia and there are two theories as to how it could have reached Avila. Some experts maintain that it arrived in

ABOVE:
Sleeve *from the traditional costume in the province of Segovia, eighteenth century. This costume is still worn by the girl elected "mayoress" on great feast days in Segovia. It is embroidered on hand-woven linen with natural dark brown wool in trellis stitch, stem stitch and back stitch over laid thread.* COLLECTION OF DOÑA CARMEN CORTON DE COSSIO.

OVERLEAF, TOP:
Sleeve *(detail), Segovia, Spain, eighteenth century. Hand-woven linen embroidered in dark brown thread with lions and birds in stem stitch and satin stitch and back stitch over laidwork.* COLLECTION DOÑA CARMEN CORTON DE COSSIO.

ancient times, while others claim that it was introduced by the Moors; the latter hypothesis now seems the more probable. In Avila the ground is of homemade linen cloth; in the early stages, the thread was of dark wool succeeding later to paler silks although all the threads were poorly dyed.

Avila work employs three techniques. First, appliqué work, using cloth both for the base and for the working, the applied pieces being sewn with back stitch. Second, quilting which derives directly from embroidery techniques of Navalcán. The third, which is peculiar to the region, is reverse embroidery, in which the background is worked leaving the motifs blank but separated by overcast or back stitch. The ground is filled with a variety of satin stitch called Spanish stitch, which creates a design reminiscent of Celtic decoration and similar to ears of corn.

Cáceres embroidery illustrates four different styles, all of which share a technique based on drawing and all of which suffer from an imperfect execution of the stitches. The whole area is covered with a coarse stitch known as Hungarian stitch, which is needed to cover the irregular ground. One Cáceres style is whitework, which is not to be confused with the white embroidery produced for the ruling classes for here the ground is of homemade linen cloth and the threads are rather coarse.

Two kinds of polychrome embroidery are produced but, with regard to technique, they share the characteristic style of appliqué work in green and red taffeta, and they are both used for outer garments. The first type is antique polychrome embroidery which was used for ladies' outer garments. The second type reveals a strong American influence which is a direct consequence of the close links between Extremadura and South America. It appeared in the sixteenth century and flourished in the seventeenth and eighteenth centuries. The decoration typically includes animals and magnificent birds, plants and large exotic flowers, as well as anthropomorphic elements. These decorations are arranged around a principal figure, from which radiate the other elements in the composition.

The third style of Cáceres embroidery consists of openwork on white linen which is strongly influenced by the openwork of Toledo. This is sometimes achieved by drawing the threads in one direction only, or from warp and weft alternately. The different techniques employed have special names: braiding open work, interlacing, antique interlacing and filigree. The decoration, arranged always in borders, draws for its subject matter on plants and animals.

Peasant Embroidery in Valencia and Majorca

Both peasant and luxury embroidery, used primarily on head-scarves, bed linen and table sets, which was developed simultaneously in Majorca, was originally worked by men, but from the nineteenth century male workers only did some of the preparatory work. Embroidery consequently suffered a decline and the workshops were reduced to a single survivor at Artà, but by the turn of the twentieth century this shop was able to increase production. New workshops were subsequently set up and the island experienced a genuine industrial revival although the old techniques suffered as a consequence.

The original ground used in Majorca was a homemade linen but this has since been replaced by a linen cambric. It has always been perfectly woven and although originally pristine white, nowadays bright colors are also employed. The thread was once of blue Turkish wool, but it is now of linen and fine cotton, to which silk and metallic threads are sometimes added. The most popular colors are various shades of red, pink, gilt and mauve, while colored grounds are worked in white.

A tambour frame and a special hooked needle are used to work the chain stitch that follows the design. In the old days the motifs were filled with chain stitch, but nowadays they are filled with cross stitches running parallel to each other and very closely set so that no ground fabric shows.

The decoration derives from plants, in particular the undulating branches of the vine, and tends to fill the entire ground. In early work the flowers were highly stylized or shown in longitudinal section while in modern work the centers of the flowers are filled with a very close cross stitch imitating lace work and producing the effect of a grille with contrasts of light and shade.

Valencian embroidery, which was

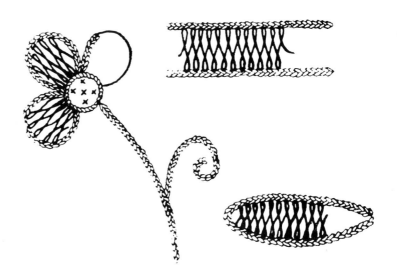

used mainly for under-garments, men's shirts, hangings and table sets, has now almost completely disappeared; few pieces have been preserved, and there is almost no documentation. The ground was of homemade linen and the thread was always of silk. Under the influence of luxury pieces the thread, which is usually very strongly colored, was worked together with threads of gold and silver and also with precious stones and pearls. The technique, based on counted threadwork, consisted mainly of satin stitch covering the surface of the cloth with interspersed chain stitch, back stitch, overcast and faggot stitch.

ABOVE, TOP:
Tablecloth *(detail)*, *Majorca, twentieth century. Crape and silk, 43in × 43in (108cm × 108cm).*

ABOVE:
Design for a tablecloth from Jajorca, *detail of above, twentieth century.*

OPPOSITE, BELOW:
Embroidered bands *(detail)*, Avila, Spain, *seventeenth century. Linen embroidered with silk, 37in × 6in, (95cm × 15cm). An example of Avila reverse embroidery.* INSTITUTE OF VALENCIA DE DON JUAN, MADRID.

Portugal

PORTUGAL, A COUNTRY ON THE IBERIAN peninsula looking out over the Atlantic from the western tip of Europe, saw a significant development in its needlework after the maritime expansion of the fifteenth and sixteenth centuries. Prior to this needlework had been slow to develop and our knowledge of what existed, if anything, is seriously limited by the lack of any documentary or material evidence.

Early Portuguese Embroidery

Dating from the fifteenth and sixteenth centuries there are a few ecclesiastical pieces which, although in a poor state of conservation, show a rare quality of workmanship; one such example being an episcopal miter (the Sacristy, Lamego Cathedral) embroidered on a white silk ground in different shades of silk and gold thread.

Embroidery was, in general, confined to the convents but there were a few secular centers of which Lamego justly became famous. These produced religious vestments and burghers' costumes.

The clothes of the upper classes were distinguished by their lavish embroidery. The royal palaces and the nobility had by then ceased to make ruinous acquisitions from the merchants of Flanders and Holland and, since 1498, when Vasco da Gama reached India via the Cape route, Portuguese merchants had controlled the trade with the Far East. The Portuguese had become a maritime nation with a chain of trading posts on the coasts of Arabia, India, Malaya, China and the islands of the East Indies. The Oriental style began to influence the design of religious vestments and the designs from the sixteenth- and seventeenth-century Persian velvets and brocades were directly adopted by the Portuguese for their coverlets and tapestries. In provincial embroidery, where female talents are so clearly evident, the Orient also showed its influence in the designs of the bedspreads of Castelo Branco and the rugs of Arraiolos.

The sixteenth century was indeed one of the best periods for Portuguese needlework. A characteristic design was a repeat of carnations, the center being worked with the Tree of Knowledge and two small figures encircled by a broad twisted band. Predominant colors used by the Portuguese in the sixteenth and seventeenth centuries were pale to bright pinks, soft greens and cream with an occasional touch of blue. Red and yellow, characteristic Spanish colors, were also employed, while a number of pieces from this period were worked in gold alone and studded with pearls and precious stones.

Perhaps among the most magnificent embroideries ever to have been executed in Portugal was the complete set of pontifical robes embroidered on the finest brocade which were given to the Pope by King Manuel of Portugal (1469–1521). The robes were decorated with a design of pomegranates of pure chased gold, while the crimson pips were represented by clusters of rubies and the flowers were entirely formed of pearls and other precious stones; the overall beauty of the robes was accentuated by the gold embroidery of the ground brocade.

A favorite type of embroidery practiced in this century in Portugal is *Bordado a Escomilha*, or crape work. Ordinary black crape was unraveled and its fine threads were used for sewing. A detailed and very accurate drawing made on white satin was then worked in such a way that when it was completed it resembled a print.

Peasant Embroidery in the Minho Region

Certain affinities with the embroidery of neighboring Spain and, in particular, the influence of the rich Spanish peasant tradition, were also apparent in Portuguese work of this period. In Portugal, peasant embroidery differs widely according to the region and in certain provinces practically none was done. In the litoral zone, for example, women do not embroider but make fine bobbin lace.

In the Minho, however, a small province in the north, there is an abund-

Peasant girl's waistcoat (detail), Minho, Portugal, nineteenth century. Red woolen ground and black velvet embroidered with polychrome wool thread in satin stitch and herringbone stitch, metal wire, glass beads and spangles, height 15in (40cm). PRIVATE COLLECTION, MEALHALDA.

ance of folk culture and peasant embroidery. The national costumes of the inhabitants of this area which they themselves both weave and embroider are among the most colorful and unusual of all those worn by the country people of Portugal. Multicolored embroideries enriched with metal wire, tiny beads and spangles decorate strips around their skirts, the back of their waistcoats and the purses which hang from their waists. Their striped skirts and their thickly woven aprons are made on a loom, a piece of equipment found in almost every Minho home. The shoulders and cuffs of their linen blouses are embroidered in blue thread, while the smocking around the sleeve is entirely individual, differing considerably from that of English smocks.

The bride's gown created by the Minhotas is a fine example of their craft: the bridal skirt and jacket made in black wool are decorated with braid stitch and braid and the velvet apron is decorated overall with bluish glass beads, which are poetically known as "moonlight beads." On her head, the bride wears a square of tulle or cambric embroidered in chain stitch with real skill.

These gifted women, for whom embroidery is almost an intuitive art, also make beautiful works of art known as "Viana da Castelo embroideries" – the homemade linen from their looms being decorated with red, blue and white cotton. Work from this area

which is in the north of Portugal, north of Oporto, also includes a national costume which is worked with wool thread on a red flannel ground and embellished with gilt-metal thread, sequins and glass beads. Stitches employed include herringbone, satin stitch and laid and couched work.

The shirts of the peasants from Guimaraês in the Minho region are decorated with embroidery for which no precedent can be found. The originality of this work does not rely on the bullion stitch, which is a familiar feature of all handmade work, but in the use that the local people make of it. The collars, shoulders and cuffs are so comprehensively worked with this intricate stitch that even when the shirts have been worn out by generations of use, their embroidery still remains intact.

A nineteenth-century shirt from Guimaraês in the Royal Scottish Museum, Edinburgh, shows that there was a certain similarity between the work produced at this time in the two countries. The embroidery of the front yoke of the Portuguese shirt resembles the front panel of a British rural smock, but whereas the British garment would in actual fact be smocked, the Portuguese shirt is embroidered on the linen ground with "tubing" and white cotton panels of wheel motifs, rosettes and foliage.

Women's clothes are not so prodigiously embroidered but there are, however, certain rather beautiful coarse

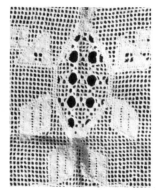

ABOVE, TOP:
Sideboard cover *(detail)*,
*Caldas da Raina,
Estremadura, Portugal,
nineteenth century.
Unbleached linen ground
embroidered with cinnamon-
colored linen thread in a
variety of stitches including
buttonhole stitch and
herringbone stitch and edged
with bobbin lace 47in × 23in
(120cm × 60cm).* PRIVATE
COLLECTION, CALDAS DA
RAINHA.

ABOVE:
Curtain *(detail)*, *Nisa,
Beira-Baixa, Portugal,
nineteenth century. Linen
ground embroidered with
white linen in drawn
threadwork, 17in × 21in
(40cm × 55cm).* PRIVATE
COLLECTION, PORTALEGRE.

sweaters of the fishermen from the north are embroidered in black and red with symbolic maritime designs such as boats and oars, anchors, fish, shells and birds, stars, Christ's cross and compasses.

The samplers of Portugal, of which the romantic period left us many attractive examples, are closely related to Spanish *dechados*, English samplers and the *Stickmustertuch* of the German schools. It is with cross stitch, which was sewn on coarse material over counted threads, that houseproud women marked their domestic linen.

Red and blue cross-stitch embroideries can be seen at the Norwegian Folk Museum in Oslo and at the Landesmuseum in Karlsruhe in Germany, with design motifs which are the counterpart to those which appear in the Portuguese "sweetheart handkerchiefs."

Crivos and Whitework Embroidery
Crivos and whitework embroidery are types of work which are widely encountered and are a characteristic feature of Portuguese embroidery, examples from Guimarães being of particularly high quality. The *crivo*, or riddle, an agricultural tool which is used for sieving cereals, has given its name to a type of drawn threadwork which has associations with Spanish *deshijados*, the Italian *sfilati* and the French *jours sur toile*. The attraction of the Portuguese classic white embroidery with its raised work is increased when it includes drawn threadwork and still more when fancy stitches are sewn over the spaces from which the threads have been withdrawn.

In Niza, in the province of Alto Alentejo, drawn threadwork is taken to an extreme of perfection. The earliest examples in which the composition is characterized by a severe formality of design succeed on account of the variety of open stitches, among which a number can be found which are similar to those used on Czechoslovakian whitework embroidery.

Tibaldinho is situated in a spa district of the Beira Alta province, where the peasant girls embroider bedclothes in poor-quality cotton. The designs are well set out with naïvely stylized motifs based on the mountain flora and embroidered in several different stitches, including eyelets and a characteristic openwork stitch.

linen waistcoats embroidered in red cotton thread. The peasant women are also fond of whitework embroidery and *crivos*, a type of drawn threadwork, while they take advantage of the picturesque designs on their waistcoats to provide inspiration for the decoration of tablecloths and other articles which are exported under the designation of "Guimarães Embroideries."

The Importance of Cross Stitch in Portuguese Needlework
Whether in Portugal or Spain, Germany or Scandinavia, Russia or the Balkans, the people in the countryside cultivate their favorite design motifs and their own folk art.

In the Minho typical peasant embroidery is the "sweetheart's handkerchief," which the young girls embroider to give to the man of their choice and which is a repository of graphic symbols of love. On a small square of material, embroidered in red and blue cross stitch, everything is expressed in the symbolic language of love: hearts, alone or in pairs, in flames or pierced by arrows; branches with tiny birds; shields topped by crowns; human and animal figures; crosses, stars and keys. The border is embroidered with a verse expressing love, a signature and a date. The spelling may not be perfect but the amorous intent cannot be denied.

Cross stitch is commonly employed throughout Portugal. It is with this stitch that the coarse white woolen

Caldas da Rainha Embroidery

A less well-known type of Portuguese embroidery is that found in Caldas da Rainha. It was not exploited commercially and appears to stem from a certain type of Oriental embroidery, though, as has been suggested, it might have been imported directly from Venice for the churches of the town, Venice being an important trading point on the route from the East. It bears a marked resemblance to certain ecclesiastical pieces which are Indian in origin and which are now deposited in the Sacristy of Braga Cathedral.

The oldest examples, which resemble filigree work, are embroidered in cinnamon-colored linen thread and are similar to certain pieces in the Museum of Decorative Arts, Madrid, and the El Greco Museum in Toledo.

The Colchas of Castelo Branco

The distinctive *colchas*, or bedspreads, worked in the Castelo Branco area of the country were made from narrow strips of homemade linen joined together at the edges and embroidered in silks with a variety of stitches, laidwork predominating. They had their origin in the province of Beira-Baixa, around the town of Castelo Branco, where both silk and linen were made. In Spain, in the areas around Cáceres and Toledo, certain works in a similar style appeared at the same time. Both Portuguese and Spanish embroidery reflected the Oriental influence dominant in all early European needlework in the fifteenth and sixteenth centuries but particularly in the needlework of the Iberian peninsula, influenced as it was by its conquests in the East. The earliest surviving examples of *colchas* date from the seventeenth century although earlier ones were certainly made.

The designs of the bedspreads were usually elaborate and in many cases very beautiful; the silks glowed with all the colors of the rainbow; stylized exotic flowers and fruit were organized in formal designs and embroidered in exotic new stitches with consummate skill. The country embroideresses with their rudimentary techniques were stimulated by such examples and adopted the learned style of these precious works of art adapting them to their own simple taste and imbuing them with a certain picturesqueness. The ingenuousness and spontaneity of their conception transformed the exotic

fauna of the jungles of Hindustan into domestic animals and poultry and the breathtaking Asiatic flora into the flowers and fruit of their back gardens.

The Tree of Life, a favorite theme in Indian art, appears in the Castelo Branco coverlets transformed into a spring sapling and decorated with leaves, flowers and fruit, and many tiny birds. The thick, straight trunk is sometimes flanked by two figures symbolizing marital bliss and representing the couple for whom the coverlet was intended. Other favorite motifs were roses, canations, bunches of grapes and tendrils, figs, pomegranates, cocks and hens, and the typically Persian motif of a stag, representing the soul, chased by a leopard, symbolic of trouble. Most of these *colchas* are embroidered entirely in laidwork, which was Eastern in origin and fascinated the embroideresses because it did not detract from the beauty of the silk, even when used over large areas. Birds and the smaller

Shoulder of a peasant girl's blouse *(detail)*, *Viana do Castelo (Minho)*, *Portugal, nineteenth century. White linen ground embroidered with blue linen thread in satin stitch, stem stitch, eye stitch, French knots and counted threadwork.* PRIVATE COLLECTION, VIANA DO CASTELO.

Handkerchief, *Minho,
Portugal, nineteenth
century. White linen ground
embroidered with linen
thread in blue and red cross
stitch, 17in × 17in (45cm ×
45cm). A typical lover's
handkerchief of the period.*
PRIVATE COLLECTION,
BARCELOS.

broidered on a pack cloth with plait stitch and counted threadwork, a type of work already familiar in the Iberian peninsula as a Moorish tradition. The woolen thread was colored with dyes extracted from wild flowers which not only produced beautiful shades but also durable colors. As the style of the rugs developed, the exotic motifs such as pine-cones, palms, clouds and lotus flowers were superseded by others which were in keeping with the taste of the country embroideress – vases with posies, animals of all kinds, keys and hearts, sweethearts and ladies seated in the traditional *Alentejo* chairs and, later on, ribbons and garlands in the rococo style. At this time, William Beckford (1760–1844), the curious English writer and collector who traveled throughout Portugal, mentioned in a letter, dated 1787, that he "had observed in *Arraiolos* more than three hundred artisans working in the manufacture of tapestry and embroidery."

Even then it was a highly successful regional industry, but in recent years it has developed considerably because of the increasing importance of the industry. Currently orders for the rugs are sometimes accompanied by modern designs which demonstrates that this kind of rug can be adapted perfectly to modern requirements.

flowers were often worked in a lighter stitch.

Over the centuries the coverlets reflected many influences, the exotic inspiration from the East being succeeded by the influence of Western decorative art, and so it was that they became a vast repository of decorative designs taken over an extended period from Europe and Asia.

The Embroidered Rugs of Arraiolos

Arraiolos is the name given to the embroidered rugs made in this town in the Alentejo province – a cottage industry both secular and ecclesiastical in origin which found its home in this region mainly because of the great flocks of sheep which provided abundant supplies of wool. The influence of beautiful imported examples from the East, whose designs it was only necessary to copy, was another factor.

The earliest examples of *Arraiolos* work date from the seventeenth century and are copies of Persian rugs brought back by the Conquistadores. The original models were made on a loom while the copies are versions made with coarse needles and woolen thread em-

The Embroidery of Madeira and St. Miguel

The island of Madeira is well known as a center for the production of embroideries, made by the peasant women from the mountainous interior of the island and by girls under the supervision of Catholic nuns in the island's convent. The earliest embroideries were English in character – heavily worked with eyelets and cutwork – which became known from the 1880s as "*broderie Madère*," or "Madeira work."

Plumetis, or whitework, of extraordinary delicacy, only comparable with the Swiss embroideries of St. Gallen in Appenzel was also produced at this time but this work has recently been superseded by the whitework embroideries imported from China.

The entrepreneurs of this profitable industry are at present exporting tablecloths and napkins in Richelieu cutwork, and small pictures in *petit point*.

Belgium

BELGIUM HAS BEEN CELEBRATED FOR FINE textiles for many centuries. Its magnificent tapestries and lace equaled, if not surpassed, those produced elsewhere in Europe and it excelled in embroidery too, particularly in the fifteenth and sixteenth centuries. In Belgian embroidery the accent has always fallen heavily on professional work. Like tapestry and lace, embroidery is a luxury trade and for it to prosper and reach high standards a large measure of professionalism is essential.

Ecclesiastical Embroidery in the Fifteenth Century

The art of embroidery seems already to have been flourishing in the Southern Netherlands in the thirteenth and fourteenth centuries, but at that time its fame was eclipsed by that of *opus anglicanum*. Nonetheless, it was already known elsewhere in Europe. Among the costly vestments given by Charles de Blois (1319–64) to Rennes Cathedral in France, for example, there were some from Bruges in addition to those from England; while in the fourteenth century there are records of Southern Netherlandish embroiderers working as far afield as Italy and Spain, as well as in France.

It was under the rule of the Dukes of Burgundy in the fifteenth century that Southern Netherlandish embroidery reached a degree of refinement and brilliance unparalleled at that time. In the Middle Ages pictorial embroidery or painting with the needle was the highest skill of the professional worker and all his technical expertise was placed at its service. The special contribution made by the Southern Netherlands was perhaps the invention and certainly the perfection, of the *or nué* technique. As a means of pictorial expression it was comparable to that of manuscript illuminations with their shimmering gold grounds.

Embroiderers in the Middle Ages invariably worked in close collaboration with painters, to whom they looked for their designs. In 1386 there is already a mention of the embroiderer Hendrik van der Leeubrugghe working with the painter Melchior Broederlam (active 1381–1409), and in the fifteenth century we find the pictorial compositions on embroideries following the styles of contemporary painting very closely.

This is nowhere better illustrated than in the most magnificent ecclesiastical embroideries to have survived from the fifteenth century, the vestments of the Order of the Golden Fleece, which were in all probability made in Brussels. The vestments do not bear any of the emblems of the Order, which was founded by Philip the Good in 1429, and it is therefore thought that they must have been started before that date, probably for the Duke's private chapel, and that he eventually presented them to the Order. They are first mentioned in the Order's inventory of 1477. The set was made during the course of the second and third quarters of the fifteenth century and thus the styles of a number of different artists are reflected in them. The altar frontal and dossal are the earliest pieces in the set and must have been designed by an artist from the school of the Master of Flémalle (1378/9–1444). The representation of the Holy Trinity on the dossal is a version of a composition by him that was widely copied. The copes and dalmatics, with their many figures of saints, reflect the style of Rogier van der Weyden (c.1400–64), while the chasuble bears scenes of the Baptism of Christ and the Transfiguration with large figures which show the influence of Hugo van der Goes (active c.1467–82). The whole set is in a remarkably good state of preservation, with even the seed pearls and precious stones still in place, and it gives an excellent idea of the splendor and richness combined with subtlety of design and execution that the Southern Netherlandish embroiderers achieved at this time.

Among other notable pieces from the period should be mentioned the embroideries from the Cope of the Seven Sacraments at Berne, which was presented to Lausanne Cathedral in Switzerland by Count Jacques de

Forte domi Gracchus geminos ut ceperat angues   Gracche, marem, uxori: Tuscus respondit aruspex: Quid non se debere tuis, Cornelia, tandem
   Maremque, faeminamque: si dimiseris,   Sin faeminam mors ingruet prior tibi.   Maritus arbitratus est uirtutibus?
      Maluit ille marem, seseque proinde, necari, Tantae superstes quam manere coniugi.

Romont, who died in 1486. The designs
for these embroideries are preserved in
Oxford. They again clearly reflect the
style of Rogier van der Weyden, as do
embroidered roundels with scenes from
the lives of St. Catherine of Alexandria
and St. Martin in the Metropolitan
Museum of Art, New York. Nothing is
known of the embroiderers of any of
the pieces so far mentioned, but at
Notre Dame in Bruges there is an
orphrey embroidered with a Tree of
Jesse design, made by Jehan Marchant

of Brussels in 1497, which in all probability was one of a number of vestments presented in memory of Mary of
Burgundy.

By the end of the fifteenth century,
there were embroidery workshops in all
the important towns and cities in the
Southern Netherlands and in some
smaller centers as well. In some places,
such as Antwerp, the embroiderers, or
acu pictores (painters with the needle),
were members of the Guild of St. Luke,
to which the painters and sculptors also
belonged, but elsewhere, as in Brussels
and Bruges, they had a guild of their
own. At Ghent, where the trade in the
Middle Ages was probably not so important as in Brussels, Bruges and
Antwerp, the embroiderers belonged to
the same guild as other groups of
needleworkers, the makers of surcoats
and the makers of quilts and mattresses.

The bulk of the professionals were
men, but there appear always to have
been a number of women workers too
and wives would often adopt their
husbands' trade. A certain amount of
embroidery was also done by nuns.
The name of Joffrauw Ridderbosch of
the small *béguinage* (convent) has been
recorded in Ghent, while at Courtrai at
a slightly later date in 1526, the nuns at
the Sion Covent are recorded as beginning to do fine needlework and embroidery. They were trained by a pro-

fessional, who at first assisted them with the finishing of ecclesiastical vestments. Later they became fully competent to work on their own and to teach the girls at their school.

The rules of apprenticeship varied from place to place, but one standard rule maintained that a trial piece had to be made before an apprentice could become a master. In an ordinance of 1408 at Ghent it was laid down that this must be a figure, while the would-be master also had to have a recommendation from a priest and pay a given sum of money. Standards and methods of work were strictly controlled. Regulations stipulated, for example, that gold thread of inferior quality might not be used in the same piece of work as the best gold, Cyprus gold; that silk thread might only be used in conjunction with gold and silver thread or on silk grounds; and that old materials or fragments of embroidery might not be used in conjunction with new.

As we shall see, there are a number of documents of the sixteenth century that shed much light on how the embroiderers worked, but it may be noted at this point that the making up of the completed embroidery was often done by another worker. For example, the vestments for which Jehan Marchant of Brussels embroidered the orphrey in 1497 were made up by Jehanne van de Smesse, while the same set also included four white velvet tunicles for choirboys made by Jehan Govaerts of Bruges and bearing the arms of Burgundy embroidered by Jehan Ghisbrecht of Bruges. It may further be noted that an important part of the work of professional embroiderers and nuns of all periods was the repair and restoration of old embroideries.

Secular Embroidery in the Fifteenth and Sixteenth Centuries

Embroiderers in the Southern Netherlands, as elsewhere, did not depend only on commissions for ecclesiastical embroidery for their livelihood in the Middle Ages. On the contrary, it seems that such wealthy patrons as the Dukes of Burgundy ordered just as much embroidery, if not more, for secular purposes. The most remarkable piece of evidence for this is the documentation of the duel that took place at Bruges in 1425 between Philip the Good and Henry, Duke of Gloucester. The Duke of Burgundy was obviously

determined to outdo his rival in splendor as well as in feats of arms. He put the whole décor of the occasion into the hands of the Parisian embroiderer, Thierry de Chastel, along with a painter and an armorer; but for the execution of the embroideries, embroiderers were called in from all over the Southern Netherlands. The names recorded include those of seven men and women from Bruges, three from Brussels, three from Lille and numerous others from Ghent, Malines, Antwerp and Tournai, many of whom had worked for the Duke in the past. Prominent among them was Simon de Brilles, the Duke's embroiderer at Bruges who, with the painter Colart de Voleur (died after 1453), designed and made horse caparisons, tabards, coats of

Canon Bernardinus de Salviatus and Three Saints (detail), by Gerard David (c.1460–1533), Southern Netherlands, 1498–1519. This detail shows St. Martin clad as a bishop in a miter richly embroidered with metal thread and cord, pearls and precious stones, and a cope with embroidered orphreys and hood. The saints and scenes under the architectural canopies, containing a mixture of gothic and renaissance elements, are typical of the early sixteenth century. NATIONAL GALLERY, LONDON.

arms, banners and the ducal tent. The latter was made of blue and white satin and embroidered with the arms of all the lands belonging to the Duke and with his motto and the Burgundian emblem of the flint and steel.

Almost no secular embroidery has survived from this period, but there is a cope which gives a good idea of how coats of arms and emblems were used to create a truly spectacular effect. It is part of a set of vestments captured by the Swiss after their defeat of the Burgundians at Murten in 1476. The booty taken on that occasion also included an embroidered flint-and-steel device which probably came from a tent. Surviving armorial work of a later period includes a tabard of the time of the Archduke Albert (1559–1621) and his wife Isabella (1598–1621) in the Byloke Museum, Ghent, and other seventeenth-century tabards in Vienna.

There are numerous other records of medieval secular embroidery and from them it is clear that the work was mainly armorial or emblematic in character. For example, in 1421 Jehan Fretelman of Ghent embroidered for Madame Dor, the Duchess of Burgundy's fool, a sleeve and hood done in pearls and another sleeve depicting a child blowing bubbles and a nutshell, both emblematic of the transitoriness and fragility of life. In addition to embroidered costume, there are also references to hangings for rooms, armorial covers for the ducal barge and similar objects.

Commissions were also forthcoming from such bodies as town councils and these often included orders for less fine work done in linen or wool. An example of this type of commission appears in a record of 1412 relating to the making of several banners for the town of Bruges by Hendrik van der Leeubrugghe; another of 1483–4 records the ordering by Ghent town council of embroidered coats of arms for hangings and cushions of green cloth; and one of 1533 records an order placed by the Clothiers' Guild of Ghent for "five shears" in embroidery for sleeves.

Ecclesiastical Embroidery in the Sixteenth Century

Early in the sixteenth century the influence of the Italian Renaissance began to make itself felt in Southern Netherlandish embroidery design as in the painting. The most beautiful

example of work in the new style is probably the altar frontal from the chapel of the old Hôtel Nassau in Brussels, which is now in the Musées Royaux d'Art et d'Histoire. It bears five New Testament scenes relating to the theme of the Eucharist executed in the most skillful *or nué* technique in designs in which some of the figures are reminiscent of the style of Quentin Massys (1465/6–1530).

The remarkable series of vestments preserved at the Norbertine Abbey of Averbode in Brabant span a large part of the sixteenth century and with them are preserved a number of documents which identify the embroiderers involved and reveal something of their methods of work. The series begins with a cope that is probably the one referred to in a document of 1523 recording a payment made to Pierre de Hesbene, an embroiderer of Lierre. The central motif on the hood of the cope is a representation of the Holy Trinity which is still rendered in the same vein as that on the Golden Fleece embroideries, thus illustrating the length of time that the gothic tradition persisted in some workshops. A later cope of *c*.1530 shows a transitional stage with a combination of gothic and renaissance elements in the architectural settings of the scenes.

Averbode's greatest patron of the arts was Abbot Mathieu s' Volders de Rethy and it was during his term of office, from 1546 to 1565, that the fully developed renaissance style emerged. Prominent among the many rich vestments commissioned by him is a cope dated 1554 with orphreys and hood bearing scenes from the life of St. Matthew, his patron saint, embroidered by François van Yeteghem of Lierre. A large part of the design consists of sumptuous renaissance ornament, foliate scrolls with flowers and fruit and grotesque masks, while the arrangement of the scenes in circular medallions was one very commonly adopted in the sixteenth century to replace the architectural settings previously in vogue. This cope may be compared with an earlier set of vestments given to St. Bavo's, Ghent, by Abbot Lieven Hugenois. They date from between 1517 and 1535 and again are illustrated with scenes from the life of the Abbot's patron saint, this time St. Livinus, the designs of which are attributed to the painter, Gerard Horenbout (*c*.1465–1540).

OPPOSITE, ABOVE:
Cope with orphreys and hood bearing scenes from the life of St. Matthew, embroidered by François van Yeteghem, Lierre, Southern Netherlands, 1554. Linen ground embroidered with silk and gold threads. The hood of the cope bears the arms of Abbot Mathieu s' Volders de Rethy of Averbode Abbey (1546–65) and must have belonged to the same set of vestments as a chasuble with orphreys bearing medallions with scenes from the life of St. Matthew which the Abbot ordered from François van Yeteghem in June 1550. This type of design with circular medallions and renaissance scrollwork was frequently used for orphreys in the second half of the sixteenth century.
AVERBODE ABBEY, BRABANT.

On one of the St. Livinus embroideries the Abbot is shown kneeling before his patron saint and Abbot Mathieu of Averbode had himself likewise depicted on another of the vestments he ordered, a chasuble dated 1564. The embroidery was the work of Jean Scherniers of Lierre, who sewed a paper into the lining of the cross orphrey bearing the inscription: "Jean Scherniers, master in the town of Lierre, embroiderer to my Lord the Prelate of Averbode and to my Lord of Tongerlo." The chasuble, together with a dalmatic and tunicle, was made to match a cope, also bearing scenes from the life of the Virgin, which had been made by Jean Scherniers in 1554 under the auspices of Barthélemy van den Kerckhoven of Brussels, an embroiderer of high repute, who is now known mainly for a set of vestments of 1562 in the church of St. Gudule in Brussels. Scherniers obviously proved himself worthy of this recommendation, for the contract of 1563 for the matching vestments is made out to him in his own right. In it the details of the subject matter and the measurements of the embroidery are set out most minutely and it is further specified that the ground is to be made of the "best, finest and smallest gold that can be worked."

More light is shed on the work of the professional embroiderer by another set of vestments at Averbode. The dalmatic and tunicle of this set, which is decorated with episodes from the life of Christ and Old Testament prefigurations of them, are known to have been made in 1561–2. They are exactly similar in style, but in fact they are the work of a number of different hands. The orphreys of the dalmatic were made in 1561 by Paul van Yeteghem, the son of François, and his sister Edbeth. When their part of the work was done, the orphreys were sent to Malines, where Gommaire Vervaren executed the faces and other flesh parts. The orphreys of the tunicle, on the other hand, were entrusted to the brothers Pierre and Antoine van Roesbroeck of Lierre, again with the possibility that the flesh parts could be done elsewhere, while the frames of the medallions and the borders were to be done in the Abbey itself.

Clearly, then, there could be a considerable division of labor, but in spite of this a unified effect was ensured by

BELOW:
Hood, *detail of cope illustrated above. This detail of a circular medallion shows the martyrdom of St. Matthew. The arms and* initials of Abbot Mathieu s' Volders de Rethy and the date appear in the border below this detail. AVERBODE ABBEY, BRABANT.

Chasuble *(detail) with orphreys showing scenes from the* Life of the Virgin *and the donor embroidered by Jean Scherniers, Lierre, Southern Netherlands, 1564. Linen ground embroidered with polychrome silks and gold thread. On the cross orphrey on the back, just below the central medallion of the* Assumption of the Virgin, *Abbot Mathieu s' Volders de Rethy of Averbode is shown kneeling in adoration. He is wearing a sumptuous cope and behind him stands a monk holding his miter. The order for the set of vestments to which this chasuble belongs is dated 1 March, 1563.* AVERBODE ABBEY, BRABANT.

the exact specifications laid down, the fact that the designs were supplied by the Abbot himself and that the contract stipulated that the work in the second vestment should be exactly the same as that in the first. The documents further reveal that the embroiderers themselves had to furnish all the materials needed for the work.

In addition to the arms of Abbot Mathieu the vestments also bear those of Abbot Mathias Valenteyns, who was elected to office in 1591. In those troubled times it was no longer possible for prelates to commission such costly work and all the Abbot could do was associate himself with the munificence of his predecessor. There is, indeed, considerable evidence of a decline in the quality of embroidery in the second half of the sixteenth century, when many embroiderers fled the country because of religious persecution. In Lierre, for example, there were about one hundred embroiderers at work in the 1550s, but by about 1580 there were far fewer; and the same is true of Mal-

ines and other centers. This did not, however, spell the end of the old tradition in the Southern Netherlands, for trade regained its old impetus once more when peaceful times returned. Moreover, there continued to be a remarkable maintenance of emphasis on pictorial embroidery, which held a dominant position almost without a break up to the end of the nineteenth century.

Whitework

Not only did the influence of the Renaissance effect changes in ecclesiastical embroidery, but it also brought a great growth of linen embroidery for domestic use. A painting of the Holy Family by Joos van Cleve (*c.*1490–1540) of Antwerp, which dates from around 1520, already shows a linen sampler bearing scattered motifs in the manner characteristic of this early period. In the Southern Netherlands, white embroidery on linen was soon to become an important luxury trade. It was, of course, closely bound up with the lace industry, which developed at the same time.

The beginnings of both industries are recorded in a remarkable set of documents relating to a shop selling fine lace and embroidered linen which belonged to the famous Antwerp printer Christopher Plantin (1514–89). It was largely run by his daughters, Martine and Catherine, who seem to have already become competent business women by the tender ages of eleven and thirteen. Among the fine white embroidery they commissioned from workers in Antwerp were borders and collars for shirts, shifts and handkerchiefs in raised embroidery in white in designs of rosettes, stars and *fleurs-de-lys* in cutwork or edged with little picots or "pearls." Their records of the makers of this embroidery are in Flemish and the workers here were all women, some of them nuns, whose status was clearly a good deal lower than that of the professional embroiderers previously discussed, although their approach to their work was no less professional for that. For business dealings with their customers, prominent among whom was Pierre Gassen of Paris, supplier of linen to the French court, French was used.

Geared to an international market, the whitework produced in the Southern Netherlands was always international in

LEFT, ABOVE:
Whitework handkerchief,
Belgium, c.1840. Muslin
ground embroidered with
linen thread, 17¾in × 17¾in
(45cm × 45cm). This
handkerchief, which bears a
crowned S and the arms of
The Netherlands and
Würtemberg, belonged to
Queen Sophie of The
Netherlands, the wife of
William II and the daughter
of the King of Würtemberg.
It is very close in style to a
whitework fichu in the
Musées Royaux d'Art et
d'Histoire in Brussels and
was in all probability made
in Belgium. It shows the
subtle effects of light and
shade characteristic of the
best whitework of the period.
RIJKSMUSEUM, AMSTERDAM,
ON LOAN FROM THE DUTCH
ROYAL COLLECTION.

style, the designers looking to other
countries for their models. It is probably significant that the only pattern
books for linen embroidery and lace
printed in the Southern Netherlands
were two books by Peter Quentel,
published by Willem Vorsterman in
Antwerp some time after 1527. In the
sixteenth and seventeenth centuries it
was largely French models that were
followed; in the eighteenth century,
southern Germany became all-important. The quality of work produced in
the Southern Netherlands remained
consistently high, however.

Among the correspondence of
Caroline d'Halluin, a dealer operating
in high-class lace in Brussels in the
eighteenth century, there are letters of
the 1740s and 1750s to a Jacques
Bassenge in Dresden, in one of which
she refuses to buy some embroidered
ruffles sent by him on the grounds that
she could obtain work that was just as
good locally. In the nineteenth century,

LEFT, BELOW:
Portrait of an Unknown
Woman by Pieter Pourbus
(?1523–84), Southern
Netherlands, c.1555–60.
Fine white embroidery and
cutwork are evident on the
collar of the lady's shift and
the undercap. Whitework of
this type was one of the
luxury trades of the Southern
Netherlands from the
sixteenth century onward. As
such it faithfully followed
international styles and was
closely linked with the
flourishing lace industry.
GEMÄLDEGALERIE ALTE
MEISTER, STAATLICHE
KUNSTSAMMLUNGEN,
DRESDEN.

Table carpet *showing the Loves of Gombaut and Macée, possibly Antwerp, Southern Netherlands, c.1600. Linen ground executed in canvas work with wool and silk, 108in × 65in (275cm × 157cm). The story shown in the borders of this table carpet was a popular subject for tapestries in the sixteenth century. Three tapestries featuring it bear Bruges marks and the exuberant pattern of its center suggests that it too is Flemish in origin.* METROPOLITAN MUSEUM OF ART, NEW YORK. COLLECTION OF IRWIN UNTERMEYER, 1954.

too, we find the Frenchman Félix Aubry, writing in his report on the lace and embroidery exhibited at the Great Exhibition of 1851, that Antwerp still maintained its old reputation for whitework.

Because of its international character, it is seldom possible to distinguish Southern Netherlandish whitework. A handkerchief with delicately delineated flowers in satin stitch, set against drawn threadwork grounds of eight different patterns of an extreme refinement of execution, was in all probability made in Belgium.

Canvas Work

As well as being a center for whitework, Antwerp was famous for its canvas work, another technique that came into prominence in the sixteenth century. The work is again international in character, which makes it difficult to distinguish Southern Netherlandish pieces unless, as rarely happened, they were signed, as in the case of a hanging of 1549 in the Victoria and Albert Museum in London, which bears the name of Rolof Vos. It has a design of vases, flowers and fruit in lozenges outlined by patterned strapwork and a border of renaissance ornament: vases, masks, acanthus scrolls, grotesques and an emperor's head in a cartouche.

Canvas work is often linked to tapestry design, as is certainly true of a table carpet which has wide borders illustrated with pictorial scenes from the story of the Loves of Gombaut and Macée, frequently employed in sixteenth-century tapestry design. The central design of flowers and fruit in vases and cornucopiae with a wreath in the center has a bold exuberance characteristic of Southern Netherlandish design.

The pictorial element remained strong in Southern Netherlandish canvas work, as in other types of embroidery. There are, for example, records relating to Maria-Jacoba Werbrouck (1721–1801), who lived in Courtrai and was famous for her canvas-work pictures. Among work by her left after her death were pictures of St. Peter and St. Paul, seven small pictures of the Virgin, pictures of an old woman, a flute player and a sleeping child and twelve chairs with upholstery representing the twelve Apostles.

Ecclesiastical Embroidery in the Seventeenth Century

Although pictorial embroidery continued to be used on church vestments in the seventeenth century, it was no longer the dominant feature as it had been previously, except in rare instances, illustrated by an altar frontal of 1642 in St. Salvator's Church in Bruges. This bears half-length representations of the Virgin and saints and the arms of Nicolaas van Troostenberghe, Abbot of Eeckhoutte. Pictorial scenes continued to reflect contemporary styles of painting, as evidenced by the chasuble with an Adoration of the Shepherds in the style of Rubens

(1577–1640) and Van Dyck (1599–1641), but they were now contained in cartouches in heavy metal thread embroidery in high relief and often accompanied by borders of flowers or scrolls. Baskets and bunches of flowers and fruit in a lush naturalistic style became the principal type of ornament on ecclesiastical vestments in the seventeenth century, while by the end of that period pictorial medallions were often replaced by sacred monograms or coats of arms.

Secular Pictorial Embroidery in the Seventeenth Century

In the seventeenth century, embroidered pictures came into use for the decoration of houses and furniture. One fine example is closely modeled on a print after a composition by Lucas van Leyden (?1494–1533), and its maker, Jan Haseloff, about whom little is known, displayed great technical skill in following every line of the engraver's burin with his needle. Certain details are executed in gold and silver thread while other materials and techniques, jet beads, knots and picots, are also used in places. Here again virtuosity was placed at the service of pictorial representation.

The making of small landscapes, seascapes and genre pictures in embroidery was another of Antwerp's specialities. They were often used to ornament the doors and drawers of cabinets for coins and medals and other small objects.

A Ghent Embroidery Workshop of the Eighteenth Century

Prominent among the embroiderers of Ghent in the eighteenth century was Jakob de Rynck (c.1680–1737). His will, which reveals him to have been a prosperous man, records that he had the best part of two hundred pounds invested in gold and silver thread. He also supplied metal threads to other embroiderers and kept a shop where they could be bought in small quantities, obtaining his supplies in Amsterdam and Lille. This illustrates the major part played by these materials in the work of the professional embroiderer. De Rynck's eldest daughter married a well-to-do Ghent painter, Frans Pilsen (1700–84), who may have supplied him and his son with designs.

From 1722 to 1732 Jakob de Rynck did a great deal of work for the Chapel of Our Lady of the Sorrows at St.

ABOVE:
David with the Head of Goliath *made by Jan Haseloff after a composition by Lucas van Leyden (?1494–1533), Southern Netherlands, known from an engraving of 1600 by Jan Saenredam. This embroidered picture is such a faithful copy that it is possible a print may actually have been pricked and pounced for the transfer of the design. The embroidery demonstrates great technical perfection, particularly in lines and details. Nothing is known about the embroiderer other than his name.*
MUSÉES ROYAUX D'ART ET D'HISTOIRE, BRUSSELS.

Banner of the Guild of St. George *made by Jakob de Rynck (c.1680–1737), Ghent, Southern Netherlands, 1728–32. Silk ground embroidered with silk and gold and silver thread. The banner, which is said to have been made to a design by Norbertus Heylbroeck, bears the arms of Bernard Jacques Coppieters, Lord of Hollebeke, who at that time was Dean of the Guild and who probably ordered it. Jakob de Rynck made banners for all three of the Ghent militia guilds at this period.* MUSÉE D'ARCHÉOLOGIE DE LA BYLOKE, GHENT.

OVERLEAF, BELOW: David with the Head of Goliath, *engraving by Jan Saenredam after Lucas van Leyden (?1494–1533), Southern Netherlands, c.1600. Used by Jan Haseloff as the model for his embroidered picture.* CABINET DES ESTAMPES BIBLIOTHÈQUE ROYALE, BRUSSELS.

Peter's Abbey, Ghent. A set of vestments still survives, which may be the one supplied by him in 1722 at a cost of a hundred pounds. The cross orphrey of the chasuble has a representation of Our Lady of the Sorrows and the other orphreys are embroidered in gold thread with a design of baskets, vases and floral ornament. In the same year Jakob's second wife supplied a chalice veil bearing the names of Jesus and Mary and a Paschal Lamb in an aureole, and there are records of further commissions in 1723 and 1732.

Jakob de Rynck also worked for the three militia guilds in Ghent, embroidering new banners for each of them between 1725 and 1737. The banner for the Guild of St. Michael done in "best blue damask with gold and silver after the model supplied," was paraded for the first time in September 1728. The center, with St. Michael and the dragon, still survives, but it is a good deal less fine in execution than the banner made for the Guild of St. George between 1728 and 1732, which cost twice as much. Jakob's pictorial skills certainly appear to advantage here. About the third banner, that for the Guild of St. Sebastian, nothing is recorded, but it is known that Jakob also made a number of embroidered pictures. Listed in his will are two battle scenes, a basket of strawberries, a representation of Flora and two figures.

After Jakob's death his business was continued by his son Michiel (born 1717), whose work was similar in style. Between 1756 and 1764 he made a good deal of embroidery for his parish church, St. Michael's. Records of 1762 concern payments to him for supplying gold thread and for his hours of work, as well as a payment made by him to the assay masters "for some burnt [melted down] gold coming from old chasubles." In 1774 he was commissioned by the Abbot of Baudelo Abbey to repair and restore some old vestments and a number of vestments were among the stock remaining in his shop after his death. In the National Army Museum, London, there is a banner embroidered by him in 1745 for an English regiment that was stationed in Ghent at about the time, and in the Byloke Museum in Ghent there are two large embroidered pictures by him, an Italian landscape signed and dated 1784 and a battle scene.

In 1807 the death is recorded of a

Italian landscape, *embroidered picture made by Michiel de Rynck (b.1717), Ghent, Southern Netherlands, 1784. Silk or linen ground embroidered with silk threads, 23in × 33in (59cm × 84cm). Embroidered pictures continued to be an important part of the output of the Southern Netherlandish professional embroiderer in the eighteenth century. There is another picture, a battle scene, by Michiel de Rynck in Ghent, while in the will of his father Jakob, five embroidered pictures are mentioned.* MUSÉE A'ARCHÉOLOGIE DE LA BYLOKE, GHENT.

Michiel de Rynck, but it is not certain whether this is the Michiel born in 1717 or whether it is his son. In either case, the embroidery business seems to have declined after that date, the family turning to selling stationery as a side-line.

The Nineteenth-century Revival

By the end of the eighteenth century pictorial embroidery was seldom used for ecclesiastical purposes and the early decades of the nineteenth century witnessed a complete decline. About the middle of the nineteenth century, however, there were signs of a revival. In this, a leading part was played by Louis Grossé the son of P. C. Grossé who had set up an embroidery workshop at Ghent in 1783. After his father's death Louis continued this business, but he also had another and much more important business in Bruges. According to the French authority, De Farcy, Bruges surpassed all the other centers in Belgium in the second half of the nineteenth century in pictorial embroidery. Examples of ecclesiastical work were shown by Grossé at the Paris Exhibition of 1867, including a "rich banner and a case of embroidered figures, the speciality of the firm." There, too, was exhibited a banner designed by William Curtis Brangwyn, who also had an embroidery workshop in Bruges. It

illustrates how closely the old techniques of medieval embroidery had been studied and followed. Grossé showed a similar banner at the Paris Exhibition of 1878 and De Farcy wrote of it: "The composition, taken from Revelations, has been most carefully studied and the execution of the angels and the elders casting their crowns at the foot of the throne of the Lamb leaves nothing to be desired."

The exactitude with which the old techniques were copied is clearly illustrated by the plates on pages 1 and 12 of De Farcy's history of embroidery, which show specimens of different techniques all worked in the Grossé workshop at Bruges. It is significant that De Farcy should have chosen professional work from Belgium rather than France to illustrate techniques in his authoritative book, but from what he writes it is clear that he had a great admiration for the work produced in the Grossé workshop and felt it far outshone anything being done in France at this time. In connection with a set of vestments by Grossé, illustrated as Plate 143, he remarked that "they could compete with the most beautiful productions of past centuries," high praise indeed from so distinguished a historian of needlework. The set in question was made in 1891 for the Bishop of Vannes to celebrate the twenty-fifth anniversary

Banner *showing the Adoration of the Lamb designed by William Curtis Brangwyn, c.1865, Bruges, Belgium. Silk ground embroidered with silk threads and gold and silver threads, 59in × 39½in (150cm × 100cm). A characteristic example of the type of ecclesiastical embroidery produced in Belgium after the revival of interest in pictorial embroidery around the middle of the nineteenth century. The central design, borders and lettering all show medieval inspiration, but are nonetheless nineteenth-century in spirit.* VICTORIA AND ALBERT MUSEUM, LONDON.

of his consecration as a bishop. The embroideries comprise elaborate scenes from the Bible and the lives of saints, together with inscriptions, all worked in a variety of techniques, including *or nué*.

An Embroidered Hanging by Henri van de Velde

Henri van de Velde (1863–1957), the famous Belgian architect and designer, began his career by training as a painter, but by the beginning of the 1890s he had begun to have doubts about pursuing a career in that direction. He had also come very much under the influence of the English Arts and Crafts Movement. After considering for some time whether or not to venture into the field of the applied arts, he eventually prepared a sketch for an embroidered hanging, *La Viellée des Anges*. The

sketch was shown at the exhibition held by the group known as "Les Vingts" in Brussels in 1893. In his autobiography Van de Velde describes how his sister and a friend of hers chose the materials for him. He began by setting to work himself, but soon realized that he lacked the necessary technical knowledge. However, he fortunately had an aunt who lived at Knokke who had trained in her father's embroidery workshop at Ghent, where she had done a good deal of ecclesiastical work. During the winter of 1892–3 she and her nephew worked together on the hanging in a room overlooking the sea and later in 1893 it was shown at the exhibition of "Les Vingts."

It seems entirely appropriate that Henri van de Velde should have turned to the pictorial needlework for which his country was so renowned. But although he was in a way following a very old tradition, his results could scarcely have been more different, as might be expected from such an innovator in the arts. He totally rejected the eclectic mode favored by contemporary professional embroiderers, who looked only to the past. Instead, his hanging shows the sinuous lines of the Art Nouveau style and is reminiscent of such contemporary painters as Maurice Denis (1870–1943) and Paul Gauguin (1848–1903) with its flat planes of color; and his use of the applied-work technique is equally innovatory. Nonetheless, the close link with contemporary painting can still be regarded as typically Belgian.

The hanging was praised as "a work of art of the first order" in a contemporary review and it certainly inaugurated a dynamic career in the decorative arts. However, apart from designing a few embroidered gowns for his wife, Van de Velde did no further work in this field and the lead he had given was not taken up in his own country. It is perhaps significant that the only Belgian contribution to the International Art Needlework Exhibition held in Amsterdam in 1886 was a display of lace. Isidore Derudder (born 1855), a sculptor contemporary of Van de Velde, who also made designs for lace, did design a number of embroidered panels which were worked by his wife and exhibited in Brussels and Antwerp in 1900, but, in the main, modern textile designers in Belgium have concentrated their efforts on tapestry and, to a lesser extent, lace, rather than embroidery.

The Netherlands

IN THE FIFTEENTH AND SIXTEENTH centuries, before the break with Spain, the Northern Netherlands followed many of the same traditions in embroidery as their more affluent Southern neighbors, although other influences were also apparent. After the north gained its independence, however, its arts developed in a completely different way.

Ecclesiastical Embroidery

The earliest surviving embroidery in the Northern Netherlands in the refined pictorial style of Southern Netherlandish work of the late Middle Ages is a dalmatic of c.1490 in the Rijksmuseum, Amsterdam, with orphreys showing various saints. This is regarded as Northern Netherlandish work, although the criteria for distinguishing it from Southern work are inevitably rather vague: namely a certain rigidity and coolness of style whereby, though the scenes may be full of deep feeling, that feeling is expressed in a restrained and sober manner.

A more reliable method of identifying Northern Netherlandish work, perhaps, is to look for associations with contemporary painters, since it may reasonably be supposed that Dutch embroiderers turned to painters for their designs like their counterparts in the Southern Netherlands. On the basis of a record in Hoorn of a commission given to Jacob Corneliszoon of Amsterdam (c.1470–1533) for a Last Judgment and other paintings in the Grote Kerk there, some vestments from Hoorn with scenes of the Baptism of Christ and the Feeding of the Five Thousand have been identified as being in Corneliszoon's style; and a further group of vestments has been associated with them on the grounds of similarities with his woodcuts. It includes vestments from Deventer, Oudewater, Loenen, Alkmaar and Amersfoort, all dating from around the first quarter of the sixteenth century. A second group of this date, which includes vestments from two churches in Leiden, has been associated with Cornelis Engelbrechtsen

of Leiden (1468–1533). All these pieces show the developed pictorial technique familiar from Southern Netherlandish embroidery, with much use of various methods of gold embroidery, including *or nué*. The designs show both gothic and renaissance elements, as was usual at that period.

There was, however, another influence at work in Northern Netherlandish embroidery, that from Germany, which, naturally, affected the eastern and northern parts of the country most. It can clearly be seen in the altar frontal made for the Boatmen's Guild of Nijmegen in c.1494 (Plate 68). This frontal achieves an imposing effect, but it is executed in a much cheaper and quicker manner than the pieces mentioned above. The boat, water and part of the flowery meadow were embroidered separately and applied to the silk damask ground, as were also the figures of the Virgin and St. Olaf, the patron saint of the Guild, which, moreover, are largely composed of pieces of silk damask. The damask background has been cut away under the applied pieces, no doubt for use elsewhere.

Ecclesiastical embroidery on linen of the type common in Germany is also found in the Northern Netherlands. From Renkum, near Arnhem, comes a fine lectern cloth embroidered in silk with the Presentation in the Temple surrounded by four angels; and another example is a small linen cloth with the Virgin and Child in glory surrounded by angels which was made for the Abbot of Aduard Abbey, Groningen, in 1541.

After the conversion to Protestantism of the Northern Netherlands and the break with Spain, the old tradition of ecclesiastical embroidery came to an end. Roman Catholic worship was still tolerated, though, as long as it was not practiced openly, and in the seventeenth and eighteenth centuries vestments, chalice veils and altar frontals continued to be made for Catholic use. They generally followed the styles current in France and the Southern Netherlands, with embroidery in high relief in the later seventeenth century

Linen cloth *showing the Virgin and Child, made for Johannes Recamp, Abbot of Aduard, Groningen, Northern Netherlands, 1541. Linen ground embroidered with polychrome silks and silver thread, 19in × 16½in (48cm × 42cm). This cloth, which shows German influence, is inscribed with the name of the abbot and the date: DOMINVS JOHANNES RECAMP ABAS IN ADWERT 1541. It bears the arms of the Recamp family on the left and Aduard on the right.* AARTSBISSCHOPPELIJK MUSEUM, UTRECHT.

Ex Vulnere Pulchrior *(More beautiful through a wound), emblematic engraving from* Proteus ofte minnebeelden verandert in sinnebeelden, *Rotterdam, Northern Netherlands, 1627. The girl appears to be embroidering a flower picture on a hand-held frame, supported by Cupid, and with the aid of contemporary embroidery accessories.* RIJKSPRENTENKABINET, RIJKSMUSEUM, AMSTERDAM.

and more delicate floral embroidery in the eighteenth. Among the more unusual pieces are a set of late seventeenth-century vestments with beadwork orphreys in the Old Catholic Church in Rotterdam, while there also survive smaller pieces of charm and interest, such as the embroidered burses used for taking the Sacraments to the sick. Mention may also be made in this connection of the fine Mantle of the Scroll of the Law which was made in the early eighteenth century for the Synagogue of the Portuguese Jews in Amsterdam and which is now in the Victoria and Albert Museum, London.

Embroidered Pictures

As a result of the religious persecution preceding the revolt against Spain, numbers of professional embroiderers from the Southern Netherlands came to swell the ranks of those in the north. Since fine pictorial embroidery was no longer in demand for church use, some other outlet had to be found for their skills and there is evidence that quantities of embroidered pictures were made in the seventeenth century. In the catalogue of Charles I's collection of pictures compiled by Abraham van Doort there is a detailed description of a

"Lanskipp peece done in Holland – with a needle in Silke," which was one of five pictures presented to the King by the States General in 1635. That pictures painted with the needle were thought of as equivalent to those painted with the brush is also clear from Dutch inventories, such as that of 1692 of Admiral Cornelis Tromp, which lists among the paintings in his house various embroidered pictures of landscapes, seascapes and pots of flowers. The close link between this type of embroidery and painting is certainly evident in the flower piece of 1650 by Wynant Haelwech. There are two other fine flower pieces, dated 1652, in the Friesian Museum, Leeuwarden.

Embroidered Cushions

Sixteenth- and seventeenth-century account books of such organizations as town councils and polder boards are peppered with entries recording payments to embroiderers for armorial

cushions, which were sometimes ordered by the dozen. From these entries it further appears that the cushions were often made up by another worker and that they were frequently backed with red leather. This branch of embroidery, at least, showed no falling off in demand after the Dutch Republic came into being (it was officially recognized by the Treaty of Westphalia in 1648). A typical cushion of this sort was made for the Delft and Polder Board. Embroidered in colored wools on a blue wool background, it clearly shows the influence of seventeenth-century tapestry – numerous cushions of this type were made in tapestry – but it is interesting to note that it is not done in canvas work, the embroidery technique most closely resembling tapestry, but in the long and short stitch type of embroidery associated with embroidered pictures. Similar cushions were also made for church use, witness three cushions dated 1703 from St. John's Church in Utrecht. The fact that they remained in use until well into the nineteenth century is demonstrated by an example, with a dark green ground bearing the arms of Utrecht, which was made in 1841 and used by the burgomaster of Utrecht until 1852.

Costume Embroidery in the First Half of the Seventeenth Century

In the first half century of the Dutch Republic's existence two distinct types of costume are to be noted among the more affluent classes. Members of the nobility and fashionable society who moved in court circles largely adopted international modes. This also applied to some of the children of the regent classes who aspired to high fashion, albeit they generally eschewed exaggerated styles and chose rather sober colors. The older members of the regent classes, however, favored a somber, puritanical style in which black predominated. Up to about 1635 this black costume, which preserved many Spanish features, might have been relieved by elaborately embroidered sleeves, while women also wore large stomachers, often richly embroidered in gold thread. After 1635 stomachers became much smaller and darker in tone, though they might still be embroidered. Examples seen in paintings show designs of formal coiling stems with flowers and birds.

From paintings by such artists as Frans Hals (1581/5–1666) and Caspar Netscher (1639–84) (Plate 70) we can also see that women wore embroidered coifs. These might be embroidered in either colored silk or blackwork and they also show patterns of coiling stems or delicate sprigs of flowers. They were often trimmed with pink ribbon and usually served as an undercap beneath a cap of fine, transparent linen.

Applied Work from North Holland

Some distinctive regional types of embroidery appeared in the Northern Netherlands in the seventeenth century. In North Holland, for example, there is a group of large covers or hangings in applied work of woolen cloth with additional embroidery in wool and/or silk. The earliest dated piece of this type is a fragment of 1622 in the Rijksmuseum, Amsterdam; the latest, a complete example of 1653 in the Bisschoppelijk Museum, Haarlem. They are all of more or less the same form with black and red grounds and embroidery in lozenge-shaped compartments outlined with patterned strapwork. The motifs include coats of arms, vases of flowers, the Sacred Monogram, horsemen and a favorite biblical subject, the Spies of Canaan; the embroideries also bear mottoes and names. Some of the names seem to be those of the people for whom the pieces were made; others, like that of Diever Edesdochter on an example of 1639 in Haarlem, those of the embroiderers involved. It has been variously suggested that these embroideries were used as palls, pew hangings or sleigh covers, but no satisfactory solution to the problem of their purpose has yet been found.

Friesian Cross-Stitch Embroidery and Whitework

Another regional speciality of the seventeenth century was the *knottedoek* found in Friesland. This was a square linen cloth embroidered in cross stitch in which a prospective bridegroom offered the girl he hoped to win a present of money when he came to ask for her hand in marriage. The cloth was pre-

Cushion *made for the Delft and Polder Board, Northern Netherlands, mid-seventeenth century. Wool ground embroidered with wool threads, $25\frac{1}{4}in \times 27\frac{1}{2}in$ (64cm × 70cm). This cushion, which is obviously influenced by contemporary tapestry cushions, bears the arms of Bavaria which were adopted by the board. In the accounts of the board there is a bill for 1652 which may relate to this cushion and in which is mentioned the name of the embroiderer, Israel Pluvier. Further mentions are one for 1665 of a payment to François van Biesen, embroiderer, for embroidering six cushions with the arms of Bavaria and one for 1668 of a payment to Nicolaes Verstraeten and Michiel Tylle for "embroidering arms and making up cushions in the yacht."* RIJKSMUSEUM, AMSTERDAM.

sented loosely knotted and if the girl
pulled the knot tight it meant that her
answer was "yes." The embroidery of
these objects shows influence from
northern Germany. They usually bear
corner motifs of stylized flowers and an
appropriate verse.

The Tree of Life motif in the center
is highly characteristic of Friesian work,
it being widely used on seventeenth-
century whitework in Friesland which
shows the same sober and very refined
taste as the *knottedoek.* The same motif
is found on handkerchiefs and sheets
between large and elaborate initials
which are often worked in eyelet holes.
A good selection of these "Friesian
letters," which may be compared with
the "Bible letters" on the *knottedoek,*
can be seen on a sampler, and it may be
noted that in the Northern Netherlands
samplers continued to serve as genuine
exercises for practical embroidery until
a surprisingly late date. Whitework
seems always to have been particularly
popular in Friesland and large quantities were made and worn there, but
from the early eighteenth century onward it was mostly in an international
style.

Furnishing Embroidery in the Seventeenth Century

As in costume, so in furnishing, two
distinct styles are detectable up to about
1660 or 1670. The regent classes do not
seem to have used embroidery in their
houses to any appreciable extent, but
in court circles it was quite different.
The inventories of the houses and
palaces belonging to members of the
House of Orange, from the sixteenth
century onward, refer to numerous
embroidered wall hangings, bed hangings and coverlets, table covers and
cushions. They seem to cover the whole

gamut of contemporary modes, although
the Dutch do not appear to have been
as fond of pictorial embroidery as some
other nationalities. Flowers were a
favorite motif, as might be expected.
In *c.*1650 Amalia van Solms, widow of
the Stadholder Prince Frederick Henry,
furnished a bedchamber in the newly
built Huis ten Bosch near The Hague
with hangings of white satin embroidered with large pots of flowers and
borders of wreaths of flowers. The bed
was hung, and the chairs, stools and
table covered, with white satin with
colored silk embroidery of "flower
work" to match.

A further notable feature of these
inventories is the wealth of imported
Indian and, later, Chinese embroidery
that they list. Some of this is heavy gold
embroidery on velvet, but much of it is
in the style of the "room hangings of
Indian stuffs of divers colors with birds
and other things wrought in them" at
Noordeinde, or the "ten pieces of
Indian white satin, embroidered all over
with all kinds of birds and wild animals
in gold and silk of divers colors" at
Buren. Oriental floral embroidery
figures prominently, too, but none of
this seems to have had much effect on
indigenous styles.

From about the middle of the century "flame" pattern embroidery in
Florentine stitch seems to have enjoyed
a vogue. There are a number of references to hangings and upholstery embroidered in this style in the Orange
inventories, and various examples survive. They include the remains of a set
of hangings from Kasteel Ysselstein,

Dolls' house *(detail)*, belonging to Petronella Oortman, wife of Johannes Brandt, Northern Netherlands, c.1700. This detail shows the "tapestry room" with silk wall hangings embroidered in Florentine stitch. Several examples of full-size wall hangings in this technique survive from the seventeenth century, while it was also popular at that period for upholstery. RIJKSMUSEUM, AMSTERDAM.

now in the Central Museum, Utrecht, a set of hangings in a doll's house of c.1700 in the Rijksmuseum, Amsterdam, and chairs and daybeds covered with Florentine stitch upholstery.

Another royal lady with a keen interest in embroidery was Princess Mary, wife of William III and later Queen of England. She was an assiduous needlewoman herself and she encouraged the ladies of the household to follow her example. She seems to have mainly occupied herself with making hangings for rooms and beds and her accounts record the frequent purchase of silks and gold thread for this purpose. The inventory made in 1700 of the palace in the Binnenhof in The Hague shows that the walls and bed in the small bedchamber there were hung with material decorated with bands of embroidery done by her, while the bed also had an embroidered tester, headboard and coverlet. Daniel Defoe's reference to the bed at Hampton Court "of her own work, while in Holland, very magnificent" is well known.

Among the Huguenot refugees who fled from France after the Revocation of the Edict of Nantes in 1685 were many professional embroiderers. In 1688 there is a reference in Princess Mary's accounts to a payment made by her at the New Year to "the French embroidery woman" and her and

William's patronage of another Huguenot, Daniel Marot (1663–1752), leaves no doubt as to their devotion to French modes. Others were quick to follow their lead, witness two fine beds of c.1700 with applied-work hangings in the style of Marot in the Rijksmuseum. One, from Kasteel Rozendaal in Gelderland, has paned hangings of multicolored and brown velvet with scrolling applied work in cream-colored *passementerie* and brown velvet; the other, from Kasteel Eerde in Overijssel, is of green silk damask with applied work also in green and it has the back and tester covered with Chinese embroidery of birds and flowers.

French fashions were to dominate Dutch taste throughout the eighteenth century in both furnishings and costume. There are, however, two types of work which deserve special mention.

Quilting
The Netherlands participated to the full in the fashion for quilting that spread throughout Europe in the late seventeenth and first half of the eighteenth century. Quilting, especially of the corded variety, was known as "Zaanland stitchery," but there is no definite evidence to connect it specifically with the area around the river Zaan, although this was then a rich and flourishing center of industry. Some of the quilted

Quilted stomacher, *Northern Netherlands, first quarter of the eighteenth century. Linen ground embroidered with linen thread, 31¼in × 10¼in × 1½in (bottom) (34cm × 26cm × 4cm). Whitework embroidery or corded quilting of this type was known in the Netherlands as "Zaanland stitchery," but it was probably not specific to the area around the river Zaan. Very neatly worked complex geometrical patterns seem to be characteristic of Dutch quilting.* COSTUME MUSEUM, THE HAGUE.

stomachers and covers that survive from this period show geometrical patterns of an exceptional fineness and neatness, which may perhaps be regarded as typical of the Netherlands.

A great deal of work was also produced in a more international style in which quilting was combined with drawn-fabric work. In addition, it may be noted that a "white satin cover" frequently crops up among lists of bedding in inventories, even when the houses concerned appear to contain little or no other embroidery, and some of these quilted covers have also survived. It is clear from paintings of the 1730s by Cornelis Troost (1697–1750) that they found an important use as covers for the cradle and bed in the lying-in room that formed an indispensable and characteristically Dutch feature of well-to-do houses.

Crewelwork

Crewelwork does not seem to have been particularly popular in the Netherlands in the seventeenth century, but in the eighteenth it was widely used for cos-

tume, notably for skirts of the kind that were worn with a jacket, often of a contrasting material. Grand ladies wore silk, but those somewhat lower down the social scale wore crewelwork of this type. The example illustrated is decorated with a sophisticated design reminiscent of the style of Daniel Marot. It is worked in long and short and stem stitches with French knots, but skirts worked with elaborate designs entirely in chain stitch are also found. In the second half of the century fine crewelwork of this type was no longer made, though a simple variety with small flower sprigs worked in chain stitch remained popular.

Peasant Embroidery

The first appearance of what were to become the traditional types of peasant embroidery occurred in the eighteenth century in the Netherlands, as was generally the case elsewhere. Though the Netherlands cannot boast of such a rich heritage of peasant work as some of the Scandinavian and Balkan countries (mainly, perhaps, because such widespread use was made of chintzes imported from the East in peasant costume), there is nonetheless an interesting variety of work, notably from the village of Marken. Until relatively recently Marken was isolated from the mainland on an island in what was the Zuider Zee and its people set great store by maintaining traditions. Many households still cherish old embroideries and garments. A bodice made of a two-colored shot material with embroidery of various motifs on the front and, on the back, a rose pattern worked mainly in greens and pale yellows, may even be brought out and worn on special occasions. The rose pattern had already become standardized by the eighteenth century and a version of it is still used on the embroidered bodices of today, which have dark grounds and are worked in much brighter, even garish, colors.

The costume of Marken exhibits in many respects the survival of modes going back to the second half of the sixteenth century and many of the embroidery techniques used in this and in other Dutch peasant work have antecedents dating from that time. A series of sixteenth-century paintings of women from villages in North Holland and from round the shores of the Zuider Zee show some of them wearing shifts

Crewelwork skirt *(detail)*, *Northern Netherlands, first quarter of the eighteenth century. Cotton ground with polychrome wool, $37\frac{3}{4}$in × $72\frac{1}{2}$in (96cm × 183·5cm). In the first half of the eighteenth century crewelwork was used mainly for costume in the Netherlands. Skirts such as these were worn with jackets, usually of a different material. The patterned strapwork and acanthus ornament are reminiscent of the style of Daniel Marot (1663–1752).* COSTUME MUSEUM, THE HAGUE.

of which the necks are embroidered in black with geometric patterns or the names of Jesus and Mary. Seventeenth-century samplers from North Holland, Friesland and Groningen have rows of border patterns in long-armed cross stitch which were used to decorate shirts and shifts. Cross-stitch borders were later used in Marken to ornament shirts, cap bands and apron bands, while other favorite motifs from samplers were used on the covers and pillow cases made for the elaborate "show" beds, which were the pride of every household and were never slept in.

Marken cross-stitch embroidery is mostly done in black and in neighboring Volendam, too, men and boys may still wear shirts with simple black cross-stitch embroidery round the neck, a survival of a much more elaborate type current in the past, which had all sorts of cross-stitch motifs embroidered on either side of the front opening, including birds, flowers and biblical subjects such as Adam and Eve and the Spies of Canaan. A more closely worked type of black embroidery is also used for baby garments in Marken and black or black-and-white work was popular in many areas such as the village of Urk or in Friesland, where undercaps were closely covered in embroidery of flowers

and birds. Similar close-packed embroidery, in black alone, is found on undercaps worn in Huizen.

An important branch of embroidery in Marken is the fine whitework, which takes many forms and is likewise based on a sixteenth-century tradition. Some of the stitches worked over the counted threads of the linen ground are still referred to as "Spanish," an indication, perhaps, of their origin. Whitework embroidery is used round the necks of men's shirts, which may perhaps also be decorated with "Friesian letters" in black or red on either side of the front opening, and it is also found on baby garments and bed linen. Other whitework techniques are drawn-fabric work, cutwork and needleweaving and all have their own repertoire of patterns handed down over the centuries through the medium of the sampler. These patterns are mostly geometric, though a bird motif is occasionally found as well.

On the subject of peasant embroidery, and the strictly practical purpose of samplers, mention may be made of the embroidered yokes worn by women in Walcheren in the latter part of the nineteenth century. They were worked in brightly colored wools on canvas with a wide variety of motifs exactly like those on contemporary samplers.

DEWYFWYZEMAAGDEN

Cover, *Marken, The Netherlands, 1868. Linen ground embroidered with silk and linen threads, in whitework and cross stitch, 24¾in × 13in (63cm × 33cm). In Marken cross stitch embroidery is nearly always worked in black. This cover shows the Five Wise Virgins, a favorite motif, and a neatly executed border in needleweaving, characteristic of the fine whitework of Marken. Such covers are used on the "show" beds in Marken cottages.* NEDERLANDS OPENLUCHTMUSEUM, ARNHEM.

Amateur Work in the Eighteenth and Nineteenth Centuries

The earliest surviving peasant embroideries may date back to the eighteenth century and peasant work may have a long tradition behind it, but there is not much evidence from before that time of amateurs having taken an interest in embroidery in The Netherlands, apart from the somewhat isolated instances of the circle of court ladies around Princess Mary or a figure such as Anna Maria van Schuurmann, the famous seventeenth-century blue stocking, whose embroideries, including book bindings, are still to be seen at Franeker in Friesland. Most seventeenth-century paintings of ladies doing needlework show them engaged in plain sewing, marking linen or sewing on lace. But in the eighteenth century a change took place and we begin to find observers commenting that, instead of plain sewing, girls are now learning "only minor kinds of needlework serving to make small ornaments or to deck themselves out." This was one of the results of the dominance of French influence, for at this time numerous "French schools" for girls were set up in the Netherlands, one of the subjects they usually offered being "all kinds of needlework."

This trend continued in the nineteenth century, when Dutchwomen followed the fashions current elsewhere, notably that for Berlin woolwork which found favor in the highest circles. There still survive chairs covered with pictorial canvas work done by Queen Anna Paulovna, wife of William II,

while at Kasteel Twickel in Overijssel there are embroidered chair covers worked by the ladies of the house.

Art Needlework

This state of affairs by no means met with official approval, however. A committee set up in 1877 to report on the state of the decorative arts in The Netherlands commented that the needlework done by women was totally lacking in good taste. A large part of the blame for this was attributed to the fact that embroidery for practical purposes had passed from the hands of professionals into those of amateurs. Steps began to be taken at once to remedy the situation, notably by the Tesselschade Society, which instituted courses in Art Needlework in industrial schools and continually strove to raise examination standards. In 1886 an International Art Needlework Exhibition was held in Amsterdam and there the Dutch entries clearly revealed a tremendous amount of study aimed at reviving old techniques: gold embroidery, holbein stitch, openwork, needlepainting and a wide variety of stitches copied from old samplers and Italian and German embroidery.

The leaders of the revival looked mainly to England for guidance, although great stress was always laid on the desirability of achieving a "national" style. One of the influential books on Art Needlework published by Johanna Naber was in fact a reworking of books by W. G. Paulson Townsend of the Royal School of Art Needlework in 1899 and by Lewis F. Day in 1900, albeit the illustrations were of work done by students of Art Needlework at schools in Amsterdam and The Hague. As in England, so in The Netherlands, a considerable part was played in the revival by architects, beginning with P. J. H. Cuypers (1827–1921), the architect of the Rijksmuseum. He designed church embroideries which were made in the workrooms he set up at Roermond. Another well-known architect, K. P. C. de Bazel (1869–1923), also designed church embroidery, a banner designed by him for St. James's Church in The Hague showing him looking back to the Middle Ages for inspiration. Another commission he received was for the curtains of Princess Juliana's cradle, for which he produced a pattern of motifs in ovals, some of them with a faintly Byzantine flavor.

Design for cross-stitch embroidery *by G. W. Dysselhof (1886–1924), from a series of three pattern books, The Netherlands, published c.1910. The peacocks are typical motifs of the period and both they and the pelicans are highly characteristic of Dysselhof's work. Other designs in the books feature fish, seahorses, animals, flowers and trees and there are also a few refined geometrical designs.* GEMEENTE MUSEUM, THE HAGUE.

"Modern Dutch needlework," wrote Johanna Naber at the turn of the century, "is characterized by an appropriate choice of materials, the avoidance of superfluous ornament, neatness of finish and well thought-out construction." These qualities were certainly clearly in evidence at the important exhibition of Art Needlework held in Haarlem in 1904. Among the designers in the field of decorative arts represented there were Chris Lebeau (1878–1945), T. Nieuwenhuis (1866–1951) and G. Dysselhof (1866–1924), who was responsible for some beautiful combinations of batik and embroidery. The work reflected the two trends present in all Dutch design of the period, including embroidery. On the one hand there were designs in a style close to that of international Art Nouveau, for example, a firescreen with a peacock by Chris Lebeau and a fan with a charming pattern of groundsel by Dysselhof's wife. These show the Chinese and Japanese influence that was one of the strongest sources of inspiration for Art Needlework in The Netherlands. On the other hand there were formal, restrained designs in canvas work or cross stitch.

Developments between the Wars

Up to the First World War emphasis was placed on the careful preparation of designs before they were worked, the drawing and planning of designs being considered just as important as subjects

of study as embroidery techniques. In the twenties, however, all this began to change as the idea of free creativity came to the fore. The break away from traditional ideas about materials is clearly to be seen in the work of Nota Homberg-Hannema, who liked to embroider in wool on thin materials such as silk shantung or crêpe, while Christina van Zeegen, in whose work Japanese influence is still clearly apparent, no longer made carefully thought-out designs in advance, but embroidered freely on the ground materials from rough studies.

At the same time stress also began to be laid on rational embroidery, the design and technique growing naturally out of the ground material or the object to be decorated. This largely applied to linen embroidery and peasant work was drawn on for models. The kind of work produced included simple applied work in squares or rectangles following the lines of the ground material, drawn-fabric work and designs based on the patterns of checked cotton.

A strong influence was exercised at this period by embroiderers trained in German art schools who came to work in The Netherlands. Notable among them was Hildegard Fischer (born 1908), who made a great deal of ecclesiastical embroidery.

The Post-War Scene

One important post-war development

OVERLEAF, RIGHT: Wilderness, *panel designed and worked by Chris Enthoven (b.1908), Amsterdam, The Netherlands, 1950s. Linen ground embroidered with linen threads, 7in × 17¾in (18cm × 45cm). Drawn-fabric work of this type, known as "Persian open-work" in the Netherlands, is one of the techniques used by present-day Dutch embroiderers. Chris Enthoven also makes small canvas-work panels, often depicting biblical subjects.* ON LOAN TO THE MUSEUM BOYMANS-VAN BEUNINGEN, ROTTERDAM, FROM THE STATE OF THE NETHERLANDS.

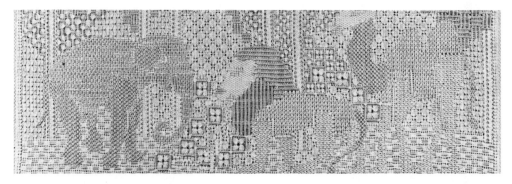

ABOVE:
Door panel, *designed and made by Christina van Zeegen, Amsterdam, The Netherlands, 1924. Silk ground embroidered with silk, 72in × 23in (183cm × 58·5cm). This panel was commissioned for Amsterdam Town Hall. Christina van Zeegen made many embroideries with designs such as this one of a deep-sea weed, which were taken from studies made in an aquarium. They show Japanese influence and were generally worked more or less freehand from a rough sketch.* STEDELIJK MUSEUM, AMSTERDAM.

in the Netherlands was a determined effort to raise standards of embroidery among amateur workers. In this the lead was taken by The Good Needlework Foundation, set up after the war, which works in conjunction with such bodies as The Countrywomen's Association. Classes are held and designs and information published in a quarterly magazine, *Bij Voorbeeld* (*For Example*), which covers an astonishingly wide range of activities and techniques. It features the work of professionals and the exercises in various techniques done by students of embroidery at art schools as well as, at the other end of the scale, creative work by children and ideas for people with failing eyesight.

Among post-war professionals some, such as Chris Enthoven (born 1908), had already been well established before the War. Her small pictorial panels show a remarkable refinement of technique and they also represent a movement that began before the War and has gathered momentum since, namely the making of embroidery for purely decorative purposes. Another important figure in this development was Ernée 't Hooft (born 1911), whose large pictorial hangings also show a very elaborate technique, often in stitches derived, for example, from crewelwork.

Since the 1950s, at least, embroidery has taken a place in The Netherlands beside painting and weaving as a form of expression and decoration. This has been recognized by artists themselves: most specialist embroiderers have had training in drawing and painting, while artists trained in the fine arts not infrequently turn to the medium of embroidery. It is also encouraged by government and local government bodies by the commissioning of embroidered hangings for such places as schools, old folk's homes, chapels and reception rooms at cemeteries and public buildings. The range of techniques in current use is enormous and they cover all degrees of fineness of finish. At one end of the scale it is possible to find the most accomplished drawn-fabric work used for abstract designs by an artist who also makes etchings; at the other, an artist using fabrics as substitutes for paint and making pictorial hangings in applied work of which the stitchery is large, clearly visible and of a fairly basic type. A development of recent years is the introduction of a three-dimensional element by means of padding or quilting, often in high relief, or even by the creation of free-standing figures and objects that are almost like sculptures.

Germany

THE BRILLIANT BEGINNINGS OF THE ART of embroidery in German territories are marked by a series of precious vestments which are historically connected with the emperor Henry II (died 1024) and his family. They are the "star mantle," which Duke Ismahel of Bari presented to the Emperor as a symbol of power comprising the whole globe; the mantle of St. Cunegund, Henry II's wife, with pictures portraying Christ's Incarnation and the chief apostles St. Peter and St. Paul, the patrons of Bamberg Cathedral; the mantle of St. Stephen of Hungary, which was given to Stuhlweissenburg (Székesfehérvár) Cathedral by Gisela, Henry II's sister, in 1031 and which eventually became the Hungarian coronation mantle; and the oldest preserved rational, probably made for Bishop Eberhard (1007–41), the first bishop of Bamberg Cathedral, which was founded by Henry II. These pieces which were of the highest quality both in design and embroidery, were created in southern Germany, where embroidery workshops must have existed at Regensburg and possibly also at Bamberg.

The gold embroidery was of the same excellent standard as the work of goldsmiths and manuscript illuminators in the eleventh century. It was carried out in very fine couched work which suited the background of dark blue silk and achieved a general impression of truly imperial dignity and splendor. The original silk ground has been preserved only where it was covered by the embroidery. The style of these vestments is that of the Regensburg illuminations of the same period, whereas the so-called "choir mantle" of St. Cunegund, which was also made in c.1010 (Cathedral Treasury, Bamberg) and depicts a ruler on his throne, is proof of the strong influence of Byzantine art.

Silk Embroidery from the Twelfth to the Beginning of the Fourteenth Century

The group of eleventh-century embroideries hold a special position in German textile art on account of the importance of their patrons and the precious materials that were employed. In romanesque times, as far as the material is concerned, such costly embroideries worked with a gold thread on a silk ground were only rarely carried out. Examples include the magnificent Rupertsberg altar frontal which is decorated with many figures and dates from the first third of the thirteenth century (Musées Royaux d'Art et d'Histoire, Brussels) and the Halberstadt chasuble with gold embroidered eagles on dark blue silk which dates from the second half of the thirteenth century (Halberstadt Cathedral).

The variety and richness of German embroidery from the twelfth century is demonstrated by embroideries in silk, linen and wool. In spite of differences in intended use, design and workmanship all these pieces rely on a large number of images and detailed narrative with one scene following another. From the monastery of St. Blasien in the Black Forest three vestments, all made within about one hundred years, have been preserved and the workmanship is so similar that it is very likely that they were produced in a monastic workshop there. After the dissolution of the monastery all three vestments were taken to Austria; two of them are in the Benedictine abbey of St. Paul in Carinthia, while the chasuble illustrating the Legend of St. Nicholas is in Vienna in the Österreichisches Museum für angewandte Kunst. The embroideries, most of them done in a regular plait stitch, completely cover the linen. The chasuble, which dates from the late twelfth century, is of conical form and the principal color has changed into a curious yellow ocher; in thirty-eight squares it shows scenes from the Old and New Testament in typological order as well as a variety of saints who were connected with the monastery of St. Blasien. The embroidered pictures on the cope are set in round medallions and portray the lives of St. Blaise and St. Vincent. The latest of the three vestments dates from the second half of the thirteenth century; its center band

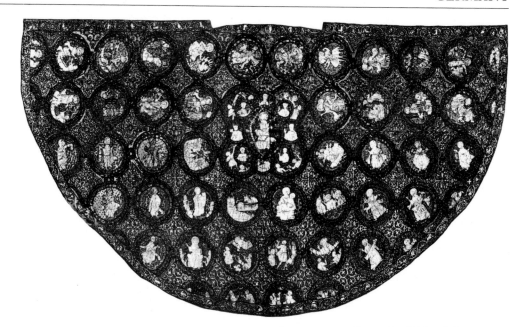

RIGHT:
Mantle of St. Cunegund,
*south Germany, c.1010.
Gold couchwork with up to
56 threads per cm. sewn
down with polychrome silk
threads, 64in × 113in
(162·5cm × 286cm). The
coat was probably donated
by Empress Cunegund to
Bamberg Cathedral. The
middle part shows the
Incarnation of Christ and
the prophecies of His coming
in the Old Testament; on
the right and left hand side
are depicted scenes from the
Lives of St. Peter and St.
Paul who were patrons of
the Cathedral. In the
sixteenth century the
embroidery was cut out and
applied on to a blue satin
ground now reinforced by
cotton.* CATHEDRAL
TREASURY, BAMBERG.

shows scenes from the Life of Our
Lord, whereas the remainder of the
vestment depicts the story of St.
Nicholas.

The earliest example of Lower Saxon
embroidery, a wall hanging of c.1160–
70, showed a richly worked series of
pictures set in four rows, one above the
other, from which only four scenes have
survived: the Resurrection, the Holy
Women at the Tomb, the Pentecost and
St. Peter healing the lame Aeneas
(Kunstgewerbe Museum, Berlin). A
cope in the Victoria and Albert Museum,
London – which has scenes taken from
various legends of saints – demonstrating the influence of English embroidery,
has the same origin. Intersecting circles
create a complicated pattern of star-
shaped compartments embroidered with
scenes, surrounded by lanceolate sections with the figures of dragons. Both
the so-called "Elizabeth chasuble"
(Erfurt Cathedral) and this cope date
from the first quarter of the fourteenth
century. In southern Germany the
beautifully worked altar frontal from
Bamberg Cathedral of c.1300 (Bayerisches Nationalmuseum, Munich),
showing the procession of the three
kings to Our Lady seated on the throne,
represents the transition to the new
formality of the gothic style (Plate 75).

Medieval Linen Embroidery

In Germany whitework embroidery was
of particular importance in the Middle
Ages. The fact that it was this type of
embroidery, *opus teutonicum*, that was
contrasted with the expensive gold and
silk embroidery, *opus anglicanum*, proves

that it was a particular feature of the German tradition in embroidery. It was for practical reasons that work with cheaper materials was often preferred to embroidery on silk with expensive metal threads; however, the choice of a simpler material made no difference to the artistic quality of the design or its careful execution. It certainly had a long tradition in the German territories as is illustrated by the archaic design of the cover from the shrine of St. Ewald (St. Kunibert, Cologne). The scenes from the Life of the Virgin on an altar cover from the Rhineland, which was in the Schlossmuseum, Berlin, until it was destroyed by fire, were comparable in their linear control to high romanesque paintings of the same period. Their mode of expression was somewhat similar to that used for a pen and ink drawing.

In Lower Saxony there are still many linen embroideries from the late romanesque and gothic periods; the numerous monasteries must have been centers of artistic skill, even though a number of these pieces came to the monasteries as donations. In the churches these linen embroideries were used in many ways; for example, as altar cloths, Lenten veils, altar frontals and hangings for lecterns. The most beautiful fully exploit all the different techniques that are possible in white embroidery alone or in combination with colored silk. On linen, which was a popular ground material in the thirteenth century, the figures were embroidered in white linen yarn, which

was enriched by details and shading in delicately colored silk.

By these simple means, a piece such as the hanging with two scenes from the Life of St. Mary Magdalene is deeply effective. This hanging might have been made in the monastery of Heiningen, near Wolfenbuettel, as was an altar cloth which is similar to it in workmanship and depicts Christ in Glory within an oval in the midst of six saints (Convent of Marienberg, Helmstedt). In the detailed rendering of the folds these pieces correspond to the characteristic jagged and spiky style of contemporary painting.

In the work of the second half of the century colored silk played a greater part in the general effect. This is demonstrated in the hanging of c.1270–80 depicting the Crucifixion with surrounding symbolical scenes and thirty-six panels with saints in Halberstadt Cathedral, or in a large embroidery made in c.1290 which illustrates the Life of Our Lord in a number of scenes, now in Brandenburg Cathedral. However, exceptions are the altar cloths and Lenten veils of Lüne Convent, which were created at the turn of the thirteenth and fourteenth centuries and which, apart from one Lenten veil in the Kestner Museum in Hanover, are still in Lüne Convent. These pieces avoid the use of any kind of color and achieve a delicate and beautiful effect solely from white embroidery partly worked in fine raised lines or in sections completely covered by embroidery. The Lenten veils, designed as church

Hanging from a reading
desk (detail), Münster,
Westphalia, last quarter of
the fourteenth century.
Brownish-dyed linen ground
embroidered with linen
thread in chain and two
types of plait stitch, 169in ×
50in (430cm × 126cm). One
of the most elaborate
Westphalian linen
embroideries, it belongs to
the group of works which is
supposed to have been carried
out in the Cistercian convent
at Münster. The ornamental
letters form when read
together, the words of the
Ave Maria, and two prayers
reading in translation, "May
God help us to grow old in
virtue" and "The Lord gives
all but for that he has not
less." ST. MARIA ZUR WIESE,
SOEST.

hangings for use in Lent, have backgrounds in openwork so that the figures
which are only partly embroidered,
seem to hover in front of them.

As the fourteenth century progressed,
Lower Saxon embroidery was worked
even more profusely with pictorial subjects and, in most cases, with richly
colored threads. An example is an altar
cover in Halberstadt Cathedral on
which even the ground is completely
embroidered.

In the early days of embroidery,
secular motifs were only represented in
coats of arms, for example in the hanging depicting the Legend of St. Margaret (Convent of Marienburg, Helmstedt), made at the end of the thirteenth
century, in which one square showing a
coat of arms alternates with a picture.
Plant and animal motifs were also employed, as illustrated by the altar cover
in the monastery at Isenhagen. In about
the middle of the fourteenth century
coats of arms were also used as independent pictorial themes in church embroidery: for example, an altar cloth of
this period is embroidered with a man

on horseback carrying a coat of arms
(Herzog Anton-Ulrich Museum, Brunswick). The simple framing used in
earlier works was replaced by a variety
of shapes such as hexagons, octofoils
(as illustrated by the altar frontal at
Druebeck), and arcading or arches
formed from scrolls and therefore
became an important part of the effect.
On the large altar cloth in Lüne the
wings of the angels touch each other to
form the ogival frames for thirty-eight
pictures illustrating scenes from
Christ's Life.

Arches in the shape of rose tendrils
which first appeared in about the middle
of the fourteenth century, form the
starting-point for a development which
is evident in works of the first half of
the fifteenth century. These plant forms
took up an increasing amount of space
within the pictorial squares so that the
importance of the depiction of figures
decreased in favor of an even decoration
of the ground. This is particularly true
of embroideries on which tendrils form
complete circles so that there is very
little space available for the small figures,
as for example in an altar cloth now in
the Museum für Kunst und Gewerbe
in Hamburg.

In addition to Lower Saxony, many
characteristic examples of white embroidery have survived in Hesse and
Westphalia. In Hesse linen embroidery
enjoyed a vogue in the second half of
the thirteenth century when Gertrud,
daughter of St. Elizabeth, was in
charge of the Premonstratensian convent of Altenberg. It is here that the
most beautiful products of the fourteenth century might have been created
since they resemble each other both in
style and workmanship with their
densely embroidered and dignified figure
style. The cover depicting royal couples
(Museum für Kunsthandwerk, Frankfurt), made at the beginning of the
fourteenth century, and a mid-century
altar cloth (Cleveland Museum of Art,
Ohio), as well as two altar cloths which
bear the names of the three nuns
Sophia, Hadewigis and Lucardis
(Metropolitan Museum, New York, and
Wartburg Collection) and made in the
first half of the fourteenth century, are
possibly all products from this convent.

The Westphalian embroideries
might also owe their origin to the workshops of convents: for example, those
showing the St. Aegidius legend might
have been made at the Cistercian con-

vent in Münster, where the church is the only one in Westphalia dedicated to that saint. These works are almost exclusively hangings for lecterns: accordingly, the cloths, some of which measure over thirteen feet (4m) in length, are normally divided into three sections. The embroidered subjects of two of these face one end and those of the third face the other, since about a third of the cloth was used to cover the top of the desk with the two thirds hanging down in front. Although these pieces were made sometime between the middle of the fourteenth and the beginning of the sixteenth century, they are closely related in technique (two or three types of stitch are used exclusively on the natural or brown-toned linen) and in the general composition as well as in individual motifs. The extremely beautiful embroidered hanging in the Wiesenkirche, Soest, dating from the end of the fourteenth century is an instance of this type of work at its best. In three quatrefoils are depicted the Annunciation, Christ and the Virgin and Christ and Mary Magdalene on a richly ornamented ground, while single decorative letters form two Latin and one German prayer. The archaic design of the arched quatrefoils which frame the scenes is retained in works of a later date, such as the hanging decorated with scenes from the Legend of St. Catherine made at the beginning of the fifteenth century (Xanten Cathedral). Important artistic influences originated from manuscript illuminations and such decorative elements as lozenges and single letters were very frequently adapted from them for needlework.

Wool Embroidery

Needlework with colored wool covering the whole ground formed the third type of German embroidery and was of equal importance. Apart from its artistic significance, its subject matter is of particular interest since secular themes have an important place in these works, even though they were mostly created in or for monasteries, and they throw considerable light on the social life of the time.

Lower Saxon convents are particularly rich in wool-embroidered hangings. In this region the earliest fine German tapestries had been woven and it is probable that from the end of the thirteenth century embroidered wall hangings took over their function.

Already in one of the earliest and at the same time most important examples, the large wall hanging with scenes from the Tristan Legend made in c.1300 (Plate 76), the individuality of this kind of embroidery is apparent. In three pictorial friezes, separated from each other by rows of coats of arms, the crowded narrative is vividly presented in a continuous sequence of scenes. A very dark blue ground forms the background against which the embroidered subjects stand out in a few deep colors. As in all other work of this kind, the so-called *Klosterstitch* (a kind of couching), which follows the contours of the drawing and densely covers the ground, was used for both the background and the figures. Here and in the Parsifal hanging, which has only survived in fragments (Herzog Anton-Ulrich Museum, Brunswick), medieval court poetry was illustrated with the same minutiae of detail as religious themes such as the Legend of St. Thomas or the *Speculum humanae salvationis*, both hangings at Wienhausen.

In characteristic fashion the decorative elements surpass the depiction of the figures in the later hangings; this was the case as early as the fourteenth century in a second Tristan hanging (Wienhausen) and in the Parsifal fragments, and it is particularly apparent in the works of the fifteenth century. The emphasis on the figures set against a neutral ground is lessened by the inclusion of plants and blossoms and wide, richly decorated bands which separate the pictorial friezes from one another to effect a compact filling, like a carpet in appearance. This change is comparable to general developments in embroidery on linen.

The hangings made by the nuns of the Lüne Convent in the years 1492 to 1508 were of an essentially different character. They treated only religious themes, explained by Latin inscriptions, and inserted the individual scenes into round medallions. The didactic theological character of these works is best illustrated by the Easter hanging of 1504–5 (Plate 77). With special reference to the liturgy of the Easter Vigil, it shows the scene of Christ's Resurrection in the center and four symbols of animals in the corners – the pelican, the lion, the eagle and the phoenix – which intimate Christ overcoming death. The seven-pointed star, the moons and the

ABOVE, RIGHT:
Adoration of the Magi,
Suebia or Franconia, c.1450.
Linen ground embroidered
with wool, white linen thread
and silver and gold thread,
39in × 53in (100cm ×
135cm). The depiction of the
figures against a dark blue
background densely filled
with scrollwork is
reminiscent of German
tapestries of the same period.
BAYERISCHES NATIONAL-
MUSEUM, MUNICH.

bells refer to Christ as the lord of time and of the seasons; angels playing music, birds and mystical animals surround the pictures, their esoteric meaning again explained by Latin inscriptions. The design for this hanging and for many others must have been made with the help of a theologian before being worked by the nuns.

There are also a few examples of colored-wool embroidery in southern Germany. The hanging of *c.*1310 to *c.*1320 which the Malterer brothers and sisters dedicated to the convent of St. Catherine at Freiburg (Augustinermuseum, Freiburg/Breisgau) is particularly attractive because of its subject matter and its bright colors. It juxtaposes the consequences of worldly love and Christian chastity in eight separate sections. The stratagems of cunning women shown in this embroidery occur frequently in late Swiss embroideries. Particular emphasis is placed on the representation of fashionable clothing in the large wall hanging at Regensburg, with medallions enclosing pairs of courtly lovers in the characteristic particolored dress. In the way that this piece bears some resemblance to Regensburg tapestries, so the beautiful embroidery made in *c.*1450 and depicting the Adoration of the Magi, is reminiscent of Frankish tapestries; and the Kalchreuth hanging of *c.*1480 worked in colored

embroidery on a black woolen ground, has scenes from the Old Testament as well as a favorite theme in tapestries – wild figures surrounded by swirling tendrils.

Pearl Embroidery

German medieval embroidery offered an extraordinary variety of techniques including pearl embroidery and appliqué work, the latter exemplified in the beautiful wall hanging depicting the Stem of Jesse made at the end of the fourteenth century, which came from Nordsteimke (Herzog Anton-Ulrich Museum, Brunswick). In the combination of corals, pearls and colored glass beads with gilt-metal plates, bright color effects were achieved which are similar to contemporary works by goldsmiths with their precious stones and enamels, as in the altar frontal from the second half of the thirteenth century at Halberstadt Cathedral and a fourteenth-century one from Marienwerder, now in the Kestner Museum, Hanover.

Gothic Gold and Silk Embroidery

Contemporary painting was an increasingly strong influence on silk and gold embroidery after the beginning of the fourteenth century, although other types of embroidery clung to their old traditions. This influence led not only to a stylistic change in the design and drawing of figures but also to a change in embroidery technique. The emphasis on the structure of the single stitch was exchanged for a concentration on delicate and smooth nuances. Chain, split and satin stitches in colored silk, often worked on a ground of couched gold, were the favorite techniques of needle paintings, and optical effects were achieved similar to those of gothic panel painting.

From the artistic and historical point of view, two works from southern Germany deserve special attention: the sumptuous rational in Regensburg Cathedral treasury and the eagle dalmatic which has been a part of the Imperial Crown Jewels since the middle of the fourteenth century (Weltliche Schatzkammer, Kunsthistorisches Museum, Vienna). The rational, the complex theological program which was strongly influenced by the corresponding Bamberg piece dating from the eleventh century, displays the most delicate silk embroidery on the gold ground, while the figures are embroidered with thin lines of colored silk so that they appear almost ethereal.

The eagle dalmatic is as sumptuous as the bishop's rational. Medallions containing eagles and embroidered in gold and silk are sewn on to the purple Chinese silk and there are wide bands of half-length figures which are interpreted from their similarity to stained-glass windows as illustrating the line of succession of the German rulers. These two works relate to Emperor Ludwig (1314–47) and his political activities. A German inscription indicates that the rational was a royal present, possibly given by Ludwig to his ally, the bishop of Regensburg, Nikolaus of Ybbs. The dalmatic, as an imperial vestment, could have been intended to symbolize the lawfulness of Ludwig's reign when he fought the Habsburg anti-king, Friedrich der Schoene in the Battle of Mühldorf who had taken possession of the old Imperial Crown Jewels.

The delicately wrought and expressive group of figures of the Crucifixion and the figures of St. Catherine and St. John the Baptist on the second altar frontal of the monastery at Königsfelden might originate from the Upper Rhine. It was possibly at the request of the royal widow, Agnes, who was living at Königsfelden, that these embroideries had added to them the figures of St. Agnes and St. Andrew – the patron saints of the Queen and her dead husband, Andrew III of Hungary – as well as those of St. Peter and St. Paul. All these figures were then applied to a red velvet ground. The beautiful altar frontal of the Coronation of the Virgin from Kamp Monastery in Westphalia demonstrates similar workmanship, with arcading delicately embroidered in gold and figures separately embroidered on linen and afterward applied to the velvet.

From the end of the fourteenth century onward the origins of embroidery can be authenticated in many parts of Germany. In this connection, it is interesting to note that the organization of guilds for embroiderers was not standardized and must have remained like this for a long time. In 1397 the Cologne embroiderers of coats of arms and the braid-weavers, since the production of both was closely connected, received a joint charter organizing them into a single guild, and this official union was retained throughout the whole of the fifteenth century. At Nuremberg, however, embroidery was practiced as a free trade and as late as 1522 the embroiderers' demand for guild regulations was refused by a decree of the town council, which pronounced "*es soll ir arbait ein freye Kunst sein, wie mit alter herkomen*" ("their work shall be a free art according to old tradition"); however, an addendum to the document insisted that "it should be seen to it that no one works that is not a citizen of the town."

At Wroclaw, now in Poland, the embroiderers were grouped with the tailors so that they are not separately mentioned either in the 1420 craftsmen's rules of the Emperor Sigismund or in the list of tradesmen, although, according to documents, quite a large number of well-to-do silk and pearl embroiderers worked in the town. At Mainz the embroiderers were listed with the tailors and cloth shearers. At Münster embroidery again seems to have been practiced as a free trade, whereas the pearl embroiderers of Duelmen in Westphalia were united in 1575 in the Guild of St. Luke with other craftsmen such as painters, glassmakers, goldsmiths and harness-makers.

Although it is rarely possible to attribute a piece of work to one of the many fifteenth- and early sixteenth-century embroiderers known by name, the fact that their names were recorded

Rational *(detail)*,
*Regensburg, Germany,
1320–30. Linen ground
embroidered with gold
couchwork and chain and
stem stitch embroidered with
silk thread, 24in × 26in
(62cm × 67cm). Fragments
of a German inscription
recording that the embroidery
was the present of a German
king to the bishop of
Regensburg indicate that the
rational could have been
presented by King Ludwig
sometime before 1328 when
he became Emperor, to his
ally, the Regensburg bishop
Nikolaus of Ybbs (1313–
40).* CATHEDRAL TREASURY,
REGENSBURG.

proves that in many German towns
professional embroiderers were at work.
Their share in the production of work
was doubtless very high; it seems that
at that time it was considerably higher
than that of the monasteries, although
these, particularly in Lower Saxony,
carried on their old embroidery traditions throughout the entire gothic
period. In the towns embroiderers enjoyed the best conditions for the
acquisition of the necessary materials
and for cooperation with the painters
who provided them with designs, or at
least with ideas for designs. In towns
they were also well placed for selling
their products and, above all, for obtaining new commissions. Although
extant medieval embroidery comprises
almost exclusively ecclesiastical work, it
is also necessary to take secular works
into account which were made for
aristocrats and the urban rich.

Today we can have only an approxi-

mate idea of the unbelievable number
and the quality of embroideries of all
types which accumulated in German
church treasuries up until the end of the
fifteenth century; they cannot have been
any less important in respect of either
quantity or value than the finest collection handed down from the baroque
period and possibly they were even
more numerous and better in quality.
The famous treasury of vestments of the
church of St. Mary in Danzig is unique:
in spite of its incompleteness, in it are
preserved more than one hundred intact
liturgical vestments which, even in the
twentieth century, give the impression
of a late medieval church treasury.

In the gothic period a change took
place in the importance of embroidery
in the decoration of church vestments.
Increasingly expensive and mainly
figured materials were used and embroidery was limited to such obvious
details as the orphrey crosses and bands.
Thus the detailed narrative series,
which had entirely covered the vestments, and large-scale compositions
more or less disappeared. After the
middle of the fifteenth century certain
designs and themes were used again
and again with only slight variations.
The most frequent theme on orphrey
crosses was, of course, the Crucifixion,
followed by the Virgin and Child; the
arms of the cross and the bands were
decorated with either single or pairs of
saints. This restriction in subject matter
together with the increase in the practice
of embroidery at that time, led to a
certain uniformity in works of mediocre
quality.

The artistic character of embroidery
is determined by stylistic movements
and regional characteristics in contemporary painting. Thus in the late
fourteenth and the early fifteenth centuries the art of Bohemia, which
achieved international importance in
both painting and embroidery, exer-
cized a fundamental influence on German needlework. The beautiful hanging
depicting Christ in the wine-press and
the Throne of Mercy, of Franconian
workmanship, shows figures typical of
this style clad in softly flowing garments
and framed in the convolutions of inscribed scrolls. The influence of Bohemian art is also apparent in Silesia and
as far afield as the Baltic coast. An echo
of this style can still be found in embroideries from the second quarter of
the fifteenth century, for example in the

OPPOSITE, TOP: Plate 67
Cope, *Southern Netherlands, c.1476. Silk and gold and silver thread applied to black velvet. One of a set of three copes from the Burgundian booty captured by the Swiss after they had defeated the forces of Charles, Duke of Burgundy, at Murten on June 22, 1476. This cope bears the arms of the Duke of Burgundy, Zeeland and* Franche Conté and the flint-and-steel device of the Dukes of Burgundy. The copes had been used at a mass held on the eve of the battle to celebrate the tenth anniversary of the death of Philip the Good. GRUYÈRE CASTLE, FRIBOURG.

OPPOSITE, BOTTOM: Plate 68
Cabinet mounted with small panels of embroidery, *the central panel showing the Fall of Man, the others, birds, animals and baskets of fruit, Antwerp, Southern Netherlands, seventeenth century. Colored silks and metal threads on silk. Small embroidered panels were often set in this way in cabinets designed to hold coins and medals. There are* two further examples in Ghent, one with landscapes embroidered in colored silks, the other with flowers embroidered in black silk. ROCKOXHUIS, ANTWERP.

ABOVE: Plate 69
Hanging "La Veillée des Anges," *designed by Henri van de Velde (1863–1957) and worked by the artist and his aunt, Knokke, Belgium, 1892–3. Applied work of silk and other materials with embroidery in colored silks, 55in × 87¾in (140cm × 223cm). The color harmonies in this hanging are greatly enhanced by the embroidered lines which consist of three rows of flat stitches worked in three different colors. The hanging was Henri van de Velde's first venture into the applied arts and shows a strong influence from contemporary painting and the Art Nouveau style.* KUNSTGEWERBE MUSEUM, ZÜRICH.

OVERLEAF: Plate 70
The Lacemaker *by Caspar Netscher (1639–84). The girl depicted in this picture is wearing a coif embroidered in black which is almost identical in the coiling stem design to an example in the Costume Museum, The Hague.* WALLACE COLLECTION, LONDON.

RIGHT: Plate 73
Woman's bodice, *Marken,
Northern Netherlands,
probably eighteenth century.
Cotton on cotton or linen,
17in × 13¼in (43·5cm ×
34cm). Many women in
Marken treasure old
embroidered bodices like this,
which are still worn on rare
festive occasions. The rose*
pattern is traditional. A
bodice like this with seven
roses would be worn by a
bride-to-be when going to
church with her future
husband on the Sunday
between the formal betrothal
and the wedding.
NEDERLANDS OPENLUCHT-
MUSEUM, ARNHEM.

OVERLEAF, TOP: Plate 71
Wall hanging, "A Day On
the Beach," *designed and
made by Leslie Gabrielse,
Rotterdam, Netherlands,
1973. Applied work of
various materials with
additional stitchery,
82½in × 118in (210cm ×
300cm). Leslie Gabrielse is
one of a number of modern
Dutch artists to use the
applied work technique. He
himself says that he works
with fabrics because he
cannot paint, but that he
derives his designs from the
drawings he makes. The
nostalgic vein in his work is
to be found in other modern
Dutch embroideries, notably
those of Ernee 't Hooft.*
ROTTERDAM
KUNSTSTICHTING,
ROTTERDAM.

OVERLEAF, BOTTOM: Plate 72
Altar frontal, *Northern
Netherlands, c. 1494.
Applied work of silk and
embroidery in colored silks
and gold and silver thread on
silk, 38½in × 86in (98cm ×
220cm). This altar frontal,
which was made for the
Boatmen's Guild of
Nijmegen and which bears
the arms of the guild and of
Gelderland and the eagle of
Nijmegen, has an
inscription which reads in
translation:* Jesus – To the
Glory of God and the
Good Saint Olaf. Maria. *It
was in all probability made
for the Chapel of St. Olaf
belonging to the Nijmegen
Boatmen's Guild, when it
was rebuilt in 1494. The
applied motifs are padded
with pieces of paper bearing
texts indicating that they
come from a religious house
near Nijmegen and it was
probably there that the
frontal was made. It clearly
shows German influence.*
GEMEENTE MUSEUM,
NIJMEGEN.

OPPOSITE, BELOW: Plate 74
Embroidered picture, *signed
and dated* W. Haelwech
1650, *Amsterdam, Northern
Netherlands, 1650. Silk on
satin, 20in × 14¼in (51cm ×
36·5cm). Wynant Haelwech
began his career as an
embroiderer, but is said to*
have applied himself to
*painting after c.1639. This
embroidered picture is clearly
linked with contemporary
Dutch painting.*
RIJKSMUSEUM, AMSTERDAM.

BELOW: Plate 75
Altar frontal from Bamberg
Cathedral *(detail), South
Germany, c.1300. Linen
embroidered with silk in
chain stitch and gold
couched work, 33in × 117in
(83cm × 298cm). The altar
frontal depicts in its four*
medallions the procession of
*the Three Kings to Our
Lady seated on a throne
with the Christ Child. In the
corners are the knights with
the coats of arms of
Bamberg.* BAYERISCHES
NATIONALMUSEUM, MUNICH.

Plate 76
Wall hanging *of the Tristan legend (detail), Lower Saxony, c.1300. Linen embroidered with wool in Klosterstich, 88in × 159in (223cm × 404cm). The wall hanging depicts the first part of the Tristan legend which is illustrated in twenty-three scenes each explained by a German inscription. This detail depicts Tristan's voyage over the sea and his fight against Marhold in the upper row and two scenes at Isolde's court in the middle row.* WIENHAUSEN CONVENT.

Plate 80
Sampler, *Nuremburg, Germany, beginning of the eighteenth century. Linen embroidered in silk with stitches which include cross,* *satin and Gobelins stitch. The figural composition and the symmetrical arrangement of the motifs are characteristic of the carefully executed and charming* *samplers of the eighteenth century.* GERMANISCHES NATIONALMUSEUM, NUREMBERG.

OVERLEAF: Plate 81
Chasuble *(back)*, *Convent of Göss near Leoben, Styria, Austria, midthirteenth century. Linen ground covered in silk embroidery, 48in × 29in (123cm × 73cm). Part of the famous pontifical set, the* Gösser Ornat, *the back of this chasuble depicts Christ on his return for the Last Judgement and the nine choirs of angels. The depiction of the Abess Kunigunde and other sections which originally belonged to the chasuble were inserted in the cope when at the end of the eighteenth century the conical-shaped chasuble was cut to the baroque shape.* ÖSTERREICHISCHES MUSEUM FÜR ANGEWANDTE KUNST, VIENNA.

ABOVE: Plate 82
Cope of the so-called Litschauer set *(detail)*, *Lower Austria, c. 1700. Silk embroidered with silks in satin stitch and silver couchwork, 51in × 101in (130cm × 256cm). The curious motif of a hailstorm and the tumbling church tower is said to be a reminder of a terrible thunderstorm with hail in Lower Austria in 1688. Probably the embroidery originally served another purpose, perhaps as wall hangings and was afterward adapted to a pontifical set.* MONASTERY OF ZWETTL, LOWER AUSTRIA.

RIGHT: Plate 83
Chasuble *(detail)*, *Austria, second half of the seventeenth century. White satin embroidered in colored silk with needle painting and relief embroidery in gold, 41in × 27in (105cm × 70cm). The naturalistic flowers executed in needle painting place this chasuble amongst the finest embroideries of this type. It is probably influenced by Friar Benno Haan who once worked in the abbey of Kremsmunster.* MONASTERY OF KREMSMUNSTER, UPPER AUSTRIA.

ABOVE: Plate 85
Wall hanging *(detail)*,
Constance, east Switzerland,
1601. The linen ground is
embroidered with colored
wool, silk, linen and metal
threads, lace, beads and
paillettes and worked in
Klosterstich, 69in × 69in
(175cm × 175cm). This
hanging of the Morell family

shows Luigia Morell with an
embroidery frame indicating
that she had embroidered
the hanging with pictures of
her family. The detail is one
of twelve medallions
depicting the children of the
Morell family.
SCHWEIZERISCHES LANDES-
MUSEUM, ZÜRICH.

OVERLEAF: Plate 84
Chasuble *(back)*, Convent
of the Ursulines, Vienna,
c.1700. Linen embroidered
with silk and gold thread
and silver couchwork, 39in
× 27in (100cm × 70cm).
Part of the rose pontifical
set which originally consisted
of more than thirty pieces,
the nuns are reputed to have

begun work on the set during
the Turkish siege of 1683
and to have continued
working on it until 1705.
ÖSTERREICHISCHES MUSEUM
FÜR ANGEWANDTE KUNST,
VIENNA.

LEFT:
Wall hanging, *Franconia,
c.1410. Linen ground
embroidered with silk thread
in stem, split and chain
stitch, 29in × 49in (75cm ×
125cm). Both themes which
are represented in this
hanging – Christ in the
mystic wine-press and the
Throne of Mercy – depict
Christ's work of redemption
in a symbolic manner
characteristic of the period.*
GERMANISCHES NATIONAL-
MUSEUM, NUREMBURG.

orphreys of a cope depicting ten
scenes from the Life of St. Mary Magdalene and several other related pieces,
which were worked in Danzig for the
church of St. Mary in that town.

Embroidery from different regions
also clearly displays characteristic
features of workmanship and their
similarity to works of other media in
the same region. This is the case, for
example, at Lübeck, where it is known
that there was a center for embroidered
vestments for more than a century, from
the last quarter of the fourteenth century onward. In northwest Germany
Cologne maintained the largest production. The close connection of embroidery with braid-weaving, which already
boasted a long tradition in Cologne, and
the influence of local painting character-
ize the needlework of that town which
reached its apogee in the second half of
the fifteenth century. The fact that the
embroiderer, Johann of Bornheim, who
belonged to one of the families which
were known for several generations as
masters of embroidery in Cologne and
in 1470 was head of the guild, and the
leading figure in Cologne painting,
Stephan Lochner, shared the same
house in 1451 is no coincidence but
substantial proof of the close connection between painting and embroidery.
The works on which embroiderers and
braid-weavers worked together were
many; the pictorial subjects woven into
the bands were supplemented by embroidery, or figures embroidered
separately were appliquéd on to the gold
band.

ABOVE:
Embroidered wings of a
reliquary-altar, *Franconia,
1519. Satin ground
embroidered with gold and
silk threads and enriched
with pearls and paillettes.
These wings which depict St.
Sebaldus and St. Ursula
belong to a small altar which
shows the Crucifixion in the
center.* BAYERISCHES
NATIONALMUSEUM, MUNICH.

OVERLEAF, BELOW:
*Orphrey band (detail),
Danzig, second quarter of
the fifteenth century. Linen
ground embroidered with
gold couchwork and split
stitch embroidered with silk
thread, 110in × 10in
280cm × 20·5cm). This
detail which depicts St.
Mary Magdalene preaching
to the apostles, is one of ten
squares illustrating scenes
from her life. Together with
other related works, it was
probably embroidered in a
Danzig workshop for the
famous vestment treasury of
the church of St. Mary in
that town.* MARIENKIRCHE,
LÜBECK.

The part of west Germany which
bordered The Netherlands, where the
luxurious *or nué* technique in embroidery had reached perfection, was also
noted for its embroideries. Not only in
Cologne and around the Lower Rhine,
but also in Westphalia, where certain
groups of embroidery represent independent achievements in the late gothic
period, the technique of *or nué* was
taken over after the middle of the fifteenth century. At first the West
prompted important artistic and technical innovations, but after the turn of the
sixteenth century the influence of
imported Netherlandish embroideries
predominated. In Cologne the finest
and most beautiful sixteenth-century
embroideries were imported rather than
local goods.

In other parts of Germany ecclesiastical embroidery was also encouraged: on the Middle Rhine there is
documentary evidence of embroiderers
working at Mainz, and also in Franconia, whose center Nuremberg seems
to have offered all that was required to
foster this art. Even a master of the
calibre of Albrecht Dürer (1471–1528)
created designs for embroiderers. There
is, for example, a drawing that he made
for the hood of a cope in *c.*1509 which

portrays the Assumption of the Virgin
and her Coronation (Victoria and
Albert Museum). A large number of
valuable embroideries which were kept
in the treasuries of Nuremberg churches
were donated by the town's patricians.

Just as embroidery had started to
imitate the colored surface effect of
panel painting in the fourteenth century,
so, in the last quarter of the fifteenth
century, it took on the character of late
gothic sculpture through the working
of figures in highly raised embroidery,
thus achieving a sculptural effect.
Although these pieces are not by any
means as numerous as fifteenth-century
orphrey crosses worked in satin stitch,
examples have survived from many
different parts of Germany. The greatest number seems to have been made in
the southern and eastern regions of
Germany and also in Austria, western
Hungary and western Poland. The
artistic quality and workmanship of
such pieces is usually very high, with
rich decoration in pearls giving a special
position of importance to such works:
the orphrey cross of Canon Helentreuter of Breslau embroidered in 1495,
which shows the Crucifixion with
angels collecting Christ's blood in the
center and on either side the half-
length figures of the Virgin and Child,
St. John the Baptist and St. John the
Evangelist, while below are depicted St.
Helena and St. Hedwig, is an example;
a miter depicting the Annunciation on
the one side and Mary and Joseph
adoring the Christ Child on the other is
another (Historisches Museum, Dresden). It is significant that in the attempt
to explore every possibility in embroidery not only vestments but also small
reliquaries were made. This illustrates
particularly well the close relationship
between sculpture and needlework at
this time, the latter assuming the functions of the former.

The Late Gothic Style in the Sixteenth Century and in Peasant Art

The artistry and skill, as well as the
variety, of German embroidery in the
Middle Ages, make it understandable
that it stimulated strong traditions
which for a long time continued to
influence styles and techniques.

In the first half of the sixteenth century German embroidery was still much
more dependent on the late gothic
style than on the current renaissance

style. This is obvious not only in church embroideries but also in the embroidery on linen and wool made in southern Germany and Alsace which shows great similarity to corresponding works in the north of Switzerland and in which a definite similarity in execution is also apparent.

Raised, figurative embroidery continued to be worked with secular themes until the end of the sixteenth century. The use in this respect of coats of arms as well as guild symbols – for example those dated 1574–5 by the embroiderer Wolf Popp from Rothenburg ob der Tauber, who worked at Passau (Plate 79) – simulate embossed and enamelled goldsmiths' work. Of particular historical interest is the hanging of 1571 on which nine figures modeled in cardboard represent in their national costume nine different nations (Museum des Kunsthandwerks, Leipzig).

In Westphalia whitework for church use was made as a "*volkstümliche*" art by peasant women and women of the middle class. Its tradition was maintained over a long period. The greater number of Lenten veils which survive mainly from the seventeenth century were not rich in embroidery but in imagery suited to the purpose of the cloths: Christ's Passion portrayed in pictures and symbols featured most frequently. *Lacis* was particularly well suited to the purpose of these cloths because the embroidered figures give

ABOVE:
Wall hanging, *south Germany, early sixteenth century. Linen ground embroidered with polychrome woolen thread in* Klosterstich, *43in × 35in (110cm × 90cm). The hanging shows four pictures from the Life of Adam and Eve namely the Creation of Eve, the Fall of Man, the Expulsion from Paradise and Adam working while Eve looks after Cain and Abel.* ÖSTERREICHISCHES MUSEUM FÜR ANGEWANDTE KUNST, VIENNA.

LEFT:
Wall hanging, *south Germany, 1544. Black woolen ground embroidered with polychrome wool thread, white linen thread and gold thread. This hanging which shows women working with flax is very similar in theme, composition and execution to contemporary Swiss works.* BAYERISCHES NATIONAL-MUSEUM, MUNICH.

ABOVE:
Linen cover *(detail), south
Germany, mid-sixteenth
century. Light blue linen
ground embroidered in white,
blue and brown linen thread
in a variety of stitches,
55in × 68in (140cm ×
172cm). This fine
embroidery which depicts the
signs of the zodiac shows the
influence of Hans Holbein
the Younger (1497/8–1543).*
BAYERISCHES NATIONAL-
MUSEUM, MUNICH.

ABOVE, RIGHT:
Coat of Duke William V of
Bavaria, *Munich, 1568.
Violet velvet ground
embroidered with gold and
silver threads, cords and
some raised work, length 37in
(95cm). Worn by Duke
William V at his wedding in
1568, this coat in the late
Italian renaissance style, is
a beautiful example of
court fashion.* BAYERISCHES
NATIONALMUSEUM, MUNICH.

the impression of hovering in front of
the openwork ground through which
the light passes. Of the Lenten veils
which have survived, the one from
Telgte in Westphalia is the most
famous because of its great size (22ft
11in × 14ft 5in; 7·4m × 4·4m) and also
because of its many embroidered scenes.
In chessboard formation thirty-three
squares of plain linen alternate with
thirty-three scenes, the last of which
bears a dedication and the date 1623.
The tradition of making Lenten veils in
Westphalia was continued until the
nineteenth century and was recently
taken up again: the Lenten veil for
Xanten Cathedral was made in 1948.

Court Embroidery in the Sixteenth Century

It is significant of the artistic situation
that in Germany, as in Austria in the
sixteenth century, almost exclusively the
works produced for royal and aristo-

cratic patrons, following their patrons'
taste, have an international character
and show, in particular, the influence of
Italian and Netherlandish decorative
forms. An excellent example is the coat
of Duke William V of Bavaria which
was worn by him at his wedding to
Renate of Lorraine in 1568. On violet
velvet, wide bands of raised embroidery
follow the contours of the coat and
present differing effects of gold and
silver; the decorative motifs follow
those of the late Italian Renaissance.
The magnificent hangings decorated
with grotesque letters, the figures of
ancient gods and allegories of the
months, which were made for the family
of the Count of Waldeck, provide a rare
example of expensive textiles used by
aristocrats for interior decoration. The
letters are richly decorated in the
Netherlandish style of so-called "*Besch-
lagwerk*" with small figures; they originate from engravings of the De Bry's
made in 1595 and reprinted in 1613.
The embroidered band of 1607 (Private
Collection) which is over sixteen feet
(5m) in length, is embroidered with
richly shaded gold and silk embroidery
on a bright green satin ground; to this
thirty-two more squares were added
sometime after 1621 which follow the
same designs.

The Seventeenth Century

In the Catholic areas of Germany the
Church again became an important
patron, as well as a recipient of expensive embroideries, after the beginning
of the seventeenth century. Such vestments as those made in the first quarter
of the seventeenth century at the time
of the Elector Prince Maximilian I of
Bavaria, now in the *"Reiche Kapelle"* of
the Munich Residenz, illustrate the
richness and versatility of these works.
The altar frontal depicting the Annunciation seems to have been derived
from a sketch by the court painter Peter
Candid (*c*.1548–1628) and is worked in
the most delicate *petit-point* embroidery
and needle painting. This Flemish
artist, who was trained in Florence,
determined the artistic character of the
Munich court to a considerable extent
in his rôle as court painter and as the
leading artist of the first Munich
tapestry manufactory. A set showing
the *arma Christi* surrounded by grotesque ornaments is similarly made;
another has heavily worked raised embroidery in gold on a dark-red velvet
ground. A miter from Mainz decorated
with pearls on a gold ground (Munich
Residenz) and the chasuble of the
Elector Prince Kasimir Anselm of
Mainz (Bayerisches Nationalmuseum,
Munich) correspond with contemporary
Italian pieces in their clear compositions
and linear control.

In the field of embroidery, Augsburg
was of primary importance for its connections with Bavaria and with neighboring Austria. Of the two interesting
Augsburg chasubles depicting death as

ABOVE:
Chasuble *(back)*, Augsburg, *c.1620–30. Black velvet ground embroidered with silk threads and applied work. Bought by the monastery of Kremsmünster in 1630 from Johann Jakob Pfalzer, a merchant of Augsburg, this chasuble depicts the triumph of death over earthly power.* KREMSMÜNSTER ABBEY, UPPER AUSTRIA.

OVERLEAF, ABOVE:
Altar frontal, *Munich, c.1620. Canvas ground embroidered with gold, silver and polychrome silk threads in* petit point *with the faces, hands and feet worked in applied white satin with satin stitch, 37in × 70in (94cm × 177cm)* RESIDENZMUSEUM, MUNICH.

century. In the many pictures decorating both the altar frontal and a chasuble, contemporary depictions of Jesuit saints are combined with designs which are strangely late medieval in character. God the Father and the Holy Spirit appear in clouds above the crucified Christ and angels collect Christ's blood in chalices; the front shows Christ as a knight in armor. The five sections of the altar frontal are divided by heavy architectural frames; the chasubles are worked with decorative tendrils of which the execution is at times too heavy, with the fruit and blossoms worked in extensive raised embroidery. With the many design motifs, heavy acanthus leaves and festoons, and the attempt to produce a sculptural effect, the embroideries of the second half of the seventeenth century directly correspond to the stucco decoration of interiors and the embossed work of contemporary goldsmiths.

The change from the delicate and light early seventeenth-century designs to the large, heavy decorations of the second half of the century also becomes obvious in the state costume of this period to which just as much lavish attention was paid. Beautiful examples made for the Saxon electors have been preserved (Historisches Museum, Dresden). The black cloak bearing the monograms of the Elector Johann Georg and his wife Magdalena Sibylle, who were married in 1607, is decorated with clear and delicate designs reminiscent of William V's coat of 1568, whereas the court robe of the Elector Johann Georg IV with the Star of the Garter, made in *c.*1693, is decorated with large tendrils and blossoms in raised embroidery on a dark-red velvet ground.

Gold and Silk Embroidery of the Eighteenth Century

The tradition of possessing fine vestments, which was particularly strong in southern Germany and gained many commissions for both ecclesiastical and lay embroidery workshops, increased to an even greater extent in the eighteenth century. Second only in importance to the magnificent works in gold embroidery, illustrated by the chasuble of the Prince-Bishop Damian Hugo Schönborn of 1730–40 (Bruchsal Parish Church) and the opulent decorations with pearls and precious stones, such as those on the miter of the Mainz archbishop and elector Johann Friedrich

a skeleton with a scythe, taken from a woodcut of a skeleton illustrated in Vesalius's book on anatomy *De Humani Corporis Fabrica*, vol 7, published in 1542, one was donated to Stams Abbey in the Tyrol in 1623 while the other was bought by Kremsmünster Abbey in 1630. This abbey in Upper Austria also possesses a magnificent pontifical set of raised gold embroidery which was made in 1672 by the nuns of the convent at Niedernburg in Passau.

Among the pieces of embroidery from ecclesiastical workshops which, as in the Rhineland, were frequently made in Ursuline convents, those of the former Cologne Jesuit Church (now the parish church) are of special interest. They were made by Johannes Lüdgens from Groningen in The Netherlands, a friar of this college, in the third quarter of the seventeenth

Karl of Ostein (Munich Residenz), worked by the Mainz court gold embroiderer Sebastian Stein, is the decorative embroidery of this time worked in colored silks and chenille thread. For the embroidery of flowers, which became increasingly naturalistic in the second quarter of the eighteenth century, work in both chenille threads and colored silk became popular. The large pontifical set worked in chenille thread and dedicated to the monastery at Wessobrunn by the Emperor's widow, Maria Amalia, in 1749 shows a strong similarity to contemporary Austrian works. This also went to the "*Reiche Kapelle*" of the Munich Residenz after the convent was closed.

Church embroideries were now produced in an international style, a tendency that was still more marked in court fashions which, in the eighteenth century were determined by French taste. The rich gold embroidery which decorated the edges and pockets of court dress for gentlemen – the dresses of ladies were mainly decorated with wide borders – indicate this predilection for international fashions almost as obviously as the expensive silks which were exported from France to the whole of Europe and used throughout Europe for the same purposes.

Petit-Point and Cross-Stitch Embroideries

The desire in the baroque period for the luxurious decoration of rooms, which led to the establishment of tapestry manufactories in many German towns, offered a new outlet to works in *gros-* and *petit-point* embroidery and also works in cross stitch, which is similar in its effect. Sets of upholstered furniture covers in colored wool and silk on canvas, of which unfortunately very few pieces have survived complete and in situ, achieved effects which were comparable to those of tapestry covers. A particularly attractive series of twelve wall hangings in *gros* and *petit point* has survived from the second decade of the eighteenth century (Germanisches Nationalmuseum, Nuremberg). The hangings, which were in all likelihood produced at Dresden, depict figures from the Italian *Commedia del Arte* in the upper section, musical instruments between half-length figures of musicians below and in the lower section, dwarfs originating from Callot's famous engravings. A series of Callot's engrav-

ings appeared in Augsburg in 1711 and it is probable that this series served as the model for these embroideries.

It is significant to the importance engravings gained as models in all areas of the applied arts in the eighteenth century that not only the famous inventions of Callot but also anonymous engravings were used several times and in different materials. The anonymous engravings used in the embroideries for the pairs Captain-Colombine and Harlequin-Harlequina served also as models for porcelain figures (Plate 78).

Whitework Embroidery

Whitework was another type of embroidery produced in the prolific period of the German baroque. The interplay between embroidery and lace had provided a stimulus to each since the sixteenth century. Whereas the earlier patterns of needle lace often betrayed their origin in double drawn work, the

Baptismal robe, *north Germany, c.1700. White cotton ground embroidered with white linen thread, height 20in (52cm). The large-scale design of this dress which is richly embroidered with piqué work and openwork is reminiscent of contemporary baroque lace.* MUSEUM FÜR KUNST UND GEWERBE, HAMBURG.

Point de Saxe, *or Dresden*
lace (detail), Germany,
second half of the eighteenth
century. Batiste ground
embroidered with white linen
thread in a·variety of
stitches, 12in × 110in (32cm
×280cm). With this type of
work, white embroidery
entered into direct
competition with lace. The
ground in open work
imitates network while the
large leaves and blossoms
give the effect of bobbin lace.
ÖSTERREICHISCHES MUSEUM
FÜR ANGEWANDTE KUNST,
VIENNA.

growing refinement and enlargement of
lace patterns increasingly influenced
eighteenth-century whitework. In the
field of fashion, delicate piqué embroideries were highly appreciated. They
corresponded to contemporary needle
and bobbin lace not only in their large-
scale baroque patterns but also in the
bold lattice patterns filling the plant
forms. Batiste embroideries, called
point de Saxe or Dresden lace, entered
into direct competition with lace even
with regard to its delicate and almost
transparent structure. After the middle
of the eighteenth century these delicate
and original works gained an international reputation. For the decoration
of elegant handkerchiefs and lingerie,
whitework – often combined with lace –
remained an indispensable part of the
fashion scene throughout the whole of
the nineteenth century.

Pattern Books

From the sixteenth century embroidery patterns were circulated in a totally
new way owing to the production of
printed pattern books. As early as 1523
a *Furm und Modellbuechlein* containing
woodcuts was published by Hanns
Schoenberger in Augsburg, and soon
afterwards it was followed by other
publications. The pattern books of
Johann Sibmacher from Nuremberg
which contained engravings were par-

ticularly popular and their influence
spread far beyond the German frontiers:
the two most influential were his *Neues
Modellbuch von allerley lustigen Modeln
neu zunehen, Zuwürcken – Un Zusticken*
(*New pattern book of all kinds of amusing
and original designs for sewing, tapestry
weaving and embroidery*) first published
in the year 1597 and the *Newes Modelbuch* completed in 1601 and published
in 1604. In addition to single motifs,
they contain patterns for small figure
compositions, friezes and lace. A considerably larger collection of designs
was offered in the *Neue Modelbuch*
(which appeared in three parts and was
published by Paulus Fuerst in Nuremberg in 1666–76), and in later and
revised editions. The pattern books
were mainly responsible for popularizing and disseminating the art of embroidery over a considerably wider area
than before because they were used by
everybody and their many different
designs and techniques could be copied,
above all by the amateur needlewoman.
This common source of inspiration was
responsible for a decrease in the regional
differences in embroidery and an international style was fostered still further.

Throughout the whole of the
eighteenth century the Nuremberg
pattern books, especially those which
were edited by Christoph Weigel's
widow and her descendants after 1734,
maintained their importance as sources
of ideas for skilled and unskilled embroiderers. Whereas the sixteenth- and
seventeenth-century pattern books contained ornamental and floral motifs
which could be used on various objects,
those of the eighteenth century often
included well-composed and detailed
designs for specific items from complete pontifical sets to fashion accessories and small objects for everyday
use. Pattern books did not lose their
significance until the nineteenth century, when the circulation of embroidery
patterns was taken over by single, often
colored, design sheets which were
printed in large numbers in Vienna,
Berlin, Frankfurt and Nuremberg.
Later on different journals and periodicals introduced ideas and gave instructions for embroidery to people working
in their homes.

Samplers

Samplers, which first appeared in the
sixteenth century, were originally made
as notebooks for patterns. Until the end

of the seventeenth century they were generally long strips of linen cloth on which the patterns were arranged in rows. In the course of their long history, which continued until the end of the nineteenth century, samplers increasingly became model pieces on which young girls proved their skill at various embroidery techniques. For this reason they frequently bear not only the date but also the monogram or the full name of the embroiderer; this development also resulted in a change in the format and the distribution of the motifs on the material. The majority of eighteenth- and nineteenth-century samplers which have been preserved are roughly rectangular in form and the designs artistically distributed in a symmetrical arrangement with particular emphasis on the center and border decorations (Plate 80). It was not until the second half of the nineteenth century, when the teaching of various embroidery techniques became a formal subject at girls' schools, that these samplers with their figures and many other motifs disappeared; often very attractive and carefully designed as well as sewn, they were replaced by sample bands, which displayed examples of stitches in single sections.

Revival Styles to the Present Day

The historical revival styles with their preference for richly decorated shapes set many tasks for the embroiderer. Needlework was used in the context of fashion and for fashion accessories and it was practiced as a hobby; and once again gold embroidery was used in interior decoration.

The phenomenal expenditure by King Ludwig II of Bavaria (1864–86) on his castles included payments for all kinds of extravagant textiles. The embroideries for Herrenchiemsee Castle number among the most splendid and, like the rest of the interior decoration of the castle, they were imitations of similar decorations at Versailles. Work on the curtains of the state bed, which were decorated with colored needle paintings of scenes from the myths of Venus and Cupid, occupied the two Munich ateliers of Jörres and Bornhauser for seven years, from 1875 to 1882. In the gold embroidery on a blue velvet and moiré ground of the curtains of this room, every possible technique in gold embroidery, including the use of relief work, was explored.

In Munich one decade later it was the embroideries of Hermann Obrist (1863–1927) that paved the way for the new ideas of Art Nouveau. Their widespread and stylized use of plant forms and their vividly flowing lines made the idea of an ornamental style, which was intentionally independent of historical models, clear to everybody. In the nineteenth century, apart from new artistic ideas, there was also an interest in the preservation and revival of old techniques, but since the turn of the century the use of different techniques for the sake of producing new and special effects has predominated. Alone, or in combination with other kinds of textile decoration, embroidery has to this day found artistic expression.

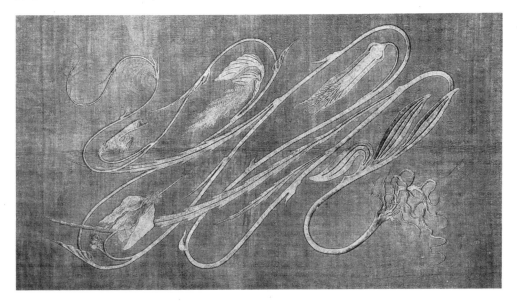

Wall hanging, *Munich or Florence, 1892–5. Light gray woolen ground embroidered with yellow-brown silk thread, 47in × 72in (119·5cm × 183·5cm). This wall hanging called* Lash *was designed by Hermann Obrist with flowing, stylized plant forms and signed with his monogram H.O. in the right hand corner.* STADTMUSEUM, MUNICH.

Austria

EMBROIDERY IN THE AREA OF PRESENT-day Austria, due to historical circumstances, produced its earliest identifiable independent works at a considerably later date than the adjacent regions of south Germany. Even in the ancient treasuries of the cathedral and the Benedictine monastery of St. Peter in Salzburg nothing is preserved which could be claimed as a characteristic product of Austrian embroidery prior to the thirteenth century.

Medieval Embroidery

The late romanesque style of the thirteenth century is represented in Austria principally by one outstanding work of great importance both artistically and historically, the set of vestments from the former convent of Göss, near Leoben in Styria. It is the only set of the period which still has all five major items – chasuble (Plate 81), cope, dalmatic, tunicle and altar frontal (Österreichisches Museum für Angewandte Kunst, Vienna). The special character of these embroideries lies in their composition, in which figure-scenes, occupying the dominant central positions, are combined with a wealth of animal figures and geometrical ornament, distributed over the remaining surfaces in a markedly asymmetrical manner. In scenes and symbols a comprehensive theological programme is here displayed and, thanks to the brilliant hues of the soft silk, achieves an immediate optical impact. Worked on undyed linen, the embroidery follows a dark-toned preliminary drawing – now visible at many points – and completely covers the ground fabric, chiefly with stepped Gobelins stitch. As is shown by a number of inscriptions and representations of the donatrix, the set was made for Abbess Kunigunde II (1239–69); in all probability, the embroidery of this monumental work was executed by the nuns of the convent.

In the fourteenth century Vienna became an important artistic center and it is highly probable that embroidery was fostered by professional craftsmen active in the city in the first half of the century, although there is no mention of embroiderers in Vienna in contemporary documents before the end of the century. The altar frontal with the *siben ziten unsers Herrn* (seven scenes from the Life of Our Lord), which Duke Albert II presented to Königsfelden Monastery in Aargau in memory of his father, now in the Bernisches Historisches Museum, Berne, is in the style of Viennese embroidery of the second quarter of the fourteenth century. It is the only large piece of embroidery to have survived practically intact from the Habsburg donations of that time. In its design and in the execution of the delicately shaded needle painting on couched gold it is of the highest quality, providing an admirable example of how embroidery could achieve similar artistic effects to painting not only in composition and the depiction of elegant figures but also in rich effects of shading. Only professional workers who were skilled in the technique of silk and gold embroidery could have created this work.

Of particular interest by way of comparison is the altar frontal from Salzburg Cathedral, now in the Österreichisches Museum für angewandte Kunst, Vienna, which is somewhat earlier in date but similar in the minute execution of different shades of silk embroidery in light colors on a gold ground. The depiction of the Life of Our Lord in twenty scenes with prophets and apostles is stylistically close to the Danubian art circle. From the inscriptions we know not only the name of the patron, Archbishop Friedrich von Leibnitz, but also the name of the embroiderer, Seidlin of Pettau.

The best pieces of southern German and Austrian embroidery are very similar and in many cases it is impossible to attribute with any certainty work to one region or the other, a case in point being the eagle dalmatic. This close stylistic connection between the two lasted for a long time. In Austria the influence of Bohemian art is also clearly recognizable in the second half

OPPOSITE, TOP:
Cope, Göss Convent, near Leoben, Styria, Austria, mid-thirteenth century. Linen ground embroidered with silk thread, 56in × 107in (143cm × 272cm). This cope which belongs to the famous pontifical set of Göss shows the Virgin and Child in the center medallion surrounded by the symbols of the four Evangelists.
ÖSTERREICHISCHES MUSEUM FÜR ANGEWANDTE KUNST, VIENNA.

of the fourteenth and early fifteenth centuries. The precious miter, originally richly decorated with pearls, depicting the full-length figures of Our Lady and three bishops from the third quarter of the fourteenth century, is unquestionably of Austrian origin and is still in the possession of the Benedictine abbey of Admont in Styria. The embroidery of a pontifical set of *c*.1410 belonging to the bishop of Trento, Georg of Liechtenstein, of which the orphrey cross and apparel of a dalmatic are in the possession of Trento Cathedral, originated in the Austro-Bohemian art circle.

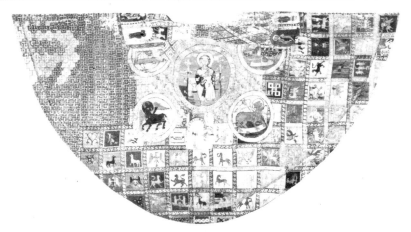

After the beginning of the fifteenth-century documentary references to embroidery become more frequent. A letter written by Duke Ernst in 1408 mentions for the first time among Viennese craftsmen the "*seydennahter*" (silk embroiderers). In the 1430 codification of Trade Law, the silk embroiderers are recognized as an organized trade, while workers with pearls were a free trade; in the guild regulation of 1446 the embroiderers appear as members of the Guild of St. Luke.

In the second half of the fifteenth century Vienna lost its political importance. However, this period saw the heyday of late gothic embroidery in the Alpine regions.

Where Austrian embroidery shows a particular similarity to German works is in the large number of church vestments which have been preserved. Throughout the whole of the fifteenth century the most popular subjects were the Crucifixion and the Virgin and Child which were worked as centerpieces of orphrey crosses while the transverse bars of the crosses were worked with the full- and half-length figures of various saints.

The basic style and subject matter of Austrian needlework remained fairly constant until *c*.1520, variations being confined to such details as the design of the frames and the gold-thread patterns used in the couched work. This period is represented by chasubles in the Diocesan Museum, Klagenfurt, which come mainly from churches in Carinthia; and other examples in the Salzburg Cathedral Museum.

In Germany as in Austria, orphrey crosses worked in relief embroidery were of great artistic importance in the second half of the fifteenth century, representative examples including the

orphrey crosses at St. Peter, Salzburg, and in the Treasury of Mariazell in Styria, in which a remarkable effect is achieved by the fine modeling of the figures as well as a meticulous technique. The Mariazell chasuble verges on statuary in the canopies extending over the figures and pinnacles which are supported by carved pieces of wood which are inserted into the embroidery

ABOVE:
Dalmatic *(detail)*, *Göss Convent, near Leoben, Styria, Austria, mid-thirteenth century. Linen ground embroidered with silk thread. Part of the pontifical set of Göss to which the illustration above also belongs.*

to support it and completely covered with embroidery. This piece of work, like the hood of a cope embroidered in Vienna in 1516–18 (Dom und Diozesanmuseum, Vienna), resembles German work of the same period in that both have as decoration the rich use of pearls. Craftsmanship of this order led embroidery into direct competition with sculpture, while in another field there is a resemblance to the art of the goldsmith, an example being the splendid miter in St. Peter, Salzburg, made at the time of the abbot Rupert Keutzl (died 1495), which is richly decorated with precious stones and pearls.

Considering the high quality of late gothic ecclesiastical embroidery still surviving and the well-documented activities of numerous embroiderers, particularly those working in Salzburg and Innsbruck, it is cause for regret that nothing of secular origin has survived. The sumptuous vestments which Frederick III had specially ordered for his coronation in Rome in 1452 have disappeared, as has Maximilian's coronation mantle – his imperial embroiderer, Master Leonhard, appointed from

Strasbourg, had decorated it in 1508 with eagles and a portrait of the Emperor Charlemagne.

Innsbruck which was Maximilian's favorite residence, gained importance in his reign as a center of the court art of embroidery. Embroiderers from Germany, The Netherlands and one from Italy worked alongside local masters, all of whom were supplied with designs by court painters such as Joerg Koelderer (c.1470–1540).

The Sixteenth and Seventeenth Centuries

The styles which developed during the second half of the fifteenth century dominated ecclesiastical embroidery in particular well into the sixteenth century. Often it was only in the details that renaissance elements occur, as in the chasuble from Steyregg in Upper Austria, dated 1576, now in the Landesmuseum, Linz. In contrast to the abundance of late gothic works, Austrian embroidery of the renaissance period is comparatively rare. Where embroidery owes its origin to court patronage and, accordingly, complies with the international taste of its patrons, whether or not it is of Austrian origin remains an open question. Such pieces are represented by the frieze decorated with the coat of arms of Archduke Ferdinand II (1529–95) between a profusion of scrolls and putti (Österreichisches Museum für angewandte Kunst, Vienna) and a chasuble with the coat of arms of the Salzburg archbishop Johann Jakob Kuen-Belasy, dated 1578 (Salzburg Cathedral).

The *Moedel Buechel Von ordenclicher Niderländischer Natterey einer wolberuehmbten Schulhalterin zu nutz Vnd der Jugendt zur ubung (Pattern book of authentic Netherlandish stitchery, useful for the well-reputed schoolmistress and for the training of the young)* which was published in Vienna in 1596, and for which Wolff Luxen made woodcuts, proves that embroidery in Austria did not lose touch with international developments in the sixteenth century. This booklet contains the earliest German designs for openwork and needlepoint lace.

Fostered by the Counter-Reformation also in those regions where the Protestant faith had been established, the second quarter of the seventeenth century was a rich period for embroidery throughout Austria. The best pieces of the time achieve their extraordinary effect solely from gold embroidery worked on a monochrome, often bright red satin, ground. The stylized plant decorations, which are arranged in uncurling spiral scrolls are enhanced by the contrasts of raised work, using any number of effects from delicate line drawing to raised, sculptural relief. In these works the absence of color, the modeling of raised sections through thick padding in soft threads, and the effect of different metals – flat lamella, small twisted cords, differently spun threads, bullion and paillettes – show a striving after heavy plastic effects and a glimmering surface, which are reminiscent of the goldsmith's art of the same time.

This type of embroidery, which employs precious materials and is superbly worked, was cultivated by professional embroiderers who had their workshops mainly in the larger towns and by monasteries which also had highly skilled craftsmen. The most important monastic workshop was that of the Benedictine abbey of Admont which developed numerous activities under the leadership of a superb embroiderer, Friar Benno Haan. In the second half of the seventeenth century and up to Haan's death in 1720 a series of large pontifical sets was produced there, which made use of the many different techniques of high baroque embroidery, combining gold relief embroidery of magnificent quality with pictorial medallions worked in delicate colored needle painting. The pontifical set of guardian angels made in 1657, that of St. Catherine worked in 1661, the Christmas set of 1680 at Admont and the so-called "pictorial pontifical set" of 1671 at St. Lambert in Styria were all made under the surveillance of Haan. This workshop also produced the larger part of the embroidered wall hangings which decorate the presbytery of Admont abbey church.

ABOVE:
Orphrey cross, *Salzburg, Austria, c.1500. Gold couchwork, the figures modeled in high relief and covered with white silk and embroidery, 50in × 26in (126cm × 67cm). Although the chasuble of which this orphrey cross once formed a part no longer exists, the cross is in very good condition. It shows Our Lord on the Cross surrounded by three flying angels and surmounted by God the Father.* ST. PETER'S ABBEY, SALZBURG.

BELOW:
Frieze *embroidered with the coat of arms of Archduke Ferdinand II, Austria (?), second half of the sixteenth century. Red satin ground embroidered with silk threads and appliqué, 15in × 66in (38·5cm × 167cm). The coat of arms of Archduke Ferdinand II (1529–95) surrounded by the chain of the Order of the Golden Fleece are embroidered between scrolls and* putti. ÖSTERREICHISCHES MUSEUM FÜR ANGEWANDTE KUNST, VIENNA.

A particularly attractive addition to the heavy raised forms of gold embroidery are the naturalistic needle-painted flowers worked in many colors which were not confined to the works of the Haan school. These flowers were generally distributed in an arbitrary fashion over the background, giving the impression of spontaneity (Plate 83). It could be that the inspiration for these realistic and picturesque embroideries was the work of Flemish embroiderers brought to Austria by Archduke Leopold Wilhelm, returning to the Viennese court after his governorship in Brussels (1657).

Peasant Embroidery in the Seventeenth Century

The wide circulation of needlework pattern books and engravings led to similar decorations appearing on modest peasant products. The most usual are spiral scroll designs combined with single large blossoms. Their simple execution, however, gives these peasant pieces an entirely different character from the more sophisticated works of the great cities and monasteries. Linen replaces the brilliant silk of the background; colored soft silk, usually scarcely twisted, is used instead of expensive gold thread for the embroidery; both the relief effect and the metallic brightness of gold embroidery are missing; a glittering surface effect is striven after here by a rich use of paillettes and by the shimmer of bright silk thread.

Professional Embroidery in the Eighteenth Century

From the beginning of the eighteenth century Vienna once again became prominent as a center for embroidery. In an area outside the city walls, which was to become the districts of Mariahilf and Neubau, and which was newly settled and flourishing again after the recent devastations of the Turkish siege in 1683, numerous embroiderers settled down alongside weavers and

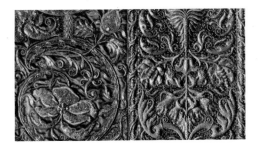

braid-makers. Professionals in these skills came from a considerable distance to work in the capital city expecting rightly to receive important commissions: for example the renowned embroiderer in gold, Johann Jakob Edlmannsperger from Melk in Lower Austria, in 1717, and Johann Sigmund Koeck from Graz in 1725.

At that time expensive commissions from the court and ecclesiastical patrons were given almost exclusively to professional men and women embroiderers, particularly in the area of gold embroidery. The influence of contemporary engravings is clearly recognizable in this type of needlework, popular throughout Europe in the first half of the eighteenth century. The light and flowing forms of French Régence ornament with its leaf designs and strapwork (*Laub und Bandelwerk*) which were popular in Austria and adapted easily to any format, were mainly worked in couched gold thread in flat relief over a cardboard or leather ground, as, for example, in the Bertholdi pontifical set at Melk and in the Leopoldi pontifical set by the same embroiderers made in 1729 and owned by the priory of Klosterneuberg near Vienna.

For many years this type of decoration was very popular and widely used, as in the gold and silver pontifical set by Maria Susanna Lindtner of 1742–3 in the abbey of Seittenstetten in Lower Austria. When, in the second quarter of the century, naturalistic flowers appeared again more frequently, the curved and broken bands of strapwork often formed their basic frame. Apart from pieces worked in colored silk in satin stitch, chenille embroidery gained importance: with its rich colors and velvet-like surface, it seemed particularly suited to the fashioning of large-scale arrangements of flowers and fruits.

In Austria the interaction of native artists on influences from outside Europe led to particularly attractive and original work. In some pieces made

ABOVE, LEFT:
Chasuble *(detail)*, Upper Austria, c.1630. Red satin ground embroidered with gold couchwork and different varieties of metal thread partly raised over cords and paillettes, 40in × 28in *(102cm × 70cm)*. This chasuble which is decorated with the coat of arms of Anton Wolfradt who was abbot of the Benedictine abbey of Kremsmünster from 1613–39 and became, in 1631, the first bishop of princely rank in Vienna, is one of the rich vestments ordered by the abbot for Kremsmünster.
KREMSMÜNSTER ABBEY,
UPPER AUSTRIA.

at the turn of the seventeenth to eighteenth century the depiction of large and exotic-looking floral designs betray the knowledge of Indian plant designs and textile decorations. These foreign attributes used in conjunction with everyday motifs produced work of great originality such as the so-called pontifical set of Litschau, which was made in *c.*1700 for the monastery of Zwettle in Lower Austria (Plate 82).

Chinoiserie, a style much favored elsewhere in Europe was not often used in Austria, but it found original expression in a large series of wall hangings at Schlosshof, a summer residence of Prince Eugène of Savoy: the wall hangings of one room, dating from 1720–30, have survived. The chinoiserie scenes are applied with pieces of colorful printed chintz on to plain white cotton and edged with white and colored braid; only the faces are embroidered in silk. The six large and thirteen small sections make up the cheerful and light-hearted decoration of a complete room and a canopy bed.

Amateur Embroidery in the Eighteenth Century

In addition to these important achievements in eighteenth-century embroidery, unskilled workers are represented by products which also show the versatile and colorful nature of Austrian embroidery in that century. Apart from the colorful silk embroidery with decorative floral patterns worked by the monasteries for their own needs, as for example the rose pontifical set from the former Ursuline convent in Vienna which was made *c.*1700 (Plate 84) and works from the Convent of the Visitation in Vienna, aristocratic ladies also enjoyed needlework. Doubtless because it was quicker and easier, these ladies seem to have preferred appliqué work. Floral designs were worked in shaded ribbons or figurative compositions using different materials for the appliqué work, as demonstrated by the attractive altar frontal depicting the Assumption of the Virgin Mary in the parish church at Linz which shows the saints dressed in mid-eighteenth-century fashion with expensive brocade clothes and high, powdered hairstyles.

During the reign of the Empress Maria Theresa, embroidery was enthusiastically cultivated at the Viennese court. The large number of works which were given by the Empress and are still in churches or monasteries are decorated with designs consisting of small colored silk cords in applied work. These characteristic pieces, which are referred to as *Ihrer Majestät Schnürlarbeit* (Her Majesty's cordwork), represent the type of needlework most enjoyed by the Empress and her ladies-in-waiting.

Peasant Embroidery in the Eighteenth Century

Peasant work also came to the fore with different kinds of embroidery at this time. Cross stitch, which had been practiced for a long time in Austria, was now to be seen on chasubles decorated with pictures worked in colored wool which are almost late medieval in character, for example the symbolic presentation of Christ's Passion through *arma Christi* on chasubles in Zwettl monastery in Lower Austria and in the Österreichisches Museum für angewandte Kunst. As for embroidery on peasant costumes, quillwork became popular in the Tyrol in the eighteenth century and remained a characteristic feature until fairly recently. The decorative use of brass nails and metal pieces fixed to the wide leather belts and braces in traditional patterns was replaced by embroidery with the quills of peacock and turkey feathers.

Late Eighteenth-Century Styles

It is characteristic of Austrian embroidery that the French rococo style only rarely found pure expression. Symmetry of composition and a certain heaviness in design were often still evident after the middle of the eighteenth century. In ecclesiastical pieces, the connection of the late baroque style with different naturalistic floral designs continued to exist as an uninterrupted tradition even after the neoclassical and Empire periods, and then, almost unnoticed, it intermingled with the general recourse to eighteenth-century motifs at the beginning of the revivalist period.

Unfortunately extant Austrian ecclesiastical embroidery in the baroque style is not counterbalanced by a similar number of existing dresses. From the Viennese court, not even a single embroidered dress from this period has survived. It is not until the last quarter of the eighteenth century that we find examples of dress coats and waistcoats embroidered in the French style with colored sprigs of flowers.

The Nineteenth Century to the Present Day

In the Biedermeier period colorful *petit point* embroidery gained in importance. The old tradition of half and full cross stitches on a regularly woven ground, which had been used on both peasant work and samplers, became a particular feature of Viennese needlework.

The important position, which Vienna gained and maintained in this field in the first half of the nineteenth century was based on the Heinrich Friedrich Müller publishing house and its embroidery patterns. Bright colors and the detailed drawing of single motifs as well as of series of decorative motifs secured an international market for these sheets of patterns at a time when the Austrian people rejoiced in carefully looked-after household effects as well as detailed handiwork. The employment of this embroidery, carried out mainly on canvas in silk and wool, comprised everything from complete sets of upholstery covers to small items of everyday use such as slippers, garters and braces.

A new stimulus to the cultivation and also to the revival of very different embroidery techniques was caused by the reform movement in all areas of the arts and crafts in the second half of the nineteenth century. Vienna contributed to this very considerably. The foundation of the K. K. Österreichisches Museum für Kunst und Industrie in 1864 was followed by the establishment of a school of arts and crafts, *Kunstgewerbeschule*, and later by similar institutions and schools throughout the whole of the Austro-Hungarian Empire. The many different techniques, including delicate whitework as well as representational gold work, were taught in courses which lasted for several years.

In the revivalist period in the second half of the nineteenth century the various types and techniques of embroidery were again employed in many different ways, from use in interior design to decoration on fashionable accessories. The movement influenced by the museums and the teaching of the schools did not only imitate earlier styles, an aspect which was predominantly welcomed by ecclesiastical bodies for church vestments, but also introduced new elements into embroidery.

Art movements in general at the turn of the century were of special importance to embroidery because of their influence on design. Textile designs were no longer regarded as equivalent to those in painting and new stylized and abstract plant decorations gained in importance. In this connection interesting design solutions were found within the Viennese School of Arts and Crafts illustrated, for example, by the large pontifical set of Our Lady which was worked in 1911 after the designs of Anton Hofer for the priory of Klosterneuburg near Vienna. It represents one of the rare examples of abstract church embroidery based on theories of the Viennese Secession. Decorative wall hangings and pictorial compositions in needlework were also successfully made, which fully employed all the possible effects of different embroidery techniques.

Up till the present day the middle

Standard for the tabernacle, Vienna, Austria, 1730–40. White silk embroidered with gold and chenille thread, 32in × 23in (82cm × 60cm). This embroidered picture was used to cover the tabernacle during the sermon. Embroidered by nuns from the Convent of the Visitation, the large flower motifs were also used by the nuns for different church vestments. CONVENT OF THE VISITATION, VIENNA.

ABOVE:
Embroidered picture, *Vienna, Austria, 1824. White canvas embroidered in* petit-point *with polychrome silk threads, 19in × 16in (48cm × 40cm). This picture which is a fine example of the* petit-point *work for which Vienna became justly famous in the first half of the nineteenth century, is signed in the lower right hand corner* "Gestickt von Katharina Dreehsen 1824." ÖSTERREICHISCHES MUSEUM FÜR ANGEWANDTE KUNST, VIENNA.

ABOVE, RIGHT:
Wall hanging, *Vienna, Austria, 1904. White silk with appliqué work in polychrome silk threads and framed with silk cord, 46in × 37in (117cm × 94cm). This hanging called* "Bird of Paradise" *was designed in the Art Nouveau style by Maria Münster who had studied at the School of Arts and Crafts in Vienna and executed by Friderike Dollmayr.*
ÖSTERREICHISCHES MUSEUM FÜR ANGEWANDTE KUNST, VIENNA.

and higher art schools, based on the nineteenth-century foundations, have been the most important centers for teaching and encouraging artistic embroidery. The Wiener Werkstätte (Vienna Workshops), founded in 1903 and supported by definite artistic theories, tried to oppose factory mass production by the creation of fine and original work also in the field of embroidery. With regard to fashion and

fashionable accessories, artists working for the Vienna Workshops such as Eduard Wimmer-Wisgrill (1882–1961) and Dagobert Peche (1887–1923), were highly productive in all fields of decorative design and used the most varied techniques of embroidery as well as of handmade lace for their sketches, thus combining new artistic theories with old and high-class professional traditions.

Switzerland

THE ART OF EMBROIDERY IN
Switzerland differs essentially from that
of the neighboring countries of Germany and Austria not only in the types
of embroidery that were favored and the
way in which they were produced but
also in the periods when particularly
original types of work predominated.
The precious and elaborate embroideries made for ecclesiastical purposes
played a less important rôle in Switzerland and the most interesting examples
of Swiss work can be found in linen and
wool in the sixteenth and the first half
of the seventeenth centuries. Even if we
take into consideration that many textiles which were in church treasuries
were destroyed during the Reformation,
nevertheless few pieces of splendid gold
and silk embroidery can have been
produced because there were no rich
aristocrats or ecclesiastical patrons to
commission such works.

Needlework in the Middle Ages
In Switzerland embroiderers did not
develop a strict guild system as in some
other countries and they could trade
freely. Thus a Zürich guild regulation
of 1489 says of silk embroiderers and
other tradesmen *"die mogen sin in der
constafel oder in welicher zunft sy
wellen, also, daz ir gewerb fry ist"* (they
may belong to a district association, or
whichever guild they prefer, so that they
may trade freely). Zürich, and probably
other Swiss towns, too, had the same
regulations for their embroiderers as the
German towns of Nuremberg or
Münster.

The Swiss monasteries provided
centers for the production of ecclesiastical embroidery during the Middle Ages
as did monasteries in other countries.
The embroideries of the Sarnen convent
and the beautiful cope of 1318 from the
Benedictine abbey of Engelberg in
Unterwalden might be the products of
the convent which was transferred from
Engelberg to Sarnen in as late as 1615.
The silk embroidery completely covering the linen ground fabric shows an
exact division into squares with a regular variation in the design of single

animal figures and ornamental patterns.
The inscription on the hood, which is of
remarkably large size and decorated
with scenes from the Life of Our Lord,
names the abbot, Walter of Engelberg
(active 1317–31); it was therefore made
at the same time as the cope although it
was not designed for it. This cope and
the altar frontals from Sarnen are traditionally associated with the widow of
Andrew III of Hungary, Queen Agnes
(died 1384), who spent many years of
her widowhood in the monastery of
Königsfelden, the memorial-place of her
father, the Habsburg king, Albert I, and
who was in close contact with the monasteries at Engelberg. It also seems
likely that the few embroidered fifteenth-century orphrey crosses which
are still extant were produced in convent workshops.

Linen Embroidery
In Switzerland embroidery on linen
with linen thread was of considerably
greater importance than silk embroidery
on linen and provided a flourishing
tradition. In old inventories this type of
work is frequently referred to as "needlework" as opposed to the "embroidery"
done in silk. Although some examples,
such as the fourteenth-century cloth
from Feldbach monastery in Thurgovia,
are artistically of high quality and
demonstrate extremely careful workmanship, the makers of these embroideries remain anonymous and often it is
not even possible to find out whether
they were intended for church or secular
purposes. Occasionally their purpose is
clear from the motifs of the embroidery, as is the case with a 1527 tablecloth, which has embroidered representations of a table set with eight
plates, cutlery, cups, bread and a bowl
of fruit in the center. In the sixteenth
and seventeenth centuries, an important
part of this output was made by women
of the middle classes who used the
pieces to furnish their living rooms or as
presents and it is likely that this was the
case as early as the Middle Ages.

The oldest preserved and at the same
time largest piece of work, a 19ft 10in

ABOVE, RIGHT:
Tablecloth *(detail),
Switzerland, thirteenth
century. Whitework
embroidered on a linen
ground with linen thread and
a small amount of silk
thread in a variety of
stitches, 41in × 264in
(104cm × 670cm). The
linked medallions are filled
with different ornamental
patterns and fabulous
animals, surrounded by an
inscription. The form of the
letters indicate a date in the
first half of the thirteenth
century.* SCHWEIZERISCHES
LANDESMUSEUM, ZÜRICH.

MIDDLE:
Tablecloth *(detail),
Monastery of Feldbach,
Switzerland, fourteenth
century. Whitework partly
worked with silk in a
variety of stitches on white
linen, 121in × 41in (308cm
× 105cm). One of the best
examples of medieval linen
embroidery. From the
disposition of the motifs in
the medallions, it is quite
clear that this piece was
designed as a tablecloth.* HISTORISCHES MUSEUM,
BASLE.

BELOW:
Detail of above.

OPPOSITE, ABOVE:
Linen embroidery *showing
the Transfiguration and the
symbols of the Evangelists,
Switzerland, beginning of
the sixteenth century. White
linen with embroidery in
white, blue and brown linen
thread, 41in × 48in
(105·5cm × 121cm).* ÖSTERREICHISCHES MUSEUM
FÜR ANGEWANDTE KUNST,
VIENNA.

(6·7m) cloth with a regular pattern of
linked medallions with different decorations and a circumscription, dates from
the thirteenth century. The elongated
shape of the cloth and the repeating
designs with medallions or scrolls remained favorite patterns on these embroideries until the fifteenth century.

Late gothic plant decoration with
its flowing forms which varied greatly
was also widely practiced. In the fifteenth century single animals and
mythological beasts and smaller figures
were added but plant decoration did
not lose its importance when larger
panels and narrative scenes were favored.

From the sixteenth century, and in particular the second half of that century from which dates the greater part of extant Swiss linen embroidery, these were the most popular motifs.

The models for these compositions were contemporary graphics, particularly book illustrations. Graphic art was especially suited to interpretation in linen embroidery, with its emphasis on outlines and the individual stitch, but it also reached great importance in Switzerland as an art form in the early sixteenth century.

Because of their clear outlines woodcuts from illustrated editions of the Bible proved very suitable for transference into embroidery patterns and examples of the work of Hans Holbein the Younger (1497/8–1543), Tobias Stimmer (1539–84), Petit Bernard (1506/10–c.61), Hans Sebald Beham (1500–50) as well as Virgil Solis (1514–62), can be traced in embroidery. On being transferred to another material, and intended for a different purpose (such as a cover or cushion), their designs were, however, altered in a distinctive way. The ground was often divided into a central picture or into the combination of a central picture with four corner medallions with scrolls forming the frame and background. These spiralling plant forms still show the influence of the gothic style far into the second half of the sixteenth century. Heavy patterning enhancing the effect of various different stitches is employed as the infilling for blossoms and leaves as well as the clothes of the figures, providing a uniform decorative texture, as in the linen cover dated 1563 depicting the young Tobias with the angel after a woodcut by Hans Holbein the Younger. The special character of these works depends on their adherence to older forms and patterns and in their transference to linen embroidery, in which the neutral background is of great importance. Their effectiveness is considerably emphasized by the sparing use of color.

In gothic work the white linen thread was mainly used in conjunction with only a small amount of colored silk but from the beginning of the sixteenth century white, blue and brown linen thread determines the overall character, with silk and occasionally even small amounts of metal thread added. On the other hand, the variety of stitches used increased considerably, especially in the

BELOW:
Linen cover *showing Tobias and the angel, north Switzerland, 1563. Half-linen ground embroidered with white, blue and dark brown linen thread, metal thread and animal hair in a variety of stitches, 54in × 63in (138cm × 161cm). This cover for which the design is based on a woodcut by Hans Holbein the Younger (1497/8–1543)*

printed in Die Gantze Bibel *(The Whole Bible) in Zürich in 1540, illustrates the way in which Swiss embroidery enlarged and adapted book illustrations to its own purposes.*
HISTORISCHES MUSEUM, BASLE.

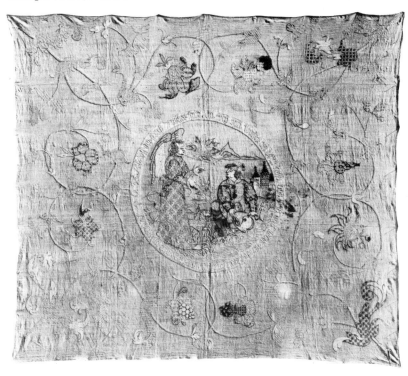

second half of the sixteenth century
when in one piece of work as many as
ten or more kinds of stitches are combined. This is illustrated by a cover
showing the Birth of Christ and the
symbols of the four Evangelists in the
Victoria and Albert Museum, London.
In essentials this type of embroidery
continued to be produced until the
middle of the seventeenth century without displaying any influence from the
baroque style.

Wool Embroidery

The same period – the sixteenth and the
first half of the seventeenth centuries –
was also the best period for embroidery
in colored wools. Apart from general
developments such as the growing wel-
fare of the middle-class population and
their interest in and contribution to
linen and wool embroidery, the gradual

decline of Swiss tapestry weaving,
which had been of great importance in
the gothic period, led to wool embroidery taking over from tapestry in both a
decorative and a functional sense. Wall
hangings embroidered in wool (because
of its light weight linen embroidery was
not suited to this purpose), formed the
most important part of this work. In
wool embroideries, with their hard-
wearing texture and bright coloring, the
intention was to produce an overall
decorative impression rather than a display of many different types of stitches.
The most popular stitch in wool embroidery, which was often used exclusively, was *Klosterstich* (a type of
couching), which followed the contours
of the design and was employed to
cover larger areas evenly and comprehensively. Much less frequently and
only after *c.*1530 cross stitch was used,
a stitch widely adopted in peasant embroidery. In the sixteenth century dark,
often black, and later undyed linen was
used as the ground fabric, which was
completely covered by embroidery.

Wool and linen embroidery are
closely related in their origin and in
their motifs. We know from letters
written in the 1570s that the daughters
of the reformer, Heinrich Bullinger
(1504–75), were particularly skilled in
all textile techniques and also made wall
hangings to order, a painter drawing the
designs for them. Similarly, signatures
on some pieces of work prove that they
were made by middle-class women and
their daughters. Thus an embroidery in
the Rathausmuseum in Lucerne, show-

ing the mystic wine-press surrounded by allegorical figures, bears the inscription *"Maria Jacobe Dorer hat gemacht dis Tuch 1603"* (M.J. Dorer made this cloth in 1603).

Next to scenes from the Old Testament and less frequently from the New Testament, moralizing subjects occur, particularly the so-called *Weiberlisten* (wiles of women), a theme which was also popular in linen embroidery, showing the defeat of famous men and heroes of both the Old Testament and classical Antiquity by clever women. A hanging of 1522 shows Virgil and the Emperor's daughter in the middle; Solomon worshipping strange gods, Samson and Delilah, David and Bathsheba and Judith and Holofernes are depicted in the corner medallions.

Occasionally a realistic depiction of daily life in a natural setting was chosen, as on the Bischofszell hanging; it shows rural activities on the banks of the streams Thur and Sitter, spanned by stone bridges, in front of an actual view of Bischofszell. Another example is the depiction of women doing their washing dated 1556 in the Schweizerisches Landesmuseum, Zürich.

The representation of a family in a multiple family portrait such as the wall hanging of the Morell family of 1601, (Plate 85) demonstrates the self-confidence of a respected middle-class family. The parents with the three youngest children are shown in the central medallion, and in twelve smaller roundels around the edge the grown-up children with their husbands or wives are depicted. A piece of work such as the carpet with the coat of arms of the Stokar and Tschachtlan families shows Swiss awareness of fashionable innovation. Here, for example, the design of west Anatolian knotted carpets, which were imported in considerable quantities into Europe in the sixteenth century mainly for use as covers on tables and chests, was imitated in embroidery.

Swiss Embroidery since the Middle of the Seventeenth Century

In the second half of the seventeenth century a radical change took place which affected fundamentally the art of embroidery in Switzerland. The two types of linen and wool embroidery with figurative decoration which had been popular thus far gradually lost their importance; under the growing influence of French taste embroideries

in an indigenous style took second place in interior decoration. It is true that embroidery on linen was done at a later period, too, but it acquired an altogether different character. With the disappearance of figurative compositions, the use of blue and brown linen thread was also abandoned; it was now that white embroidery, or whitework, in the proper sense of the word, was taken up. The decoration, which is mainly limited to plant motifs, shows a resemblance to the baroque samplers which were worked in Switzerland, as they were in other countries, as demonstrations of expertise in needlework.

A flourishing tradition of embroidery on linen appeared in the folk art of Grisons, where until recently the same motifs were used more or less unchanged. It relied predominantly on cross stitch which was particularly suited to the geometrical, stylized forms, worked straight on the cloth without the help of a drawn design.

Carpet *with the coat of arms of the families of Stokar and Tschachtlan, Schaffhausen, 1533. Linen ground embroidered with polychrome wool in cross stitch, 72in × 54in (183cm × 138cm). One of the earliest examples of cross stitch to be found in Switzerland, this carpet which shows the influence of near-eastern knotted carpets was made in memory of Alexander Stokar-Tschachtlan (d.1519), whose brother as a pilgrim to Jerusalem, had probably introduced Oriental carpets to Schaffhausen.* SCHWEIZERISCHES LANDESMUSEUM, ZÜRICH.

Altar frontal *(detail)*,
Ursuline Convent, Lucerne,
Switzerland, c.1700. White
satin ground, embroidered
with silk thread in satin
stitch and couched gold,
35in × 110in (90cm ×
280cm). This embroidered
picture showing the voyage
of the eleven thousand
virgins over the sea is the
left-hand part of an altar
frontal embroidered by the
nun Anna Maria Marzohl
for the altar of St. Ursula in
her convent chapel. It bears
the coat of arms of the
families of Krus and Dorer.
URSULINE CHURCH,
LUCERNE.

The baroque influence was evident
in church embroideries, which were
made in Switzerland by secular as well
as monastic workers as was, for example, the rich antependium made in 1620
for the priory of the Augustinian
Canons in Beromünster by the Lucerne
silk embroiderer, Johann Jakob Ackli. A
series of rich gold and silver embroideries are recognizable as the work of
Sister Scholastica An der Allmend
(died 1722), who worked for more than
five decades at the convent at Olsberg
as an embroiderer of church vestments.
The spontaneous pleasure in narrative,
which had been characteristic of the
early figurative embroideries in Switzerland, is only rarely found in ecclesiastical work as, for example, in the original
embroideries of Anna Maria Marzohl.
In her years as an Ursuline nun (1665–
1712) at Lucerne, she made a series of
embroideries for the convent chapel:
a chasuble depicting the Tree of Jesse
and three altar frontals for the high
altar as well as the altars of St. Joseph
and St. Ursula. The style of their many
figures can be attributed to the influence
of engravings.

In east Switzerland, in such places
as St. Gallen, where linen weaving and
the linen trade had flourished for many
centuries and where the manufacture of
cotton reached a high degree of refinement in the eighteenth century, white
embroidery underwent a strong revival
after the middle of the eighteenth century. In the seventeenth century, a preference for lace had predominated over
white embroidery in the field of fashion.

The new fashion at the end of the
eighteenth and the beginning of the
nineteenth centuries often substituted
white linen or cotton for the heavy silks
which had been previously used. Thus
a revival of white embroidery was
favored in the Empire.

Appenzell and St. Gallen, whose
hinterland extended to the east across
the country frontier of Vorarlberg,
achieved an international reputation for
their white embroidery. The white
embroidery on handkerchiefs and
underclothes of cambric and muslin
was carried out by organized teams of
outworkers and was exported, at first to
France in particular and then across the
whole of Europe. Owing to growing
industrialization, outworkers gradually
came to rely on embroidery machines,
but this type of Swiss embroidery still
maintained its importance and renown.

Sweden

ONLY A FEW SWEDISH EMBROIDERIES have survived from early medieval times and before. Fragments of needlework found in Viking graves in the trading center of Birka, near present-day Stockholm, indicate that commercial and cultural connections existed with eastern Europe and Byzantium besides the important links with western European countries. Western influences grew stronger during and after the thirteenth century, as demonstrated by Swedish ecclesiastical architecture in particular but also by Swedish embroideries. The backwardness in style due to the geographical situation of Sweden was naturally less pronounced in ecclesiastical textiles and in textiles from workshops where there was a knowledge of contemporary foreign needlework.

Late Medieval Embroidery

In founding a religious order at Vadstena in 1370, St. Birgitta stipulated that some of the nuns should devote their time to decorative needlework. The embroidery workshop at Vadstena became famous throughout the Scandinavian countries as both its products and a knowledge of the techniques that were used there were disseminated.

Ecclesiastical textiles from the late Middle Ages have been preserved in much greater quantity in Sweden in proportion to the size of the population at that time than in any other European country. Small provincial churches often took over works of art from the larger ones which could afford to renew their vestments and church furnishings. Chasubles, stoles, antependia and other altar coverings, chalice veils and funeral palls are among the surviving treasures from the Middle Ages, some imported – from north Germany, The Netherlands and England, in particular – and some Swedish work, such as was produced at Vadstena and at other convents.

In addition to the embroidery done by religious foundations and in private houses, there were a number of independent workshops. The best-known workshop of those in Stockholm was that of Albert the Embroiderer, also known as Albertus Pictor (Plate 86).

Of the medieval embroideries that survive, three principal types may be distinguished: silk embroideries generally executed freehand, with the design unrelated to the threads of the fabric; patchwork embroidery combined with appliqué work in wool; and counted threadwork in, for example, cross stitch or long-armed cross stitch or darning in wool on a thin fabric, usually linen.

The first is the largest category, comprising most of the ecclesiastical textiles that survive. The stitches most commonly employed were satin and split stitch, but there are also examples of laid and couched work. In early needlework geometric patterns predominate but later the patterns were freer and the stitches laid in different directions to simulate painting. Split stitch was used in the earliest embroidery from Vadstena as in *opus anglicanum*, and in some pieces it covered the entire pattern surface.

Outlines might be emphasized by thicker threads or seams and the appearance of velvet was sometimes imitated in embroidery. A special effect was achieved with threaded pearls, stitched on to the ground; and sometimes pearls covered the whole pattern area. Relief effects obtained by the use of different stitches, gold, silver and brilliantly colored threads and beads gave to late medieval textiles the sumptuous appearance of embroidered pictures.

Some embroideries which have been preserved appear to have been donated to churches after they had been used in secular ceremonies and festivals. Among these are coverlets with patchwork embroidery and couched threads or gilt membrane strips between shaped patches in contrasting colors. The oldest known coverlet of this type was probably made for a wedding in 1303. It bears the crest of a German princess, which has been regarded as evidence that this kind of embroidery was introduced from Germany. There are also cushion covers ornamented in a similar way or in appliqué work combined with woolen embroidery.

Counterpane, *from Dalhem Church, Småland, Sweden, probably early fifteenth century. Red, green and black wadmal with intarsia embroidery, 9ft 1in × 6ft 7in (2·7m × 2·1m). Swedish embroideries were not infrequently presented to the church after they had served some secular purpose.* STATE HISTORICAL MUSEUM, STOCKHOLM.

Medieval textile furnishings included wall hangings (often in the form of friezes), tablecloths and cushion covers. These were usually worked on counted threads, in cross stitch or long-armed cross stitch or darning on a thin ground of tabby or extended tabby weave. Common motifs were stylized lilies, trees, stars and birds, arranged diagonally or symmetrically with a central axis and often in a polygonal framework. These were also typical of ecclesiastical textiles. Darning, which produced an effect resembling that of brocading, was usually worked in wool on linen, and there are also examples of medieval embroidery in existence worked in holbein stitch, drawn threadwork and darning on knotted net.

Some medieval needlework is difficult to date since the techniques and patterns, composed of stylized natural motifs, continued to be employed long after the fifteenth century.

The Sixteenth and Seventeenth Centuries

After the Reformation in Sweden, and the dissolution of the religious foundations at the beginning of the sixteenth century, the larger workshops for secular embroidery gained in importance. The Swedish kings, wishing to live like renaissance princes and demonstrate their power, interested themselves in ceremonial display. They ordered dresses, saddle cloths and other textiles from abroad and also employed court embroiderers of their own; and the aristocracy followed suit.

Beds were important pieces of furniture in the houses of the rich and wedding beds received special attention even in humbler homes. The whole wooden frame was sometimes covered in fabric, which was often embroidered, and there were two types of coverlet, one for when the bed was not in use. The patterns on these were generally freehand designs.

The influence of foreign embroidery is discernible in the sixteenth and early seventeenth century, principally of German work. Subsequently the influence of French textiles became increasingly apparent until and after the emergence of the full baroque style. The techniques employed were many and various, even on a single object, especially during the seventeenth century. The flat style of embroidery of the sixteenth century gave way to raised work or padded satin stitch. Large, bold shapes were worked in appliqué or patchwork while the outlines and edges were decorated with metal, lace and

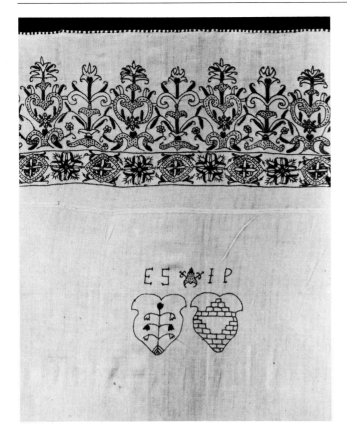

fringes. Velvet and other thick fabrics were used in furnishings, both secular and ecclesiastical, and for dresses.

The quality of embroidery on sheets and pillowcases was regarded as an indication of the owner's social position. In the sixteenth century the design had definite outlines possibly worked in stem stitch, with filling-in laidwork or darning patterns, while geometrical satin stitch and cut and drawn threadwork were also used in white embroidery. Later, ornament was composed of curving rather than right-angled forms. Characteristic motifs on bed linen were flowers, leaves, pomegranates and heraldic animals with the crests and initials of the owners.

Appliqué work was favored on cushion covers for hard chairs and benches, though in the seventeenth century upholstered seat furniture became increasingly popular in the houses of the prosperous. Representative of middle-class furnishing of this period are some cushions embroidered by a minister's daughter in wool with appliqué decoration. It was needlework such as this that served as a model for popular decorative needlework.

Tablecloths were ornamented with appliqué work in the same manner as the bed coverlets but also with cross stitch or long-armed cross stitch on linen fabrics. A special type of tablecloth, made of white material, was embroidered in red or black silk with stem stitch for the outlines and sometimes with back stitch, drawn threadwork and holbein stitch, such as were also used on linen garments. Another kind of cloth, a "ceiling cloth," often made of white linen with openwork ornament, sometimes made of netting with a darned pattern, was hung over the big dining table at festivals.

Eighteenth-Century Embroidery
The art of embroidery continued to flourish in the eighteenth century. Both silk and woolen yarns were employed for colorful and picturesque motifs, and long and short satin stitch was used with increasing frequency.

While appliqué work was rare in the eighteenth century, quilting, a technique that makes for warmth even when the fabrics are thin, became more common. At this period silk and white cotton materials found favor for fine embroidery.

Flowers and tendrils were typical decorative motifs, deriving from English and Dutch examples and ultimately from Oriental patterns. In the mid-century naturalistic versions of these

ABOVE, LEFT:
Sheet, *detail of the border, worked with the coats of arms and initials of Erik Stake and Ingeborg Posse, Sweden, 1590s. Linen embroidered with red silk in stem and satin stitches, 7ft 7½in × 9ft (2·32m × 3m). Beds were important pieces of furniture and bed linen, especially for the bride's bed, was beautifully embroidered.*
NORDIC MUSEUM, STOCKHOLM.

ABOVE:
Cushion cover, *worked by Maria Krok, a minister's daughter from Villstad, Småland, Sweden, and embroidered with her name and the year 1680. Red wadmal with appliqué and laid linen cords, 21¾in × 21¾in (56cm × 56cm). Appliqué work was popular for the decoration of cushion covers for seat furniture.*
NORDIC MUSEUM, STOCKHOLM.

were used for all forms of furnishing,
even carpets, and particularly on
dresses. Long and short satin stitch,
cross stitch and *point d'hongrie* were
popular and, for furnishings, *petit point*.

During the latter part of the
eighteenth century flower borders be-

came narrower, smaller leaf forms were
used and floral motifs were often combined with bands and festoons. Whitework again became popular after the
colorful rococo period with chain
stitch and tambour work predominating.

Young girls, who learnt to embroider
as part of their education, made samplers with letters of the alphabet and
decorative motifs which served as
patterns for them later. Needlework
pictures, simulating paintings, were
made for fire screens and other pieces
of furniture.

Needlework in the Nineteenth Century

Professional embroiderers, of whom
there were still a considerable number
in the eighteenth century, became increasingly rare and were principally
occupied in the making of uniforms.
However, there were plenty of amateurs
working at home, embroidery was
taught in schools for girls and, toward
the end of the century, a number of
special workshops and schools were set
up.

Of the many needlework techniques
that were practiced, cross stitch on a
canvas ground following patterns made
in Germany was among the most
popular. Neckerchiefs and shawls were
often embroidered with white yarn on
machine-made net. In spite of the
growing industrial and domestic use of
the sewing machine in the latter part of
the nineteenth century, hand embroidery was still done, often to supplement
machined work.

In 1874 the association Handarbetets vänner (Friends of Handicraft)
was founded, followed by Svensk
Hemslöjd (Swedish Handicraft) in
1899. At the same time antiquarians
set to work recording surviving pre-
industrial forms of art which in turn
encouraged textile designers to study
ancient Scandinavian ornament and
folk art. Old patterns were the inspiration for new ones. The influence of
William Morris and his fellow-thinkers
in England was also felt in Sweden, but
not before the end of the century.

Swedish Folk Embroidery

In Scania, the southernmost province
of Sweden which until 1658 belonged
to Denmark, a great many embroidered
pieces still exist that were made in the
eighteenth and nineteenth centuries in a
style passed on from one generation to

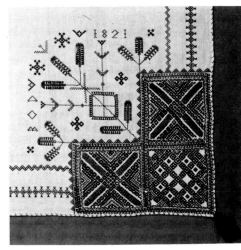

LEFT:
Neckerchief, *detail of a corner, Leksand, Dalecarlia, Sweden, worked with the initials BOD and the date 1821. White linen embroidered with black thread in geometric satin, holbein and cross stitches. This was part of the formal dress for women in Dalecarlia.* NORDIC MUSEUM, STOCKHOLM.

FAR LEFT:
Wall hanging, *worked with the initials POS HMD, Sweden, early nineteenth century. White linen tabby embroidered with cotton thread in surface satin and stem stitches, 8ft 3½in × 2ft 8½in (252cm × 82cm). The stitches are worked predominantly in blue and pink thread.* NORDIC MUSEUM, STOCKHOLM.

the next since the renaissance and early baroque periods. These were times of prosperity for farmers in this region and their conservative taste since has ensured the survival of the old patterns and handicrafts. Typical of this part of the country is a type of *reticella* work on fine linen.

Cushions for chairs, benches and carriages were stored by many families in chests, as were large woolen coverlets with rich wool embroidery in many colors on a dark ground. The pattern, generally baroque in character, was composed of flowers, wreaths, hearts,

stars and trees and figures of men and animals (Plate 87). Items were often embroidered for a marriage and where this is so it is indicated by the use of hearts and doves as decoration. A lion represented the man, a deer the woman. Characteristic stitches were long and short satin stitch combined with stem stitch. The oldest needlework of this type dates from *c*.1700, but most surviving pieces are from the nineteenth century.

Eighteenth-century cushion covers from Scania, and from other parts of the country, were worked in long-armed cross stitch or appliqué. While houses in the country still had unupholstered furniture, cushions were required. Many families brought these out only for festivals and for this reason they are in a good state of preservation.

In the two provinces closest to Scania a characteristic type of house consisted of a low central building with a chimney and one or two higher buildings at the side. For festivals it was the practice to dress the bare wooden walls and the sloping ceilings with decorative friezes and hangings, either woven, painted or embroidered. In the western district, the province of Halland, the hangings were embroidered with stylized plant forms in, among other stitches, herringbone stitch. It is a characteristic of much folk embroidery that the colored thread forming the design is more in evidence on the front of the cloth than on the reverse, an economical use of the expensive thread.

In the eastern district, the province of Blekinge, there were embroiderers who, from the eighteenth century onward, made to order a particular type of wall hanging, usually of linen. The pattern, which derived from eighteenth-

metric satin stitching, and in Dalecarlia holbein stitch was also used. On woolen garments the embroidery was generally freestyle and often worked by tailors and other professional needleworkers.

In Hälsingland, east of Dalecarlia, they specialized in linen weaving from the Middle Ages onward and farmers regarded fine bed linen as particularly important. A traditional embroidery pattern used on the short side of the pillowcase, on the top sheet and on a hanging sheet which covered the lower part of the bed front was executed during the nineteenth century and earlier in red thread in satin or cross stitch. About 1800 a new, freer type of decoration appeared, relating in style to earlier folk embroidery found on the Continent, from where it seems to have been introduced. In the nineteenth century this type of embroidery, mostly in surface satin stitch, became especially popular in the district; and in the twentieth century throughout the country.

The Lapps embroidered in an archaic and recognizable manner: thin threads of tin were laid and fastened to the cloth with threads made of reindeer sinews.

The Twentieth Century
Many excellent artists worked as teachers in the handicraft schools founded in the nineteenth century; and early in the twentieth century a number of small textile workshops were set up. With the revival in secular embroidery came a renewed interest in ecclesiastical embroidery and for this special workshops were established as well as a textile conservation institute.

Art Nouveau was the principal style in Swedish textile design in c.1910, known by the German name, "*Jugendstil.*" Plant forms and patterns with swirling lines replaced the Nordic decoration of the previous century. *Jugendstil* was adopted at an early date by the embroidery designers of Handarbetets vänner.

In the twenties there was a return to a more formal style of decoration, which was often restricted to narrow borders. The vogue for functionalism, with the desire for plain surfaces, brought about a decline in embroidery.

Shops selling the materials and patterns for home needlework were set up in the nineteenth century and they exist still. The designers stressed the

ABOVE:
Wall hanging, *detail of the frieze, worked with the initials ALND and the date 1842, Sweden. White linen tabby embroidered with cotton thread in braid, stem and cross stitches, 17ft 8in × 1ft 2½in (538cm × 37cm). Linen wall hangings of this type were generally made for an occasion such as a wedding.* NORDIC MUSEUM, STOCKHOLM.

RIGHT:
Sample of embroidery, *designed by Gunnar G:son Wennerberg for Handarbetets vänner, Stockholm, Sweden, 1901. Embroidered with green, gray and pale yellow linen thread in stem stitch with the outlines in red, 38in × 26½in (96cm × 66cm). A design in the Art Nouveau style that was used for a variety of different types of textiles.* NORDIC MUSEUM, STOCKHOLM.

OPPOSITE, TOP LEFT:
Bed with two pillows, *from Gräsbo, Hälsingland, Sweden. The top pillowcase is decorated with drawn work and darned red stars, the lower one is embroidered with a red star pattern in satin stitch.* NORDIC MUSEUM, STOCKHOLM.

century models of English origin, was of flowers, scattered over the surface or in groups. Embroidered dates and initials indicate that they were made for a festival, usually a wedding.

The folk costume from Scania and Dalecarlia, in the northwestern area of central Sweden, are some of the most distinctive. The ornament on the linen garments of the traditional dresses is often executed in drawnwork and geo-

importance of good-quality materials;
and they often turned to traditional
patterns for inspiration. In recent years
needlework, often worked by a group of
embroiderers, has been commissioned
to decorate public buildings. This contemporary work is characterized by the
use of unconventional materials and
techniques.

ABOVE:
"The Lion Bride," *detail of
a wall hanging, one of nine
pieces for a room in the
Swedish ship,* Jor Britannia,
*designed by Gösta Werner
and embroidered by
Handarbetets vänner, 1974.
Sailcloth decorated with
appliqué work and machine
embroidery, 27½in × 59in
(70cm × 150cm).*

LEFT:
Cardboard stencils and
templets, *used in the
nineteenth century for a
type of embroidery, mostly
in satin stitch, popular in
Hälsingland, Sweden.*
NORDIC MUSEUM,
STOCKHOLM.

FAR LEFT:
Collar of a Laplandish
woman's costume, *worn in
the nineteenth century. Blue,
red and green wadmal with
silver jewelry and tin-
embroidered turned-up
collar. This type of collar
was worn on festive occasions.*
NORDIC MUSEUM,
STOCKHOLM.

Denmark

IN DENMARK, ONE OF THE EARLIEST embroidered textiles to survive is a woolen blouse worn by a young woman of the Bronze Age whose body was unearthed in its coffin, made from a hollowed-out tree trunk, at Skrydstrup, south Jutland, in 1935. Around the neck and across the sleeves is woolen button-hole stitching of remarkable quality. It is, however, only from the period of the Renaissance onward that enough examples of Danish needlework still exist to study its history and development.

In contrast to the outstanding embroideries done in expensive materials in monasteries and workshops throughout Europe, Danish needlework has a character of its own that is expressed in a particular simplicity both in the choice and the representation of motifs. Furthermore, it is typified by a sparing use of the embroidery materials. Excellent embroideries for chasubles, uniforms and other items were, of course, manufactured by professional workers in Denmark as elsewhere, but what was, and still is, characteristically Danish is the tradition among women to embroider their clothes and objects for the home.

Needlework of the Upper Classes
Dating from the late sixteenth century are a number of pieces intended as altar cloths or for domestic use in the houses of the nobility. They were usually worked in red silk on linen. Scenes from the Bible and symbolic subjects predominate following the fashions in design of that period. In one example, four female figures symbolize the Virtues: Charity, Justice, Prudence and Fortitude. The other three of the Seven Virtues – Faith, Hope and Temperance – which were often depicted in those days – are supposed to have been embroidered on the borders of the cloth which have since disintegrated. Apart from these figures, the composition includes a variety of flowers, birds and animals (Plate 88), all of which, as pointed out by Georg Garde who has made a detailed study of the patterns for these embroideries

in his book, *Danske silkebroderede lærredsduge*, derive from different sources and yet are typical of Danish design at this period. The cloth is signed by the embroideress Wiveke Friis with her own and her parents' names. She herself died in *c*.1655, so it is possible to give the needlework an approximate date.

Danish silk-embroidered linen table-cloths followed the European fashions in embroidery and are related to English blackwork, the linen embroidery of Switzerland and silk embroidery done in Italy, Spain and France. However, the direct inspiration came from the German embroideries of the sixteenth century. At that time Denmark and the entire northern part of Europe entered a period of prosperity, which was reflected in the style of works of art. Furniture decorated with rich carving became popular and noblewomen based their embroidery patterns on the many new motifs adapted for furniture and designs in printed books which from that time were being enthusiastically collected by members of the aristocracy. With the conservatism that is so typical of textile design, the new style did not find its way into the design of embroidery until about ten or twenty years after it had appeared in the design of furniture.

Transferring the patterns to the cloths was mainly carried out by the women who intended to stitch them, but often the hand of a professional is discernible in the composition. Differences in the quality of the needlework may also be apparent between one part of the cloth and another which indicate that the work was started by a skilled embroideress, who left other parts of the embroidery to be done by less experienced women. The housewife, her daughters and the servant girls, it would appear from diaries and letters of that period, took part in the work as equals. The collaboration of the many women of a household and the assistance of, for example, a painter resulted in the special character of Danish silk-embroidered linen cloths. As many as

seventy pieces are preserved to this day.

Among the upper classes the earlier styles of needlework continued throughout the eighteenth century and there is reason to believe that the manner of embroidering textiles for the home did not change radically. The baroque design of the flower border of a sheet dated 1789 suggests a much earlier date in the same century. It belonged to several generations of a family of rectors. Even though there are many pieces of needlework from the eighteenth century in Danish museums which show the acceptance of rococo and later styles and of other techniques, it must be supposed that many women went on working with the patterns and stitches with which they were familiar and which they appreciated.

Peasant Embroidery

During the eighteenth century the peasants developed a style of their own, or at least from that time to the end of the nineteenth century the peasants formed a more distinctive social class than in earlier periods.

The peasants as well as the nobility needed linen for their homes and clothes and in certain parts of the country social and economic conditions allowed the women to carry out the production of high-quality textiles. Their needlework developed into a splendid branch of Danish folk art. The peasants' liberation from serfdom, or at least from the bonds of traditional land tenure, was an important social factor. The peasants in those districts which produced the most elaborate

Sheet (details), Denmark, 1789. Linen embroidery on linen, 9ft 3in × 4ft 9in (281cm × 144cm), the border 7in (18cm). This formerly belonged to a family of Danish rectors and formed part of a set, of which there is a pillowcase in a similar style dated 1796. DANISH FOLK MUSEUM, COPENHAGEN.

LEFT:
Scarf (detail), Amager, Denmark, first half of the nineteenth century. Silk and silver threads on silk, 32in × 32in (82cm × 82cm). Known as Barcelona scarves, the woven pattern on the imported scarves was copied in the embroidery by smallholders' wives. DANISH FOLK MUSEUM, COPENHAGEN.

Mette Olsdatter, *a
photograph of her in her
home at Heden, near
Copenhagen, Denmark,
1917. The towels and
pillowcases are worked in
Hedebosyning and were
part of her trousseau since
they bear her initials. She
was married in c.1860. A
few days after the
photograph was taken the
farm was burned to the
ground.* DANISH FOLK
MUSEUM, COPENHAGEN.

needlework had comparatively large
herds of livestock: in summer the cows
were milked by the maids on the common land far away from the villages; in
winter the work with the livestock was
limited to a minimum and the milkmaids could spend a good deal of their
time spinning and doing needlework.
Outstanding embroideries are to be
found from the island of Amager and on
Zealand in the neighborhood of Copenhagen, the district called Heden. Work
from various regions may be distinguished by the differences in the technique and design of their needlework.

Peasant women hardly ever used
metal or silk thread or commercial
fabrics in their needlework. Generally
the stitching was worked on linen with
a bleached linen thread. The linen was
used for shirts and shifts, men's and
women's undergarments and it was also
used for towels and bed linen for festive
occasions.

Renaissance pattern books from Italy
and Germany were an important influence on style and technique and from
about the second decade of the nine-

teenth century the influence of the
baroque also became apparent. The
delay in its adoption may seem remarkable, but parallels may easily be found
in many central and eastern European
countries. Furthermore, the conservatism of textile design as a whole, which
may be noticed in Danish embroideries
of the upper classes, should be
remembered.

A particular kind of silk embroidery
was done on the isle of Amager on
scarves. Because of the precious
materials that were employed, it was
done almost as professional work by
local smallholders' wives. In order to
spare the expensive silk, the stitches are
fastened over only a couple of the
threads of the fabric on the reverse
side. Known as *Amagersyning* (Amager
needlework), this type of embroidery
has acquired an international renown.

The peasant women of Amager also
did remarkable needlework on linen, in
which the influence of Friesian work is
apparent. About one hundred families
from Friesland, in the northern part of
the Netherlands, settled on Amager in

the sixteenth century and, as ship-owners, they kept in touch with their home country.

The Nineteenth Century

During the first half of the nineteenth century woven tulle became available and was readily accepted by Danish peasant women as a substitute for the expensive bobbin laces from Flanders or from Tonder in Denmark. Tulle drawn work was popular until *c.*1850. The patterns were often copies of the Tonder laces, though in some cases the patterns were freely adapted for needlework. These imitations of lace appear to be peculiar to Denmark and the tulle network was a purely individual product.

During the same period linen embroidery became a highly developed art among the peasants, as demonstrated by a shift with needlepoint lace round the collar and embroidery on the collar and sleeve. It was worked in Heden, near Copenhagen.

After the middle of the nineteenth century the needlework from Heden became fashionable in Copenhagen and some examples left the country as presents to friends and family. At the end of the century *Hedebosyning* (Hedebo needlework) was described in ladies' magazines.

Woolen materials were also used by the peasant women. The imitation of the fashionable shawls, known in Denmark as "French shawls" or "Paisleys," resulted in the many excellent pieces of work that were carried out in the middle of the nineteenth century.

At the end of the nineteenth century, when peasant art was about to disappear, a group of architects and designers in Copenhagen realized that a rich source of inspiration lay in traditional embroideries. They started collecting what pieces were available and using the patterns in their designs. Most embroidered textiles up to that time were imported from Germany, but this new interest resulted in a change in style. The designs, traced on to the background material, could be obtained from several workshops. Today, many needleworkers design their own pieces as they always did in the past. Of the various techniques that are practiced, patchwork is among the most popular (Plate 89), bearing witness to the traditional Danish skills with the needle and thread.

ABOVE:
Shawl *(detail)*, Funen, Denmark, *c.1860–70. Wool embroidery on woolen tabby, 6ft × 4ft 1½in (180cm × 105cm). The patterns for shawls such as this were derived from French woven ones, adapted for embroidery. There are often different motifs in the corners, one in gay colors, the other in somber colors for mourning.* DANISH FOLK MUSEUM, COPENHAGEN.

LEFT:
Shift *(detail)*, Heden, Denmark, 1844. Linen embroidery on linen, width of collar approx. 8in (20cm). This bears the initials SLD of the original owner, the daughter of a prosperous peasant family in the neighborhood of Copenhagen.* PRIVATE COLLECTION.

ABOVE:
Cap, *Jutland, Denmark,
c.1840. White tulle with
Tonder lace and silk ribbon
and embroidered with cotton,
width of the pleated wings
5in (12cm). Woven tulle
first became available in
Denmark in the early part
of the nineteenth century. It
is here used with the bobbin
lace for which it was often a
substitute.* DANISH FOLK
MUSEUM, COPENHAGEN.

ABOVE, RIGHT:
Cap, *Funen, Denmark,
c.1840. Tulle with white
cotton embroidery, width
from front to neck, 10in
(25cm). The tulle cap was
worn over a cap of silk,
often, as in this example,
embroidered in silk with a
flower motif. This was a
substitute for the French silk*

*brocades that were much
admired in Denmark but
unobtainable after the
French Revolution.* DANISH
FOLK MUSEUM,
COPENHAGEN.

RIGHT:
Cap, *worked by Dorte
Sørensen, a professional
peasant embroideress, North
Zealand, Denmark, c.1850.
Gold thread and spangles on
silk, width of embroidered
ribbon on the front, 4in
(10cm). The cap is
particularly richly decorated
as not only the neck but the
ribbon on the front are
covered with embroidery.*
ROSKILDE MUSEUM,
ZEALAND.

Norway

Norwegian decorative needlework survives from medieval times onward, executed by both professionals and by amateurs. Embroidery in towns followed the general trends in European fashions, whereas the needlework done in country districts has its own particular character and is thus of special interest.

Medieval Embroidery

From ancient legends and ballads it is known that the art of embroidery was highly regarded throughout the Middle Ages. However, there is today little evidence of work produced in Norway, as most of the preserved embroidery of this date was imported. The needlework wall hanging depicting the three Magi from Höylandet Church is one of the few medieval pieces that is assumed to be of Norwegian origin, and it probably dates from the first half of the thirteenth century. To the left the kings are riding to Bethlehem, then comes the presentation of the gifts to the Infant Jesus, and to the right the kings' dream. The background is of red woolen fabric in extended tabby and, of what must have been a considerably larger piece of needlework, a length of about seventy-eight inches (205cms) remains. Remnants of loops indicate that the piece was hung on the wall for decorative purposes.

The outlines are elegantly executed in white linen yarn in stem stitch, and the figures filled in with pattern darning in blue, yellow and green woolen yarn and in white linen. Several patterns are used in the execution of a single figure. It is skilled work, probably carried out in a workshop.

The long, slender figures with naturalistic expressions, the firm outlines and the poses relate closely to manuscript illuminations from St. Albans Cathedral in Hertfordshire. It is thought that the designer of this hanging might have had access to English patterns, though the design was not directly copied, as the kings' costumes are not known from pictorial representations outside Norway.

The Höylandet wall hanging seems to be the work of a professional embroiderer and this may also be the case with three tablecloths from western Norway which probably date from the close of the fifteenth or the beginning of the sixteenth century. One piece was not known about until 1977. It is made of fine white tabby woven linen, about 150 inches (391cms) long, and quite narrow. Five bands in pattern darning run across the material with a single rhomboid figure at one of the short ends. Each band is of a different pattern consisting of geometrical designs and birds in conventionalized trees. The patterns are arranged so that the guests all sitting along one side of a narrow table see the design the right way up. Woolen yarn in red, blue and brown is used, the colors varying within the borders to give a lively and pleasing effect.

The embroidery seems to have been carried out with great precision, but on careful inspection it may be seen that there are some inaccuracies in the thread counting. Every mistake is, however, cleverly adjusted so that the pattern is properly maintained. This freedom in the handling of the work proves that the embroideress knew her craft.

The Seventeenth Century

From the seventeenth century, in contrast to the Middle Ages, several pieces of needlework are known. An example of popular textile art is the cloth of traditional type from the Narom farm in Sigdal which would have been used to cover the bread, carried in a neatly decorated basket, which the guests brought with them to feasts. It is dated 1682 and has the owner's initials, KKS, and the name of the farm between geometrical motifs. Similar owner's marks with dates are frequently to be found on decorative textiles and occasionally on costume.

The embroidery is in dark blue, red and yellow wool on a ground of tabby woven white linen. Three kinds of stitches are used: holbein stitch predominates, with minor details in cross

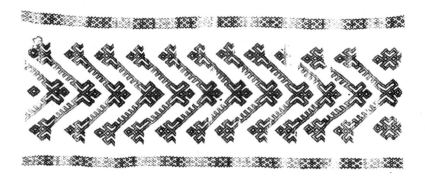

stitch and inscriptions and dates in
chain stitch. The main pattern has three
rows of diamond motifs that are linked
together and filled with crosses. The
design is spacious, and the contrasts of
colors make a pleasing effect.

As in the tablecloth the thread counting has not been carried out accurately,
but in this case the faults have not been
adjusted, the effect of which is particularly visible on the left-hand side. Perhaps our ancestors did not find it
necessary, as we do, to stick strictly to a
regular design.

Eighteenth-Century Needlework

The eighteenth century is a rich period
in the history of Norwegian embroidery,
particularly with regard to costume and
interior decoration for festive occasions.
Cushion covers form one of the most
important types of embroidered textiles
preserved from this period. Seat furniture in farmhouses consisted of hard
wooden chairs and benches and cushions therefore served both a useful and
a decorative purpose.

Embroidered cushion covers were
made from the second half of the seventeenth century until the early nineteenth
century, different districts developing
individual designs. A group of items
dating from 1747 to 1786 made in the
valleys of Hallingdal and Numedal
have easily recognizable designs,
exemplified by a cushion cover with a
pattern composed of a vase with flowers
stretching out toward the four corners.
Between the main flowers in the corners
are three peacocks and a deer eating
fruit and leaves. The year and the
owner's initials, J A S, appear between
the flowers.

Blue, green, pink, yellow and white
wool is used on a blue woolen twill
ground. The animals and flowers are in
satin stitch and laidwork, with the outlines and other details in stem stitch,
couched and split stitch. Colored floral
embroidery of this type worked independently of the threads of the background is known in Norway as "rosesaum." The models were frequently
derived from different sources but were
often varied and the result depended on
the embroiderer's skill and imagination.
In this example the design spreads
harmoniously over the surface and the
colors are excellently balanced.

The embroiderer of a glove from
Telemark possessed a strong sense of
color and design. The glove, which was
a gift from the bride to the bridegroom,
is dated to the close of the eighteenth
century. The tradition of the bride
bringing gifts to her fiancé and his
family prevailed in certain parts of the
country up until recent years. They
were made by the bride herself and
embroidered gloves and mittens were
popular items.

Here the glove is made of white
knitted wool with a simulated plush
wristband. A large rosette covers the
back and small tendrils extend along
the fingers. The colors are bright, the
flowers in red and orange and the leaves
in shades of green with smaller dashes
of light blue, dark blue and black, and
the woolen yarn has a silky gloss. The
choice of technique – predominately
satin stitch, and stem stitch and
couched stitch for the outlines – displays well the texture of the yarn.

Floral embroidery became especially
popular for traditional festive costumes
and was used on various articles such as
headdresses, jackets, bodices and skirts,
stockings and mittens. No doubt the

ABOVE, LEFT:
Cushion cover, *Hallingdal, Norway, 1772. Wool embroidery on wool, $23\frac{5}{8}$in × $21\frac{5}{8}$in (60cm × 55cm). The floral patterns worked on such cushion covers were generally in bright colors on a blue, red, green or yellow ground.* NORWEGIAN FOLK MUSEUM, OSLO.

ABOVE, RIGHT:
Glove, *Telemark, Norway, late eighteenth century. Knitted wool with wool embroidery, length $9\frac{1}{4}$in (23·5cm). Embroidered knitted gloves were traditionally used for festive occasions.* NORWEGIAN FOLK MUSEUM, OSLO.

BELOW, LEFT:
Collar *(detail), Nordmöre, Norway, 1830–40. Counted-thread embroidery in linen on cotton and linen, $4\frac{5}{8}$in × $6\frac{7}{8}$in (11·75cm × 17·5cm). Nordmöre embroideries were sometimes executed in a free style with naturalistic motifs.* NORWEGIAN FOLK MUSEUM, OSLO.

BELOW, RIGHT:
Apron, *detail of the border, western Norway, nineteenth century. Linen embroidery on linen, $7\frac{5}{8}$in × $10\frac{13}{16}$in (19·5cm × 27·5cm). Hardanger embroidery, as this type of work is called, was inspired by Italian reticella work.* NORWEGIAN FOLK MUSEUM, OSLO.

embroidery of eighteenth-century fashion dresses had a certain influence on country costumes.

At a funeral it was traditional in many parts of Norway to place the coffin, covered by a woven coverlet or shawl, in the living room before the procession moved to the churchyard. In Telemark a special type of embroidered linen cloth, placed on top of the woven cloth, consisted either of two pieces laid crosswise or of a single piece with arms fastened to either side to form a cross.

Such coffin cloths were often richly decorated, as was the one embroidered with the date 1796 (Plate 91). The ground of white tabby woven linen is embroidered in blue, green, red, yellow, pink/beige and black wool and silk. There is a greater variety of stitches than in any of the other items that are illustrated – pattern darning, holbein stitch, cross stitch, satin stitch, stem and buttonhole stitch – each type forming an individual row or part of the central design. In this may be recognized the pattern darning that appears on medieval tablecloths and the diamond patterning on the traditional cloth used for covering a gift of food. Eighteenth-century floral embroidery and cross stitch, new and old motifs, all blend together.

The borders in darning stitch enclosing the central design were used in Telemark for the neckbands and wristbands of shirts. The end of the eighteenth century also saw coverlets embroidered in this way, closely imitating the woven textiles in weft-patterned tabby known as "opphämta."

Nineteenth-Century Whitework and Colored Embroidery

In the nineteenth century whitework predominated in certain districts of western Norway such as Nordmöre. Extant embroidery of this type dates from 1750 to the 1870s, reaching its peak in the years between 1820 and 1845. A collar dating from this period is worked in linen on a ground of tabby woven cotton, lined with a heavy tabby woven linen. Some of the stitches go through both layers; some only through the cotton fabric.

The design consists of eight-pointed stars, the St. Andrew's cross and geometric motifs arranged in three rows running lengthwise and separated by back stitching. The main pattern is

executed in satin stitch standing out prominently from a ground of punched work. Between the motifs the fabric is perforated with punched eyelets producing a fine contrast between the dense embroidery and the more or less transparent background.

This effect is even more striking in embroidery from the Hardanger district in western Norway. The whitework here is always in geometric counted-thread embroidery, whereas the Nordmöre stitching is often freely worked. An apron border has hem stitching, needleweaving, punch stitch, cutwork, kloster

Cloth, *Sigdal, Norway, dated 1682. Wool embroidered on linen, 40in × 23¼in (104·5cm × 59cm). This type of cloth was used to cover a basket containing a gift of food. The owner's name and the name of his farm are embroidered on this cloth as well as the date.* NORWEGIAN FOLK MUSEUM, OSLO.

blocks and English eyelets embroidered in linen on tabby woven linen. The main pattern is composed of diamonds, each one filled with a large St. Andrew's cross and four smaller Greek crosses. A narrow eyelet border and a somewhat broader band of crosses and eight-pointed stars enclose the center piece.

Like the colored embroideries, white-work was also limited to textiles for festive use such as shirts for the bride and bridegroom, aprons, kerchiefs and headdresses, bridal sheets, pillowcases, tablecloths and towels. Generally the work was carried out by young girls and old women and most of it was intended for their own use, though sometimes the articles were for sale.

In Telemark floral embroidery was also used in the nineteenth century on garments. The design of an apron, according to tradition made by a twenty-year-old girl, is common to the district, with the pattern concentrated in a border above the hemline. From the central motif the pattern runs symmetrically to either side of it and terminates in corner motifs. Each embroiderer developed her own variations of a standard pattern and, if the design were successful, others might adopt it; but exact copying never occurred. The apron is of black woolen tabby embroidered with wool in shades of red, ranging from purple to pink, and light yellow and light blue-green. The flame-like embroidery has the usual flowers and leaves worked in satin stitch and twigs and outlines worked in stem stitch.

The Twentieth Century

The valley of Setesdal is where traditional folk costume has survived longer than elsewhere in the country. Until recent years old people were still to be seen working in the fields in the everyday dress of this kind. Now, however, folk costume is used only for festive occasions and even then not by everyone. The costume is made and the embroidery traditionally worked without any underlying design by specialists within the area, very few women now maintaining the tradition of sewing their own costume.

The two decorated parts of the male costume are the trousers and the waistcoat (Plate 92). The embroidery shown here, made in 1970, is done in strong colors – red, green, blue, and white wool and the same colors with the addi-

ABOVE, TOP:
Women from Voss, western Norway, in traditional costumes, *1933. The aprons and one of the skirts are worked in Hardanger embroidery; the headdresses are in blackwork and the plastrons embroidered with pearls.* WILSE COLLECTION, NORWEGIAN FOLK MUSEUM, OSLO.

ABOVE, BOTTOM:
Apron *(detail), Telemark, Norway, nineteenth century. Wool embroidery on wool, 6⅛in × 13¾in (15·5cm × 35cm). Embroidered aprons were often worn by women as part of their traditional costume, the decoration confined to the border or scattered over the background.* NORWEGIAN FOLK MUSEUM, OSLO.

Girls from Setesdal, *Norway, 1910. The traditional costume of Setesdal consisted of two skirts. For everyday use they used to wear a white skirt; for festive occasions a black skirt used to be worn over the white one.* NORWEGIAN FOLK MUSEUM, OSLO.

tion of black in glazed cotton – on a black woolen twill ground. Satin stitch, stem stitch, threaded punch stitch and threaded cross stitch are the main features of the geometric patterning. Triangles, diamond and zigzag designs predominate with some floral embroidery in between to achieve an informal effect.

The costumes are never exactly alike, although during recent years the style has stagnated. The design is coarser and the range of colors more uniform, while as a whole the technique has been simplified. To obtain quicker results thicker yarn is used, the sewing-machine adds to the speed of the work.

It is difficult to tell what the fate of the traditional embroidery in Norway will be. Local handicraft practice following regional traditions has been replaced by handicraft organizations. The embroidery executed by Norwegian women today either follows international trends, which change with fashions, or is the result of individual artistic skill. During recent years a renewed interest in traditional needlework has become apparent, but the items which were embroidered formerly have largely ceased to be used and modern embroidery must find new functions.

Finland

When Finland came under Swedish rule in the twelfth century, and thus under the influence of the Roman Catholic Church, the country developed strong cultural ties with the West. These continued to exist even after 1809, when Finland was annexed to the Russian Empire as an autonomous state. In 1917, as a result of the Russian Revolution, Finland gained her independence.

These historical changes have influenced all aspects of Finnish culture. Under Swedish rule fashions and styles were brought in by the upper classes from Sweden, especially Stockholm which was the capital of the realm, and there was some contact with northern Germany as well.

Medieval Needlework

Because of the ravage of wars between West and East there are very few examples of textiles left in Finland from the era prior to the Great Northern War (1700–21). The medieval textiles still in existence are ecclesiastical and most of them were imported from abroad. It is known that as early as the fourteenth and fifteenth centuries, the bishops of Turku (Åbo) were importing expensive silk cloth from Venice and a few silk vestments have survived. Following the ecclesiastical fashions of the later Middle Ages, chasubles and copes made of Italian velvet with pomegranate designs and with embroidered orphreys were imported from northern Germany and Flanders.

Some examples of Finnish needlework of the Middle Ages are provided by the textiles from the Brigittine convent at Naantali, founded in 1438. According to the rules of the Brigittine order the nuns themselves wove and sewed textiles for the convent and embroidered works for ecclesiastical use following the example set by the mother convent at Vadstena in Sweden. Textiles for furnishings were embroidered in long-armed cross stitch in wool or ornamented with intarsia work or applied work using thick woolen cloth (Plate 93). The only signed work is an altar frontal with the initials "b a" of the nun Birgitta Anundsdother (daughter of Anund). This is a needle painting with fourteen scenes from the Lives of the Virgin Mary and Jesus, worked with colored silks on linen in split stitch and couched in silver-gilt and silver thread. In some silk and gold embroideries symbolic flower and animal designs and symbolic letters and short sentences cover the background in confused profusion to avoid empty spaces. Furnishing textiles with large designs in wool and intarsia embroidery in woolen cloth show the influence of the Byzantine silk fabrics from which the stylized lions, peacocks and griffins were copied. In intarsia work carried out on coarse woolen cloth the designs were embellished with applied work and the contours emphasized with gilt-leather strips couched with linen thread.

Gilt-leather counterpanes and cushions made of intarsia squares were used in Finnish castles and manor houses as late as the sixteenth century as wall hangings and as long cushion covers. Daughters from the manor houses who were educated at the convent of Naantali probably helped to spread the skills of embroidery to western Finland. In the churches of some manorial parishes these gilt-leather counterpanes and cushions were in use as funeral palls until as late as the beginning of the seventeenth century.

The Church, impoverished during the Reformation, was unable to support the art of embroidery and for a long time churches did not acquire any new and valuable textiles. It was not until the seventeenth century, when Sweden was at the height of her power, that the churches in Finland were again decorated with valuable ecclesiastical textiles, usually gifts from influential people and often the spoils of war from Central Europe.

The Renaissance in Finland

Little is known about secular embroidery during the Renaissance. Both French and German professional embroiderers worked at the Castle of

RIGHT:
Chalice cover *(detail),*
Finland, early seventeenth
century. Linen embroidered
in green and yellow silk in
in satin and stem stitches and
in silver-gilt thread, 1ft
9½in × 1ft 5½in (56cm ×
45·5cm). This was formerly
in Seili Church. NATIONAL
MUSEUM OF FINLAND,
HELSINKI.

MIDDLE:
Altar frontal or wall hanging
(detail), from the
Brigittine convent at
Naantali, Finland, early
sixteenth century. Coarse
linen embroidered in
polychrome wools in long-
armed cross stitch, 2ft 7½in
× 7ft 1in (80cm × 217cm).
The predominant colors are
red, yellow, green and blue
of various shades. NAANTALI
CHURCH.

BELOW:
Chalice cover, *Finland,*
mid-seventeenth century.
Linen embroidered in green
and yellow silk in satin and
stem stitches, 10in × 1ft 11in
(26cm × 60cm). This was
formerly in Pöytyä Church.
NATIONAL MUSEUM OF
FINLAND, HELSINKI.

Turku (Åbo), then the administrative
center of Finland, where their main
duty was to embroider the costumes of
their masters (in the sixteenth century
sometimes members of the ruling
Swedish family of Vasa) in the fashionable Spanish arabesque style. There
are also documents to prove that during
the seventeenth century there were professional embroiderers in the city of
Turku. It is possible that in some Finnish churches chalice covers and chasubles embroidered by Hebla, Eskil or
Maria, embroiderers mentioned in
mid-seventeenth-century documents,
are still in use. Professional embroiderers fell on hard times, however, after
embroidery using gold thread was for-
bidden in Sweden-Finland by the
Luxury Edict of 1644, passed because
the garments worn by noblemen and
their ladies were considered too
sumptuous.

Domestic Needlework of the Seventeenth Century

The traditions of needlework were nonetheless carried on in the seventeenth century in the form of domestic needlework by the mistress of the house and her maids. Few examples of this work have survived and these are mainly in churches. Designs from the embroidery pattern books of the Renaissance can be seen in chalice covers of linen embroidered in stem and satin stitch in silk and sometimes in metal thread. Their corners are usually decorated with a stylized flower or a chandelier. Some of them were, perhaps, originally intended to be used as handkerchiefs. Linen hand towels were embroidered with red silk thread in bands of double-running stitch, the heraldic patterns of these conforming too with the designs of embroidery pattern books. Toward the end of the seventeenth century embroidery with colored silk threads was replaced by whitework on household linen, and this is seen, for instance, on pillowcases, parts of which are so skillfully embroidered in white that they closely resemble professional work.

Furnishing textiles were still usually of canvas embroidered with colored woolen thread, mostly in cross stitch, long-armed cross stitch and tent stitch. The background was sometimes covered in a geometrical diaper pattern. Hungarian stitch was also popular for embroidered chair covers and embroidery in cross stitch and tent stitch was favored for upholstery because of its resemblance to tapestry.

Chairs were sometimes covered in colorful woolen cloth embroidered with large scattered flowers in the baroque style using stem stitch, satin stitch and long and short stitch.

The Eighteenth Century

From the eighteenth century onward embroidered household textiles have survived in greater quantity. The daughters of upper-class and burgher families were brought up to be skilled with a needle and thread from an early age and girls were often sent as boarders to Stockholm to be educated in the feminine arts. For that purpose they were usually equipped with embroidery materials, a frame and threads, and encouraged to make samplers on which to practice cross stitch and tent stitch, various kinds of whitework and also

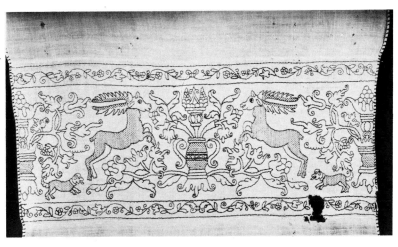

darning stitches. Thanks to these samplers, ancient designs from embroidery pattern books have been passed from one country to another and from one generation to the next. The designs were gradually popularized until they finally found their way into the repertoire of patterns in general. In these samplers it is possible to find patterns such as the common palmette and the geometrical diaper that were often used for chair covers. They were worked with wools in cross stitch.

During the eighteenth century furnishing textiles were usually embroidered in colored wools either on woolen cloth or on canvas. The patterns were international, during the first half of the century in the late baroque style and in the second half in the brilliant colors of rococo floral designs.

The florid patterns of the rococo period were at their best in silk embroidery which had to compensate for the fact that the importation of expensive foreign silks was prohibited. Bouquets of flowers embellished the fronts

ABOVE:
Hand towel, *detail of a decorative band, Finland, seventeenth century. Linen embroidered in red silk in running and double-running stitches, 9in × 20in (23cm × 52cm). This was formerly in Kiikka Church.* NATIONAL MUSEUM OF FINLAND, HELSINKI.

LEFT:
Armchair covered with embroidery on canvas *(detail), Finland. Linen canvas, worked in polychrome wools in cross and tent stitches, 1ft 11in × 1ft 9¾in (61cm × 55·5cm). This has the appearance of tapestry. A similar design with acanthus scrolls became popular on the bridal rugs woven in parsonages in the second half of the eighteenth century. The chair was formerly at Hermansaari Manor, Lokalahti.* NATIONAL MUSEUM OF FINLAND, HELSINKI.

OPPOSITE, RIGHT:
Altar border *(detail), signed by Birgitta Anundsdother, a nun at the Brigittine convent at Naantali, Finland, late fifteenth century. Linen embroidered with colored silks in split stitch and couched in silver-gilt and silver thread, the pearls from the arcades having disappeared, approx. 6in × 6ft 10in (15cm × 210cm). The border depicts scenes from the Life of the Virgin and of Christ and was formerly in Huittinen Church.* NATIONAL MUSEUM OF FINLAND, HELSINKI.

ally to the restrained single-color chain patterns typical of the neoclassical period.

The numerous stitches of whitework, practiced on samplers, were used mainly on garments such as caps, scarves, cuffs and petticoats. For bedcovers and on ladies' garments it was often combined with quilting and it was used on women's bodices, skirts, stomachers and ladies' caps, and on christening robes for babies as well as on waist-coats and night caps for gentlemen.

Under the influence of the classical revival embroidery patterns changed during the last quarter of the eighteenth century and became more delicate, while the colors employed were generally

of gentlemen's silk waistcoats, flowers burst out from cornucopiae on the ornate pocketbooks embroidered by young maidens for their sweethearts. Colorful embroidery in silks was often used in conjunction with quilting. In the cold climate quilted petticoats were popular and their embroidery shows clearly how fashions changed from the band ornament in the style of the French designer Jean Bérain (1640–1711), popular at the beginning of the eighteenth century, to the picturesque floral patterns of the rococo and eventu-

paler; the embroidery was often mono-chrome. Chain stitches and stem stitches in silk were embroidered on white or pale-colored satin grounds with motifs of classical urns, garlands of flowers, pillars and the Altar of Love. Topographical subjects carried out in black silk or using hair to simulate engravings were popular as decoration for commemorative panels and fire screens. Numerous silk-embroidered wallets, purses, handbags, muffs, belts and garters bear testimony to the inter-est in needlework among ladies of social standing, and articles embroidered in silk were popular gifts. Eyelet work and drawn threadwork were favored in the embroidery of linen because they complied with the tastes of the period.

The Biedermeier Style

The magnificent metal-thread embroidery of the Empire period never gained popularity in Finland. Not until the 1820s were there signs of a new style in needlework, the distinctive techniques employed being woolwork cross stitch and beadwork. In the main German originals were copied, as indicated by the adoption of the German term "Biedermeier" in Finland at that period. Berlin woolwork patterns swamped the market and in boarding schools girls were taught cross-stitch and tent-stitch embroidery using colored wools and German patterns printed on squared paper. In addition to animal and flower designs, elaborate pictorial designs of religious, historical and romantic subjects were favored and these can be seen in many of the furnishing textiles: cushions, fire screens, runners for rocking chairs, tablecloths and rugs. Upholstery for neo-rococo sofas and chairs was ornamented with curling leaves and flowers in brilliant, harsh colors. Toward the end of the century various kinds of beadwork were combined with wool embroidery and small objects were often embroidered with glass beads on perforated cardboard.

Household linens were skillfully decorated using *broderie anglaise* and

ABOVE:
Needlework picture, *worked by Agnes Fr. Leffrén, Finland, 1799. White silk with hair embroidery, 14½in × 19in (37cm × 49cm). This depicts the Russian fleet outside Hanko in 1788 and was copied from an engraving.* NATIONAL MUSEUM OF FINLAND, HELSINKI.

LEFT:
Apron petticoat *(detail), Finland, c.1750. Whitework on linen, 4¾in × 7¾in (12·5cm × 23cm).* HISTORICAL MUSEUM OF THE CITY OF TURKU.

FAR LEFT:
Pocket book, *worked by Elisabet Aejmelaeus aged thirteen, Finland, 1799. Pink satin embroidered in polychrome silks mainly in satin, stem and chain stitches, 10in × 8in (25·5cm × 20·5cm).* NATIONAL MUSEUM OF FINLAND, HELSINKI.

RIGHT:
Carpet *(detail), presented
to Countess Louise Armfelt
by her friends, Finland,
second quarter of the
nineteenth century.
Polychrome wool
embroidery on canvas, 9ft
10½in × 11ft 9in (93·04m ×
3·58m). The design of the
carpet is of panels of animals
and flowers.* NATIONAL
MUSEUM OF FINLAND,
HELSINKI.

ABOVE:
Coif of a Greek Orthodox
woman, *parish of Sakkola
on the Karelian Isthmus,
Finland, nineteenth century.
Linen with traditional
eastern peasant embroidery
of double-running and long-
armed cross stitch in red,
yellow and blue thread,
height of front piece, 5¾in
(15cm).* ETHNOGRAPHICAL
COLLECTION, NATIONAL
MUSEUM OF FINLAND,
HELSINKI.

eyelet embroidery. Brides' handkerchiefs of fine embroidered linen or
cotton cloth were often masterpieces of
whitework. For these, patterns of an
international character, embroidered
on fine cambric in white thread with
needlework fillings, were used.

Nearer the end of the century, due
to needlework and fashion magazines,
international embroidery patterns became more widely known and houses in
Finland boasted furnishing textiles that
were inappropriate and showed lack of
imagination and taste. With the support
of primary schools and adult education
institutions embroidery had gradually
become a hobby even in rural homes.

Folk Embroidery and Karelian Needlework

The rural population of Finland was
self-supporting as far as textiles were
concerned, for it had always woven and
prepared its own everyday textiles and
ornament had been confined mainly to
woven patterns. Folk embroidery was
principally limited to garments, to the

decoration of headdresses, aprons and
shirt collars, and the designs used were
those favored by gentlefolk. The embroidery on the bridegroom's shirt was
the traditional way of demonstrating
the sewing skills of the bride.

The exceptionally rich geometrical
patterns used by Greek Orthodox
women in what was South Karelia, in
eastern Finland, belong to a different,
eastern culture. The styles originated
in Byzantium and came to eastern
Europe with the Greek Orthodox faith.
They are based on the ancient diamond
and cross patterns. The long Karelian
hand towels with their embroidered
bands of double-running stitch in red
silk, show the influence of the pattern
books of the Renaissance, though with
some distortion. The folk embroidery
of Karelia bears interesting testimony
to the fact that on the fringes of a cultural area old traditions can survive for
a surprisingly long time.

During the early nineteenth century,
in the Swedish-speaking coastal areas of
South Ostrobothnia, bed and sleigh
coverlets were used with large, simple
flower and geometrical patterns worked
in multicolored wools covering the
ground material, usually black woolen
cloth. The style was undoubtedly of
Swedish origin and, spread by professional seamstresses, it reached the
Finnish-speaking parts of Ostrobothnia
and Satakunta. Descriptions survive of
the way in which these designs were
drawn freehand on the cloth. Covers
with folk embroidery have recently
been "rediscovered" and their unusual
designs have inspired textile designers
to revive these techniques.

Suomen Käsityön Ystävät – The Friends of Finnish Handicraft

The founding in 1877 of Suomen
Käsityön Ystävät (Friends of Finnish
Handicraft) represented the beginning
of a new era in Finnish needlework.
The initiative came from the painter
Fanny Churberg, (1845–92), who was
inspired by the formation in 1874 in
Stockholm of Föreningen Handarbetets vänner, a society which aimed at
the revival of needlecraft traditions in
Scandinavia. The founding of Suomen
Käsityön Ystävät was closely associated
with the nationalist revival that took
place in Finland toward the end of the
nineteenth century. It was felt important to create a national identity, to take
an interest in the country's past, to

study its history, its folklore and its folk culture. Inspired by Swedish example, student unions had already started a few years previously to collect ethnographical objects and costumes which later formed the basis for the ethnographical collections of the National Museum of Finland in Helsinki. Members of the Suomen Käsityön Ystävät, among them artists and wealthy society ladies as well as ethnologists, took an interest in the folk textiles collected by these students. Particularly admired were the geometrical patterns on the headdresses and aprons of Karelia, homeland of the Finnish national epic, *Kalevala*. In their enthusiasm, these patterns on the garments of Greek Orthodox women were mistakenly assumed to be of ancient Finnish origin. Through the efforts of Käsityön Ystävät they were copied and modified to suit furnishing textiles and sold either as finished needlework or in the form of partly prepared handwork. In addition, pattern books of indigenous motifs were published and the designs could be used either for cross-stitch embroidery, still popular for furnishing textiles, or woven materials.

Art Nouveau to Functionalism

However, people gradually began to tire of the patriotic themes and the English Art Movement and Art Needlework already had a following in Finland in the 1890s. Members of Käsityön Ystävät realized that merely to copy national patterns was pointless. It was necessary to create original patterns, based on Finnish traditions, and to this end competitions were arranged and exhibitions held. The exhibit by Suomen Käsityön Ystävät at the World Exhibition in Paris in 1900 was a turning point, signaling the beginning of the Art Nouveau movement in Finland. The architect Eliel Saarinen (1873–1950) designed the Finnish Pavilion, the textiles of which were commissioned from Axel Gallén-Kallela (1865–1931), the most prominent Finnish painter of the national-romantic era. He chose a spruce twig with its cones rendered in appliqué work as the theme for the textiles in the Finnish Pavilion.

Most of the best-known Finnish artists took part in designing patterns for Käsityön Ystävät in the early part of the twentieth century. Motifs were taken from nature. Ecclesiastical textiles were included in 1904 in the pro-

LEFT:
Coverlet, *parish of Parkano, Finland, c.1830. Peasant embroidery of buttonhole, and herringbone, stitches and couching in polychrome wools on black woolen cloth, 6ft × 3ft 2in (1·8m × 1·3m).* NATIONAL MUSEUM OF FINLAND, HELSINKI.

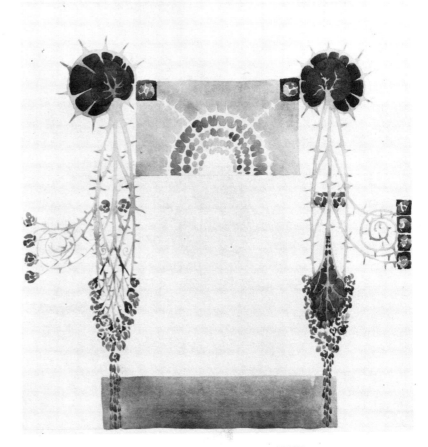

gram of Käsityön Ystävät on the initiative of the architect Armas Lindgren (1874–1929). Finnish Art Nouveau architects aiming at a complete and unified work of art began to take responsibility for the textiles in the churches they designed. Most were in appliqué work, with good clean lines, with stem-

ABOVE:
Design for an altar frontal, *by Professor Armas Lindgren (1874–1929), Finland, 1904. The architect, Professor Lindgren, was a leading figure in the Art Nouveau movement in Finland.* SUOMEN KÄSITYÖN, YSTÄVÄT, HELSINKI.

stitch and satin-stitch embroidery. In addition to religious symbols, flower motifs, usually roses, were employed.

This golden age of embroidery lasted until the First World War. Needlework done at home included tablecloths, tray covers, curtains for windows and doors, wall hangings, runners for rocking chairs, not to mention cushions (Plate 94) and coffeepot covers. The work was mostly based on patterns by Käsityön Ystävät which were available even in country areas through a network of agents.

Finland's Independence in 1917 added the embroidery of flags to the activities of Käsityön Ystävät. Designs for flags and ecclesiastical textiles were for a long time the responsibility of the textile artists, Toini Nyström (1887–1967) and Greta Strandberg (1895–1941). At the same time, however, interest in the embroidery of domestic tex-

tiles was lessened by the fact that the new, functional style did not encourage unnecessary ornament. Woven fabrics were more in keeping with the times and so the work of Käsityön Ystävät was modified to suit these requirements.

During the past fifty years the interest in needlework in Finland has been lukewarm. Käsityön Ystävät have tried to provide encouragement by arranging competitions, but results have mainly been limited to patterns suitable for the embroidery of cushions and coffeepot covers by amateurs. In the 1940s some textile designers showed an interest in embroidery because it offered some scope for personal expression, and domestic art magazines and ladies' journals have helped to make artists' patterns available for needlework in the home. The art of the needle has nowadays been reduced to a hobby for the few – a therapy for the soul.

Iceland

ICELAND WAS SETTLED LARGELY FROM Norway in the period from A.D. 874 to *c.*A.D. 900. A few settlers came from other parts, mainly from the Scottish Isles and Ireland. The first republic was established in 930, lasting until 1262, when the Icelanders surrendered to the king of Norway. Iceland remained under Norwegian rule until *c.*1380 when, together with Norway, it became subject to the Danish crown. Partial autonomy was acquired in 1918, but it was not until 1944 that Iceland gained complete independence from Denmark with the establishment of the second republic.

Christianity was adopted as a state religion in Iceland in the year 1000. In 1056, a bishopric was established in Skálholt in southern Iceland; a second see for northern Iceland was founded at Hólar in 1106. Iceland remained Catholic until the middle of the sixteenth century, but since 1550, when the Catholic bishop Jón Arason of Hólar was executed, the state Church has been Lutheran. This date, 1550, marks the end of the Middle Ages in Iceland.

Extant Embroideries
The largest and most varied collection of traditional Icelandic embroideries is housed in the National Museum of Iceland in Reykjavík. Outside Iceland a most important collection is in the Danish National Museum in Copenhagen, with works of significance also in the Victoria and Albert Museum, London; the Royal Scottish Museum, Edinburgh; the Nordic Museum, Stockholm; the Cluny Museum, Paris; and the Twenthe Museum, Enschede in the Netherlands.

Although written medieval sources tell of secular needlework as well, only ecclesiastical embroidery has survived in Iceland from the Middle Ages, and the oldest pieces probably date back no further than from the latter half of the fourteenth century. From after the Reformation (1550) and at least as early as the seventeenth century both ecclesiastical and secular work exists. Among the church embroideries are altar frontals, altar cloths, chasubles, chalice veils and burses; while secular examples range from coverlets, bed valances, saddle cloths and cushion covers to various items of costume, such as women's skirts, jackets, collars, kerchiefs, and mittens, as well as children's caps. The embroideries are worked in a variety of techniques, several of which – together with the materials, colors and designs employed – may be said to lend a special character to old Icelandic needlework.

In this context it should be noted, however, that for the last hundred years or so most of the embroidery executed in Iceland to a great extent has followed the fashion in embroidery of neighboring countries. Where designs and, to some extent, materials are concerned, though less so as regards embroidery techniques, some work has been done along traditional lines.

Embroidery Designs and Materials
Traditional Icelandic embroidery designs are characterized by circular and polygonal frames enclosing various motifs such as animals and plants, hunting scenes, scenes from the Bible and from the lives of saints. This design feature dates back to Byzantine silk fabrics and even earlier and was widely used in northern Europe during the Middle Ages. Developing in Iceland in a distinctive way, it remained popular into the nineteenth century.

It is of interest to note the close relationship of medieval embroidery designs with contemporary Icelandic illuminations. No doubt artists of the day undertook to draw embroidery patterns. This is at least strongly indicated by a sketchbook, dating partly from the fourteenth, partly from the fifteenth century and *c.*1500, in which there are a number of drawings apparently intended as embroidery patterns, some even quite closely resembling surviving medieval needlework. In addition, recent research has established clear connections between prints of the early sixteenth century and designs on late medieval embroideries.

From extant work of more recent times, it is evident that Icelandic needlewomen had access to foreign embroidery designs, including the printed pattern books of the sixteenth and seventeenth centuries. None of these books is known to have survived in Iceland, but a few manuscript pattern books of local production exist, dating from the seventeenth to the early nineteenth century. These books contain a variety of geometric, floral and animal motifs, mostly based on squared patterns intended for counted threadwork, some of them exact copies of designs found in the early printed pattern books of Germany.

The greater part of old Icelandic needlework is executed in homespun woolen yarn of natural color or dyed with vegetable dyes, with only occasional use being made of silk, linen and metal thread. The grounds used for the embroideries are mainly domestic woolen and imported linen fabrics, more costly imports such as silks and velvets being employed more rarely. The linens are plain tabby, the woolens mainly a loosely woven tabby or extended tabby (basket weave) for counted threadwork, and closely woven tabby or twill for free embroidery.

Laid and Couched Work

Among the most remarkable of the Icelandic embroideries is the laid and couched work, best known from altar frontals from the later Middle Ages. This work was called *refilsaumur* (*refil* embroidery), a term found only in Icelandic sources. In *refilsaumur*, motifs were first outlined in stem stitch, chain stitch, split stitch or couching, whereupon they were filled in with laid and couched work. In the National Museum of Iceland there are five couched frontals as well as a frontlet, a cross orphrey on a chasuble and a portrait, the latter three examples being seventeenth-century work, however, while another six medieval works, five frontals and a long horizontal wall hanging – a *refill* – found their way to museums abroad during the nineteenth century. The majority of the frontals are completely covered with stitchery, which is worked mainly in polychrome woolen yarns, with some blue and white linen yarn found in most pieces. Occasionally silk and metal thread is introduced to highlight important details and, in one instance, a frontal is worked entirely in silk and metal thread. The ground used is most often tabby woven linen, but in three of them it is woolen extended tabby (basket weave).

The designs on the frontals are freestyle pictorial renderings of a religious nature, with three of the frontals illustrating lives of saints through a succession of scenes set in circular frames. On the frontal from the parish church at Draflastadir in northern Iceland, framed in barbed quatrefoils, are depicted the Virgin and Child, various saints and three bishops, possibly sainted. It is worked mainly in wool on a now off-white linen ground with some details in blue and white linen thread. The color scheme of the embroidery, blue, green, red, and white against a faded yellow background, is typical of much Icelandic embroidery, both medieval and of a later date.

Straight Darning and Pattern Darning

From post-Reformation times long white linen bed valances embroidered with polychrome woolen yarns are particularly prominent. Extant valances of which the museum in Reykjavík possesses eleven complete examples and parts of two others – six are known to be in foreign museums – are all dated to the seventeenth and eighteenth centuries. Most of these are executed in a straight darning stitch, *glitsaumur*, a technique also found in some minor details of two late medieval altar frontals. The valances, generally measuring from about 20in to 24in by 138in to 158in (50cm to 60cm by 350cm to 400cm), usually carry designs consisting of rows of decorated round or polygonal frames enclosing flower and bird (Tree of Life) motifs, biblical scenes, human figures and various animals. As a rule the borders above and below the frames have the words of evening hymns. A detail from an eighteenth-century bed valance, *rekkjurefill*, from eastern Iceland, worked in blue, red and faded yellow, shows two mounted warriors or hunters. In the left circle, the inscription TIRPINN BISKUP indicates that the figure is meant to represent bishop Turpin, one of Charlemagne's paladins.

An apparently earlier form of *glit* embroidery is a type of pattern darning, also called *skakkaglit* (slanting *glit*) in seventeenth- and eighteenth-century sources. Like straight darning, slanting *glit* is worked with wool on a white

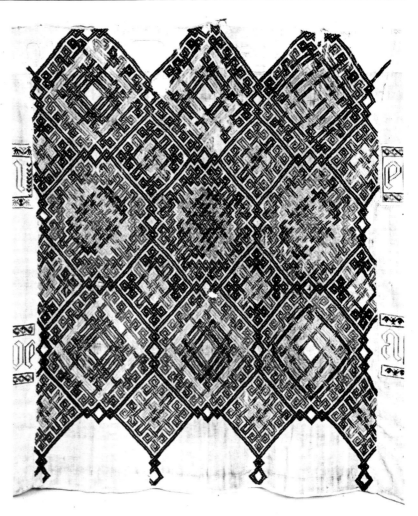

linen ground. A few of the bed valances
are executed in this technique but it is
found also, at times in conjunction with
other types of embroidery, on six altar
frontals dating from late medieval times
to the end of the seventeenth century.
A pre-Reformation example from an
unknown church has a center panel
executed in blue, blue-green, red and
yellow which has a rather complicated
interlaced design, typical of these
embroideries.

Long-Armed Cross Stitch, Eye Stitch and Florentine Stitch

Also characteristic of post-Reformation
needlework are woolen coverlets completely covered with long-armed cross
stitch. The old term employed for the
stitch was *krosssaumur* (cross stitch);
today, however, that word designates
ordinary cross stitch, while the long-
armed variety is referred to as "old
Icelandic cross stitch," or *fléttusaumur*
(braid stitch). The technique first
appeared as a supporting stitch on a
few late medieval church embroideries
and it is found used in this way or on its
own on ecclesiastical as well as secular
work of later periods.

The museum in Reykjavík possesses
six complete cross-stitched coverlets
and parts of three others, while three
are known to exist elsewhere. Dating
from the seventeenth to the beginning
of the nineteenth century, they
measure from about 59in to 67in by
39in to 49in (150cm to 170cm by 100cm
to 125cm) and are embroidered with
multi-colored woolen yarns on a woolen
ground in a loose tabby or, more often,
extended tabby weave. Of special note
among those in the museum in Reykjavík is perhaps the seventeenth-century

coverlet popularly known to visitors as
Riddarateppid, the Coverlet of Knights,
because of the central design of gentlemen and mounted horsemen or knights
– all, incidentally, in sixteenth-century
dress – set in octagonal frames. The
color scheme, common to most of the
coverlets and similar to several of the
medieval couched frontals, consists of
red, blue, green and white against a
faded yellow background.

Occasionally eye stitch, *augn(a)-
saumur*, was employed for small motifs
and borders on the cross-stitched coverlets. One of these, worked in polychrome
wools on a basket-weave ground and
dated to the seventeenth century, was
apparently part of the furnishings at
the bishop's seat at Hólar in the late
eighteenth century. The main design
consists of decorative frames encircling
biblical scenes – the Nativity, the
Baptism, the Crucifixion and the Burial
of Christ – while in the half-circles may
be seen Noah's Ark and the Tree of
Life. The surrounding inscription is
part of an evening prayer. The letters,

ABOVE, LEFT:
Bed valance *(detail)*,
*Espihóll, northern Iceland,
eighteenth century.*
Rekkjurefill *worked in*
glitsaumur, *a type of
straight darning, with
polychrome wools on linen,
size of detail 16in × 16in,
(40cm × 40cm).* NATIONAL
MUSEUM OF ICELAND,
REYKJAVÍK, Inv. No. 1808.

ABOVE:
Center panel of altar frontal,
*Iceland, late medieval.
Linen embroidered with
polychrome wools in pattern
darning,* skakkaglit, *33in ×
27in, (84cm × 68cm).*
NATIONAL MUSEUM OF
ICELAND, REYKJAVÍK, Inv.
No. 2371.

together with some details in the spandrels, are worked in eye stitch.

There exist four coverlets and parts of a fifth, together with five cushion covers, which are completely covered with eye-stitch embroidery executed in wool on wool, but this distinctive needlework – apparently unique to Iceland – was evidently not as widely practiced as long-armed cross stitch. One of the cushion covers dating from the eighteenth or early nineteenth century, is worked on a tabby ground primarily in ordinary eye stitch, with a border in one of the two rarely seen diagonal varieties. The cover measures about 16in by 18½in (40cm by 47cm), a size common for traditional cushion covers. The main motif is a rather intricate form of the eight-pointed star, *áttabladarós,* a popular design in Icelandic folk art.

The indications are that during the seventeenth and eighteenth centuries coverlets and cushion covers were also executed in wool on wool in Florentine stitch, or *pellsaumur* as the technique apparently was called, worked from diamond-shaped pattern drawings with four stitches to each diamond. Only three small pieces of such embroidery have, however, survived.

Drawn Work and Darned Net

Examples of traditional embroideries executed in whitework in linen on linen that have survived are comparatively few and seem to date mainly from the seventeenth and eighteenth centuries, although one or two pieces may be medieval, at least in part. Some of these embroideries are executed in drawn work, others in darned net (*lacis*), both types having apparently been called *sprang* and the latter occasionally *rid-sprang* (net *sprang*). No examples or traditions of the plait work which is now called *sprang* in other countries are known in Iceland. Of the Icelandic *sprang* embroideries, handkerchiefs which were an accessory to women's church dress are particularly notable among the secular work. One of the most striking examples of *sprang,* however, is a hanging for a baptismal font from an unknown church, possibly in western Iceland. Executed in drawn work, it has a design resembling those of the darned bed valances and because of this is dated tentatively to *c.*1700.

Floral Embroidery

Very different in character from the various types of counted threadwork is the free-style floral embroidery known as *blómstursaumur* which came into vogue during the seventeenth century and retained its popularity into the nineteenth century. Whereas in the early work a variety of stitches were employed – such as split, stem, and long-and-short stitches, as well as French knots – split stitch became increasingly favored as time passed, so much so that today *blómstursaumur* has come to mean embroidery worked almost entirely in split stitch, regardless of the type of design. The technique, executed in polychrome woolen yarns on a closely woven woolen ground, found varied uses, both ecclesiastical and secular. Some early altar frontals in bold colors and designs are on display in the museum in Reykjavík.

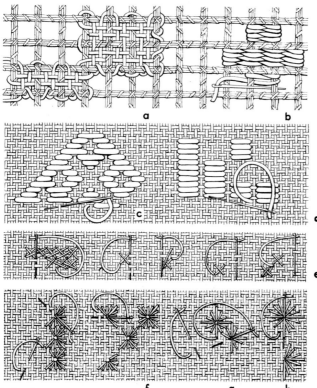

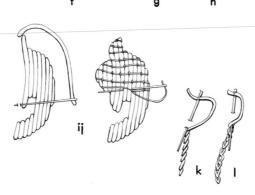

ABOVE:
Diagrams of stitches from Icelandic embroideries. a) and b) sprang, drawn work. *c)* skakkaglit, *pattern darning. d)* glitsaumur, *straight darning. e)* fléttusaumur *(old Icelandic cross stitch),* long-armed cross stitch. *f, g, h)* augn(a)saumur, *eye stitch. i)* refilsaumur, *laid and couched work. k)* varpsaumur, varpleggur, *stem stitch. l)* blómstursaumur, *split stitch. Drawings: Gunnlaugur S. E. Briem.*

During the eighteenth century it became fashionable to decorate the skirts of women's festive dress above the hemline with wide floral borders of richly colored *blómstursaumur* and, during the nineteenth century, cushion covers worked in this technique were particularly popular.

Other Embroidery Techniques

Very few pieces of appliqué work have survived although late seventeenth- and eighteenth-century documents indicate that a number of such embroideries, mainly ecclesiastical, were then in existence. The work was not designated by one specific term, it seems, but only as being of "cut-out cloth" or something similar; the word *skorningur*, found in medieval inventories, may be an early term describing this technique. The most remarkable surviving example of appliqué work is an altar frontal from the parish church at Reykir in

northern Iceland, which in all probability dates from the end of the Middle Ages. The main panel of the frontal has a central motif of the Virgin as the Queen of Heaven, surrounded by smaller designs framed by interlaced circles. The work is composed of pieces of gilt leather and multi-colored woolen, linen and silk fabrics applied with white linen thread to a dark blue woolen tabby ground.

Another piece of church embroidery dating from this period is a possible frontal from Skard church in northwestern Iceland, worked in polychrome wools on white linen, entirely in stem stitch, *varpsaumur*, *varpleggur*, a technique frequently combined with other stitches but rarely used alone. On the frontal are depicted six saints set in

LEFT:
Font cloth, *probably from a church in western Iceland, c.1700. Linen worked in drawn work,* sprang, *approx. 31½in × 67in (80cm × 170cm).* NATIONAL MUSEUM OF REYKJAVÍK, Inv. No. 1924.

BELOW:
Woman's skirt *(detail), embroidered by Gudrún Skúladóttir in Videy, southern Iceland, c.1790. This detail of a skirt which was part of the costume of a bishop's bride in 1806, shows a section of the hemline border embroidered with polychrome wools on wool in split stitch,* blómstursaumur, *width of border approx. 6in (15cm).* NATIONAL MUSEUM OF ICELAND, REYKJAVÍK, Inv. No. 2868.

Altar frontal *from Reykir Church, northern Iceland, probably first half of the sixteenth century. Wool and linen worked in appliqué in wool, linen, silk and gilt leather, size of main panel 37in × 31½in (95cm × 80cm).* NATIONAL MUSEUM OF ICELAND, REYKJAVÍK, Inv. No. 4797.

rectangular frames with the name of each saint inscribed below.

During the eighteenth century, and right up to the present time, silver and gold embroidery, *baldýring*, has been used to adorn parts of women's national costume, such as the jackets, bodices and collars. How far back this custom goes has not been established. In early sources terms such as *gullsaumur* (gold embroidery) are used. The word *baldýring*, which does not appear until the second half of the seventeenth century, seems to have been used first as a general term for embroidery; not until the middle of the eighteenth century is it used in connection with gold and silver work.

With the exception of one example from 1779 and remnants of another, perhaps from the seventeenth century, the few known Icelandic samplers are nineteenth-century work, and all are practically devoid of national characteristics in design as well as in execution. An interesting variation on the sampler dating from 1795 has been preserved, however, in the form of a chalice veil from Brekka church in eastern Iceland. Although intended for church use from the beginning, the veil executed in colored silks on linen is nevertheless worked in the manner of a sampler, in a great variety of stitches: cross, long-

armed cross, straight darning, double running, Florentine, stem, satin, counted satin and buttonhole stitches.

Needleworkers and Needlework Centers

In some cases it is possible to identify the worker, owner or donor of a piece of Icelandic embroidery, but on the whole little is known about the women who planned, supervised and executed the work. This is especially true of the medieval period. Little is known, too, about the places where the medieval embroideries were executed, but the laid and couched frontals, for example, certainly indicate the existence of needlecraft centers or schools. No doubt the art of the needle was practiced in the two convents in Iceland with no less diligence than in convents in other countries. Documentary evidence of this is very meager, however, and no existing embroidery can be ascribed to them with complete assurance, although two of the laid and couched frontals, from the churches at Grenjadarstadur and Reykjahlíd, may perhaps be ascribed to the convent at Stadur in Reynines in northern Iceland; and an inscription on the stem-stitched altar frontal from Skard church containing the name and residence of abbess Sólveig Rafnsdóttir, indicates some connection with the same convent.

Ecclesiastical embroideries were almost certainly produced from the earliest days at both the episcopal residences, Skálholt and Hólar. At Hólar, in the time of its first bishop, Jón Ögmundsson, a maid named Ingunn studied there and stayed on to teach Latin and correct Latin books which were read to her while she embroidered, wove or in other ways wrought pictures of the lives of saints. Produced at Hólar, although more than three hundred years later, may be three of the couched frontals, among them the one from Draflastadir. There are indications that they were worked there by or under the auspices of Helga Sigurdardóttir, mistress of Jón Arason, the last Catholic bishop, during the second quarter of the sixteenth century. Written sources also reveal that the cathedral church at Hólar in 1725 possessed a riddell, one of a pair now lost, which carried an inscription relating that Thóra Tumasdóttir, who has been identified as Helga's granddaughter, had embroidered them to the glory of the Virgin Mary. Besides this, the name of an otherwise unidentified needle-woman, Ingibörg, is found in a late medieval inscription on an embroidered riddell from Hólar.

After the Reformation, when the convents were dissolved, besides the bishops' seats, the homes of other high officials and people of wealth and education became the main centers of artistic needlework. Extant embroideries with inscribed dates and often identifiable names or initials are not uncommon. Written sources are also more common and much more detailed, consisting mainly of inventories giving information about both extant embroideries and others which are now lost.

Many of the larger or more impressive pieces of work were associated with women of comparative means, position and leisure, such as the wives and daughters of bishops, ministers, sheriffs and magistrates. The study of needlework was considered a necessary part of the upbringing of young girls; one of the bishops of Hólar in the second quarter of the seventeenth century is even reported to have sent for a teacher from England in order that his daughter might receive the best possible education in the feminine arts. To her and her teacher is attributed an embroidered portrait of her father, unique among Icelandic needlework.

A predominantly cross-stitched altar frontal, executed in polychrome wool on white linen, is the oldest known piece of Icelandic embroidery, still extant, to have borne a date, 1617, which has now worn off. It also bears the remains of the name Brettefa Tómasdóttir, probably that of the embroideress, daughter of the minister who donated the frontal to the church at Háls in northern Iceland in 1631. Another altar frontal, from Laufás church in northern Iceland, worked predominantly in pattern darning, carries an inscription which relates that in the year 1694 Ragnheidur Jónsdóttir presented the frontal to the church. Ragnheidur, twice married to bishops of Hólar, was a frequent donor of church embroideries, several of which carried her name or initials. Furthermore, she was active in teaching needlework and the oldest of the Icelandic pattern books mentioned earlier seems to have belonged to her. One of Ragnheidur's pupils was Thorbjörg Magnúsdóttir, wife of a magistrate, an

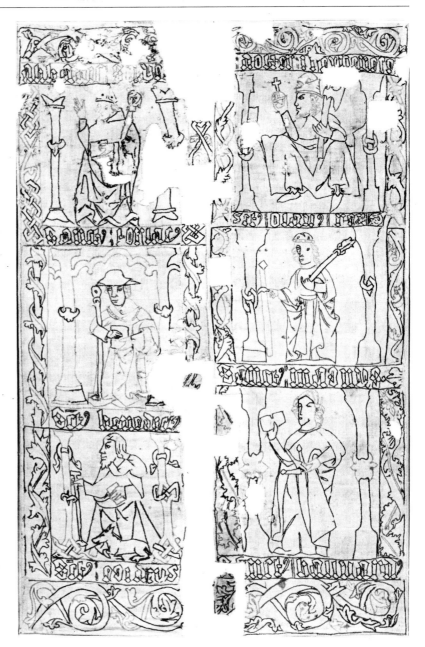

able needlewoman who worked a long-armed cross- and eye-stitched coverlet that is now in the Victoria and Albert Museum in London. Yet another renowned needlewoman, working semi-professionally during the late eighteenth and early nineteenth centuries, was Gudrún Skúladóttir, who augmented her pension as a sheriff's widow by embroidering, mainly, it seems, the then fashionable floral borders on women's skirts.

In general, women of lesser means would of necessity have been restricted in their output of fancy work; however, from extant embroideries, large and small, it is evident that women from all walks of life found opportunity, to a greater or lesser degree, to enhance

Altar frontal from Skard Church, northwestern Iceland, first half of the sixteenth century. Linen embroidered with polychrome wools in stem stitch, varpsaumur, varpleggur *approx, 45in × 30in (115cm × 75cm).* NATIONAL MUSEUM OF ICELAND, REYKJAVÍK, Inv. No. 2028.

their surroundings in this manner. The majority of Icelandic needlewomen of the past must be forever anonymous, but the beauty and distinctive character of the embroideries they left to posterity remain. By patiently adding stitch to stitch through the centuries, these women created some of Iceland's finest works of art.

BELOW:
Coverlet, *northern Iceland, seventeenth century. Woolen, basket-weave ground embroidered with polychrome wools in long-armed cross stitch and eye stitch, 58in × 41in (148cm × 105cm).* NATIONAL MUSEUM OF ICELAND, REYKJAVIK, Inv. No. 1065.

ABOVE:
Chalice veil, *Iceland, dated 1795. Linen worked with colored silks in a variety of stitches, cross, long-armed cross, straight darning, double running, Florentine, stem, satin, counted satin and buttonhole stitches, 8in × 7½in (20·5cm × 19·5cm).* NATIONAL MUSEUM OF ICELAND, REYKJAVÍK, Inv. No. 7177.

Central and Southeastern Europe

THE INHABITANTS OF THE LARGE AREA stretching from Poland to Greece were prolific embroiderers, partly by tradition, partly because cheap manufactured materials were less readily available to them than they were in the West. Nevertheless, it is impossible to look on these embroideries as a cohesive group. Rather, the area must be regarded as one of contrast, where opposing strands of historical development blended or separated and were reflected in the arts, as in the lives, of the people.

The Peoples of Central Europe

Only the Albanians and the Poles and, from early Classical Antiquity, the Greeks and the Romanians, appear to have been native to the lands they occupy today. The present racial composition of the area dates mainly from the waves of nomadic migration from northern Europe and the steppes of central Asia which took place from the sixth to the tenth centuries A.D. These invasions eventually left settled populations of Slavs from the North in present-day Bulgaria, Yugoslavia and Czechoslovakia, while from central Asia came the Bulgars and Magyars: the first to merge in the seventh century with the existing Slav population of Bulgaria and the second to settle during the ninth century in the lands along the middle Danube, that is to say approximately in modern Hungary. Even this ancestral division has left a trace in embroidery patterns in the constant preference of the Slav populations, wherever they may be found in Eastern Europe, for abstract geometric design.

From the Middle Ages onward two major historic events have combined to draw the line between East and West and to set up a continuing interaction between the artistic influences on either side. In the first place the spread of Christianity during the ninth century, urged forward by the rival proselytizing of the eastern and western branches of the Church, forced rulers to make the choice which would in the end mold the sphere of the Roman Catholic Church and the Holy Roman Empire on the one side and the Greek Orthodox Church and Byzantium on the other, a choice which would in the end mould not only a nation's politics but every aspect of its life, whether secular or religious, artistic or domestic. In many cases geographic proximity and the attachments of the ruling prince decided his choice. Bohemia and Moravia, Poland, Hungary and Croatia were drawn toward Rome, partly because the Papacy offered the most effective curb on German power. Greece was from the beginning a part of the Christian Byzantine Empire. Serbia, Bulgaria and the Romanian principalities, while some of their earlier rulers dallied cautiously with Rome, ultimately opted for Byzantium. These denominational differences hardened after the great schism between the eastern and western Churches in the middle of the tenth century and the Crusades.

In the second place the thrusting invasions into Europe of the Ottoman Turks from the fourteenth to the seventeenth centuries simultaneously widened the gulf between East and West and created greater opportunities for the exchange of cultural ideas. Well before the sixteenth century the whole of southeastern Europe, that is to say mainland Greece, Bulgaria, Albania and the southern half of modern Yugoslavia, had been conquered by the Turks and held in strict subjection. Parts of the population, particularly in Albania and Bosnia, became converted to Islam. In the eastern half of the area only the principalities of Wallachia and Moldavia retained some degree of independence under princes paying tribute to the Turks. By the middle of the sixteenth century the Turks had extended their occupation over the greater part of Hungary and established a third principality in Transylvania under Hungarian princes. Intermittent and confused frontier warfare only ended with the final expulsion of the Turks from central Europe by the imperial Austrian army in 1688.

Trade as well as war played a large part in importing Middle Eastern influences into central Europe, since it must be remembered that it was here that the great river highways linking the East and South with northern Europe, met and crossed.

Meanwhile, in the West, successful rulers from the Middle Ages onward who wished to strengthen their ties with the papal authority and at the same time make a display of their material wealth turned in the main to Italy, that fount of artistic inspiration and renovation, for successive generations of architects and painters to adorn their cathedrals and castles and train their own court artists. A counterpoise was again supplied by the master craftsmen of German cities such as Nuremberg, whose close proximity to the courts of central Europe ensured that their talents also would be imported there. At the same time tentacles of European influence penetrated the eastern world of the Adriatic and Aegean in the train of Venetian conquests.

All these threads, woven together in harmony and contrast, combined to affect the life and arts of the different nations of this area and may be followed in embroidery as in other spheres.

Church Embroidery in the West

The earliest embroidery to survive, in this part of Europe as elsewhere, is the fine work made for the Church in the Middle Ages. The deep contrast between East and West, between the different theological approach of the two arms of the Church, and between the romanesque, gothic and renaissance models of the West on the one hand and the distinctive Byzantine blend of Hellenistic and Anatolian art on the other, is immediately evident.

In writing of embroidery for the Catholic Church in central Europe it is necessary to mention briefly the splendid bell chasuble embroidered in laid gold threads with figures of Christ with saints and prophets which is connected with St. Stephen of Hungary (957?–1038) and his wife Queen Gisela and

dated 1031. It was later cut into the form of a cope and used as the coronation mantle of the kings of Hungary. This is one of the major early embroideries of Europe and could hardly have been made in Hungary at this period. Both technically and artistically it conforms to other embroidered works made at the court of the Emperor Henry II (951–995), Gisela's brother, at Bamberg, and it must be considered to have its origins there.

Most of the early church embroideries in this area appear to have been the work of convents. In Bohemia many religious foundations of the eleventh and twelfth centuries were provided by their founders with workrooms for the spinning and weaving of linen, as well as for embroidery and other crafts, to ensure a sound economic base for the monastery's finances. The workers were girls employed for the purpose, not necessarily the nuns themselves. The convents of St. George and of Břevnov in Prague were both famous for their embroideries.

A frontal, thought to have been made in the convent of the Poor Clares at Cheb for the chapel of the castle there, clearly illustrates the links between the craft of embroidery and the architecture as well as the painting of the period. The long altar frontal with a double row of arcades framing figures of saints became a classic design of the fourteenth century, while the same concept was widely used on the orphreys of copes and chasubles in the West and on stoles in the Orthodox Church. The style of the embroidered arch was closely modeled on the actual architecture of the period.

The frontal at Cheb, which dates from about 1300, has round-headed romanesque arches supported on slender pillars. In fact the drawing of the figures themselves introduces an element of gothic grace in the stance and draperies, but this is practically negated by the fact that the whole frontal is embroidered entirely in pearls, coral, beads and small metal plaques, a rich but somewhat cumbersome technique which enhances the archaic appearance of the piece. The embroidery has been transferred to a background of later date.

Many medieval embroideries were decorated with pearls, but the freshwater pearls fished in the rivers of Bohemia and Saxony were particularly

OPPOSITE, ABOVE:
Altar frontal, *detail of St. Catherine, Bohemia, c.1300. Embroidery in pearls, colored beads and metal plaques, whole frontal 34¾in × 90in (88cm × 228cm).* MUNICIPAL MUSEUM, CHEB, CZECHOSLOVAKIA.

OPPOSITE, BELOW:
The Pirna altar frontal, *detail of the Coronation of the Virgin with St. John the Evangelist and St. John the Baptist, Bohemia, c.1360. Polychrome silks in split stitch and couched work with some gold thread, whole frontal 37½in × 132in (95cm × 335cm).* STATE ART COLLECTIONS, DRESDEN, EAST GERMANY.

freely used in the countries of central Europe. Among many other examples a late fourteenth-century set of apparels in the treasury of Prague Cathedral may be mentioned and, in Poland, a prayer-book binding belonging to Ann Jagiello which is dated 1582.

Two further Bohemian frontals serve to emphasize the effect of the cosmopolitan influences brought together in Prague in the second half of the fourteenth century. On the one hand, an important arcaded frontal from a church in Pirna, which is now in Dresden, has as the central scene the Coronation of the Virgin, supported on each side by five saints under gothic arches. This sophisticated work from about 1360 stands in direct succession to a line of Italian frontals of the first half of the century, in particular a famous Florentine piece worked by Jacopo Cambi to which the Pirna frontal bears a marked resemblance. This frontal must owe its existence to the Italian artists brought to Prague in the second half of the fourteenth century by the Emperor Charles IV (1316–78), but the figure drawing is closely allied to Bohemian court art of the period and it seems likely that it is indigenous work. It is worked in colored silks in split stitch and couching, with some laid gold in the background.

In a quite different style, bearing witness to German rather than Italian connections, is another frontal dating from toward the end of the century (Plate 97). Worked in colored-silk split stitch on a couched gold background, it shows in rectangular compartments the figures of the Virgin and Child, Christ as Man of Sorrows, the Pelican in her Piety and the arms of the Rožmberk family, placed between half-length figures of apostles and saints bearing scrolls. The realism of these couched figures with downcast eyes, which give the impression of portraits taken from the life, and the broad folds of their garments, stand in direct contrast to the idealistic Italianate style of the Pirna frontal. They are closely related to the work of the painter Master Theodoric (active 1348–68), who decorated the chapel at Karlstejn Castle during the 1360s, while the layout of the frontal and the use of scrolls rather than arcades to set off the figures calls to mind an earlier German tradition in embroidery, which can be seen among other examples in a set of vestments

Epitaphios signed by donors, the Serbian princesses Euphemia and Euphraxia, Serbia, late fourteenth century. Silk ground embroidered with couched gold and silver threads and silk split stitch, 43¾in × 67in (111cm × 170cm). This piece shows strong Byzantine influence in the attitudes of the angels. The stars decorating the background have replaced the crosses often found in Byzantine work of the period. MONASTERY OF PUTNA, ROMANIA.

made at Göss in Styria in the third quarter of the thirteenth century, and was continued in the wool-embroidered convent hangings of Saxony.

In general, the German tradition in embroidery is more evident in central Europe than the Italian. In Germany during the fourteenth century a crucifixion had become the standard motif for the back of a chasuble, in earlier works applied directly to the vestment and later worked on a cross orphrey. By the end of the century it was customary to bring together the figures of the Virgin and St. John, normally standing on either side of the Cross, so that they too could be encompassed by the narrow width of the orphrey. This style was taken up and developed in Bohemia, where the group of figures was enlarged in numbers, and at the same time composed even more closely into a vignette filling the orphrey space at the foot of the Cross. One of the best-known examples is a chasuble cross from the end of the fourteenth century, now in the Moravian Museum of Decorative Art at Brno, in which Mary is supported in the arms of St. John with other figures, colorfully embroidered in silk split stitch. Another example in the Victoria and Albert Museum, London (Plate 98), is perhaps slightly earlier, probably 1370–80. The two saints are shown standing close to the Cross within the orphrey. The figure of Christ is particularly fine, with features which have been worked with great expertise and sensitivity. The introduction of a certain amount of modeling beneath the silk embroidery pays tribute to a growing desire for three-dimensional effect at

this period. This is further accentuated by the shading of the colored silks into broad folds shaped by strong highlights which were a feature of Bohemian painting at the court of Charles IV.

Two chasubles in the same artistic style illustrate the increasing elaboration of scenes on orphreys. The first, from the Collegiate Church at Rokycany, which dates to the late fourteenth century, has a fine late gothic Virgin and Child supported by angels filling the whole angle at the top of a Y orphrey, and below it an Annunciation, which was probably transferred from the front of the chasuble, most cleverly folded into the width of the orphrey band. The second, in the Louvre in Paris, can be dated to the beginning of the fifteenth century and shows scenes from the Life of the Virgin more conventionally divided into architectural compartments.

These must be among the last of the sophisticated works of Charles IV's court embroiderers. That monarch's excessive expenditure on ecclesiastical ceremony and luxury was at least in part responsible for the outbreak of the Hussite movement in the fifteenth century, which brought the Reformation to the Czech lands a hundred years before the advent of Calvin and Luther.

During this period embroiderers catered for a bourgeois taste, and turned again to the earlier style of German Crucifixions. The desire for the effect of perspective in art was no longer translated in the painterly fashion already adopted in the Bohemian chasubles of the late fourteenth century, and carried still further in the supreme masterpieces of light and shade in the *or nué* technique worked in Flanders and Italy at this time. Embroiderers in both Bohemia and Hungary turned rather to sculptured forms and attempted by means of raised embroidery to create actual three-dimensional forms, using figures carved in wood and padded, or shaped in papier-mâché before being covered in silk or couched work. Folds were outlined in braid or by couching over thick string, and embroidery lost the elegance of the earlier period. An elaborate exercise in the style is the figure of St. Wenceslas on the back of a chasuble dated 1487 from Brno Cathedral.

The three-dimensional style reached fresh heights in Hungary during the second half of the fifteenth century, when impetus was given to all artistic

activity during the reign of Matthias Corvinus, king of Hungary from 1458–90. A series of chasubles of a much higher technical standard than the padded crucifixions show saints framed in architectural canopies of great elaboration. Parallel with these sculpted embroideries a number of orphreys were still worked in the traditional split stitch on gold backgrounds. A fine example with scenes of the Passion which shows in the center of the orphrey the figure of Christ scourged, stepping forward from the background with hands bound to the pillar, appears to have been inspired by the slightly earlier work of the painter Tómas de Koloszvár, who was active in 1427.

Relations between the court of Matthias Corvinus and Italy produced by the end of the century a series of orphreys in a strongly Italianate manner, showing small scenes or busts of saints in roundels applied to orphreys embroidered with renaissance ornament in raised gold thread.

In the first half of the sixteenth century Sigismund I of Poland (1467–1548) also used Italian architects to rebuild and decorate the castle of Wawel in the renaissance style but brought goldsmiths, carvers and embroiderers from south Germany, especially from Nuremberg. An advanced example of a chasuble cross in the elaborate manner akin to the German carved polyptych altarpieces is one given to the Wawel Cathedral at Cracow by the Voivod

Piotr Kmita about 1504. Fully developed scenes from the Life of St. Stanislas (1030–79), the patron saint of Poland, are modeled in high relief and embroidered in couched gold threads and silks over silk and linen.

An Italian element is introduced into Polish embroidery by an altar frontal of a very different type. This piece, which is also in the treasury of the Wawel Cathedral, shows scenes from the Lives of Christ and the Virgin under arcades surrounded by renaissance ornament (Plate 99). It is worked in colored silks in long and short stitch with no attempt at modeling but a suggestion of perspective, and appears to be an essay in the new manner by a local workroom, or perhaps a convent, since the drawing of the arcading and ornament lacks authority and the scene of the Flight into Egypt has been reversed from the traditional direction, suggesting that the tracing was mismanaged. The scenes are probably taken from engravings, as yet unidentified, and the whole makes a bright and colorful impression.

The influence of the Reformation, whether Hussite, Calvinist or Lutheran, the wars against the Turks and in Bohemia the Thirty Years' War from 1618 to 1648, which led to the final cession of the Bohemian crown to the Habsburgs and a period of great impoverishment in the country, all combined to make the later sixteenth and first half of the seventeenth centuries a

ABOVE LEFT:
Cross orphrey, *detail showing a scene from the life of St. Stanislas, Poland, c.1504. Raised embroidery with laidwork and pearls. The gift of Piotr Kmita.* TREASURY OF WAWEL CATHEDRAL, POLAND.

ABOVE:
Saccos, *or church vestment, worn by a Patriarch, embroidered with the Transfiguration and the Communion of the Apostles on the shoulders. Dark blue silk ground embroidered with couched gold and silver threads and the faces in split stitch, length 64in (162cm). Greek (Byzantine), probably made in Constantinople, midfourteenth century. The crosses scattered on the background are typical of Byzantine work of this period. The sprig decoration in the lower part of the scene is a later addition.* TREASURY OF ST. PETER'S, ROME.

Epitaphios *embroidered in Vienna to a design by the Serbian monk, Hristofor Žefarović, 1752. The traditional iconography of the Orthodox Church is combined in this piece with west European baroque decoration.* MUSEUM OF ART, BUCHAREST.

style of their vestments and the type of decoration used on them.

Against the background of the renewal of artistic inspiration which took place under the Palaeologus emperors of Byzantium between 1260 and 1453, embroidery in the Greek Church itself reached the height of its flowering in the fourteenth century, showing a subtle mastery of a potentially somewhat rigid gold-thread technique which was fully capable of interpreting the new free elegance of figure drawing, introduced by artists in mosaic and fresco painting.

The characteristics of the style developed in Constantinople at this time differed greatly from that of the West in the type of vestment chosen for decoration, in the iconography, in technical modifications to stitches which were basically the same everywhere at this period and, of course, in artistic inspiration.

The only garment worn by a priest of the Orthodox Church to be decorated with embroidery was the patriarchal *saccos*, a vestment which has no precise equivalent in the Western Church, cut in the shape of a straight tunic and worn in the Middle Ages only by a patriarch but later by all bishops. The Greek equivalent of the priest's chasuble was seldom, if ever, embroidered, but the priestly insignia, the bishop's pallium, miter and cuffs, and the stoles of priest and deacon, were elaborately decorated, a priest's stole normally having embroidery down its whole length, even though it would not be seen when he was fully vested.

The altar frontal as a display piece was unknown, since the altar was much smaller and was in any case hidden from the congregation by the iconostasis (or screen), but the communion veils were appropriately decorated and above all a large veil known as the "*epitaphios sindon*" (the sepuchral linen) showing the Lamentation over the Body of the Crucified Christ, which is carried in procession in the services of Good Friday. This is one of the chief vehicles for embroidery in the Orthodox Church and many examples have survived, particularly from later periods. Apart from this, a number of curtains and hangings for the iconostasis were embroidered and, in some instances, palls to cover the tombstones of royal or aristocratic persons.

All the embroideries were figure

period of little activity in the church arts. By the second half of the seventeenth century, however, the Counter-Reformation, led by the Jesuits in central Europe, brought about a further period of self-confidence and a deliberate revival of ceremonial in the Church.

Throughout this period and into the eighteenth century, vestments everywhere in Europe were strongly influenced by the Italian style. Many vestments relied entirely on the brocaded silks of the period for their ornament. In embroidery the patterns were either in a severe style of baroque ornament in gold thread or in the more exuberant rococo floral style. A very good example in the colorful floral manner of the mid-eighteenth century, which is worked against a background of couched gold threads, is in the church of Sv. Mikuláš in Prague. Only in Poland was an archaizing style of figure embroidery continued through the seventeenth century.

Embroidery in the Orthodox Church

The countries of southeastern Europe which embraced Orthodox rather than Latin Christianity followed Byzantine models in the arts as in law and government. Their autonomous churches were shaped in every sense as daughters of the Greek Orthodox Church, giving their allegiance to the Patriarch in Constantinople and drawing from the Greek Church their doctrine, liturgy and forms of religious art, including of course the

Plate 86
Chasuble, *detail of the
middle part depicting the
Virgin Mary, workshop of
Albert the Embroiderer,
Sweden, late fifteenth
century. Embroidery in gold,
silver and silk thread and
pearls. Of the independent
workshops in the late
medieval period, that of
Albert the Embroiderer in
Stockholm was the most
famous.* UPPSALA CATHEDRAL.

Plate 87
Cushion cover, Åkarp,
Skåne, Sweden, marked
NISIBD, Ano 1814. Black
domett embroidered with
colored wool and white
cotton thread in stem, chain
and knot stitches, 43in ×
approx. 19½in (110cm ×
approx. 51cm). The design
is of the Fall of Man, the
Expulsion from Paradise
and the Creation of Eve.
NORDIC MUSEUM,
STOCKHOLM.

RIGHT: Plate 88
Tablecloth *(detail)*, *signed by Wiveke Friis, probably the embroideress, Denmark, c.1650. Linen with silk embroidery, the fragment 5ft 5½in × 5ft 5½in (1.65m × 1·65m). The motifs are derived from pattern books published in Arnhem and Amsterdam in the early seventeenth century.* NATIONAL MUSEUM, COPENHAGEN.

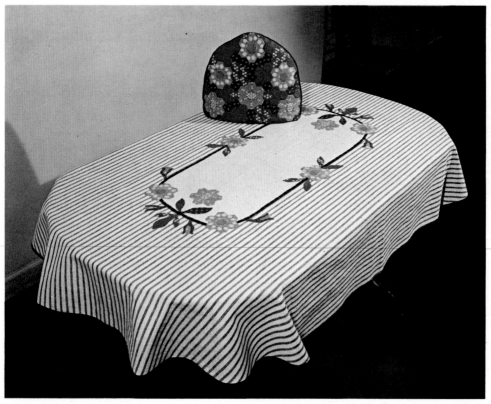

LEFT: Plate 89
Table cloth and tea cosy, *designed and worked by Mrs. C. Rønne-Lotz, Vedbæk, Denmark, 1975. Patchwork of Austrian printed cottons, 6ft 1in × 4ft 1in (1·85m × 1·25m). Born in Germany, the embroideress has adopted the style of contemporary Danish needlework.* PRIVATE COLLECTION.

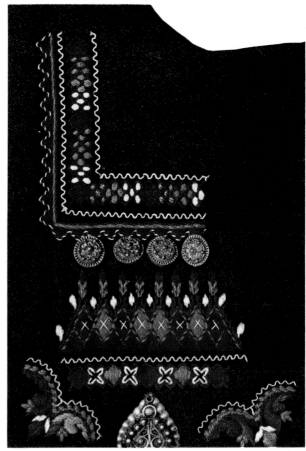

ABOVE, LEFT: Plate 91
Coffin cloth, *Telemark,
Norway, dated 1796. Linen
with embroidery in colored
wool and silk, 16½in × 13in
(42cm × 33cm). In Norway
coffin cloths were often richly
embroidered. This one
belongs to a group from
Hjartdal in Telemark.*
NORWEGIAN FOLK MUSEUM,
OSLO.

ABOVE, RIGHT: Plate 92
Man's waistcoat *(detail),
Ingebjörg Bö, Setesdal,
Norway, 1970. Wool with
embroidery in wool and
cotton, 5¹³⁄₁₆in × 6¼in
(12·9cm × 7·1cm).
Waistcoats are still worn as
part of men's festive costume
in Setesdal.* MRS. SIGNE
KJELLBERG, OSLO.

LEFT: Plate 90
Sampler *(detail), Denmark,
1754. Woolen canvas
embroidered with colored
silk in tent, cross and satin
stitches, 12in × 13in
(31cm × 32.5cm). This is
typical of the embroidery
worked by Danish
noblewomen in the eighteenth
century.* DANISH FOLK
MUSEUM, COPENHAGEN.

OPPOSITE, TOP: Plate 93
Wall hanging *(detail)*,
worked by the nuns at the
Brigittine convent at
Naantali, Finland, c.1500.
Wool intarsia embroidery
with black and green cloth
panels, 15½in × 15½in
(70cm × 70cm). The white,
yellow, red, violet and green
appliqué work is of
broadcloth; the seams are
joined with strips of gilt
membrane, also used for the
decorative design. This was
formerly in Masku Church.
NATIONAL MUSEUM OF
FINLAND, HELSINKI.

OVERLEAF, BOTTOM: Plate 94
Design for a cushion cover,
by Väinö Blomstedt (1871–
1947), Finland. Watercolor.
Blomstedt worked as a
designer for Suomen
Käsityön Ystävät (The
Friends of Finnish
Handicraft) between 1900
and 1903 and this design is
representative of his work in
the Art Nouveau style.
SUOMEN KÄSITYÖN YSTÄVÄT,
HELSINKI.

OVERLEAF: Plate 95
Coverlet, Iceland,
seventeenth century.
Embroidered in long-legged
cross stitch with polychrome
wools on a woolen, basket-
weave ground, approx.
63in × 51in (approx.
160cm × 130cm). NATIONAL
MUSEUM OF ICELAND,
REYKJAVIK.

ABOVE: Plate 96
Altar frontal from
Draflastadir Church in
northern Iceland, first half,
probably second quarter, of
the sixteenth century.
Embroidered in laid and
couched work, refilsaumur,
in wool and some linen on
linen, 43in × 46in (109cm ×
117cm). NATIONAL
MUSEUM OF ICELAND,
REYKJAVIK.

LEFT: Plate 97
Třebon altar frontal
(detail), Bohemia, c.1370–
80. Silk split stitch on a
background of couched gold
threads, complete frontal
27¾in × 47½in (60cm ×
120cm). This section of the
frontal shows Christ as the
Man of Sorrows, St.
Matthew and St. John.
NATIONAL MUSEUM, PRAGUE.

ABOVE: Plate 98
Cross orphrey, Bohemia,
late fourteenth century.
Embroidered in silk split
stitch on a couched gold
background with the
Crucifixion, the Virgin and
St. John and angels. The
cross is mounted on a
chasuble of fifteenth-century
Italian velvet, length 43¾in
(116cm). VICTORIA AND
ALBERT MUSEUM, LONDON.

LEFT: Plate 99
Altar frontal (detail),
Poland, sixteenth century.
The Flight into Egypt,
embroidered in colored silks
with some metal threads.
TREASURY OF WAWEL
CATHEDRAL, POLAND.

BELOW: Plate 101
Skirt border *(detail), Crete, mid-eighteenth century.* Linen/cotton mixture embroidered in colored silks with Cretan feather, satin, chain, ladder and stem stitches, height of border, 10in (25·5cm). *The sirens and flower vase patterns show Italian influence.* VICTORIA AND ALBERT MUSEUM, LONDON.

RIGHT: Plate 100
Military tent *(detail), Poland, eighteenth century.* Applied work on linen. Tents made in Poland were copies of Persian and Turkish originals which were greatly sought after. STATE ART COLLECTIONS, WAWEL CASTLE.

Plate 102
Woman of Joannina in the
nineteenth century, *costume
sketch by Athena Tarsouli,
1946. Joannina in northern
Greece has always been
famous for its goldsmiths
and jewelers as well as its
embroiderers as is
demonstrated by this lady's
magnificent full-skirted,
sleeveless coat.*

Plate 103
Woman's costume, *from the region of Peć (Metohija), late nineteenth century.*
NATIONAL ETHNOGRAPHICAL MUSEUM, BELGRADE.

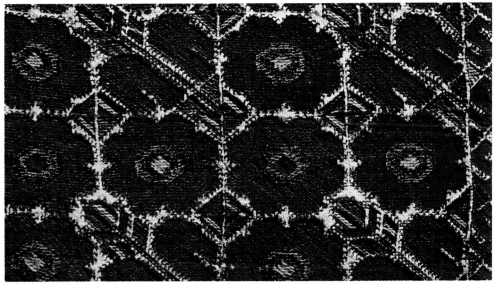

ABOVE, LEFT: Plate 104
Women from Bitola and
Skopska Crna Gora *in
Yugoslav Macedonia. After
a watercolor by Nikola
Arsenović, second half of the
nineteenth century. Fine
examples of the rich
geometric patterns of the
Slav peoples of Macedonia
and southern Serbia.*

BELOW, LEFT: Plate 105
Sleeve embroidery *(detail
of Plate 103), from the
region of Peć (Metohija),
late nineteenth century.
Cotton embroidered with
wool in Gobelins stitch.
These closely worked
patterns are found over a
wide area of Macedonia and
the southern parts of Serbia.*
NATIONAL ETHNOGRAPHICAL
MUSEUM, BELGRADE.

ABOVE: Plate 106
Sleeve embroidery on a
woman's dress *(detail)*,
*Attica, late nineteenth
century.* BENAKI MUSEUM,
ATHENS.

RIGHT: Plate 107
Woman's cap, *Bosnia,
Yugoslavia, nineteenth
century. Embroidered with
silk thread and some metal
thread in cross stitch. The
rose is a stylization of a
Turkish embroidery pattern.
Length 8¾in (22cm).*
VICTORIA AND ALBERT
MUSEUM, LONDON.

OPPOSITE: Plate 108
Inditia or altar cloth,
*Godunov School, Russia,
1601. This altar cloth is a
typical product of the
Godunov School and
represents Christ sitting
enthroned between the
Virgin and St. John the
Baptist with the Saints,
Serge and Nicon Radonezh
kneeling at his feet. Legend
ascribes this work to Ksenia,
Boris Godunov's daughter.*
THE HISTORY AND ART
MUSEUM, ZAGORSK.

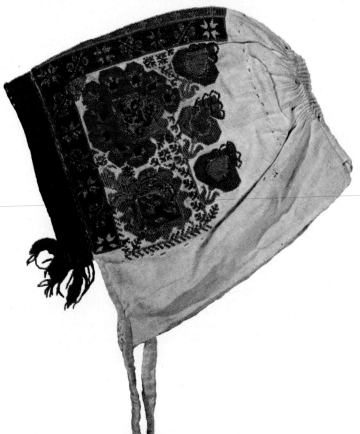

ABOVE: Plate 109
Towel end, *south Russia,
nineteenth century.
Needleweaving and counted
threadwork in silk on linen
90in × 30½in (229cm ×
79cm).* VICTORIA AND
ALBERT MUSEUM, LONDON.

RIGHT: Plate 110
Woman's peasant costume,
*Cheremes tribe, Russia,
eighteenth century. The
Cheremes, a non-Slavonic
minority living alongside the
Russians, were noted for
their dress, the upper part of
which was often embroidered
in colored wool and
decorated with coins.*
VICTORIA AND ALBERT
MUSEUM, LONDON.

embroideries illustrating for the most part scenes from the biblical texts. The Orthodox Church laid great stress on the symbolic meaning given to various vestments and an ancient tradition dictated the scenes considered appropriate in each case. The actual portrayal of any scene depended on the even more rigid rules laid down for iconographical interpretation of the texts, and artists were given no latitude for personal invention. A stole would be embroidered with scenes illustrating the Twelve Great Feasts of the Church, or alternatively with apostles and saints, or the Early Fathers, each standing under an architectural arcade. A deacon's stole carried angels in their rôle of deacon or heavenly servitor. Veils for covering chalice and paten showed Christ administering Communion to the Apostles, traditionally used in preference to the more realistic illustration of the Gospel story of the Last Supper. Examples of the *epitaphios* from the fourteenth century simply show the Body of Christ lying on a bier guarded and mourned by angels. From the end of the fifteenth century the Virgin and other mourning figures from the Gospel stories are added. Traditionally the Four Evangelists are placed in the corners of the veil.

Orthodox church embroidery employed virtually unchanged throughout its history the technique of surface-couched gold or other metal threads for all figure subjects and ornament, using silk split stitch only for the flesh parts of figures. Colored silks were used very sparingly and then as an adjunct to the metal threads until late in the post-Byzantine period. Sophisticated refinements of this basic technique employed by the professional embroiderers of the earlier periods included the laying of the gold threads at slightly different angles in adjoining sections to catch the maximum play of light on the metal surface, and also the setting of the couching stitches in herringbone and other patterns to give still greater variety.

A further subtlety, which is characteristic of eastern church embroidery but which was not practiced in the West, was the use of gold or silver thread lightly twisted with a colored silk and laid and couched in the same way as a solid metal thread, so that the brilliance of the gold was infused with a faint sheen of color. Orthodox embroid-

erers did not hesitate to undertake quite long inscriptions, labeling scenes and figures, dedicating the vestment, or quoting from scripture or the liturgical texts. In some cases this lettering provided a decorative element in its own right.

Unfortunately no information has yet come to light about the conditions in which these embroideries were worked. It may be assumed that the finest of them were made in Constantinople. Since we know that the craft guild system was strongly established there, and since monastic life in the Orthodox Church embraced fewer subsidiary activities than that of the West, it also seems probable that these highly professional artefacts were made in secular workrooms, probably often in those under imperial control. In the emerging states of southeast Europe, the guilds, which were essentially a part of city life, could hardly have operated and here it seems more likely that workrooms were run under the auspices of religious houses, or under the direct patronage or management of a lady of the ruling house.

The two great monuments to the skill of Byzantine embroiderers during the fourteenth century are a patriarchal *saccos* in the Vatican, which was at one time known as the "Dalmatic of Charlemagne," and the "Salonica" *epitaphios*, so-called because it was discovered in that city, and which is now in the Byzantine Museum in Athens. The *saccos* has on the front the scene of the Last Judgment composed in a roundel, and on the back a freer composition of the Transfiguration. On the shoulders are the twin scenes of the Communion of the Apostles, and the intervening background is powdered with crosses in circles, as happens in so many of the fourteenth-century embroideries. The vestment is made of a heavy dark blue satin and embroidered almost entirely in gold and silver with touches of colored silks, used mainly to mark the lines of the figure drawing. The very high degree of technical skill employed on this piece fully matches its artistic sophistication, which rivals the greatest mosaics of the period.

The *epitaphios* is the finest of its kind in existence. It is unusual in that the whole background, as well as the figures, is worked in gold and silver thread and it is the earliest existing example of the technique of twisting

Priest's stole *(detail)*, *worked by the Greek embroideress, Despoineta of Constantinople, 1696. Apostles, saints and donors on a pale blue, silk ground embroidered with metal threads, polychrome silks and pearls. The pretty decorative style was a feature of Greek church embroidery of the eighteenth century.* MUSEUM OF ART, BUCHAREST.

colored silk (in this case blue) with the metal threads. The mourning angels in particular are drawn with a fluid grace which clearly conveys their anguish. Their style strongly influenced a number of *epitaphioi* of the period, among them one signed by the Serbian princesses Euphemia and Eupraxia which is discussed below.

In southeast Europe the self-confidence and the resources necessary for the production of luxury works of art were present in the two Bulgarian kingdoms of the tenth and later of the thirteenth and fourteenth centuries, but unfortunately no embroideries survive which can be called Bulgarian.

From the medieval kingdom of Serbia, however, two *epitaphioi* of the fourteenth century exist in the monasteries of Mount Athos, and a third which by its inscription was the gift of the Serbian King Stephen Uroš II Milutin to an unknown church. Several embroideries from the end of the fourteenth century are connected with the Serbian princess Euphemia, one of which is the *epitaphios* already mentioned which was later taken to Moldavia in northern Romania and is still there, in the monastery of Putna.

Serbian embroidery was highly professional work in the Byzantine manner. It is possible that the city of Ohrid, where the donation of many embroideries to the church of St. Clement was recorded in an inscription in the church itself, was a center for their production. Even those which name Euphemia as their donor, which were probably made after the defeat of the Serbs by the Turks at the Battle of Kossovo in 1389, are strongly Byzantine in style, iconography and technique. A feature of her *epitaphios*, on which the name of Eupraxia is also recorded, is the transmutation of the crosses of the Byzantine backgrounds into a thick cluster of stars, and this detail was later copied by Romanian embroiderers at Putna, for whom the *epitaphios* may well have served as a model.

Christianity was brought to the Romanian lands during the tenth century by followers of the Byzantine missionary, St. Cyril (827–69), operating from Bulgaria. When the two principalities of this area, Wallachia and Moldavia, emerged into independence during the fourteenth century, church art, as in Serbia, followed

Byzantine traditions, and the earliest embroideries were the work of Greek craftsmen. By the end of the fifteenth century Stephen the Great of Moldavia appears to have established a court workroom, either in his capital at Suceava or under the auspices of the monastery he founded at Putna, where many of the embroideries of his reign and his son's survive. They include three *epitaphioi*, a number of stoles and other small pieces, and a set of large veils illustrating scenes from the Gospels and the Life of the Virgin. These in particular are true successors of the more elaborate Byzantine style. They show a strong affinity with Moldavian fresco painting of the period and are carried out with a bolder but still masterly handling of twisted gold and silk threads to produce gold-flecked areas of color, and careful directional changes in the gold to ensure a play of light. The mixture of gold and color became a marked feature of Moldavian embroidery, but by the middle of the sixteenth century had become coarser, using a greater proportion of crudely colored silk to the amount of gold and showing considerably less subtlety in the handling.

Another characteristic of the Moldavian embroideries of this period is the development of the inscriptions, particularly in the *epitaphioi*, into fine decorative borders. Both script and language were not the vernacular Romanian but the Old Slavonic originally introduced to the area and established there as a necessary tool of their trade by the missionaries from Bulgaria. It remained the language of Church and State in Romania until well into the seventeenth century. In the hands of Stephen's artists, the script took on an almost Islamic appearance and vied with Islamic calligraphy in refinement. These must be the most elegant inscriptions ever carried out in embroidery, which does not as a rule lend itself successfully to the recording of the written word.

Church embroidery in the sister principality of Wallachia, which achieved independence half a century earlier than Moldavia, followed very similar lines, relying in the earliest years on Byzantine pieces, among them a magnificent stole heavily adorned with pearls which is in the monastery of Tismana.

As Turkish political supremacy

increased its hold on both countries during the sixteenth century, further evidence of near-eastern influence can be seen in the embroideries, even though these remained basically true to their Byzantine models in all but decorative detail. On stoles, the rounded arch harboring the figure of a saint was often replaced by a tri-lobed ogee arch. The imported Turkish silks which had become part of fashionable upper-class dress were faithfully reproduced in embroidery, for example on the tomb covers of the Movila princes of Moldavia at the end of the sixteenth century. Later, broad borders of floral ornament in Turkish style surrounded curtains and veils.

With its territory totally submerged by the invading Turks, the Greek Church held steadfastly to its traditions as a means of preserving its identity and providing a national focus for its people. The aristocratic classes who had previously commissioned embroideries had largely disappeared, to be replaced by a bourgeois class of small-town merchants and officials. Embroideries continued to be made in small individual workrooms or convents which clung tenaciously to the old style and technique but with ever-deteriorating finesse, so that the earlier mastery of light and shade was lost.

By the turn of the seventeenth and eighteenth centuries, however, the Church itself, in Greece in particular, was waking from its hibernation, cautiously renewing contact with the West, and reassuming its rôle as a leader of education. Briefly, from the last years of the seventeenth century until about the middle of the eighteenth, this refreshing breeze touched the world of church embroidery, fanned by a Greek embroideress in Istanbul, whose work in a pretty decorative style revived older standards of technical perfection and embodied many iconographical touches borrowed from Italian Catholicism. She had a number of followers, mostly in the Greek cities of Asia Minor.

Similarly in the 1750s, one Hristofor Žefarović, a monk in the service of the Serbian Patriarchate, which at that time had taken refuge from the Turks at Karlovci in the Austrian Danubian provinces, designed a number of embroideries which combined the traditional Orthodox iconography with pure baroque ornament. It is thought that

his designs were carried out in a Viennese workroom. Unfortunately this spirit of innovation was not maintained and the nineteenth century was a period of sad decline.

Secular Embroidery from the Sixteenth to the Nineteenth Centuries

The sixteenth century saw throughout Europe a great upsurge of elaborate embroidery on fashionable dress, a trend which was naturally shared by those countries of central Europe with western affiliations. In Poland, at this time, the ready availability of freshwater pearls ensured that they were used not only on church embroidery but also in immense quantities on the dress of the court and the aristocratic classes. This type of embroidery was exclusively the work of professionals, always men, who were sometimes described as "stringers of pearls" rather than "embroiderers."

In the first half of the sixteenth century, during the period of Sigismund I's (1467–1548) rebuilding of the Wawel Castle, a professional team of male embroiderers, mainly under German leadership, worked under the orders of the Warden. At the same time a workroom under Sigismund's Italian queen, Bona Sforza, was staffed by young girls. Both undertook embroidery for the Church, for the embellishment of the Castle, and for the royal dresses, but whereas the male team specialized in pearl embroidery and the heavier type of gold-thread work, the women worked on finer embroideries on linen.

From 1525 a certain Jan Holfelder of Nuremberg is recorded as court embroiderer, mainly engaged on pearl embroidery on royal dresses. Later another German, Sebaldus Linck, held the post. He worked for some forty years in the service of Sigismund I and II (1520–72) and Ann Jagiello, sister of Sigismund II, who at the end of the century took over the royal patronage of embroidery. Many pieces were credited to her hand.

The royal workrooms were closed in 1545, when the court moved to Vilna, but professional embroiderers still operated in the city of Cracow. At this time, however, they do not appear to have had any professional organization. The guild system for embroiderers did not reach Poland until the middle of the seventeenth century, when they

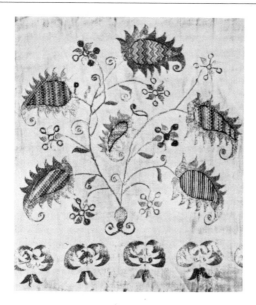

Border of a kerchief, *Hungary, seventeenth century. Embroidery in polychrome silks and some metal thread. The flower sprays show strong Turkish influence.* MUSEUM OF APPLIED ARTS, BUDAPEST, HUNGARY.

were first granted charters in Lwów and Lublin, which was very late in comparison with other countries.

In Hungary the same division of labor operated between professional workers in gold threads, who were organized into guilds in the cities from the end of the fifteenth century, and in amateur workrooms in the castles of the aristocracy, where girls of good family were sent to complete their education and worked with the castle's maids or hired embroideresses under a professional seamstress on the lighter type of embroidery.

In the well-appointed Hungarian aristocratic household of the late sixteenth and seventeenth centuries everything possible was embroidered. Ladies took a personal interest in the activities of their workrooms and corresponded frequently with their friends over the exchange of patterns and samplers. Very high standards were achieved on shifts and shirts for men and women, on bed linen, sheets, pillows and curtains, and on the most elaborate table linen, which included a cloth, a center runner, a valance fastened to the edge of the table to show below the cloth and numerous napkins for the use of guests and servants. Embroidered handkerchiefs were used on all occasions, less in the mundane sense of a handkerchief than as gifts, and especially at weddings, when a particularly fine one was worked by the bride for her betrothal ceremony and others were presented to the guests. Portraits show young married women carrying their betrothal handkerchiefs, and also kerchiefs placed in the hands of the dead for their lying-in-state.

These formal portraits of the departed, which were regularly commissioned by leading Hungarian families in the late seventeenth century, give an excellent idea of embroidery on bed linen and dress.

Light church embroideries, particularly chalice veils, were worked on fine linen in much the same style, with the addition of a Christian symbol such as the Lamb in the center.

All these embroideries were worked in floral patterns in light, brightly colored silks, sometimes with the addition of a little gold thread. The principal stitches were satin and long and short, although many others were added and an inventive variety of filling stitches can be found in leaves and petals. A favorite stitch used in this way is the arrangement of satin stitch variously known as flame stitch, Irish stitch (in England) and, later, Florentine stitch and Hungarian point. Although it was used in Hungary for the most part as a filling in fine silk embroidery, it was more often used elsewhere in Europe in the seventeenth and eighteenth centuries as a ground-covering stitch for large wool hangings.

This is an area in which the combination of eastern and western influences is particularly marked. The reign of Matthias Corvinus in the second half of the fifteenth century had established strong cultural links between Hungary and Italy. Hungary, like the rest of Europe, adopted Italian embroidery patterns with the dissemination of Venetian printed pattern books during the sixteenth century, and also borrowed from Italian silk design as trade in these luxury materials increased. The Hungarian embroideries, therefore, include many Italian motifs such as wave and scroll patterns, vases of flowers, detached diagonal leaf shapes, and a classic renaissance arrangement of formal flower and stem patterns. On the other hand Hungary, unlike the rest of Europe, assimilated during the sixteenth and seventeenth centuries an influx of Turkish designs which affected embroidery especially. Turkish motifs such as the pomegranate and tulip were blended with the Italian to produce a uniquely Hungarian style. At the same time, it must be remembered that during the sixteenth century the interchange of influence between Turkish and Italian silk designs was very strong, so that when embroiderers drew on this source it is not always possible to separate the two strands.

The Turkish occupation of a large part of the country for a century and a half between 1542 and 1699 placed Hungary in the forefront of Europe's defense lines against the Turks, but the constant border skirmishes of this period did not prevent her trading with Turkey and employing Turkish labor. Turkish embroidery could be bought in Buda as early as 1500; large quantities of Turkish embroidery silks were imported as well as fine linen and cotton materials, while the demand for Turkish gold thread was so great that eventually Armenians were brought to Hungary to manufacture it. Turkish seamstresses were even employed in Hungarian households and played a large part in introducing Turkish patterns.

The better to harass their enemies in frontier warfare, Hungarian troops discarded their heavy western-style armor and adopted the Turks' own mode of dress, a tight-fitting frogged tunic with long wide skirts and a long overmantle with shoulder slits for the arms to pass through, allowing exceptionally long and narrow sleeves to hang free, which the Turks in their turn had taken from Persian medieval costume. Shortened to thigh length, the tunic (*dolman*) and the loose overmantle (*mente*) became the national costume of the Hungarian upper classes during the sixteenth and seventeenth centuries. The *dolman* in particular could be for festive occasions a very showy garment. By the seventeenth century they were not only made of brocaded silks but also of velvet or satin completely covered in raised gold-thread embroidery or applied gold braids in patterns which recall the heavy Italian laces of the period. By the nineteenth century these garments were shortened again to become the typical braided hussar uniform. A garment peculiar to Hungary was a short loose shirt of thin silk worn directly over the shirt proper by young men and over the *dolman* by their elders. It was embroidered at home in the domestic style with flower sprays in gold and colored silks.

Gold embroidery became increasingly influenced by Turkey. Turkish horse trappings captured on the battlefields started a fashion among military commanders for embroidery in gold and silver and pearls on saddles and saddle cloths and every possible item of harness.

ABOVE:
Saddle, *Hungary,*
seventeenth century.
Embroidered in silver in the
Turkish manner. The fashion
in central Europe for
embroidering horse

trappings with metal threads
was copied from Turkish
saddlery captured in battle.
HUNGARIAN NATIONAL
MUSEUM, BUDAPEST.

Woman's underdress, *Oltenia, Romania, nineteenth century. Embroidery in pink and black silk with metal thread and sequins, length 51in (129cm).* VICTORIA AND ALBERT MUSEUM, LONDON.

Poland's relations with the Middle East were both of longer standing and more direct in that the Vistula and Dnieper had formed part of the river trade routes linking the north of Europe with the East since the early Middle Ages. Armenian embroiderers were brought to the country as early as the beginning of the sixteenth century to work in gold and pearls and, by the seventeenth century, Persian works of art had become extremely fashionable. Fine Persian carpets and woven silk sashes were imported in large numbers.

Not only horse trappings but also military tents were captured from the Turks and taken over by their opponents. These portable pavilions, which were made mainly in northwest Persia in the region of Tabriz and also in Anatolia and Armenia, were lavishly decorated with colorful applied work and embroidery, in patterns which were often based on a *mihrab*, or prayer niche, closely related in design to Turkish ceramic tile compositions. They became so popular with the Polish court and aristocracy, by whom they were used for journeys of state and summer entertainment as well as for military purposes, that they were not only imported from Persia via the Black Sea ports but also manufactured in Poland itself, for the most part by Armenian and Jewish embroiderers working in Lwów and Brody. Polish tents were similar to their Oriental prototypes but they were less elaborate in technique and the principle of the design was sometimes misunderstood so

that the effect is less assured (Plate 100).

In spite of these flourishing trade connections, Polish embroidery as a whole in this period was less affected by Oriental design and more in keeping with fashionable trends in western Europe. An example is the embroidered skirt border of Zofia Sieniawska, which is decorated with floral groups and small architectural motifs in the rococo chinoiserie style. Vases and baskets of flowers deriving from Italian silk designs also became very popular in embroidered hangings as well as in Polish-made carpets.

It cannot be said that any particularly characteristic style emerged in Bohemia and Moravia during the seventeenth and eighteenth centuries as it had in the Middle Ages. The annexation of these provinces to the Habsburg Crown in the 1630s was followed by the emigration of much of the Protestant population of all classes and an influx of German nobility. Their wealth and desire for display meant that the sumptuary arts were no less in demand, but as the style of church furnishing was dictated by Rome, so secular taste, for the decoration of town houses for example, was inspired by Germany. It is perhaps worth mentioning the very fine white embroidery worked on linen in a myriad of drawnwork fillings which is principally associated with Dresden in the first half of the eighteenth century but which was also taken up in Czechoslovakia, where it was eventually assimilated into peasant art.

The pattern of life in southeast

Europe was very different from that of the West. During the height of Turkish power in the sixteenth century the ruling classes over most of the area were either Turks or indigenous Moslems who adopted Turkish manners and customs. Equally, the princes and aristocracy (the *boyars*) of the Romanian principalities, the wealthy landowners of the Morea in southern Greece, the merchants of Salonica and the Black Sea ports, all followed a way of life which was perhaps Near Eastern rather than specifically Turkish, but depended nevertheless on Turkish fashions in dress and domestic luxury. Since this was the period when the Turkish silk industry was at its most prolific and inventive, these textiles were greatly sought after for clothes, particularly ceremonial robes, and furnishings. Large numbers of them were imported into Wallachia and Moldavia. Embroidery everywhere seems to have played a lesser part.

In the principalities donor portraits in church frescoes show aristocratic women of the late sixteenth century wearing underdresses with sleeves decorated in stripes, either woven or embroidered. This is a style which is characteristic of the area and which persisted in peasant dress into the twentieth century. Some fine blouses embroidered in silk and gold thread still survive from the eighteenth and nineteenth centuries which are evidently in the older tradition.

By the early years of the nineteenth century a middle class began to emerge in the towns of southeast Europe sufficiently wealthy and self-confident to display a certain luxury in dress, while at the same time earlier Turkish regulations forbidding any form of ostentation in the dress of the conquered peoples were relaxed. At the same period Turkish dress, particularly for the middle and lower classes, underwent a change from the long caftan for men and women to shorter jackets and waistcoats, which were increasingly decorated with gold embroidery. These fashions were taken up with great enthusiasm in the Turkish European possessions and embroiderers in gold were much in demand.

A considerable center for the work was Joannina in northern Greece, at that time the capital of a Turkish administrative district and a town of considerable wealth, famous, as it still

is, for its goldsmiths and jewelers as well as embroiderers. Bourgeois ladies of Joannina wore long, full-skirted sleeveless coats, magnificently embroidered in raised laid gold threads and applied gold braid and ribbon (Plate 102), with short vests to match. These garments were exported as far as Albania and Montenegro (now in Yugoslavia) where they were also fashionable in the towns. It is not clear whether such towns as Shkodër in Albania and Cetinje in Montenegro had their own workrooms, although this must be the supposition, or whether all coats of this kind were imported from Joannina. Elsewhere in southeast Europe short velvet jackets and waistcoats also embroidered in gold were popular with both men and women. The sketches of Popp de Szathmary and a portrait of a lady by Katarina Ivanović illustrate this fashion in Belgrade.

At this period also the Greek War of Independence fostered enthusiasm for a national dress based on the Albanian costume of the freedom fighters from Souli, in the Pindus north of Joannina. Basically this consisted of the *fustanella*, or full white cotton kilt, and a short jacket with hanging sleeves and a sleeveless waistcoat which lent themselves ideally to gold embroidery. It is splendidly illustrated in the portrait of Byron in Greek dress by J. B. Phillips. This did in fact become the national dress of Greece and, later in the century, traveling tailors went from place to place working on the embroidery. After the establishment of Greek independence and the institution of the monarchy the fashion was encouraged at the court and in upper-class circles by the example of Queen Amalia. Gentlemen wore the full panoply of *fustanella* and gold embroidery, while the ladies wore over their fashionable dresses a tight-fitting, somewhat Europeanized form of short jacket, embroidered in gold or applied colored cords, which were in any case sometimes substituted for gold in the bourgeois costume. A middle-class blend of European fashion with this semi-Turkish style can be seen in a portrait in Joannina of the 1860s by Pierre Billet of an elderly lady wearing a wide-sleeved velvet jacket. Her European blouse is trimmed with a profusion of *bibila* lace, those elegant chains of needlemade flowerets made in Turkey and all around the shores of the Aegean in bright colors, but here worn in white.

TOP:
Wool embroidered wall hanging *(detail)*. *Now an altar frontal. Poland, late seventeenth century. Vase patterns derived from Mediterranean decorative traditions were popular in Poland during this period and during the eighteenth century.* NATIONAL MUSEUM, CRACOW.

ABOVE:
Churching shawl *(detail)*, *Moravia, 1790. Embroidered with cream-colored silk threads in satin and buttonhole stitches with pulled and drawn work, 60 in × 90.7 in (150 cm × 244 cm). A churching shawl was used to carry a baby to the mother's churching ceremony after the birth. The fine whitework is derived from the famous white embroideries made in Dresden in the eighteenth century.* NATIONAL MUSEUM, PRAGUE.

The Greek Islands, for historical reasons, can be regarded as a special case. The islands of the Aegean were under Venetian domination throughout the later Middle Ages until the middle of the sixteenth century, by which time most islands had fallen to the Turks except Crete, which remained Venetian until 1669. This is therefore another area where Italian and Turkish influences vie with each other, but the results are very different from those produced by the combination of the same influences in Hungary.

The embroideries of these islands cannot exactly be described as peasant work, at least until the end of the eighteenth century, since they were made in a bourgeois society which enjoyed at various periods a fair prosperity. All of them are worked in silk on linen or cotton grounds with very little gold thread except occasionally in Turkish-style scarves. Nearly all are for household use, particularly bed furnishings, with a certain amount of embroidery on underdresses. The more elaborate of these embroideries were often the work of professionals, in this case women rather than men, while dresses and smaller pieces were made by girls for their dowries.

Crete was one of the few islands where the outer dress was elaborately embroidered. During the eighteenth century the long full overskirts of western Crete, which hung from the shoulders on narrow straps, were richly decorated at the hem with a deep border worked in bright colors and a great variety of stitches, Cretan feather being the most usual, with herringbone, satin, chain and French knots (Plate 101). They were sometimes signed and dated by their workers and were the only island embroideries where this occurred. Crete's Venetian associations are reflected in the patterns, which are more often than not based on the vase of carnations so frequently found in Italian silk design and also, as we have already noted, in Turkish silk design.

Household embroideries concentrated mainly on furniture for the marriage bed such as curtains, valances and cushion covers, and in the Dodecanese splendidly embroidered bed tents, designed to give a newly married couple some privacy in the one-roomed house on their wedding night. It is known that such tents were offered for sale in Rhodes toward the end of the fourteenth century, but the few existing examples are not thought to be earlier than the seventeenth century.

These tents and the large curtains embroidered in pattern darning from the southern Cyclades and Dodecanese seem to have attempted to provide a homely substitute for the admired Turkish silks, and it is possible to trace a relationship between the repetitive designs of the embroideries and silk patterns, although in the embroideries this is almost lost in the severely diagrammatic form imposed by the technique. A stronger Turkish influence is found in the northern Sporades, where the bedspreads and cushion covers bear a marked likeness to the floral decoration of Iznik pottery. Embroideries which were very similar in style were made in Joannina, which has already been mentioned in connection with the gold embroideries. The finest pieces here were marriage cushions showing bride and groom with their attendants in a setting of flowers and vegetation.

The strongest links with Italian embroidery were in the Cyclades and Ionian Islands, which had the closest relations with Venice. In these groups whitework on drawn threads and borders with renaissance wave and scroll patterns worked in red silk in long-armed cross stitch are in effect coarser copies of Italian sixteenth- and seventeenth-century pieces.

The making of fine embroideries in the islands seems to have died out during the course of the eighteenth century, when many of them suffered a period of great poverty owing to raids by pirates and by Turkish press gangs seeking manpower. The nineteenth century saw in some cases the debasement of the old patterns and occasionally the substitution of a more popular style. This can be seen in bright cross-stitch skirt borders from Astypalaia with patterns of birds and ships (both traditional motifs in the islands) and in Cretan popular textiles, both woven and embroidered, depicting heroes of the struggle against Turkish domination, which persisted there until the end of the nineteenth century.

Peasant Embroidery in the Nineteenth Century

The nineteenth century saw an explosion of embroidered decoration on peasant dress in central and southeast Europe, due in part to a greater prosperity among the peasant classes and also to a rising desire for an expression of national feeling directed against foreign rulers, whether these were the Habsburgs or the Turks. Some distinctive features in peasant dress date back to very old traditions, but these are often matters of cut rather than decoration. Examples are the cut of men's trousers, wide or narrow, the heavy square-hooded shepherd's mantle so typical of the Hungarian plains, the long shirt worn over the trousers in Romania and Hungary, and the set of the sleeve in women's underdresses, straight at the shoulder and narrow, a direct heritage from Byzantium in the south, and in the north a full sleeve gathered at neck and wrist, the descendant of the sixteenth-century fashionable shirt.

Early illustrations such as seventeenth-century woodcuts indicate these characteristics in cut, but nevertheless give the impression that clothes were something to be worn as body covering without any pretensions to style. As time goes on it can be seen that the distinctive cut is deliberately emphasized and worn with an air which consciously declares the wearer's identity, but even as late as the middle of the nineteenth century contemporary engravings show in the main only very modest embroidery, usually a narrow band on the cuffs and neck of blouse or shirt. As the century progressed a growing self-confidence found expression in an ever more exaggerated style of personal adornment. By the last few decades peasant fashions, especially in central Europe, had reached an extreme of fantasy, decked out as much with lace and commercially woven ribbons as with hand embroidery.

All over the area the usual distinction prevailed between professional work in heavy materials done by men, and lighter personal and household embroideries made at home by women. Village tailors made and decorated the fur and sheepskin coats of the north of the area, as well as the felt coats and mantles of the Danube, and sleeveless felt coats for women and men's short jackets and trousers in the south. Women were responsible for the weaving of cotton and linen fabrics and the making of household articles such as bed curtains, cushions and towels and of personal linen such as men's shirts and their own underdresses or blouses,

ABOVE:
Woman's sleeveless coat, *Joannina, northern Greece, nineteenth century. Dark blue cloth embroidered with gold thread and gold braid.* MUSEUM OF GREEK POPULAR ART, ATHENS, GREECE.

LEFT:
Man's jacket *(detail of embroidery), Croatia, late nineteenth century. Colored felt applied and embroidered.* ETHNOGRAPHICAL MUSEUM, ZAGREB, YUGOSLAVIA.

which were naturally especially finely worked for a wedding.

Virtually no evidence exists to show how far the tradition of embroidery went back, and it is very possible that the weaving of simple patterns on household articles was an earlier craft. Some church embroideries illustrate home-woven fabrics, for example a cushion in the Annunciation on the Rokycany chasuble, and covers on the bier in certain Romanian and Greek *epitaphioi* of the sixteenth century. It seems probable that diamond and wave patterns with swastika and S forms, which are everywhere present in embroidery, originated in weaving. It must be open to question whether they are in fact a heritage from the nomadic past of the Bulgars, Slavs and Magyars, or whether their universal popularity is merely due to the ease with which they can be produced on a primitive loom.

On the other hand patterns which were the currency of central Asiatic and Mediterranean textile design from the sixth to the sixteenth century and later, do recur constantly in the peasant embroideries all over this central European area. The ancient Assyrian Tree of Life motif with birds or wild animals, which was transmitted to the Mediterranean area through Persian, Byzantine and Islamic silk weavings, and later appeared in Italian domestic weaving and embroidery, survives very frequently in peasant embroideries, as do the Italian renaissance wave and vase patterns.

Floral designs are by far the most popular, whether in natural form or severely stylized by the technical demands of cross-stitch and other counted-thread techniques. It has been suggested that many flower patterns evolved from repetition and misunderstanding of earlier cult motifs and "signs" associated with fertility, the spring renewal of fruitfulness and the warding off of evil spirits. These motifs were normally

objects known in everyday life, originally represented on everyday articles for a magical purpose, and continually repeated as a partially understood superstition through many centuries of Christianity. Thus, in the end, in embroidery patterns the sun was transformed into an open rose, the snake into a wave pattern with flower sprigs, various agricultural tools took leaf bract forms and bees and ants became mere dots. This form of transmutation worked in a double sense in that an embroideress could take a much-worked traditional motif which had lost its original meaning and rework it according to her fancy to resemble some quite different object. In the same way names from the home and farm could be given to patterns, not because the worker was trying to create, for example, a hen, but because a known motif reminded her of one. It seems in fact that peasant designs were virtually always based on a decorative tradition, whether this was handed down from an aristocratic art or evolved from ancient popular practice, and seldom if ever actually copied from a natural object.

In this huge area not only every country but every district and even every valley and village had its small distinctions in embroidery patterns. They can be divided into two categories: those of strictly geometric character, which are mostly abstract in form but can also include severely stylized flower patterns, and freer, more naturalistic floral embroideries. As a very broad generalization it can be said that the first group comes from the south and east of the area and from the Slav population of eastern Czechoslovakia, while the second belongs to the north and west.

Among the geometric embroideries the rich thickly worked patterns (Plate 104) of the Slav peoples of Macedonia and southern Serbia are the most impressive. They are worked in silk or wool in dark colors, usually rich reds and black, on the heavy straight-cut dresses of the area. The sleeves in particular are rigid with embroidery from wrist to elbow. The most usual stitch is a form of tent or gobelins stitch, worked diagonally from the back, which is called locally "half-stitch" (Plate 105). Details are added in satin stitch or chain. Many of these embroideries are solidly conceived blocks of abstract pattern, suggesting tribal origins by

Skirt and sleeve borders, *the neighborhood of Samokov, Bulgaria, late nineteenth century. Embroidery in cross stitch and holbein stitch.* BULGARIAN ACADEMY OF SCIENCES, ETHNOGRAPHIC INSTITUTE, SOFIA, BULGARIA.

their likeness to Turcoman and Caucasian carpets. Others are made up of severely stylized flowers. Dresses of the same cut were worn all over Greece but the embroidery was usually lighter in character. In Attica, however, where much of the population was Albanian by origin, the deep borders on skirts and sleeves were decorated with a mosaic of rich reds and purples (Plate 106). A sketch of the costume of Attica by the archaeologist Baron Otto von Stackelberg, made as early as 1811, shows the deep band of embroidery on hem and sleeves. It is worth noting also that the costume illustrations made by Nikola Arsenović after the middle of the nineteenth century suggest that Macedonian costumes were very heavily embroidered, while those from the central and northern parts of present-day Yugoslavia were much less decorated than they later became.

Dress embroidery in Bulgaria, as well as in Bosnia, Herzegovina and parts of Romania, is characterized by stylized flower patterns which are worked in a lighter style than those of Macedonia. Many of them are recognizable adaptations of the Turkish forms of carnation, tulip and rose. In particular the essentially Turkish motif of a rose spray curled into a curved leaf was widely copied and modified on dress borders and scarf or towel ends over the whole area of the Turkish occupation.

Floral embroidery in the west and north of the area, that is in western Czechoslovakia and in Poland and Hungary, is much more naturalistic and more influenced by changing western European fashions. Traces of rococo and Biedermeier styles are frequently apparent in peasant embroidery and, in Hungary, wool embroidery on household articles was directly descended from the domestic embroideries of the upper classes in the seventeenth and eighteenth centuries. The patterns of these embroideries survived into the late nineteenth century in a greatly coarsened form in the Hungarian districts of Transylvania (now part of Romania) where they were worked in red or blue cotton in thick ladder or chain stitches.

Another technique taken from upper-class fashion was the whitework which, as we have already seen, was based in the north on the fine white embroideries associated with Dresden in the eighteenth century. White embroidery

Sleeve border *(detail), the neighborhood of Sofia, Bulgaria, late nineteenth century. Embroidered with cotton thread in cross stitch, mainly in red.* BULGARIAN ACADEMY OF SCIENCES, ETHNOGRAPHIC INSTITUTE, SOFIA, BULGARIA.

was very widely used on the costumes of Poland, Czechoslovakia, Hungary, Croatia and Slovenia for caps and blouses, which became more and more elaborate as the century wore on. At the same time the embroidery itself became less fine until the cutwork often called *"broderie anglaise"* almost entirely usurped the beautiful and varied fillings. This method was also very popular in Hungary for the wide-sleeved shirts worn by the herdsmen of the plains. A somewhat different style of cut and drawn work derived from Venetian patterns of the sixteenth century was made on the Dalmatian coast, which had a long historical association with Venice.

During the eighteenth century a type of floral embroidery based originally on baroque flower forms developed in colored leather appliqué on fur and sheepskin jackets and sleeveless coats and waistcoats for both men and women, which were worn with the pelt to the inside and the skin, often richly decorated in the eighteenth and nineteenth centuries, to the outside. Such jackets are worn in Hungary, Poland, Czechoslovakia, Romania and Croatia, and the decoration was always the work of male furriers. The appliqué technique later gave way to wool and silk embroidery worked on strips of soft leather and applied to the garment.

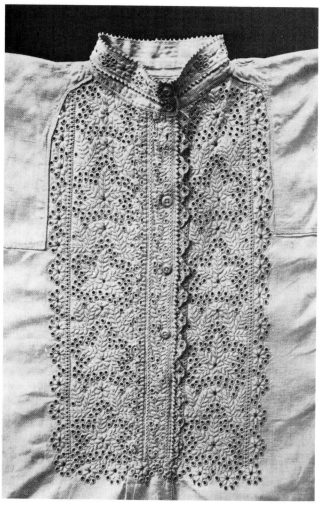

ABOVE:
Man's shirt front, *Csököly,
western Hungary, nineteenth
century. Embroidery in
white* broderie anglaise.
HUNGARIAN NATIONAL
MUSEUM, BUDAPEST.

ABOVE, RIGHT:
Leather jacket *(detail),
southeast Hungary,
nineteenth century. Appliqué
and embroidery.* HUNGARIAN
NATIONAL MUSEUM,
BUDAPEST.

RIGHT:
Man's trousers, *detail of
applied braids on the front
pocket, Moravia, 1950s.
This type of braiding,
usually in black, was found
in the nineteenth century
in all the areas of eastern
Europe where such felt
trousers were worn.*
NATIONAL MUSEUM,
PRAGUE.

This type of appliqué and floral embroidery was copied during the nineteenth century in Hungary by the makers of the heavy felt coats (called *szür*) which were the traditional wear of shepherds and herdsmen. Similar coats were common in many areas of southeast Europe, but only in nineteenth-century Hungary were they richly decorated. It was among the families of furriers that the fashion first started, using colored cloth for the applied work and, later, embroidery in satin stitch. The decorated *szür* was a greatly prized garment, often given to a young man for his wedding.

The working *szür* and felt coats elsewhere were often finished with narrow braiding, and applied braid decoration of a much more elaborate kind was worked on the type of men's suit which consisted of short jacket and waistcoat of felted cloth with trousers fitted close to the leg. Narrow trousers (as opposed to the voluminous Turkish style and the wide-legged linen garment of the Hungarian plain) were worn in the mountains of southern Poland and in the north of Romania, in Czechoslovakia and parts of Hungary, and farther south in Bosnia, Herzegovina and Albania. In the latter part of the nineteenth century elaborate braided patterns, often in black, were worked on the jackets and waistcoats and on the front pockets and flaps of the trousers, sometimes on the front of the thighs too.

This also was the work of village tailors, as was the colored braiding and applied work on women's sleeveless felt coats in Macedonia and Greece which contributed still more to the massive effect of the heavily embroidered dresses.

The twentieth century saw some adaptation of traditional patterns and occasionally the introduction of new ones, more often the use of totally new colors as imported commercially dyed thread became more readily available, but technical advances, and the social change inevitably produced by two world wars, have contributed to the near-extinction of traditional peasant dress, although it is still worn in some areas for festival occasions.

Deathbed portrait of Gáspár Illésházy, *1648. The cushion cover and the handkerchief are typical examples of Hungary domestic embroidery of the period.* HUNGARIAN NATIONAL MUSEUM, BUDAPEST.

Russia

In Russia the most important and interesting types of needlework were medieval church embroidery and, in the category of secular work, peasant embroidery, which was the inspiration for town embroidery. A serious study of the subject calls for inspection of the material held by Russian museums; relatively little is held in the West. The State Art Museum in Zagorsk, the State Russian Museum in Leningrad, the State National Museum and the State Historical Museum in Moscow and the museum in the Kremlin of Novgorod all own particularly fine collections of textiles.

Ecclesiastical Embroidery

As Christianity, which became the state religion in 988 when Prince Vladimir of Kiev was converted, came from Byzantium, it is not surprising that Russian church embroiderers followed the Byzantine tradition – and ultimately Greco-Roman traditions – in design, technique and choice of material. The medieval style lasted until the end of the seventeenth century, when Western influences were assimilated.

Most early Russian textiles have now perished and are known only by repute. For example, it is recorded that in 1183 many pieces embroidered with gold and pearls which belonged to the Ipateev monastery in Vladimir were destroyed, the sheer number of pieces attesting to a well-established tradition. They hung on two ropes which stretched from the Golden Gates (the main entrance of the city) to the Cathedral of the Assumption, a distance, according to Baedeker, of half a mile, and from there to the archbishop's residence. Presumably, the embroideries lined the processional route of the clergy on feast days. The earliest extant examples of Russian embroidery date from the first half of the fourteenth century.

In the eleventh century the daughter of Prince Vsevolod who had become a nun gathered together a group of girls and taught them to design (or write), to sing and to sew. The wife of Rurik, a prince of Kiev who died in 1215, is said to have applied herself to embroider in gold and silver; and further evidence shows that in the houses and estates of princes and rich merchants special workrooms were set aside for embroidery. In the sixteenth century one prince employed forty embroideresses and, in the seventeenth, as many as eighty worked for the tsaritsa. A Swedish traveler writing during the reign of Boris Godunov (1598–1605) speaks of the mistress of the house in which he is living as being herself a trained embroideress, presiding over the work.

Before the seventeenth century designs were drawn directly on the background by a *znamenshchik* (limner), who was governed by the same strict rules as those which applied to the iconography of icons and frescoes. Frequently the border of the larger pieces was an appropriate text, drawn by another specialized artist, which made full decorative use of Slavonic lettering. Embroidered pieces include ecclesiastical vestments, furnishings and banners; in Russia and Romania tomb covers and icons were also frequently embroidered, and occasionally whole *iconostases*.

Materials were often imported. The favorite ground material was ready-woven silk from Persia or brocade from Italy. So frequently were pearls used to enrich the work that the supply from northern Russian rivers was insufficient and they were brought along the caravan routes from India and Persia. Silk threads from Persia or China were employed, either loosely or tightly twisted. Occasionally silk, usually red, green or blue, was twisted for variety with a gold or silver thread which was also imported, probably from the West.

Metal threads limited the variety of stitches that were used, the goldwork in Russian medieval embroideries being mainly couched. The most common stitches sewn in silk were satin, split and a slanting stitch, used generally to depict the face, hands and other exposed flesh. In small pieces the stitches depicting the face are horizontal or vertical but in larger pieces there is an attempt to follow the contours.

Boris Godunov's wife was in charge of his embroidery workrooms and in the last years of the sixteenth century they produced works of outstanding technical quality. After Godunov ascended the throne in 1598 the embroideries were elaborately decorated with precious stones and worked on sumptuous materials to emphasize the wealth and prestige of his dynasty.

The *inditia*, or altar cloth (Plate 108), is a typical product of his workshops. It was embroidered in 1601 and in 1602 was presented to the Monastery of the Holy Trinity at Zagorsk. Christ sits enthroned between the Virgin and St. John the Baptist and at his feet kneel the saints Serge and Nicon Radonezh.

In the seventeenth century a change began to manifest itself. The standard of technique remained high but the designs lost their elegance through a tendency to rely too much for their effect on precious materials and ornamentation. In 1806 Catharine Wilmot wrote of a service in a monastery near Smolensk: "On the Robes of the Priests I observ'd a little ticket which I asked the meaning of, and they told me 'twas a Memorandum of the pounds weight of pearl on the embroidery of the Robe. Sometimes 'twas 8 pounds, sometimes 10, and sometimes 12. The Communion Cloths are work'd and fringed with real pearl & there are several dozen of them. . . ."

When Peter the Great (1689–1725) opened his "window on the West," Western traditions penetrated even church embroidery and after this, though a few well designed and executed pieces were still made, embroidery does not in general have the impact of work of the earlier period.

Peasant Embroidery

The great collections of Russian peasant embroidery in the State Historical Museum in Moscow and the State Russian Museum in Leningrad date, with a few earlier exceptions, from the nineteenth century. Valuable evidence of eighteenth-century peasant costume is given by the illustrations to Charles Müller's *Description de toutes les Nations de l'Empire de Russie*, which was published in St. Petersburg in 1776, and by the diaries of the Wilmot sisters written between 1803 and 1806. The tradition established by that time lasted throughout the century and was still recogniz-

able in the twentieth, though much modified.

Embroidered objects were part of a Russian peasant girl's dowry and demonstrated her ability to sew. Towels, bed curtains and valances display some of the most characteristic and interesting designs, but clothing, including shifts, pinafores and caps, was also embroidered. The designs were so localized that Martha Wilmot was able to say: "In the village you may distinguish newcomers from old inhabitants as neither party will alter a single point in conformity to the other."

Embroidered towels were used to decorate carts and sleighs on ceremonial occasions. They were also tied to sacred trees, hung in the corner of the room where the icon was displayed and used to cover the icons in church. When Martha Wilmot visited the house of some Old Believers, she remarked that "their room is all adorned with embroyder'd towels." On another occasion she wrote: "If a Young Woman presents you with a bowl of milk or eggs . . . you will always find hanging on her arm or covering the little basket a towel embroidered at each end, either with white thread in imitation of lace, or with red ditto, and worked with a delicacy to which few ladys could attain."

The variety and imagination which was lavished on headdresses defy description. *Kokoshnik, kichka, koruna* are but three of the many types. It was considered immodest for a married woman to show her hair, so female ingenuity devised caps which were lovingly embroidered and decorated. Sometimes they were a woman's only treasure. Martha Wilmot again makes an interesting social comment: "The mother of Pashinka is a degree above the lowest peasants. That is, instead of their horn'd headdress, she wears a handkerchief."

Both the Wilmot sisters comment on the highly decorated headdresses of the peasant women whom they saw on Princess Dashkov's estate near Smolensk. Catherine says that the headdress "differs in every Government, even in every village sometimes and here it is precisely like a pair of budding Horns subdued by bandages which nevertheless are gaudily decorated with gold and spangles and a deep fringe upon their Pole in place of hair." Without doubt the horns referred to are the curious

Woman's headdress, *Cheremes tribe, province of Viatka, Russia, nineteenth century. Linen ground embroidered with wool in slanted satin stitch, 19in × 10in (48cm × 25cm).* ROYAL SCOTTISH MUSEUM, EDINBURGH.

excrescences, covered in pearl beads, which were characteristic of the Smolensk district.

The type of cap a woman wished to have was stipulated in particular by the wet nurse, to whom it was customary to give not only money but a complete outfit of clothes and household linen.

Her status was reflected in the magnificence of her attire and in the clothes of her charge, whom she would always carry even when prams were in general use.

The illustration here shows the summer headdress of the Cheremes, a non-Slavonic minority living alongside the Russians in the provinces of Kazan, Nizhni, Novgorod and Viatka. The donor of this exhibit describes the rest of their attire as consisting of "a long chemise of coarse linen, the upper part embroidered with colored wool and coins." The embroidered cap which comes from Viatka is worked in a slanting satin stitch in dark rust, medium rust, dark blue and light green worsteds on a coarse linen ground. The embroidery is typical of the late nineteenth century.

Particular care was taken with the embroidery on women's sleeves, possibly showing a superstitious attitude toward the arm. It is obvious, however, that what might once have been regarded with superstition was soon forgotten and the designs became purely decorative. Whereas in the early part of the nineteenth century the sleeves of women's shifts were almost completely covered with embroidery, by the end of the century stitchery was limited to a band at the top of the sleeves and the wrist and neck bands.

In the first half of the nineteenth century, especially in the central and southern regions, linen and cotton threads were used in conjunction with gold and silver and colored silk but, by the end of the century, linen and silk had been replaced by cotton and wool, and aniline dyes had superseded natural dyes.

That the predominant color is red, ranging in shade from mulberry in the north to orange in the south, is not purely fortuitous. The root of the Russian word for "red" is also that of their word for "beautiful" and the corner in a peasant's house where the icon stood was known as the "red corner." The color red was supplemented by dark blue, green and yellow. Only in the provinces of Tambov and Voronezh was black used.

The designs may be divided into two main groups: the one comprising geometrical patterns and the other animals, birds and human figures. This latter group includes the embroideries produced in the towns.

Geometrical Designs

In the central and southern Russian provinces of Smolensk, Orlov, Ryazan, Voronezh and Tambov geometric designs predominated, with combinations of squares and stripes and the swastika, a sign of good omen. A diamond with extended "rusticated" sides is particularly characteristic of the first three regions mentioned above as well as of Vladimir and Tula. The piece illustrated is probably a *shirinka*, a large kerchief which was a customary wedding present from the sixteenth century onward and made either with elaborate gold embroidery for members of the aristocracy, or, in a simpler form, by the peasants for their own fraternity. It was carried in the hand as an essential part of ceremonial dress.

Designs with Animals, Birds or Human Figures

V. V. Stasov (1824–1906), the great Russian ethnographer, was one of the first to make the obvious point that Russian embroidery illustrates ancient legends and long-forgotten beliefs. Especially common is the design with a central female figure facing forward and holding in each hand a bird or the reins of horses. She is probably intended to represent a mother goddess or the spirit of fecundity and can be seen in truncated form in the border of a towel where, in the main design, female figures support what appears to be a stylized eagle with a small bird in its middle.

In the northern regions of Russia, Archangel, Olonets, Vologda and Novgorod, designs which are evidently ancient are preserved with local variations in technique and color. Geometric designs occur rarely and, when they do, are usually implemented in narrow borders.

Embroidery was often worked so that it was reversible. The most characteristic stitches were cross stitch worked by counting threads and stitches worked on a drawn-thread ground, including Russian overcast and drawn filling and a weaving stitch.

Town Embroidery

A special kind of embroidery began to appear in the middle of the nineteenth century when the peasants began to drift to the towns. The embroideress no longer employed only traditional patterns and stitchery but with enthusiasm

and originality drew on her own experience and view of life. Some of the figures which she worked were pictorial representations of well-known types of people: ladies with umbrellas, and on towels and valances soldiers and coachmen appear looking like the illustrations to a fairy tale or the work of a Russian Grandma Moses.

Although many of the designs originated from traditional stylized patterns, the symbols were altered almost beyond recognition. In many examples the tradition of representing animals in profile but people full face was retained, although the subject was treated naturalistically. In some embroideries of this type the counted-thread technique was still used. The illustration here shows a lively hunting scene which, despite its naturalism, retains the traditional central motif, in this case a stylized eagle, with a symmetrical design on either side. The animation of the scene is remarkable: a duck which has just been shot throws its head back before it falls to the ground. The hunter's face is, unusually, in profile.

Another is also naturalistic in style. Curtains fall in deep swags and are swept aside to reveal a curious rustic scene. A strange column has been embroidered in the center, perhaps a reference to a forgotten myth or another obscure symbol for the mother goddess. To the left and right lions stand beside

Kerchief, *or* shirinka *(detail), Russia, twentieth century. Linen ground worked in drawn threadwork with linen thread, 35in × 28in (89cm × 71cm).* EMBROIDERERS' GUILD, LONDON.

ABOVE:
Towel end, *south Russia,
nineteenth century. Linen
ground worked with silk
thread, mainly in red, in*
*needle weaving and counted
threadwork, 13½in × 90in
(34cm × 229cm).* VICTORIA
AND ALBERT MUSEUM,
LONDON.

BELOW:
Valance, *province of St.
Petersburg, Russia,
nineteenth century. Linen
ground worked in drawn
threadwork with linen thread
and a border of bobbin lace,
72in × 33in (183cm ×
84cm).* VICTORIA AND
ALBERT MUSEUM, LONDON.

ABOVE, RIGHT:
Towel end, *Russia, early
nineteenth century. Cotton
ground embroidered with
white cotton thread in chain
stitch and drawn threadwork,
20in × 93in (236cm ×
51cm).* VICTORIA AND
ALBERT MUSEUM, LONDON.

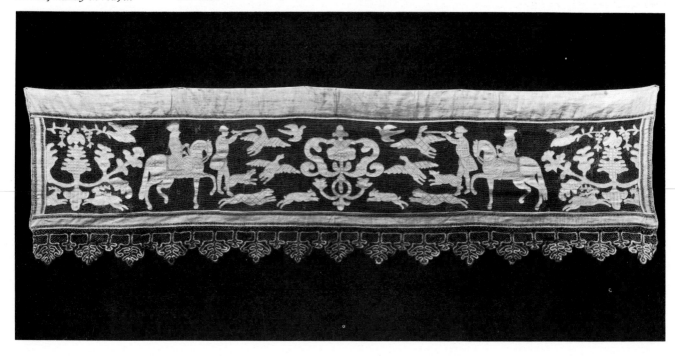

Border for a bed curtain, *Russia, nineteenth century. Linen ground embroidered with silk and linen thread in double running stitch and drawn threadwork.* ROYAL SCOTTISH MUSEUM, EDINBURGH.

beehives. Butterflies fly in the intervening spaces. The comparatively coarse thread embroidered in free stitchery on fine lawn gives the work a bold three-dimensional quality which contrasts dramatically with the fine stitches of the pulled work used for the leaves of the bushes in the foreground.

Two other works illustrated here are interesting because they incorporate formal and naturalistic elements in the same design. Both these pieces are embroidered in the traditional stitches of Russian peasant embroidery. The formalized buildings are said to be the temples of an unknown goddess and in their arcades stand stylized female figures. Other elements of the designs are characteristic of the town embroideries: for example, the coach with the passenger and footman and the "factories" with smoke rising from the chimneys.

By the 1880s interest in traditional Russian culture had been stimulated by the group of artists in Moscow known as the Wanderers and by the World of Art movement in St. Petersburg. In 1880 Sergei Mamontov, a railway tycoon, had set up a workshop on his estate at Abramtsevo to encourage cottage industries. His example was quickly followed by other landowners. The catalogue of the All Russias Exhibition held in St. Petersburg in 1913 lists patrons from every part of the country. Not only did the patrons provide facilities for work but they also helped to design the artefacts, basing their designs on traditional patterns.

The final work illustrated is representative of many such embroideries. They were made so that the piece could be cut up to decorate the *rubashka*, a man's shirt. The broad piece would be stitched

Panel, *Russia, nineteenth
century. Linen ground
embroidered with brown and
red silk thread mainly in
cross stitch, 42in × 16in
(107cm × 41cm).* VICTORIA
AND ALBERT MUSEUM,
LONDON.

Shirt trimmings
*(unfinished), linen ground
embroidered with silk thread
in satin and double running
stitch, twentieth century,
14in × 4in, 14in × 2in,
12in × ¾in (36cm × 10cm,
36cm × 5cm, 31cm × 1·7cm).*
AUTHOR'S COLLECTION.

vertically to the shirt front; the two narrow borders edged the sleeves and the other piece made up the collar. Many of these were doubtless sold in Madame Pogorsky's Russian Peasant Industries shop which was established at 41 Old Bond Street in London in 1911 and continued to operate until 1920.

In Russia at the beginning of the twentieth century it became fashionable in the countryside to wear a pastiche of peasant costume. However, these products can quickly be recognized, for their designs are taken from imported pattern books and although worked in cross stitch, the stitches have been made not by counting threads but over a base of embroidery canvas which was subsequently removed.

Despite two major wars and a revolution, the tradition of embroidery has not died in the Soviet Union. In the cities most women go out to work as well as look after their homes and families and have little time for handwork, but the designs and techniques evident in the cushions and table linen produced today still convey the Russian heritage of embroidery. In the villages where the long winter nights provide ample time for leisure, the tradition lingers on and pieces of embroidery made in the countryside are offered for sale in many shops in the major cities.

Glossary

Stitches

With the naming of stitches, the same name may refer to different stitches in different countries; and, equally, different names may apply to the same stitch. Also, small differences in the manner of working may alter the name of the stitch. Some stitches are generally, and some often, called by their foreign name in English although there may be an English equivalent: for example, *petit point* and *gros point*. The words *point*, *punto* and *ponto* mean stitch.

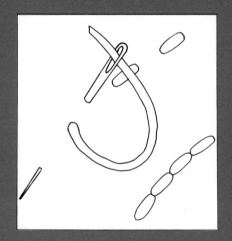

Algerian eye stitch	See eye stitch.
Algiers stitch	See plait stitch.
Back stitch	Used in most countries in the world either as a basic stitch in plain sewing or as a decorative stitch. The stitches may either touch or have a space equivalent to the stitch length between each.
Bargello stitch	See Florentine stitch.
Blanket stitch	A looped edging stitch resembling buttonhole stitch (q.v.) but worked with a space between each stitch.
Block satin stitch	See counted satin stitch.
Braid stitch	See long-armed cross stitch.

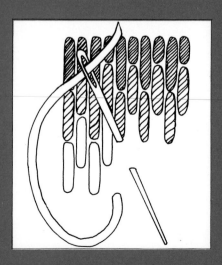

Brick stitch	Can be used as a canvas stitch or can be another name for long and short stitch (q.v.). The principle is that the stitches should be the same length but placed alternately, as in a brick wall.

Bullion stitch	A knot stitch which gives texture to a design.	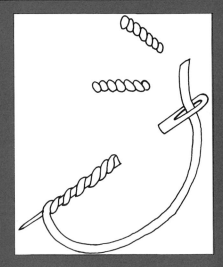
Buttonhole stitch	A looped stitch which when worked closely is frequently used to stabilize raw edges, either as a scalloped edge to a piece of work or as the finish to raw edges in drawn threadwork (q.v.) and some cutwork (q.v.). Detached buttonhole is also used as a filling stitch.	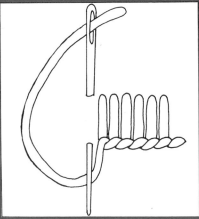
Chain stitch	Used all over the world and worked with the needle, tambour hook (q.v.) or 'ari (India). It is used as an outline stitch or to fill large spaces.	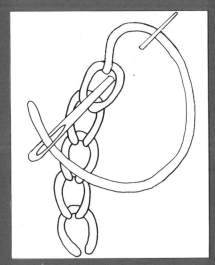
Chevron stitch	Used for wide lines or as a filling stitch. There are several varieties including diagonal, raised and stem-stitch chevron.	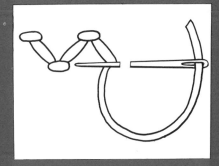

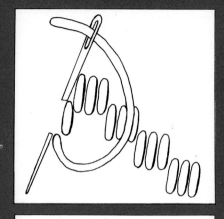

Counted satin stitch (block satin stitch, geometrical satin stitch)

Variation of satin stitch (q.v.) where the stitches are worked by the counted thread and make a regular pattern, either as a border or as a filling.

Cretan feather stitch

Much used in eastern Europe. The angle of the side threads make it suitable for representing feathers, and it is also used on borders.

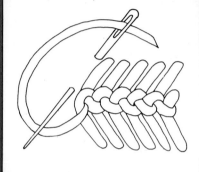

Crewel stitch

See stem stitch.

Cross stitch

A stitch universally used, worked by the counted thread. It consists of two diagonal lines of equal length crossing each other in the middle. Although it can be used as a line stitch it is more usually worked in blocks.

Darning stitch (pattern darning, straight darning).

Darning consists of a thread taken over and under threads of the ground fabric. It may be regular with each row alike, patterned with each row different but forming a regular pattern, or patterned in motifs rather than rows.

Double back stitch	A stitch which shows either two rows of back stitch (q.v.) on the front of the fabric or when reversed, a row of closed herringbone (q.v.) It is used to hold a cord in corded quilting (q.v.); and on fine fabric, when the herringbone shows faintly through the fabric, it is known as shadow work.	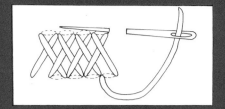

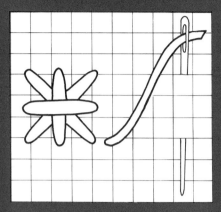

Double cross stitch (Irish stitch, railroad stitch, railway stitch)	Quickly worked canvas stitch popular in the second half of the nineteenth century. It consists of a double cross stitch, one set diagonally with another set straight over the first, giving a raised effect. The two stitches could be worked in different colors.

Double running stitch (holbein stitch)	Very popular in the sixteenth century and frequently used since, especially in peasant embroideries. It is sometimes known as holbein stitch because it is so frequently seen in the embroideries in portraits by the painter of that name.	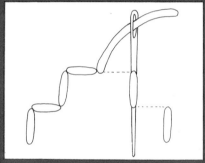

Eye stitch (Algerian eye stitch)	Worked by the counted thread with a series of stitches radiating from a common center leaving a hole or eye in the middle. In Iceland whole pieces of work were embroidered in eye stitch but in most European countries it is used in conjunction with other counted-thread stitches.	

Feather stitch (plumetis)	Wide looped stitch which gives a light feathery look while covering a fair amount of ground. There are many variations, used all over Europe and the United States.	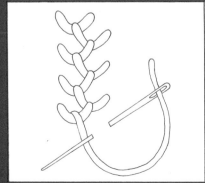

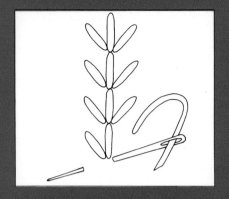

Fern stitch

Sharply angled line stitch which can be used for sprays, light veinings or borders. It is made from three spokes of equal length.

Flame stitch

See Florentine stitch.

Flesh stitch

See long and short stitch.

Florentine stitch (bargello stitch, flame stitch)

See also Hungarian stitch. Used all over Europe and in the United States. It is worked by the counted thread and consists of upright stitches of varying lengths used in a design which rises and falls, giving the effect of flames.

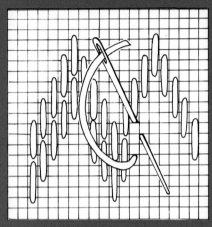

French knots

Stitch consisting of small isolated knots which can be used individually or else tightly grouped giving a solid, textured effect. Found in most countries.

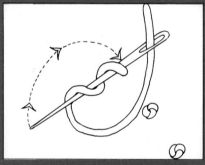

Geometrical satin stitch

See counted satin stitch.

Gobelins stitch

Stitch worked by the counted thread, named after its nineteenth-century use to simulate woven tapestry. In its most usual form it consists of a tall tent stitch (q.v.) worked over two threads up and one to the right, but there are many variations, all self-explanatory, such as upright, staggered, encroaching, straight.

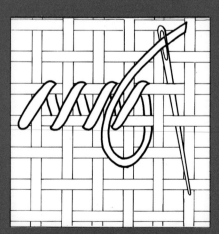

Half cross stitch	See tent stitch.	
Hemstitch	Used to secure a hem or form a decorative line when combined with pulled-fabric work (q.v.).	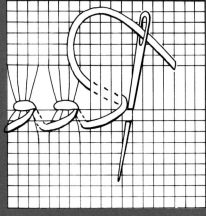
Herringbone stitch	One of the most useful stitches, employed in plain sewing and dressmaking as well as embroidery. It can be worked with each stitch fairly wide apart or with each stitch touching the previous stitch, when it becomes the reverse side of double back stitch (q.v.).	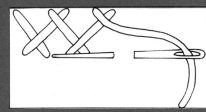
Holbein stitch	See double running stitch.	
Hungarian stitch *(point d'Hongrie)*	Canvas grounding stitch consisting of a short upright stitch covering two threads followed by one covering four threads and one covering two threads and then a space of one thread. Each block is followed by a space into which the block of the next row fits. See also Florentine stitch.	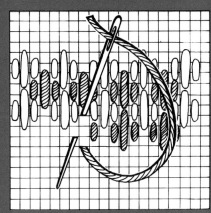
Italian cross stitch (two-sided Italian cross stitch)	Variation of cross stitch (q.v.) which consists of a diagonal cross surrounded by a square. Besides being a dense and strong stitch, it is the same on both sides of the fabric.	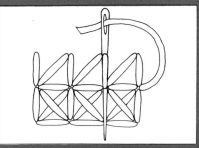
Ladder stitch	Used for bands and borders especially in central Europe.	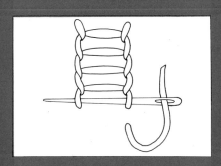

Long stitch

A form of counted satin stitch (q.v.) where the blocks, of whatever size and shape, are meshed in together making a solid, patterned ground.

Long and short stitch (flesh stitch, shading stitch)

Stitch with a number of names, used universally to produce a smooth, dense surface which may have innumerable shades of color. It is, therefore, used particularly for figure embroidery, drapery and for the shading of flowers. See also brick stitch.

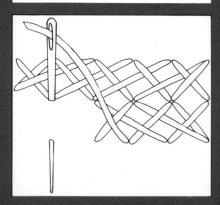

Long-armed cross stitch (braid stitch, long-legged cross stitch, old Icelandic cross stitch)

Variation of cross stitch (q.v.) which is very strong and hard wearing. It is worked in horizontal rows, sometimes with each row starting from the same end; sometimes from alternate ends. It resembles plait stitch (q.v.).

Long-legged cross stitch

See long-armed cross stitch.

Old Icelandic cross stitch

See long-armed cross stitch

Outline stitch

Resembles stem stitch (q.v.) except that the thread is taken to the left of the needle instead of to the right, resulting in a finer line.

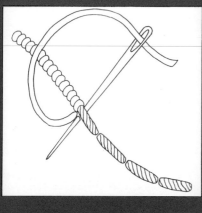

Overcast stitch

1. Embroidery stitch where a thread is laid or run and a series of small tight stitches are worked over it.

2. Plain sewing stitch used particularly in patchwork (q.v.) where the edges are sewn together with a small stitch joining them.

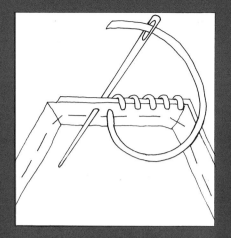

3. Also an edging stitch.

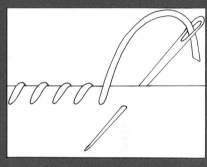

Pattern darning   See darning stitch.

Petit point   See tent stitch.

Plait stitch (Algiers stitch, Spanish stitch)   Form of cross stitch (q.v.) resembling long-armed cross stitch (q.v.) but with the initial stitch covering fewer threads. The stitch is very strong and may also be used for edging rugs.

Plumetis   See feather stitch.

Plush stitch   Counted-thread stitch making a series of detached loops which may or need not be cut according to the type of embroidery and the design. Each loop is held by a cross stitch (q.v.). Used in the seventeenth and nineteenth centuries for sculptured effects in embroidery, it is also used for pile rugs.

Point d'Hongrie   See Hungarian stitch.

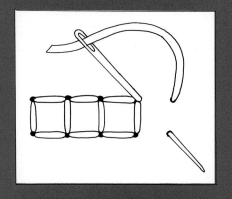

Punch stitch

Drawn-fabric stitch which can be used as a line stitch for seams, applied lace and other decoration, or can be used to cover the ground. In the latter case it is worked slightly differently and becomes single faggot stitch (q.v.).

Railroad stitch

See double cross stitch.

Railway stitch

See double cross stitch.

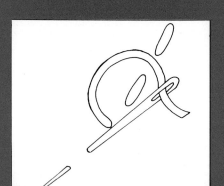

Running stitch

The simplest of all stitches, formed by the needle passing in and out of the fabric at equal intervals.

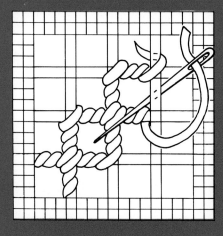

Russian overcast and drawn filling

Drawn-thread stitch where two threads are drawn and two are left both vertically and horizontally. The remaining threads are overcast in an upward step direction which is Russian overcast filling, and when the square holes are subsequently worked with a light filling, this becomes Russian drawn filling.

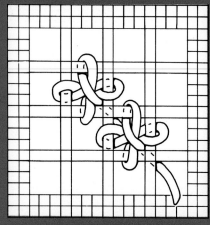

Satin stitch	Universal stitch which gives a smooth, even texture. It can be worked to fill an uneven shape such as a petal or a leaf, or it can be worked in regular blocks when it becomes counted, block or geometrical satin stitch (q.v.).	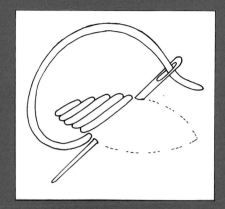
Shading stitch	See long and short stitch.	
Single faggot stitch	Filling stitch made from the four lines of a square. It closely resembles punch stitch (q.v.).	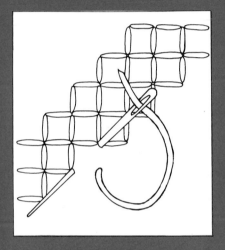
Spanish stitch	See plait stitch.	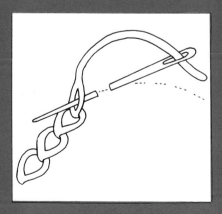
Split stitch	Used universally where a fine, delicately controlled line is required. In *opus anglicanum* (q.v.) split stitch was used for faces (often worked in a spiral), hands and fine detail.	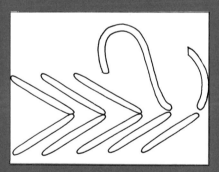

Stem stitch (crewel stitch)

Line stitch universally used, especially in crewelwork (q.v.), and many kinds of flower embroidery. It is worked the same way as outline stitch (q.v.), except that the thread always lies to the right of the needle.

Straight darning

See darning stitch.

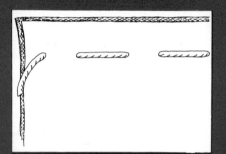

Tacking

The temporary joining of two or more pieces of fabric with a long stitch.

Tent stitch (half cross stitch, *petit point*)

Stitch which under these and several other local names has been one of the most generally used canvas stitches for several centuries. The names may vary according to the country using the stitch, and may also refer to minute differences in the manner of working, but the effect is always the same: a flat, hardwearing surface with stitches small enough to permit detailed variations in color and drawing.

Underside couching

Medieval method of couching gold thread. The gold thread is pulled through to the back of the work where it is secured by the couching thread.

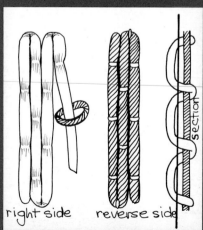

Techniques

The names of identical techniques may vary in different countries, and generic terms are often used in place of specific ones and vice versa. Sometimes it is difficult to tell if it is the stitch or the type of work which is referred to as the two are often interchangeable. With the terms couching, Florentine and *petit point* for example, the word may apply to either the work or the stitch of the same name.

Amagersyning

Embroidery from the Danish island of Amager, Denmark, using silk threads on silk (q.v.). In the eighteenth century it was used in particular for large kerchiefs or scarves.

American crewelwork

Basically the same as crewelwork (q.v.) but worked with a lighter and freer design. Thread was scarce in North America in the eighteenth century and so the designs were not as dense as those worked in England. Stitches were chosen where most of the thread was evident on the surface of the fabric.

Applied work (appliqué work)

Embroidery in which one fabric is superimposed on another, and fastened invisibly or with decorative stitches. The technique has been used from earliest times in most countries of the world and is still popular. Applied work was frequently used on heraldic banners and surcoats; combined with patchwork (q.v.) and used for coverlets (q.v.); and in present-day collage, fabrics and materials of every kind, particularly net (q.v.), are applied to make a decorative panel or picture.

Appliqué work

See applied work.

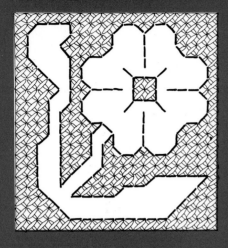

Assisi work

Nineteenth- and twentieth-century embroidery derived from early designs worked in a technique where the design is left in reserve on the linen (q.v.) while the background is filled with plain or long-armed cross stitch (q.v.). The ground is often worked with a blue thread.

Ayrshire embroidery

Type of whitework (q.v.) which contained both surface stitching and needle-lace filling stitches on muslin (q.v.). It was practiced particularly in southwest Scotland and Northern Ireland in the early and mid-nineteenth century.

Beadwork

The application of beads to fabric. The seventeenth and nineteenth centuries were two periods when the use of beads in embroidery was particularly favored, either to highlight a motif or to make a complete design.

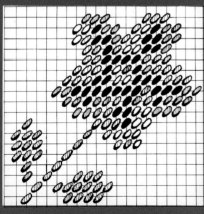

Berlin woolwork

Embroidery which was very popular from c.1810 to the 1880s, reaching its peak in 1840–50 in Europe and the United States. It consisted of working designs in colored wools on canvas using a chart which was ruled in squares with each square representing a stitch. Both the charts and the wools were originally produced in Germany. The designs varied throughout the century with flowers, animals and the reproduction of famous paintings and biblical scenes being especially popular.

Blackwork	Embroidery in black thread which was particularly favored in the sixteenth century. It was used on articles of clothing and household linen, and consisted of outline and filling stitches in geometric patterns and designs of coiling tendrils with leaves, fruit and flowers worked in a black thread on linen (q.v.) Occasionally a metal thread was added.

Bordado a Escomilha	See Crape work.
Braidwork	The use of braids to form decorative patterns either by themselves or in addition to embroidery. In nineteenth-century Europe and America braids were used on many articles of clothing.

Broderie anglaise (eyelet work)	Type of cutwork (q.v.) popular in the nineteenth century in most countries of Europe and in the United States. A formal pattern of round or oval holes was worked with white thread on a white cotton (q.v.) ground. The holes were overcast and any added decoration was worked in padded satin stitch (q.v.). Used on underclothes, children's clothes and blouses.

Broderie perse	Type of applied work (q.v.) of the eighteenth and early nineteenth centuries in which shapes of, for example, birds, animals and figures were cut from plain and printed cottons (q.v.) and applied to a plain ground. There was no attempt at scale, and seldom any relationship between the motifs.

Burato embroidery

Darning on a heavy linen (q.v.)
cloth with an open gauze weave.
The embroidery resembles darned
net (q.v.) but the ground is
woven not netted.

Canvas work

Generic term for all types of embroidery worked on canvas (q.v.) by
the counted thread. It includes
Berlin woolwork (q.v.), Florentine
work (q.v.), and tent stitch (q.v.).
In America canvas work is
wrongly known as needlepoint,
and in England it is sometimes
wrongly called tapestry work.

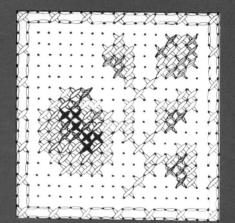

Cardwork

Simple form of embroidery current in Britain and America in the
mid-nineteenth century. It consisted of working texts or messages
in colored silks or wools on card
which had been prepared with
holes cut in regular lines.

Corded quilting

Type of quilting (q.v.) in which a
cord is used to define the design.
The cord, at the back of the work,
is sewn on with a closed herringbone stitch (q.v.) which produces
a row of back stitches (q.v.) on
either side of the cord on the surface. In the Netherlands this
method is known as Zaanland
stitchery.

Cordwork

Various types of needlework
involving the use of cords. This
may be using colored cords made
of various yarns to edge applied
work (q.v.), or couching (q.v.)
them in pattern, or twisting fine
cord round bodkins to make flat
rosettes which can then be joined
in pattern.

Counted threadwork	Any type of embroidery which is worked on a fabric where the threads can be counted and where the design depends on the regularity of these threads. The main types are linen embroidery and canvas work (q.v.).
Couching	A technique which consists of one or more threads being tied down by another thread. It is a technique particularly suited to metal and other intractable threads which need not be taken through the ground fabric. It can be used as an outline or as a filling stitch.

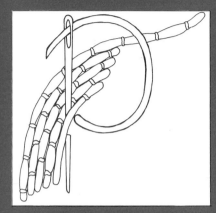

Crape work	Portuguese embroidery of the fifteenth and sixteenth centuries. Black crape, which is woven from very tightly spun yarn, was unravelled and the thread used for stitching fine designs on white satin. This technique, called *Bordado a Escomilha* (q.v.), resembled the printwork (q.v.) of the early nineteenth century.
Crazy patchwork	See patchwork.
Crewelwork	Embroidery where crewel wool (q.v.) is used, especially referring to the free embroidery on bedhangings and curtains of the seventeenth and eighteenth centuries. A favorite stitch in this work was stem stitch (q.v.), sometimes known as crewel stitch.

Crivos embroidery	Type of embroidery practiced in Portugal, particularly in the Guimaraẽs district in the north. It is whitework (q.v.) which has a raised effect obtained by the use of bullion stitch (q.v.), in particular, and it is often combined with drawn work (q.v.) which softens the rather hard effect of the raised stitches.

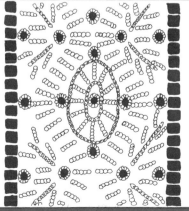

Cutwork	Technique where part of the fabric is cut away and the space left is crossed by threads which are strengthened by buttonholing. Later the term was widened to include any embroidery which involved holes being made in the fabric as part of the design. See also *broderie anglaise*.

Darned net (*filet, lacis*, network)	Type of work which has been done all over Europe from the Middle Ages to the present day. On a hand-made, square-meshed netting some of the squares are closely filled with darning, this forming the pattern. Since the nineteenth century machine-made net (q.v.) has also been used.

Découpé (reverse appliqué)	Applied work (q.v.) in reverse, the top layer of fabric being cut away in a pattern to show a contrasting fabric underneath.
Drawn-fabric work	See pulled-fabric work.
Drawn work (drawn threadwork)	Type of embroidery where certain threads are removed from the fabric and the spaces left are filled with stitchery. This definition applies to many named types of work in different countries such as Hardanger embroidery (q.v.), various forms of hemstitching (q.v.) and needle weaving (q.v.).

Dresden work (*point de Saxe*)	Form of pulled-fabric embroidery (q.v.) developed in Dresden in the eighteenth century and copied in many European countries. It gave the light, lacy look to muslin (q.v.) accessories such as ruffles, aprons and kerchiefs that was so much in fashion, and was in fact a cheaper version of the very expensive bobbin laces.

Etching embroidery	See printwork.
Eyelet work	See *broderie anglaise*.
Façon d'Angleterre	Ecclesiastical embroidery of the fifteenth century made in England. It continued the tradition of the earlier *opus anglicanum* (q.v.) but was heavier, coarser and more mechanical in its interpretation.
Filet	See darned net.
Filigree work	Embroidery which because of its fineness, overall patterning and light lacy look, resembles the filigree work seen in metalwork and jewelry.
Fishskin appliqué	Technique employed by the Aleutian Eskimos to decorate the seams of their sealskin parkas. Bands of seal gullet are applied with moosehair embroidery.
Flanders style embroidery	Late medieval embroidery in England which attempted to copy in needlework two Flemish techniques: tapestry weaving and the new-style easel painting.
Glit embroidery	Medieval embroidery in Iceland worked with wool on linen. The stitch used was darning (q.v.) and it could be worked either straight or in pattern.

Gold embroidery	Frequently used for ecclesiastical embroidery and also for sumptuous secular work. Thread made of gold or gilt metal wound round silk was used in a variety of techniques including *or nué* (q.v.) and underside couching (q.v.) in conjunction with polychrome silk threads. Although gold embroidery was at its height in the Middle Ages and Renaissance, it has never died out and is being much used today. Other metals such as silver, copper and aluminium are also used.

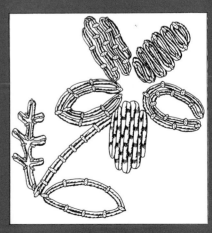

Hardanger embroidery

Drawn threadwork (q.v.) and counted threadwork (q.v.) from Norway. It is worked on an open-weave double-thread linen (q.v.) with a thick cotton (q.v.) or linen thread, and the designs include areas of drawn-thread squares surrounded by blocks of satin stitch (q.v.). The technique is decorative and hard wearing and is used for many household articles.

Hedebosyning

Embroidery from Heden in Denmark characterized by surface stitching combined with drawn work (q.v.) in white cotton (q.v.) on homespun linen (q.v.).

Incised embroidery

Form of patchwork (q.v.) involving counterchange, where light and dark in ground and pattern exchange rôles in different sections or panels.

Intarsia work

Embroidery design which resembles the elaborate inlaid wood-work of the Italian Renaissance. In Finland the work was carried out in inlay appliqué, either of wool (q.v.) or leather.

Kells embroidery

Irish embroidery of the last half of the nineteenth century in which designs were based on the illustrations in the Book of Kells and other Celtic manuscripts. It was a form of Art Needlework (q.v.) and was sponsored by the Donegal Industrial Fund.

Lacis

See darned net.

Laidwork	Type of embroidery usually worked in silk where threads are laid down on the ground fabric and tied in pattern with other threads. Although it has been used in most countries at different periods, it is especially popular in Spain and Portugal.

Log cabin patchwork	See patchwork
Madeira work	Development of *broderie anglaise* (q.v.) with more surface embroidery. The technique was taken by nuns to Madeira and became so popular for household articles, that the style became known by the name of the island.

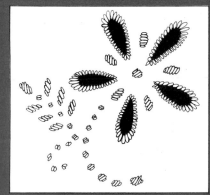

Metal embroidery	See gold embroidery
Moravian embroidery	1. Embroidery from Moravia in Czechoslovakia which was a type of Slav peasant embroidery using geometrical satin stitch (q.v.) as well as chain and stem stitches (q.q.v.). 2. Needlework done and taught by Moravian sisters who settled in Bethlehem (Pennsylvania) in the 1740s.
Mountmellick work	Devised in Ireland in the 1840s to help relieve the impoverishment due to the famines. It consisted of work on white satin jean (q.v.) using a thick white cotton (q.v.) thread in a variety of stitches and textures.

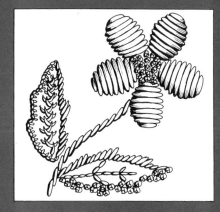

Needle painting	Technique of making embroidery stitches appear as much like painting as possible. This has been in and out of fashion in most countries from at least the fourteenth century, although it is currently out of favor.

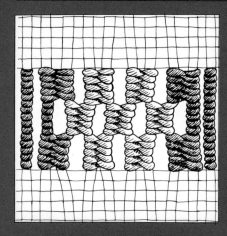

Needlepoint	Generic term for needle-made laces, sometimes mistakenly used for canvas work (q.v.).
Needle weaving	Form of drawn work (q.v.), especially popular in Scandinavia and eastern Europe, in which colored threads are woven or darned in pattern to take the place of those withdrawn.
Network	See darned net.
Openwork	Term referring to any embroidery where the ground fabric has threads removed or pulled apart, thus giving an open effect. It includes darned net (q.v.) pulled-fabric work (q.v.), drawn work (q.v.), Dresden work (q.v.) and *broderie anglaise* (q.v.).
Opus anglicanum	English ecclesiastical embroidery famous from the tenth to the fifteenth centuries with specific characteristics. These include the excellent and dramatic drawing of the figures, the use of underside couching (q.v.) and the modeling of the faces in split stitch (q.v.) with the cheeks worked in a spiral.
Opus teutonicum	Term used for German needle-work of the Middle Ages.
Or nué (shaded gold)	Technique of the Middle Ages using gold thread couched (q.v.) down with colored silks (q.v.) either close or far apart, making a shaded pattern on the gold. It was seen at its best on Flemish embroideries in the fifteenth century.
Padding	See raised work.
Patchwork	Term which includes various techniques and is broadly divided into onlay and inlay. Onlay includes all applied patchwork where pieces of fabric are applied in pattern to a ground fabric. See applied work and *broderie perse*. Inlay consists of pieces of fabric cut out and so shaped that they will fit together and can be sewn

without a backing. This is also known as mosaic or pieced patchwork. The box pattern in this group is made up of three diamonds of differing tonal values joined into a hexagon. These hexagons, when joined, resemble boxes or steps. Two other types must also be included although they do not fit into either inlay or onlay: crazy, where shapes of any kind are laid one over the other and sewn down with hemstitch. This type generally has the seams decorated with feather stitching (q.v.); and log cabin, where narrow strips are joined in extending squares which are then sewn together in various combinations to make the whole.

Pattern darning

See darning stitch.

Pearl embroidery

Embroidery using the freshwater pearls found in abundance in the rivers of Russia and eastern Europe. Many embroideries from these and other European countries, made for both the nobility and the Church, were heavily decorated with pearls in the Middle Ages and later.

Pile needlework

Though it can be worked on canvas of any size, the term is usually applied to rugs stitched or knotted on canvas (q.v.), with a pile.

Plush technique (sheared-pile technique)

Embroidery using plush stitch (q.v.) to make a raised pile. The stitches are worked closely together on canvas, the loops are cut, and the resulting pile is cut into any shape. It was a popular embroidery in the nineteenth century and was used for example, for the bodies of birds.

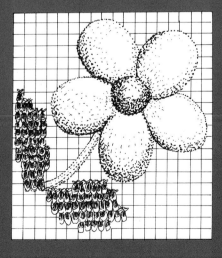

Printwork (etching embroidery)

Fine stitchery worked in a black thread or sometimes hair, which copied prints. It was a popular form of needlework in the late eighteenth and early nineteenth centuries and was revived in the late nineteenth century as etching embroidery.

Pulled-fabric work (drawn-fabric work)

Embroidery on fine cotton or linen (q.q.v.) where the stitches are pulled tight and the design is shown as much by the holes and the spaces as by the threads. In some cases, such as Dresden work (q.v.), it simulated the expensive laces of the eighteenth century.

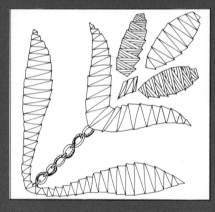

Quillwork

Embroidery worked by the Canadian and American Indians using porcupine or bird quills on birch bark or hides. The quills which were dampened and softened were held in place by hidden stitches using sinew as thread. In Austria the term refers to the decoration of materials with bird quills and feathers in the nineteenth century.

Quilting

One of the earliest and most universal embroidery techniques, consisting of stitching two or three thicknesses of fabric together in pattern. See also corded quilting.

Raised work

Any kind of embroidery which is given a three-dimensional effect by means of padding. This padding at different times and with different techniques has consisted of wooden molds, cotton, wool (q.q.v.), string, paper, card or felt. See also stumpwork.

Raised woolwork	See plush technique and plush stitch.

Relief embroidery	See raised work.
Renaissance embroidery	Nineteenth-century form of white-work (q.v.) loosely based on six-teenth-century lace designs. The pattern is cut out of the ground fabric and the raw edges are covered with buttonhole stitch (q.v.). The bars which join and strengthen parts of the pattern are also covered with button-holing.

Reticella	An early type of needlepoint lace or cutwork (q.v.). It could be worked by withdrawing threads from the fabric and using those remaining as a basis on which to work patterns in buttonhole stitch (q.v.), or by working the stitch on threads laid as a foundation.

Reverse appliqué	See découpé.
Richelieu embroidery	Similar to renaissance embroidery (q.v.) with the addition of picots (q.v.) which decorate the joining bars.

Rosesaum

Peasant embroidery from Norway consisting of swirling rows of satin stitch (q.v.) worked in bright wool (q.v.) which form roses and other flowers. This type of work is used to decorate household articles and clothes.

Sheared-pile technique

See plush technique.

Silver embroidery

See gold embroidery.

Smocking

The control of fullness by means of gathers. In England equal gathers are drawn up and held by rows of ornamental stitching; in America the gathers are drawn and ornamented in one process, while in Portugal and in parts of Italy rows of running stitches (q.v.) are taken along the fabric in pattern and are then drawn up and fastened so that the pattern is in the gathering rather than in the ornamental stitch.

Soft sculpture

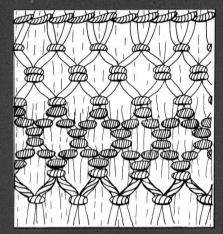

Modern type of needlework particularly current in the United States. Three-dimensional objects and forms are made, both realistic and bizarre in design, and many different materials are used. It is a type of Pop Art.

Strapwork

Embroidery of the sixteenth and seventeenth centuries which followed the fashion for the same type of design in woodwork, plasterwork and metalwork. It consisted of interlacing bands and was carried out in applied work (q.v.), patchwork (q.v.) and other techniques.

Straw embroidery

Embroidery using straw (plaited or plain) as a thread. It could be couched (q.v.) down or sewn on to a loosely woven fabric.

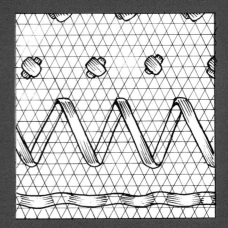

Stumpwork

A form of raised work (q.v.) (which it is more properly called), popular in the middle of the seventeenth century in England. Most of it is representational, Old Testament stories being very popular and parts of the design, generally hands, faces and some architectural details, are heavily padded, giving a three-dimensional effect.

Tambouring

Embroidery worked with a tambour hook (q.v.) which forms a chain stitch (q.v.) on fine fabric very quickly. It was a fast method of decorating the muslin (q.v.) of the late eighteenth and early nineteenth centuries before machine embroidery was invented. In America the same technique using a larger hook and coarser materials was used for making rugs.

Tapestry work

See canvas work.

Tulle drawnwork

Form of pulled-fabric work (q.v.) on tulle (q.v.) practiced in Denmark and elsewhere. It simulates French bobbin net laces.

Turkey work

Form of carpet knotting of the sixteenth and seventeenth centuries, in the technique of Oriental carpets. It was used particularly for hassocks and chair and cushion covers. It was also used for table carpets.

Whitework

Generic term for all types of embroidery worked in white on white. These can include pulled-fabric work (q.v.), drawn work (q.v.), pattern darning (q.v.), cutwork (q.v.).

Zaanland stitchery

See corded quilting.

Miscellaneous

Acanthus

A conventional representation of the elegant leaf of the plant *Acanthus spinosus* seen frequently on Corinthian capitals and also used in many of the decorative arts.

Agnus Dei

The Lamb of God. A symbol for Christ showing a lamb adorned with a halo and carrying a staff with a pennant. It refers to the saying of John the Baptist, "Behold the Lamb of God."

Alb

Vestment of white linen or cotton (q.q.v.) worn by priest, deacon and sub-deacons when celebrating Holy Communion in Christian churches. It is full length, has long sleeves and is sometimes decorated with apparels (q.v.) at cuffs and hem.

Album quilt

Patchwork (q.v.) quilt made and signed by different people, given as a tribute to some member of the community. Although the idea is occasionally used in other countries, it is chiefly American.

Altar cloth (fair linen cloth)

Length of white linen (q.v.) which exactly covers the altar and almost touches the ground at the sides. Often the ends are embroidered in white thread and there may be five crosses worked on the top — one in each corner of the altar and one in the middle.

Altar frontal (*antependium*)

Richly decorated fabric which hangs in front of the altar. As the altar is the focal point for the main services of the Christian Church, all the resources of skill, money and materials have always been lavished on its decoration and from very early times the frontal has been associated with superb embroidery.

Altar frontlet (super frontal)	Piece of fabric, the length of the altar, approximately six inches (15cm) deep which hangs over the top of the frontal, and is generally embroidered to match. Alternatively it may be made of lace.	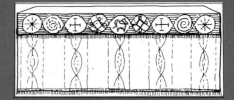

Antependium See altar frontal.

Apparel Decorative rectangular panel applied to a vestment.

Arabesque style	Embroidery of the sixteenth century using patterns of scrolls and curving lines derived from Islamic art. The style penetrated into most European countries and was widely used in fashionable embroideries.	

Art Deco	Style of ornament of the 1920s and 1930s characterized in embroidery by a highly stylized and often angular rendering of the human figure, flowers etc., and by the use of unnatural colors.	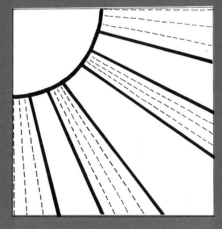

Art Needlework Embroidery which was produced in the late nineteenth century in revolt against the tastelessness of some of the prevailing styles. It stressed line and color and the involvement of the worker in interpreting the design.

Art Nouveau	Art movement in Europe and America particularly between 1890 and 1910. It was a reaction against nineteenth-century fussiness in design. In embroidery it was exemplified by a move away from canvas work (q.v.) and a strong emphasis on line.	

Aumonière See Saracen purse

Banner	Standard or ensign used by armies and the Church, and today used by many societies and movements. The Pulaski Banner was carried by the dragoon legion of Count Pulaski (1745–79) in the American War of Independence. It was of red silk embroidered by the Moravian nuns of Bethlehem (Pennsylvania).

Baroque	Type of design prevalent in Europe between c.1630 and 1710. It was florid and extravagant in style and was expressed in embroidery as well as in every other art form.
Basket weave	See extended tabby.
Bed rug	Form of bed covering made chiefly in New England, America, during the eighteenth and early nineteenth centuries. They were generally worked in wool on a wool or linen (q.q.v.) foundation, using a stitch consisting of a series of running loops.
Bed tent	Bed curtains used in houses on the Greek Islands. These were tapered strips of embroidered linen (q.v.) which were fastened on to a wooden ring at the top.
Bed valance	See valance.
Bell chasuble	See chasuble.
Bell pull	Long, narrow strip of fabric, often embroidered, terminating in a decorative handle or tassel. It rang a bell summoning servants.

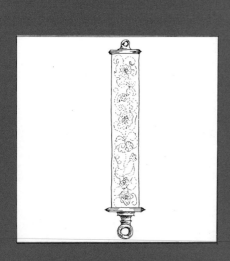

Bibila lace (*bebilla*)	Form of needlepoint lace (q.v.) made in Armenia, Cyprus, Palestine and eastern Mediterranean countries. It consists of small motifs, mainly flowers and leaves, worked with a needle using a particular knot, not unlike a fisherman's knot. It can be stiffened with wire and worked with thick or thin thread in bright colors or plain white.

Bible cover	Loose embroidered cover made to protect a Bible.
Biedermeier	An artistic style that existed in Germany, Austria and Scandinavia between about 1814 and 1848. It was essentially bourgeois, comfortable, realistic and pleasant.
Book cushion	Used to support a prayer book, or Bible on the altar, pulpit or prayer desk in a church. While it may be made of a plain fabric it is often decorated with embroidery, especially when used on festal occasions.
Book of Hours	Devotional book used by men and women particularly in the Middle Ages. Some commissioned by royalty and the nobility were exquisitely illuminated and others had beautifully embroidered covers and bindings.
Brocade	Type of patterned textile, often with gold and silver thread.
Bullion	Bullion is a special kind of tightly coiled metal thread. Bullion embroidery is the generic term for embroidery worked entirely with metal threads.
Bureau scarves	American term for dressing-table runners.

Burlap	American term for sacking or hessian.
Burse (corporal case)	Square pocket in which the corporal is kept when not in use during the service of Holy Communion. It is usually about nine inches (23cm) square, stiffened with cardboard, and it matches, in color and embroidery, the altar set in use.

Byzantine	To do with Byzantium or Constantinople but generally indicating art and architecture practiced in the Eastern Empire from the sixth to the fifteenth centuries.
Camblet (camlet)	Fabric which has changed its component yarns (q.v.) many times over the centuries, goat hair, silk, wool (q.q.v.) and other fibers having all been used at different periods. Watered camlet has been put through rollers to produce the watered pattern.
Cambric	Originally a fine linen fabric made at Cambrai in Flanders, but now it may be of fine linen or cotton (q.q.v.) or a mixture of both.
Camlet	See camblet.
Candlewick	Soft cotton (q.v.) thread traditionally used for the wicks of candles, also used for embroidery, both as a thread to be couched (q.v.), and, when made in several plies, worked in tufts for counterpanes and other domestic articles.
Canvas	Fabric originally made from hemp, but which is now also made of cotton, flax, hemp, jute or wool (q.q.v.). In embroidery today the word refers to an open-weave fabric which is used as the foundation for most work done by the counted thread.
Caparison	Decorative horse cloth, saddle and harness, often embroidered.
Carded wool	Wool (q.v.) prepared preparatory to spinning. The cards are flat pieces of wood with handles and are studded with nails: the wool is worked between the two cards to remove tangles and straighten the fibers.
Cartoon	Preliminary study or drawing on which a work of art will be based. The finished work may be tapestry, embroidery, fresco etc.
Cartouche	Ornamental frame enclosing an element in a larger composition. Any ornament in the form of a scroll.
Casement curtains	Inner curtains which hang from the top of the window frame and only reach to the sill. They are usually made of a very light fabric.

Chalice veil	Covering for the chalice when it is used at the service of Holy Communion. The veil is made of a supple fabric and may be embroidered to match the burse (q.v.).	
Chasuble	Vestment generally worn by the officiating priest in the Western Church. It derives from the Roman *paenula* and originally was a circular garment with a hole for the head. As it became heavily embroidered and bejeweled, and thus stiffer, it impeded the movement of the arms and so the sides were gradually cut away. The earlier, fuller forms are known as bell chasubles (q.v.); later forms in which the stoles were cut away to the shoulders are known as fiddle-back chasubles.	
Chenille	Round thread with a pile made of silk or wool (q.q.v.). Pulling it through the ground fabric damages the pile and so it is generally couched (q.v.) or worked in long satin stitches (q.v.).	
Chevron	The shape made when two beams meet at an angle in a roof. In embroidery the word is used to describe a stitch or a pattern in that shape.	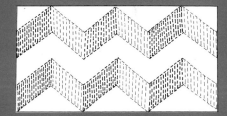
Chinoiserie	Foreigners' exercise in the Chinese style or manner. The fashion for all things Eastern reached Europe in the middle of the seventeenth century and continued through the eighteenth, but the designs in Europe bore little resemblance to the original Chinese.	
Chintz	Originally the name for painted or stained cloths imported from India. Now the word refers to cotton (q.v.) cloth printed with designs of flowers. It is generally glazed.	
Coffin cloth	See pall.	

Coif

Close-fitting head covering generally made of linen (q.v.). They were worn in the Middle Ages by both men and women in many countries, and continued for men as part of the dress of lawyers until the middle of the nineteenth century. Women's coifs were often beautifully embroidered, especially in the sixteenth and seventeenth centuries.

Colchas

Bedspreads, especially those worked in Portugal, Spain and New Mexico. In Portugal they were usually embroidered in brilliant colors in silk laidwork (q.v.), while in New Mexico a special couching stitch (q.v.) called *colchas* stitch was used which gave the impression of laidwork (q.v.).

Cope

Cloak worn by ecclesiastics which derived from the ordinary protective outer garment of the Romans. It is semi-circular and still often has a vestigial hood, or a shaped piece of stiffened fabric, often heavily ornamented. The straight bands in front, generally embroidered, are the orphreys (q.v.) and the cope is fastened across the chest.

Coronation robes

Special dress worn by royalty at their coronation. It is usually traditional in style and sumptuous in fabric and decoration.

Cotton

The generic name for a wide range of fabrics and sewing threads made from the fiber of the cotton plant. The main areas of cultivation are India, Egypt, and Georgia in the United States. The quality of yarn (q.v.) varies but it can be woven as fine as muslin (q.v.) or as heavy as sail canvas.

Counter-Reformation

Religious offensive mounted by the Roman Catholic Church in the sixteenth century to counter the Protestant Reformation which had obtained a strong hold in northern Europe.

Coverlet (counterpane)	Bed covering which in many countries has been one of the most decorative features of a bedroom. They are often skillfully embroidered.
Counterpane	See coverlet.
Crewel wool	Lightly twisted, worsted yarn (q.v.) used by embroiderers. It is strong and can be used with one, two or three strands: it is suited to all types of work on canvas, linen (q.q.v.) and many other fabrics.
Cross orphrey	See orphrey.
Cushion cover	Embroidered cover for cushions of every type used for chairs, kneelers, books, benches and carriages. The cushion cover lends itself to nearly every type of embroidery.
Cyprus gold	Fine quality gold thread imported from Cyprus in the Middle Ages. It was considered to be the best and purest metal thread and there was a prohibition against its being mixed with *laten de Spayne* (alloy from Spain).
Dalmatic	Vestment worn by a deacon assisting the priest at the Eucharist and other solemn services; by a bishop under his chasuble (q.v.); and by a monarch at his coronation. It is a straight tunic with wide sleeves which do not quite reach the wrist.

Damask	Reversible fabric, originally of silk, woven with an ornamental and generally self-colored design.
Diaper pattern	Small geometric pattern often forming diagonal lines. The pattern is frequently used in simple weaving and also in gold couching (q.v.) and as a decorative filling.

Dimity	Cotton (q.v.) fabric, generally with a raised line in the weave. It is hardwearing and light and was used for bedhangings in the eighteenth century as well as for curtains, petticoats and light dresses.
Domett	Type of flannel woven of wool and cotton (q.q.v.) and used as an interlining or a backing in various forms of embroidery.
Dossal	Curtain or cloth which is hung behind the altar of a church.
Doublet	Close fitting jacket of the fifteenth to seventeenth centuries worn by both men and women.
Drizzling (*parfilage*)	Polite amusement of the eighteenth century which consisted of un-picking metal threads and laces and selling the gold and silver. Though, as in the case of the French emigrés, it could be for financial necessity, generally speaking it was a strange pastime of the aristocracy in both Britain and France.
Embroiderers' Guild	British society with many local and overseas branches which exists to further the knowledge of all types of needlework. It has an extensive library and portfolios of techniques which are available to members; and in addition it runs many classes and study courses and publishes the journal *Embroidery*.
Evenweave	American term for fabric woven with warp and weft (q.q.v.) of the same thickness and all threads equidistant.
Extended tabby (basket weave)	The weave generally known as basket weave, that is, simple tabby (q.v.) weave extended over two or more threads.
Fichu	Light muslin (q.v.) costume accessory worn round the neck and shoulders in the eighteenth and nineteenth centuries, often beautifully embroidered.

Fire screen	A movable screen either for protecting the face from the heat of the fire or for standing in the fireplace during the summer.
Flax	See linen.
Flowerers	Women and girls who embroidered muslin (q.v.) in Scotland and Ireland in the late eighteenth and early nineteenth centuries. The work included tambour work (q.v.) as well as pulled-fabric techniques (q.v.).
Gathering	One method of controlling the fullness of fabric. Even running stitches (q.v.) are made and the fabric pulled up to the required length.
Gauntlet	That part of a glove which flares out from the wrist. Originally it was the whole glove as worn with medieval armor, but later the word referred only to the piece extending from wrist to forearm which was often embroidered.
Gin	A machine for separating the downy fibers of the cotton plant (q.v.) from the hard seeds. In 1793 the American, Eli Whitney, invented a toothed cotton gin which speeded up the process.
Girdle	Belt worn round the waist to hold garments in place. They could be made of any material, plain or decorated, and were worn by either sex.
Greek fret pattern	Pattern from ancient Greece re-introduced into all kinds of ornament in the neoclassical or American Federal period, approximately 1780–1820.

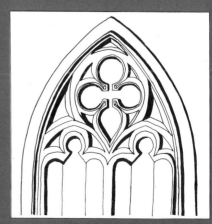

Gothic	The style of architecture common to western Europe from the twelfth to the sixteenth centuries. This style, known primarily for its pointed arch, was also seen in embroideries, carvings and other crafts.

Grotesque	Decorative work of art or ornament based on Roman wall paintings in which architectural and many other elements are fantastically mingled.
Hemp	Plant whose fibers can be made into rope or woven into strong cloth or canvas (q.v.). Today it is principally made into hessian or burlap (q.v.).
Herm	Plain tapering pillar surmounted by a carved head.
Hooked rug	Type of rug made in many homes in America from the 1850s onward, which was made by pulling strips of cloth through burlap (q.v.) with a hook, leaving loops on the surface. In England known as rag rugs.
Iconostases (ikonostases)	Curtains used in Greek and Russian Orthodox churches to screen the sanctuary from the congregation.
Infilling patterns	Patterns, often geometrical, used to fill in the outlines of flowers, leaves and other shapes on a piece of embroidery. They might be of pulled stitches or surface stitches in crewelwork and blackwork (q.q.v.)
Jean	A strong twilled cloth used in the eighteenth and nineteenth centuries chiefly for boots and in the corset trade, and in the twentieth century for cotton (q.v.) jeans or pants.
Kirtle	Gown worn by women in the middle ages, but later a skirt or a petticoat which was designed to show at the front.
Kloster blocks	Blocks of geometrical satin stitch (q.v.) which edge the cut threads in Hardanger embroidery (q.v.).

Kunstgewerbeschule	German word for a school of industrial art.

Lambrequin	Piece of fabric often with a scalloped or vandyked (notched) border made to hang from a mantelpiece, cornice or shelf. It was often embroidered or made of crazy patchwork (q.v.).
Lappets	Pairs of hanging bands forming part of ecclesiastical miters (q.v.) and many ladies' caps.

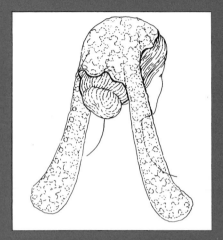

Lectern cloth	Covering for the lectern or reading desk in churches. It covered the bookstand, sometimes hanging down to the ground.
Lenten veil	Part of the set of cloths, sometimes called the Lenten array, which covers all gilt and colored objects in a church during Lent. The set includes the altar frontal (q.v.), burse (q.v.), veil and pulpit fall. The veils are free hanging, and in Germany were generally worked in white on white, but black or red thread might be used.
Linen	Fabric woven from the fibers of the flax plant, *Linum usitatissimum*.
Maniple	Vestment frequently worn by bishops, priests, deacons and sub-deacons at the service of Holy Communion. It consists of a strip of cloth resembling the stole (q.v.) but shorter, and is worn over the left forearm. It represents the towel with which Jesus wiped the disciples' feet.
Mantle	Outer garment or cloak originally worn by either sex. The word now applies to outer garments worn on ceremonial occasions such as a coronation or investiture and, in the Jewish religion, refers to the covering of the Scroll of Law.

Mantua (*Manteau*)

Gown for women, fashionable in the late seventeenth and eighteenth centuries. It was an open robe worn with a decorative petticoat, with the bodice unboned and the skirt trained and sometimes looped or pinned up.

Miter

Headdress worn by a bishop. In the Eastern Church it originated as a round-flat-topped cap and evolved into a beehive shape. In the Western Church it was originally a circlet, then a cap, and eventually a high-pointed cap with curved sides.

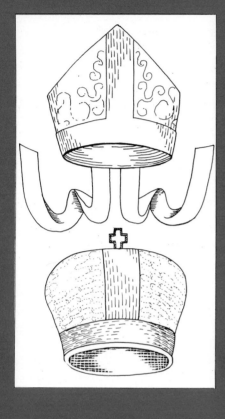

Mary, Queen of Scots

Mary Stuart (1542–87), who became Queen of France and then Queen of Scotland. She was imprisoned for nineteen years before her execution and solaced her distress and boredom with embroidery.

Medicine bags

Used by the "medicine-men" of the North American Indian tribes for their cures and charms. They were often decorated with quill-work (q.v.).

Memorial pictures

Embroidered pictures of the eighteenth and nineteenth centuries commemorating the death of a public figure or a near relation. They were often worked in a fine black silk (q.v.) on a cream silk ground and the design usually incorporated an urn, a weeping willow and a mourning figure. These pictures were particularly prevalent in North America, where they were embroidered in schools, especially those run by the Moravians.

Mocassin	Soft shoe of leather chiefly worn by the North American Indian. They are often decorated with beads, moosehair or purcupine quills.
Muslin	Fine fabric woven from cotton (q.v.) thread, originally imported from Persia and India but since the late eighteenth century woven in many European countries.
Needle	Steel implement with a point at one end and an eye at the other used for drawing a thread through material. It is the main tool used in all forms of sewing.
Needlepoint lace	Lace made with a needle. It developed in the sixteenth century from the cutwork (q.v.) embroideries of that time.
Net	Openwork fabric made by hand or machine which consists of knotting or twisting threads to produce meshes of various sizes.
Orphrey	Band of contrasting fabric, often embroidered, on the front edges of copes (q.v.), the backs and fronts of chasubles (q.v.) and sometimes on altar frontals (q.v.). The word derives from the Latin *auriphrygium* (gold embroidery). Orphreys on chasubles are cross shaped (cross orphrey), Y-shaped (Y orphrey) or straight (pillar orphrey).

Paillettes	Small metal pieces with holes for stitching on to fabric. They differ from spangles (q.v.) in that they can be of various shapes.
Pall	Cloth covering a coffin, hearse or tomb. Those made for rich families or Livery Companies were beautifully and heavily embroidered.
Pallium	Vestment worn by bishops and archbishops deriving from the ancient Greek robe which was thrown over the left shoulder. This robe conferred great dignity to its wearer which was why, when it was adopted by the Western Church, it was worn only by high ecclesiastics. In the course of time it became folded and smaller and now somewhat resembles a stole (q.v.).

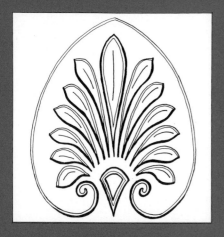

Palmette — Ornament in architecture or any of the decorative arts which resembles a palm leaf in shape.

Parfilage — See drizzling.

Passementerie — Generic term for gold and silver lace, fringes, braids, tassels, gimps (wire or stiff cords), beaded edgings and trimmings.

Pattern book — Book of designs printed for the use of lacemakers or embroiderers. The first known pattern book was published at Augsburg in 1523, since when they have been published in large numbers.

Pew-hanging — Fabric used in some churches to furnish pews and to give warmth and privacy.

Picot — Small loop of twisted thread often forming an edging to lace or embroidery, but also sometimes being an integral part of the technique as in Richelieu work (q.v.).

Pin — Thin piece of wire with a sharp point at one end and a small knob at the other used as a temporary expedient to hold two pieces of material together.

Plate — Narrow strip of metal, generally gilded, which is used in gold and metal embroideries. It is couched (q.v.) down on to the surface of the embroidery.

Pockets — Accessories worn underneath the dress in the eighteenth and nineteenth centuries. A pair of pockets was attached to tape and tied round the waist under the dress and petticoat. They held all feminine necessities such as keys, handkerchiefs and purses.

Pocket book — Wallet which held letters and papers. They were often home-made and embroidered and given as presents. In America it describes a handbag.

Pouncing	Method by which a design is marked out on a fabric. Small holes are pricked in the cartoon (q.v.) and then a fine powder (pounce) such as powdered charcoal or cuttlefish is rubbed through. After the cartoon has been removed the design is fixed by painting over the little heaps of pounce which are then blown away.
Portière	Curtain hung over a door, doorway or arch for privacy or warmth.
Predella	Painting or sculpture at the back of an altar forming part of the altarpiece above it.
Putti	Representations of small naked children or cherubs found in many forms of art from the fifteenth century onward.
Quilt	Bedspread, coverlet or counterpane (q.q.v.) made by joining two, or more generally three, layers of material by stitching them together in a pattern. The top may, in some quilts, be patchwork (q.v.).
Quilting bee	Social gathering of the pioneer days in America when neighbors would meet in order to stitch together the quilt which the hostess had made. In the north of England these gatherings were known as quilting feasts or quilting parties.
Rational	Ornament of metal or embroidered cloth formerly worn over the chasuble (q.v.) and pallium (q.v.) by bishops of certain sees when saying Mass.
Rep	Fabric which can be made from silk, cotton or wool (q.q.v.) and is characterized by ribs which run horizontally. Generally used for furnishing.
Riddell	An altar curtain, generally hung from a movable wooden or brass arm which swings from riddell posts on either side of the altar.

Rococo

Style originating in France and prevalent in most European countries between *c.*1720 and 1770. It was characterized by the shell motif and light asymmetrical ornament.

Romanesque

Medieval architectural style preceding the gothic, at its height in the eleventh century. The designs in subsidiary arts such as embroidery were often based on this architectural style.

Roundel

Round part of an embroidery design; also a circular piece of embroidery sewn on to a ground.

Royal School of Needlework

Founded in London in 1872 as the School of Art Needlework, later becoming the Royal School of Art Needlework and now known as the Royal School of Needlework. It was to supply "suitable employment for Gentlewomen" and to restore "Ornamental Needlework to the high place it once held among the decorative arts."

Russian linen

Form of linen (q.v.) made in Russia which is slightly rough in texture and makes an attractive background fabric.

Saccos

Vestment worn by patriarchs and bishops in the Orthodox Church. Though not precisely the same, it resembles the dalmatic (q.v.) worn by bishops and deacons in the Western Church and is a straight, sleeved tunic, often heavily embroidered.

Saddle cloth

Cloth put over the back of a horse or other animal underneath the saddle.

Samplers	Collection of techniques, patterns and stitches put together for easy reference. They have been, and still are, worked in all European countries and America, although nowadays the decorative element is generally more important than the practical.
Saracen purse (scrip, *aumonière*)	Bags or purses used at the time of the Crusades for bringing back relics from the Holy Land. Alms purses had been used in Europe before this time by the wealthy but their use became so general during the Crusades that a special guild was set up in France to make them for the pilgrims.
Scissors	Tool consisting of two sharp blades which, when placed either side of a piece of material and brought together, cut through it. They are used all over the world and there are many different patterns and types.
Scrip	See Saracen purse.
Sealskin thimbles	Thimbles (q.v.) worn by the Eskimos when sewing. They consist of an oval piece of sealskin with a slit across one end. The forefinger is put through the slit so that a pad of tough sealskin rests on the pad of the finger.
Seed pearl	Tiny pearl resembling a seed, with a hole drilled through, used to embellish embroideries.
Shawl strap	One of a pair of straps joined by a handle, used for carrying a shawl. They were often embroidered in Berlin woolwork (q.v.) and were used particularly in the United States.
Silk	Fabric woven from the fiber spun by the larvae of some of the bombycine moths. It was originally produced in China and came from there to Europe. The richest and most luxurious fabrics have been made from silk.
Sleigh-cover	Decorative material which covers and pads the hard inside parts of a sleigh.

Slips

Embroidery motif popular in the sixteenth and seventeenth centuries, consisting of a flower with its foliage, stem and a small piece of heel attached. It might have fruit as well as flowers as part of the same motif.

Slumber throw

Used in America to describe a small light rug used as a covering when taking a nap.

Society of Decorative Arts

American society founded by Candace Wheeler (1828–1923) and a group of ladies in 1877. Its formation was inspired by the work of the Royal School of Needlework (q.v.) in England. The Society spread until it had more than thirty branches.

Spangles

Small flat shiny metal disks used to add brilliance to embroidery. They are round with a hole in the middle for sewing them down.

Stole

Vestments worn by priests round the neck and by deacons over the left shoulder at the service of Holy Communion. It is a long narrow piece of fabric which may be embroidered either along its whole length or only at the two ends. Also a garment worn by ladies.

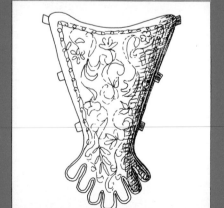

Stomacher

Fabric, often richly decorated and sometimes stiffened, which filled the V-shaped opening in the bodice of open robes.

Sumpter cloths

The covering of a pack horse, richly decorated on ceremonial occasions.

Szür

Coat of frieze or felt worn in Hungary. Though made like a coat, it was worn like a cape and was heavily decorated with applied work (q.v.) and wool (q.v.) embroidery.

Tabard

In general, a short, loose overgarment with short or no sleeves. In particular it could be worn by a knight over his armor emblazoned with his arms. Now it generally refers to the garments worn by the Heralds of the College of Arms on ceremonial occasions.

Tabby

The most common of all weaves, sometimes called plain weave. It consists of warp threads interlaced with weft threads in a regular over and under sequence, the return being under and over.

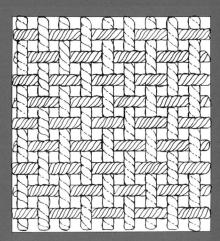

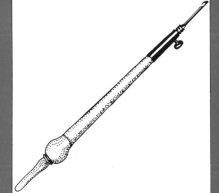

Tambour hook (tambour needle)

Tool resembling a crochet hook but much finer, always of metal, with a sharp end to the hook. Though utilitarian, they frequently have mother-of-pearl or ivory handles and are often found in eighteenth- and nineteenth-century sewing boxes.

Tambour needle

Another term for the tambour hook (q.v.) used in tambouring (q.v.).

Tester	The canopy over a bed generally supported by four posts. Originally the word referred to the vertical head of the bed and the canopy was known as the *celure*, but tester is now used to describe the canopy.
Thimble	Small protective tool made from some hard material and covered with indentations which is worn on the second finger of the hand which holds the needle (q.v.). It helps to push the needle through the material.
Tönder lace	Bobbin lace made at Tönder in South Jutland, Denmark. It was based on Flemish designs. In the eighteenth century drawn-muslin work resembling Dresden work (q.v.) was also made in the district, and this type of white-work is sometimes mistakenly called Tönder lace.
Tree of Jesse	Design used in ecclesiastical embroideries and in stained glass in the Middle Ages in which a tree grows from the body of Jesse. On each branch is one of his descendants including David and Solomon with Jesus Christ on the uppermost branch.
Triptych	Set of three pictures or carvings, hinged together. The two sides can fold over the central and more important picture or can be swung open. They are generally used as altarpieces.
Tulle	Originally silk net (q.v.) named after the town in France. Later the machine-made net was much used for evening dresses and bridal veils.
Tunicle	Vestment worn by subdeacons and clerks at the service of Holy Communion. It resembles the dalmatic (q.v.) worn by deacons but may have narrower sleeves and less embroidery.
Twill	Weave in which a diagonal line is apparent in the fabric. It is formed by the weft (q.v.) threads crossing the warp (q.v.) in a regular sequence with the return journey made in the same sequence but one or two threads along.
Valance	Horizontal band of fabric hanging from the tester (q.v.) and base of a bed, or from the top of a window frame. In both cases it usually matches the curtains.

Velvet	Fabric made from silk, wool, cotton (q.q.v.) or nylon with a short dense pile. It was first woven in the East and was introduced into Europe in the Middle Ages when it was – and it still is – used for the richest garments and vestments.
Vienna Secession	Movement of artists and architects away from the realism of the Imperial Academy of Vienna. It was started by the painter Gustav Klimt (1862–1918) and nineteen students in 1897. Its motto was *Der Zeit ihre Kunst, der Kunst ihre Freiheit* (To the era its proper art, to art its proper freedom).
Volute patterns	Patterns having a spiral or twisting form.
Wadmal	Coarse cloth, often twilled, used for the dresses of the very poor, for covering the collars of cart-horses or lining the ports of ships of war, for example. It was used in Europe from the fourteenth century, and probably earlier, to the eighteenth century.
Warp	The strong foundation threads of a woven fabric which are fastened lengthwise in the loom and across which the weft (q.v.) is worked.
Water camblet	See camblet.
Weft (woof)	The threads which cross from side to side of a woven fabric at right angles to the warp (q.v.) threads with which they are interlaced.
Woof	See weft.
Wool	Hair from the fleece of sheep and other animals which is cleaned, combed or carded, and spun into lengths ready for weaving, knitting, crochet and embroidery.
Worsted	Fabric made from the long-stapled fibers of a sheep's fleece, combed parallel and woven into smooth-faced fabric. The word also applies to the yarn (q.v.).
X orphrey	See orphrey.
Y orphrey	See orphrey.
Yarn	Thread spun from any fiber. The word embraces silk, wool, cotton hemp (q.q.v.), jute, flax, rayon and other man-made fibers.
Ystoires	Pictorial subjects in French embroidery.

Bibliography

UNITED STATES

BOLTON, Ethel Stanwood and Eva Johnston Coe, *American Samplers*. Boston, 1921.

DAVIS, Mildred J., *Early American Embroidery Designs*. New York, 1969.

DAVIS, Mildred J., *Embroidery Designs*. New York, 1971.

FINLEY, Ruth E., *Old Patchwork Quilts and The Women Who Made Them*. New York, 1929.

HANLEY, Hope, *Needlepoint in America*. New York, 1969.

HARBESON, G. B., *American Needlework*. New York, 1938.

HOLSTEIN, Jonathan, *The Pieced Quilt: An American Design Tradition*. Greenwich, Conn., 1973.

ICKIS, Marguerite, *The Standard Book of Quilt-Making and Collecting*. New York, reprinted 1959.

KENT, William Winthrop, *The Hooked Rugs*. New York, 1930.

ORLOFSKY, Patsy and Myron, *Quilts in America*. New York, 1974.

PETO, Florence, *Historic Quilts*. New York, 1939.

STEARNS, Martha Genung, *Homespun and Blue, A Study of American Crewel Embroidery*. New York, 1940.

STEPHENS, Mrs. Ann S., *The Ladies' Complete Guide to Crochet, Fancy Knitting and Needlework*. New York, 1854.

WADSWORTH ATHENEUM, *Bed Rugs*. Hartford, Conn., 1972.

WHEELER, Candace, *The Development of Embroidery in America*. New York, 1921.

WILSON, Erica, *Crewel Embroidery*. New York, 1962, London, 1964.

GREAT BRITAIN

Arts Council of Great Britain, *Opus Anglicanum*, catalogue of the exhibition at the Victoria and Albert Museum. London, 1963.

Birmingham Museum and Art Gallery, *British Embroidery from the 13th to the 19th Century*, catalogue of the exhibition. Birmingham, 1959.

BRETT, Katharine B., *English Embroidery in the Royal Ontario Museum: 16th–18th Centuries*. Toronto, 1972.

BUCK, Anne, "The Countryman's Smock," *Folk-Life*, Vol. I. 1963

CHRISTIE, Mrs. Archibald H., *Samplers and Stitches*. London, 3rd edit. 1934.

CHRISTIE, Mrs. Archibald H., *English Medieval Embroidery*. Oxford, 1938.

COLBY, Averil, *Patchwork*. London, 1958.

COLBY, Averil, *Quilting*. London, 1972.

CROMPTON, Rebecca, *Modern Design in Embroidery*. London, 1936.

DODWELL, C. R., "The Bayeux Tapestry and the French Secular Epic," *Burlington Magazine*, Vol. CVIII. November 1966.

GIROUARD, Mark, *Hardwick Hall*, National Trust guide book. London, 1976.

GROVES, Sylvia, *The History of Needlework Tools and Accessories*. London, 1966.

HOGARTH, Mary, "Modern Embroidery," *The Studio*, Special Spring Number. 1933.

HUGHES, Therle, *English Domestic Needlework 1660–1860*. London, 1961.

IRWIN, J., "Origins of the 'Oriental' Style in English Decorative Art," *Burlington Magazine*, Vol. XCVII. April 1955.

KENDRICK, A. F., *English Needlework*. London, 2nd edit. (revised by Patricia Wardle) 1967.

KING, D., *Samplers*. London, 1960.

Keele University, *The History of the Leek Embroidery Society*. Keele, 1969.

City of Leicester Museum and Art Gallery, *Mary Linwood*, catalogue of the exhibition. Leicester, 1951.

LEVEY, Santina, *Discovering Embroidery of the Nineteenth Century*. Tring, Herts, 1972.

MACQUOID, Percy, *A Record of the Collections in the Lady Lever Art Gallery, Port Sunlight*, Vol. III, "English Furniture, Tapestry and Needlework of the XVIth–XIXth Centuries." London, 1928.

McROBERTS, D., "The Fetternear Banner," *Innes Review*. 1956.

MANN, Vivian B., "Architectural Conventions on the Bayeux Tapestry," *Marsyas*, annual journal of the Institute of Fine Arts, University of New York. New York, 1974–5.

MARRIOTT, Charles, *British Handicrafts*. London, 1943.

MORRIS, Barbara, *Victorian Embroidery*. London, 1962.

Needlework Development Scheme, *An Account of its Origins and Aims*. Glasgow, 1951.

NEVINSON, J. L., "Peter Stent and John Overton, Publishers of Embroidery Designs," *Apollo*, Vol. XXIV. July to December 1936.

NEVINSON, J. L., *Catalogue of English Domestic Embroidery of the Sixteenth and Seventeenth Centuries*, Victoria and Albert Museum. London, 2nd edit. 1950.

ODDY, R., *Catalogue of Embroideries given to the Museum by the Needlework Development Scheme*, catalogue of the exhibition at the Royal Scottish Museum. Edinburgh, 1965.

PAYNE, F. G., *Guide to the Collection of Samplers and Embroideries*, National Museum of Wales. Cardiff, 1939.

SELIGMAN, G., and HUGHES, T., *Domestic Needlework*. London, 1926.

STRONG, Roy, *The English Icon: Elizabethan and Jacobean Portraiture*. London, 1969.

SWAIN, Margaret H., *The Flowerers*. London and Edinburgh, 1955.

SWAIN, Margaret H., *Historical Needlework: a Study of Influences in Scotland and Northern England*. London, 1970.

SWAIN, Margaret H., *The Needlework of Mary Queen of Scots*. New York, 1973.

Swain, Margaret H., "Mrs. J. R. Newbery 1865–1948," *Embroidery*, Vol. XXIV, No. 4. Winter 1973.

SWAIN, Margaret H., "Ann Macbeth 1875–1948," *Embroidery*, Vol. XXV, No. I. Spring 1974.

SWANSON, M., and MACBETH, A., *Educational Needlecraft*. London, 1913.

Tate Gallery, *The Elizabethan Image*, catalogue of the exhibition. London, 1969.

Victoria and Albert Museum, *Notes on Applied Work and Patchwork*. London, 2nd imp. 1949.

Victoria and Albert Museum, *Victorian and Edwardian Decorative Arts*, catalogue of the exhibition. London, 1952.

Victoria and Albert Museum, *Victorian Church Art*, catalogue of the exhibition. London, 1971.

Victoria and Albert Museum, *The Needle's Excellency*, catalogue of the traveling exhibition. London, 1973.

WADE, N. Victoria, *The Basic Stitches of Embroidery*, Victoria and Albert Museum. London, 1960.

WARDLE, Patricia, *Guide to English Embroidery*, Victoria and Albert Museum. London, 1970.

WINGFIELD, Digby, G. F., "Lady Julia Calverley: Embroideress," *The Connoisseur*, Vol. XXIV. March and April 1960.

WINGFIELD DIGBY, G. F., *Elizabethan Embroidery*. London, 1963.

FRANCE

AUBRY, Felix, *Rapport sur les dentelles, les blondes, les tulles et les broderies . . . à l'exposition universelle de Londres en 1851*. Paris, 1851.

CHRISTIE, Mrs. Archibald H., *English Medieval Embroidery*. Oxford, 1938.

COX, Raymond, *L'Art de Décorer Les Tissus d'après Les Collections du Musée Historique de la Chambre de Commerce de Lyon*. Paris, 1900.

COX, Raymond, *Les Soieries d'Art depuis les Origines jusqu'à nos Jours*. Paris, 1914.

DESVALLÉES, André et RIVIÈRE, Georges-Henri, *Arts Populaires de France*. Paris, 1976.

FARCY, Louis de, *La Broderie du Onzième Siècle jusqu'à nos Jours. . . .* Paris, 1890–1919.

GAUTHIER, Joseph Stany, *L'Art Populaire Français : costumes paysans*. Paris, 1930.

GEIJER, Agnes, "Broderies françaises du haut-gothique conservées en Suède," *Festschrift Ulrich Middeldorf*. Berlin, 1908.

GEIJER, Agnes, "Franska 1200-talsbroderier," *Fornvannen*, 4. 1964.

HACKENBROCH, Yvonne, *English and other needlework, tapestries and textiles in the Irwin Untermeyer Collection*. Harvard, 1960.

IKLE, E., *La Broderie mécanique, 1823–1930*. Paris, 1931.

JARRY, Madeleine, *La Tapisserie art du XXième siècle*. Paris, 1974.

JARRY, Madeleine, *Tapisserie pour vos sièges*. Paris, 1975.

LEMOINE, Pierre, "La chambre de la Reine à Versailles," *Revue du Louvre*, 3. 1976.

LEROUDIER, Emile, *Les Dessinateurs de la Fabrique Lyonnaise (1754–1825)*. Lyons, 1908.

LESPINASSE, René de, *Les Métiers et Les Corporations de la Ville de Paris*. Paris, 1879–97.

MARQUET DE VASSELOT, J. J., and WEIGERT, R. A., *Bibliographie de la tapisserie, des tapis et de la broderie en France*. Paris, 1935.

MIGEON, Gaston, *Les Arts du Tissu*. Paris, 1909.

Musée des Arts Décoratifs, *Nouvelles Collections de l'Union Centrale des Arts Décoratifs*. Paris, 1906.

Musée Historique des Tissus, Lyons : *Broderie de la Fin de l'Époque Louis XVI et de l'Époque Napoléonienne*. 1905.

SAINT-AUBIN, Charles-Germain de, *L'art du brodeur*. Paris, 1770.

SCHUETTE, M., and MULLER-CHRISTENSEN, S., *The Art of Embroidery*. London, 1964.

STANDEN, Miss E., ed, *Metropolitan Museum of Art Bulletin*, New York. 1950–1. Vol. IX, p. 131: "Le Roi-soleil et ses enfants." Vol. XIII, p. 144. "Embroidery in the French and Chinese taste." 1954–5, Vol. XV, p.165 "A picture for every story," 1956–7, Vol. XXII, p. 143, "A boar-hunt at Versailles," 1963–4.

VERLET, Pierre, *Versailles*. Paris, 1961.

WEIGERT, R. A., "Le Meuble Brodé de la Salle du Trône du Grand Roi à Versailles," *Revue de l'art Ancien et Moderne*, p. 96. November, 1932.

Exhibition Catalogues :

"L'Art Européen vers 1400." Kunsthistorisches Museum, Vienna, 1962.

"Les Trésors des Églises de France." Musée des Arts Décoratifs, Paris 1965.

"Le XVIe Siècle Européen, Tapisseries." Mobilier National, Paris 1965–6.

"L'Europe Gothique." Palais du Louvre, Paris, 1968.

"L'Ecole de Fontainebleau." Grand Palais, Paris, 1972–3.

"Raiment for the Lord's Service." Art Institute, Chicago, 1975.

"Broderie au Passé et au Présent." Musée des Arts Décoratifs, Paris, 1977.

ITALY

BINETTI-VERTUA, Caterina, *Trine e donne Siciliane*. Milan, 1911.

GARZELLI, Annarosa, *Il ricamo nella attività artistica di Pollaiulo, Botticelli, Bartolo di Giovanni*. Florence, 1973.

MORAZZONI, G., *Ricami Genovesi*. Milan, 1952.

MORTARI, Luisa, *Il Tesoro della Cattedrale di Anagni*. Rome, 1963.

"Peasant Art in Italy," *The Studio*. Special Number. 1913.

PODREIDER, Fanny, *Storia dei Tessuti d'Arte in Italia*. Bergamo, 1928.

RICCI, Elisa, *Ricami Italiani*. Florence, 1925.

SANTANGELO, Antonio (trans. Peggy Craig), *The Development of Italian Textile Design from the 12th to the 18th Century*. Rome, 1959; London, 1964.

SCHWABACHER, S., *Die Stickereien nach Entwurfen von Antonio Pollaiuolo in der Opera di S. Maria del Fiore zu Florenz*. Strasburg, 1911.

TOSCHI, P., *Arte Populare Italiana*. Rome, 1960.

SPAIN

ALFAYA y LÓPEZ, M. C. y M. P., *Los bordados populares en Segovia*. Madrid, 1930.

Broderie au passé et au présent, catalogue of the exhibition held 28 April to 18 July, 1977. Musée des Arts Décoratifs. Paris, 1977.

CALLEJO, C., *El Monasterio de Guadalupe*. Madrid, 1958.

DURAN I SANPERE, A., *Barcelona i la seva història*, III. Barcelona, 1973.

ERNEST, H., *Broderies populaires espagnoles*. Paris, 1923.

FLORIANO CUMBREÑO, A. C., *El bordado*. Barcelona, 1942.

FOCHIER-HENRION, A., "La broderie au fil du temps," *L'Estampille*, No. 85 Paris, 1977.

GONZALEZ MENA, M. A., *Catálogo de bordados del Instituto Valencia de Don Juan*. Madrid, 1974.

MIGUEL I BADIA, F., "Historia del bordado," Vol. VIII, *Historia general del Arte*. Barcelona, 1897.

SCHUETTE, M., and MULLER-CHRISTENSEN, S., *The Art of Embroidery*. London, 1964.

STAPLEY, M., *Popular Weaving and Embroidery in Spain*. London, 1924.

TACHARD, P., *Collection de broderies anciennes Moyen-Age et Renaissance de M. Célestin Dupont*. Barcelona, 1907.

TURMO, I., *Bordados y bordadores sevillanos* (sixteenth to eighteenth centuries). Seville, 1955.

PORTUGAL

DAY, Lewis, and BUCKLE, Mary, *Art in Needlework*. London, 1900.

CARDOSO, Ribeira, and CHAVES, Luis, *Subsidios par a Historia Regional da Beira – Baixa*. Castelo Branco, 1944.

Catálogo Guia da Secçao de Tecidos, Bordados, Tapeçarias e Tapetes do Museu Machado de Castre. Coimbra, 1943.

DILLMONT, T. de., *Encyclopedia of Needle-work*. Mulhouse, 1930. Reprinted, Philadelphia, 1972.

LACOMBA, Maravillas, *Tejidos e Bordados Populares Españoles*. Madrid, 1924.

SPRATLEY, Mildren, *Tejidos e Bordados Populares Espanoles*. Madrid, 1924.

VASCONCELOS, Joaquim de, and GOMES, Marques, *Exposiçao Distrital de Aveiro*, 1882. *Volkskunst in Europa*, Berlin, 1941.

NETHERLANDS

GRAAF, J. J., "Noordhollandsch borduurwerk van 1639," *Bulletin van den Nederlandschen Oudheidkundigen Bond*, no. 6, Vol. X. Leiden, 1917.

HEMERT, M. van, *De handwerken op het eiland Marken*. Netherlands Open-Air

Museum, Arnhem, 1967. (English edition in preparation.)

HOBIJN, M., and JARVEN, O., *Textiel in Beeld*. De Bilt, 1974.

JANSEN, B., *Laat Gotisch Borduurwerk in Nederland*. The Hague, 1948.

JONG, J. de, *Weef- en Borduurkunst*. Rotterdam, 1933.

JONG, M. C., de, "Iets over de historie en het gebruik van Zaans stikwerk," *Bij Voorbeeld*, No. 2, Vol. 1. IJmuiden, 1969.

JONG, M. C., de, "Crewel-werk," *Bij Voorbeeld*, No. 2, Vol. 3. IJmuiden, 1971.

JONGE, C. H., de, *Het Costuum onze Voorouders*. The Hague, 1936.

MEULENBELT-NIEUWBURG, A., *Embroidery Motifs from Dutch Samplers*. London, 1974.

NABER, J. W. A., *De Borduurkunst*. Haarlem, 1901.

NABER, J. W. A., *Rechlindis. Het Kunstnaaldwerk*. Haarlem, 1911 (1st ed. 1887).

NIEUWBURG, A., "Handwerk toegepast op streekdrachten," *Ars Folklorica Belgica*. Antwerp/Amsterdam. 1956.

ROGGE, E. M., *De Tentoonstelling van Kunstnaaldwerk in het Museum van Kunstnijverheid te Haarlem*. Haarlem, 1904.

ROGGE, E. M., *Naaldkunst, Kantwerk en Handweven*. Rotterdam, 1923.

SCHENK, L. G., "Needlework Revival in Holland," *Embroidery*, Vol. V. London, 1954.

THIENEN, F. van, *The Great Age of Holland, 1600–60*. London, 1951. (One of the series *Costume of the Western World*.)

TORDAY, S., "Three Dutch Embroidery Artists," *The Studio*, Vol. 144. London, 1952.

WARDLE, P., "Embroidery in Miniature," *Embroidery*, No. 4, Vol. 27. London, 1976.

YSSELSTEYN, G.T., van, "Het Schippers Antependium in het bezit van het Gemeente Museum te Nijmegen," *Bulletin van de Koninklijke Nederlandse Oudheidkundige Bond*, No. 2, 6th series, Vol. 4. Leiden, 1951.

BELGIUM

CALBERG, M., "David Vainqueur de Goliath. Tableau brodé en 1651 par Jan Haseloff," *Bulletin des Musées Royaux d'Art et d'Histoire*, Vol. XXIV. Brussels, 1952.

CALBERG, M., "Les broderies historiées de l'abbaye d'Averbode," *Revue Belge d'archéologie et d'histoire de l'art*," Vol. XXIII. Brussels, 1954.

DUVERGER, G., "De Gentse borduurwerkers Jakob en Michiel de Rynck," *Miscellanea Jozef Duverger*, Vol. II. Ghent, 1968.

DUBERGER, G., "Borduurwerkers en borduurwerk te Gent. Een bijdra ge," *Artes Textiles*, Vol. VIII. Ghent, 1974.

DUVERGER, J., and VAN GELDER, H. E., ed. *Kunstgeschiedenis der Nederlandens*, Vol. III Utrecht/Antwerp, 1954.

DUVERGER, J., and VERSYP, J., "Schilders en borduurwerkers aan de arbeid voor een vorstenduel te Brugge in 1425," *Artes Textiles*, Vol. II. Ghent, 1955.

FARCY, L. de., *La Broderie du XIe siècle jusqu'à nos jours*. Angers, 1890–1919.

FREEMAN, M. B., "The Legend of St. Catherine told in Embroidery," *Bulletin of the Metropolitan Museum of Art*, Vol. XIV. New York, 1955–6.

FREEMAN, M. B., "The St. Martin Embroideries," *Bulletin of the Metropolitan Museum of Art*, Vol. XXVI. New York, 1968.

HAUWERMEIREN-GROSSE, J. van., "Een Brugs kunstatelier," *West-Vlaanderen*, Vol. II. 1953.

MACLEOD, C., "Fifteenth-century Vestments in Waterford," *Journal of the Royal Society of Antiquaries of Ireland*, Vol. LXXXII. Dublin, 1952.

MERTENS, J., "Bij een antependium," *'t Land van Reyn*, Vol. X. 1960.

RISSELIN-STEENEBRUGEN, M., "Caroline d'Halluin, marchande de dentelles à Bruxelles au XVIIIe siècle," *Annales de la Société Royale d'Archéologie de Bruxelles*. Brussels, 1956–7.

RISSELEN-STEENEBRUGEN, M., "Les débuts de l'industrie dentellière – Martine et Catherine Plantin," *De Gulden Passer*, Vol. 39. Antwerp, 1961.

SCHLOSSER, J. von., *Der Burgundische Paramentenschatz des Ordens vom goldenen Vliesse*. Vienna, 1912.

STANDEN, E., "The Shepherd's Sweet Lot," *Bulletin of the Metropolitan Museum of Art*, Vol. XVII. New York, 1959.

VIAENE, A., "Borduurwerck met de tapijtsteek van Maria-Jacoba Werbrouck," *Biekorf, Westvlaamsarchief*, Vol. 62. 1961.

VELDE, H., van de, *Geschichte meines Lebens*. Munich, 1962.

WYSS, R. L., "The Dukes of Burgundy and the encouragement of textiles in the Netherlands," *The Connoisseur*, Vol. 194. London, 1977.

GERMANY

BRAUN, J., "Ein Kölner Nadelmaler des XVII. Jahrhunderts," *Zeitschrift für Christliche Kunst*. 1905.

DREGER, M., *Die Künsterlische Entwicklung der Weberei und Stickerei*. Vienna, 1904.

ENGELMEIER, P., *Westfälische Hungertücher*. Münster, 1960.

GRÄBKE, H. A., "Eine westfälische Gruppe gestickter Leinendecken," *Westfalen* 23. 1938.

HAGER, L., "Die Paramentenkammern," *Die Residenz zu München, Bayerland*. April 1960.

HEINEMEYER, E., *see* Austria.

HUBEL, A., *Der Regensburger Domschatz*. Munich-Zürich, 1976.

KLINGELSCHMIDT, F. Th., "Mainzer Seidensticker am Ende des Mittelalters," *Zeitschrift für Christliche Kunst*. 1916.

KLUGE, D., "Westfälische Kaselstäbe des 15. Jahrhunderts," *Westfalen* 37. 1959.

KLUGE, D., "Stoffe, Stickereien und Wirkereien," *Kunst und Kultur im Weserraum 800–1600*, Ausstellungskatalog. Corvey, 1966.

KROOS, R., *Niedersächsische Bildstickereien des Mittelalters*. Berlin, 1970.

KURTH, B., "Die europäische Bildstickerei im Mittelalter," *Ciba-Rundschau*, No. 48, 1941.

MANNOWSKY, W., *Der Danziger Paramentenschatz*. Berlin, 1931–8.

MULLER-CHRISTENSEN, S., "Uber drei Stickereien im Bayerischen Nationalmuseum," *Pantheon*, Vol. XXVIII. 1941.

MULLER-CHRISTENSEN, S., "Passauer Reliefstickerei des 16. Jahrhunderts," *Pantheon*, Vol. XXIX, 1942.

MULLER-CHRISTENSEN, S., *Sakrale Gewänder des Mittelalters*, Ausstellungs Katalog, Bayerisches Nationalmuseum. Munich, 1955.

REICHERT, L., *Spätgotische Stickereien am Niederrhein*, Kunstgeschichtliche Forschungen des Rheinischen Vereins für Denkmalpflege und Heimatschutz Band II. Bonn, 1938.

SCHELLENBERG, A., "Bortenwirker, Messgewänder in Schlesien," Schlesiens Vorzeit in Bild und Schrift N.F. IX = *Jahrbuch des Schlesischen Museums für Kunstgewerbe und Altertümer*. 1928.

SCHELLENBERG, A. "Bortenwirker, Seiden – und Perlenhefter in Schlesien," Schlesiens Vorzeit in Bild und Schrift N.F.X. = *Jahrbuch des Schlesischen Museums für Kunstgewerbe und Altertümer*, 1933.

SCHUETTE, M., *Gestickte Bildteppiche und Decken des Mittelalters*. Vol. 1, 1927; Vol. II, 1930.

WILCKENS, L.V., *Aus dem Danziger Paramentenschatz*, Ausstellungskatalog,

Germanisches Nationalmuseum.
Nuremberg, 1958.
WILCKENS, L. V., "Hessische
Leinestickereien des 13. und 14.
Jahrhunderts," *Anzeiger des
Germanischen Nationalmuseums
Nürnberg 1954–9.* Nuremberg, 1960.
WILCKENS, L. V., "Zwölf gestickte
Wandbehänge aus Dresden,"
Pantheon, JG.XX. 1962.
WILCKENS, L. V., "Ein Jahrhundert
Lübecker Gold – und Seidenstickerei
seit 1365," *Anzeiger des Germanischen
Nationalmuseums Nürnberg.*
Nuremberg, 1970.
WILCKENS, L. V., "Textilien" in
Bayern, Kunst und Kultur,
Ausstellungskatalog. Munich, 1972.
WITTE, F., *Die kiturgischen Gewänder
und kirchlichen Stickereien des
Scnütgen Museums Köln.* Berlin, 1926.
WITTE, F., *Tausend Jahre deutscher
Kunst am Rhein.* Leipzig, 1932.

AUSTRIA
BRACHER, K., "Der Stifterin-Altar und
der Stifterin-Ornat zu Göss," *Blätter
für Seckauer Diözesangeschichte,* Heft
6. 1948.
DREGER, M., *Die künstlerische
Entwicklung der Weberei und
Stickerei.* Vienna, 1904.
DREGER, M., "Der Gösser Ornat,"
Kunst und Kunsthandwerk XI. 1908.
EGG, E., "Die Kunst der Seidensticker
im Umkreis des Innsbrucker Hofes,"
Schlernschriften 228. Innsbruck, 1963.
FIEDLER, F., "Admonter
Kunststickereien und der Sticker J. S.
Köck," *Grazer Volksblatt.*
Festbeilag, 1.1.1927.
HEINEMEYER, E., *Süddeutsche
Stickereien des 13. und 14.
Jahrhunderts,* Dissertation. Munich, 1958.
HEINZ, D., *Linzer Paramente.* Vienna
and Munich, 1962.
HEINZ, D., *Kunstschätze aus dem
Kloster der Heimsuchung Mariae,*
Austellungskatalog. Vienna, 1967.
HEINZ, D., "Textilien" in *Gotik in
Osterreich,* Ausstellungskatalog.
Krems, 1967.
HEINZ, D., *Meisterwerke barocker
Textilkunst,* Ausstellungskatalog.
Vienna, 1972.
KRAUSE, A., *Das Blasiusmünster in
Admont.* Linz, undated.
KURTH, B., "Eine Hochreliefstickerei
des 16. Jahrhunderts im Wiener
Diözesanmuseum," *Jahrbuch der
Kunsthistorischen Sammlungen in Wien*
N.F. IX. 1935.
KURTH, B., "Die Europäische
Bildstickerei im Mittelalter," *Ciba-
Rundschau* No. 48. 1941.
LIST, R., *Kunst und Künstler in der
Steiermark.* Ried. 1967.

SWITZERLAND
DREGER, M., see Germany.
EGLI, E., "Schweizer Handstickerei im
16. Jahrhundert," *Zwingliana* I.
1897–1904, Heft. 4.
FALKE, O. V., "Gestickte Bildteppiche
der Ostschweiz," *Pantheon,* IX. 1932.
KURTH, B., see Germany.
RAPP, A., "Schweizerische
Mustertücher," Schweizerischen
Landesmuseum 40. 1976.
REINLE, A., *Luzerner Volkskunst.*
Berne, 1959.
SCHNEIDER, J., "Schweizerische
Bildstickereien des 16. und 17.
Jahrhunderts," Schweizerischen
Landesmuseum 14. 1960.
SCHNEIDER, J., "Schweizerische
Leinenstickereien," Schweizerischen
Landesmuseum 32. 1970.
SCHUETTE, M. and MÜLLER-
CHRISTENSEN, S., *The Art of
Embroidery.* London, 1964.
SUTER, R. L., "Scholastica An der
Allmend. Eine Luzerner
Paramentenstickerin der Barockzeit,"
*Zeitschrift für schweizerische
Archäologie und Kunstgeschichte,* 25.
1968.
SUTER, R. L., "Die Altarornate des
Stiftes Beromünster," *Zeitschrift für
Schweizerische Archäologie und
Kunstgeschichte,* 30. 1973.
TRUDEL, V., "Leinenstickerei in der
Schweiz," Ciba-Rundschau, No. 86.
1949.
TRUDEL, V., "Schweizerische
Leinenstickereien des Mittelalters und
der Renaissance," Schweizer
Heimatbücher No. 61/62. Berne, 1954.

SWEDEN
BRANTING, Agnes, and LINDBLOM,
Andreas, *Medieval Embroideries and
Textiles in Sweden.* Stockholm, 1932.
DANIELSON, Sofia, *Om Handarbetets
vänner* (English summary). Stockholm,
1975.
DILLMONT, T. de., *Encyclopedia of
Needle-work.* Mulhouse, 1930.
ESTHAM, Inger, *Figurbroderade
mässhaker från reformationstidens och
1600–talets Sverige.* Stockholm, 1974.
FRANZÉN, Anne Marie, *Prydnads-
sömmar under medeltiden.* Stockholm,
1971.
FISCHER, Eivor, *Svensk broderikonst.*
Stockholm, 1953; Paisley, Scotland,
1953.
FISCHER, Ernst, *Skånska yllebroderier :
i fria sömsätt,* Yearbook II. Malmö,
1971.
GEIJER, Agnes, *Die Textilfunde aus den
Gräbern,* Book III. Stockholm, 1938.
GEIJER, Agnes, *Albertus Pictor,
målare och pärlstickare.* Stockholm,
1949.

GEIJER, Agnes, *Textile Treasures of
Uppsala Cathedral.* Uppsala, 1964.
GEIJER, Agnes, *Ur textil konstens
historia.* Lund, 1972.
HENSCHEN, Ingegerd, *Svenska
broderier.* Stockholm, 1950.
KARLSON, William, *Stât och vardag i
stormaktstidens herremanshem.* Lund,
1945.
NYLÉN, Anna Maja, *Broderier från
herremans och borgarhem : 1500–1850.*
Stockholm, 1950.
NYLÉN, Anna Maja, *Hemslöjd.* Lund,
1969; New York, 1976.
PYLKKÄNEN, Riitta, *The Use and
Traditions of Mediaeval Rugs and
Coverlets in Finland.* Helsinki,
1974.
SCHUETTE, M., and MULLER-
CHRISTIANSEN, S., *The Art of
Embroidery* (trans. D. King). London,
1964.
STAVENOW-HIDEMARK, Elisabet,
Svensk Jugend. Stockholm, 1964.
WALTERSTORFF, E. von, *Swedish
Textiles,* Stockholm, 1925.
WOLLIN, Nils G., *Svenska textilier.*
Stockholm, 1930.

DENMARK
ANDERSEN, Ellen, "The Costume and
Textile Collection in the Danish Folk
Museum," *Dansk Folkemuseum &
Frilandsmuseet, History & Activities.*
Copenhagen, 1966.
ANDRESEN, Gudrun, *Danske bondesk-
jorter fra ca. 1770 til ca. 1870.* Jelling,
1974.
ANDRESEN, Gudrun, *Særke. Danske
bondekvinders særke og oplod fra ca.
1770 til ca. 1870.* Copenhagen, 1976.
BUSCH, Ebba, "Kniplingsimitationer i
tyllstrækning," *Arv og Eje,* yearbook
for Dansk Kulturhistorisk
Museumsforening. Odense, 1965.
DALGAARD, Hanne Frøsig, *Hedebo.*
Copenhagen, 1977.
GARDE, Georg, *Danske silkebroderede
lærredsduge fra 16. og 17.
århundrede. Med særligt henblik på de
grafiske forbilleder.* Copenhagen,
1961.
KRAGELUND, Minna Holm, "Gammelt
på en ny måde – almue-inspirationen
i nytidens tekstiler," *Nationalmuseets
Arbejdsmark.* Copenhagen, 1971.
MYGDAL, Elna, *Amagerdragter,
Vævninger og Syninger.* Copenhagen,
1932.
Nationalmuseet, *Fra Fruerstuen paa
Slotte og Herregaarde,* catalogue of the
exhibition. Copenhagen, 1953.
WANDEL, Gertie, *Klassiske Korssting.*
Copenhagen, 1971.
WANDEL, Gertie, *Vor Tids Korssting.*
Copenhagen, 1972.

NORWAY

ASTRUP, E., MOLAUG, R. B., and ENGELSTAD, H., *Sting og Söm i gammelt og nytt broderi.* Oslo, 1973.

DEDEKAM, H., *Hvitsöm fra Nordmör.* Trondheim, 1914.

ENGELSTAD, H., "Veöy-duken. Et klosterarbeid fra slutten av middelalderen?" *Viking*, Vol. XVIII. Oslo, 1954.

FRANZÉN, A. M., "Höylandteppet," *Det kongelige norske videnskabers selskab Museet*, Yearbook 1960. Trondheim, 1960.

GEIJER, A., "Broderi," *Kulturhistorisk leksikon for nordisk middelalder*, Vol. II. Oslo, 1957.

MOLAUG, R. B., "Se Norges Blomsterdal. Broderte putetrekk fra norske bygder," *By og Bygd*, 1948–49. Oslo, 1949.

SJOVOLD, Aa. B., *Broderikunst og prydsöm. En liten historisk oversikt.* Oslo, 1976.

STEWART, J. S., *The Folk Arts of Norway.* New York, 1972.

STUELAND, G., *Hardangersaum.* Oslo, 1960.

FINLAND

BRANTING, Agnes, and LINDBLOM, Andreas, *Medeltida vävnader och broderier i Sverige*, I. Stockholm, 1928.

NORDMAN, C. A., *Klosterarbeten från Nådendal.* Finskt Museum, Helsinki, 1943.

PYLKKÄNEN, Riitta, *The Use and Traditions of Mediaeval Rugs and Coverlets in Finland.* Helsinki, 1974.

CENTRAL AND SOUTH-EASTERN EUROPE

Albania

IKBAL, Mustafa, *Albanian Popular Motives in Textiles and Needlework.* Tirana, 1959.

Bulgaria

CHOUKANOVA, Rossitsa, *Bulgarian National Embroidery.* Sofia, 1957.

Czechoslovakia

DROBNÁ, Zoroslava, *Les trésors de la broderie religieuse en Tchécoslovaquie.* Prague, 1950.

VACLAVIK, A., and OREL, J., *Textile Folk Art.* London, 1960.

Greece

JOHNSTONE, Pauline, *A Guide to Greek Island Embroidery.* London, 1972.

WACE, A. J. B., *Mediterranean and Near Eastern Embroideries from the Collection of Mrs. F. H. Cook.* London, 1935.

ZORA, Popi, *Embroidery and Jewellery in Greek National Costume.* Athens, 1966.

Hungary

FÉL, Edit, *Hungarian Peasant Embroidery.* London, 1961.

GERVERS-MOLNÁR, Veronika, *The Hungarian Szür, Royal Ontario Museum.* Ottawa, 1973.

VARJÚ-EMBER, Maria, *Hungarian Domestic Embroidery.* Budapest, 1963.

Poland

MANKOWSKI, Tadeusz, *Polskie Tkaniny i Hafty XVI–XVIII w. (Polish Textiles and Embroidery, 16th–18th century.)* Breslau, 1954.

PIETKIEWICZ, K., *Haft o Zdobienie Stroju Ludowego (Embroidery and Decoration on Peasant Costume).* Warsaw, 1955.

Romania

BANATEANU, Tancred (and others), *Folk Costumes, Woven Textiles and Embroideries of Roumania.* Bucharest, 1958.

Yugoslavia

POPSTEFANIEVA, M., *Broderies nationales macédoniennes.* Skopje, 1953.

START, Laura E., *The Durham Collection of Garments and Embroideries from Albania and Jugoslavia, Bankfield Museum, Halifax.* Halifax, 1939.

Orthodox Church

JOHNSTONE, Pauline, *The Byzantine Tradition in Church Embroidery.* London, 1967.

RUSSIA

BOGUSLAVSKAYA, I. Ya., *Russkaya Narodnaya Vyishivka.* Moscow, 1972.

HOLME, Charles, ed., *Peasant Art in Russia.* London, Paris and New York, 1912.

JOHNSTONE, Pauline, *The Byzantine Tradition in Church Embroidery.* London, 1967.

MAYASOVA, N., *Drevnerusskoye Shit'o.* Moscow, 1971.

MULLER, CHARLES, *Description de toutes les nations de l'empire de Russie.* St. Petersburg, 1776.

OKUNEVA, Irene, "Russian Embroidery," *Embroidery*, Vol. IV, No. 2. London, 1936.

SVIRIN, A., *Drevnerusskoye Shit'o.* Moscow, 1963.

WILMOT, Martha and Catharine, *Russian Journals 1803–1808*, ed. the Marchioness of Londonderry and H. M. Hyde. London, 1934.

ICELAND

ELDJÁRN, Kristján, *Hundrád ár í Thjódminjasafni.* Reykjavík, 1962. (Thirteen sections out of one hundred are concerned with embroideries in the National Museum of Iceland, Reykjavík. English summaries.)

GESTSSON, Gísli, "Altariskloedi frá Svalbardi," *Arbók hins íslenzka fomleifafélags 1963.* Reykjavík, 1964. (pp. 5–37. Embroidered medieval altar frontal. English summary.)

GUDJÖNSSON, Elsa E., "Altarisdukur Ara á Sökku. Ensk áhrif í íslenskum útsaumi á 17. öld," *Minjar og menntir. Afmoelisrit helgað Kristjáni Eldjárni Eldjárn 6. desember 1976.* Reykjavík, 1976. (pp. 130–44. English influence on Icelandic embroidery in the seventeenth century. English summary.)

Gamle islandske motiver til korssting. Copenhagen, 1965. (Old Icelandic designs for cross stitch. Introduction in Danish and English.)

Icelandic Embroidery. Domestic Embroideries in the National Museum of Iceland, Reykjavík, 1973.

"Icelandic Mediaeval Embroidery Terms and Techniques," *Studies in Textile History. In memory of Harold B. Burnham*, pp. 133–43. Toronto, 1977.

Islenzk sjónabók. Gömul munstur í nýjumbúningi : (Traditional Icelandic embroideries and patterns.) Reykjavík, 1964.

"Islenzkur dýrgripur í hollenzku safni," *Andvari:* (Icelandic altar frontal in a Dutch museum. English summary in offprint pp. 127–38). Reykjavík, 1962.

Saumakver. Íslenskar útsaumsgerðir (Icelandic embroidery techniques.) Reykjavík, 1975.

"Stafaklútar," *Húsfreyjan*, 28:3:25–7 (Samplers, particularly Icelandic ones. Offprint with mimeographed English summary.) 1977.

"Traditional Icelandic Embroidery," *The Bulletin of the Needle and Bobbin Club*, 47:4–31. 1963.

JÓNSDÓTTIR, Selma. "Gömul krossfestingarmynd," *Skímir.* (pp. 133–47. The relation of a medieval illumination to embroidered altar frontals. English summary.) Reykjavík, 1965.

KALF, E. J., "Een interessant borduursel in het Rijksmuseum Twenthe," *Textilhistorische Bijdragen*, 1:50–70. (An embroidered altar frontal from Iceland. English summary.) 1959.

THÓRDARSON, Matthías. "Islandsk folkekunst navnlig i 17. og 18. aarhundrede," *Nordisk kultur*, XXVII. (pp. 446–58. Folk art in Iceland, mainly in the seventeenth and eighteenth centuries.) Stockholm, 1931.

"Islands middelalderkunst," *Nordisk kultur*, XXVII. (pp. 324–45. Icelandic medieval art, including embroidered textiles.) Stockholm, 1931.

WANDEL, Gertie. "To broderede billedtœpper og deres islandske oprindelse," *Fra Nationalmuseets arbejdsmark*. (pp. 71–82, English translation, "Icelandic Origin of Two Embroideries," *Embroidery*, 15. 78–83, 1964. Reprinted from *Danish Handcraft Guild*, Vol. II, No. 1.). Copenhagen, 1941. *For Additional Illustrative Material on Icelandic Embroideries see the following:*

BLÖNDAL, Sigfússon, and Sigurdur Sigtryggsson. *Alt-Island im bilde*. Jena, 1930.
ELDJÁRN, Kristján. *Icelandic Art*. New York, (1960?).

Biographies

Aldyth Cadoux (Russia)
Aldyth Cadoux was educated at Manchester University, England (B.A. 1948) and after her marriage took a second degree (M.A. with Honors in Russian) at the University of Edinburgh. She taught Russian in Edinburgh, and was on the National Committee of the Association of Teachers of Russian. For many years she has cultivated an interest in the history and literature of needlework, especially lace and embroidery, and has an extensive collection of samples, tools and books. She has written reviews for the *Journal of the Association of Teachers of Russian* and for *Embroidery*.

Pamela Clabburn (Glossary)
Pamela Clabburn has worked as a lingère, dressmaker, embroiderer, conservator of textiles and teacher of all these activities. Until recently she was assistant keeper of social history at the City of Norwich Museum, where she had special responsibility for textiles.

Grace Rogers Cooper (United States)
Assistant and associate curator of the Division of Textiles, the Smithsonian Institution, from 1947–61, Mrs. Cooper was appointed curator in 1961, a position she held until her retirement in 1976. She was department editor and advisor on textiles to the *Eldjáni Eldjárn 6. desember 1976.* and was appointed textile consultant in 1973, a position she still holds in conjunction with a contract as Museum Consultant to advise the Smithsonian Institution, the Wisconsin Veterans Museum and various other museums in American textiles. She has written a number of books including *The Scholfield Wool-Carding Machines* (1959), *The Invention of the Sewing Machine* (1968) and *Thirteen-Star Flags: Keys to Identification* (1973; reprinted in paperback, 1976). She has contributed articles on a variety of textile subjects to *The Encyclopedia of Victoriana* (1975), *A Nation of Nations* (1976) and *The Dictionary of American History* (1976). Mrs. Cooper has also mounted a number of exhibitions on American textiles.

Hanne Frøsig Dalgaard (Denmark)
Since 1966, Hanne Frøsig Dalgaard has been a curator at the Danish Folk Museum, Copenhagen, in charge of the costume and textile collections. She was previously assistant curator at the Open Air Museum in Sorgenfri. The author of a book and several articles on Danish textiles, she has an M.A. degree from the University of Copenhagen.

Elsa E. Gudjónsson (Iceland)
Born in Reykjavík, Elsa Gudjónsson later studied at the University of Washington, Seattle, where she majored in clothing and textiles and took a Master of Arts degree.
Since the formation of the post in 1963, she has been Curator of Textiles in the National Museum of Iceland. Prior to this, in 1947, she planned and established the Department of Clothing and Textiles at the Icelandic Teachers' College where she lectured in textiles and embroidery for a number of years. A member of CIETA since 1962, Elsa Gudjónsson is on the editorial board of the quarterly *Húsfreyjan*, is a contributor to *Kulturhistorisk Leksikon for Nordisk Middelalder* and was a collaborator responsible for Icelandic terms on the textile vocabulary, *Nordisk Textilteknisk Terminologi* (1974).

Dr. Dora Heinz (Germany, Switzerland, Austria)
Dr. Dora Heinz studied Art History, History, Archaeology and Philosophy at Vienna University. Professor of Art History at Vienna University from 1949 to 1976, Dr. Heinz was also curator of the Textile Department of the Austrian Museum of Applied Art in Vienna.
She has written a number of books on many aspects of the history of textiles, including *Old Oriental Carpets* (1958), *Linz Vestments* (1962), *European Tapestries* (1963) and *Masterpieces of Baroque Textile Art* (1972). She has also contributed many articles to journals and exhibition catalogues.

Pauline Johnstone (Italy, Central Europe and South eastern Europe)
Pauline Johnstone has worked in the textile department of the Victoria and Albert Museum for the last eight years. She lectures on embroidery and her publications include *Greek Island Embroidery* (1961), *The Byzantine Tradition in Church Embroidery* (1967) and *A Guide to Greek Island Embroidery* (1972).

Anne Kjellberg (Norway)
Having studied weaving for several years, Anne Kjellberg took her M.A. degree at Oslo University in 1975 with Art History as her principal subject. Since 1970 she has worked at the Norwegian Folk Museum in Oslo, first as a research assistant and then as curator of the department of textiles. She has written articles on textiles and on medieval art.

Maria Clementina Carneiro de Moura (Portugal)
Educated at the Lisbon Fine Arts School, Maria Carneiro de Moura is a painter who has had a number of exhibitions of her work, and is also an expert on textiles. In 1946, she was commissioned to write *Traditional*

Embroideries of Portugal and, in 1966, *Castelo Branco Coverlets and Embroidery* which was also published in Lisbon. She has contributed a number of articles to periodicals, including articles on Peniche lace, rugs and embroideries in Portuguese folk art and Castelo Branco coverlets.

Gertrud Grenander Nyberg (Sweden)

A teacher of European ethnology, weaving and textile history, Dr. Grenander Nyberg has made a special study of folk art. She has worked in the provincial museums at Uppsala, Umeå and Västervik, and at the Nordic Museum in Stockholm, and she has written books and articles on weaving and embroidery.

Linda Parry (Great Britain)

After studying weaving, embroidery and art history at Liverpool College of Art and the Central School of Art and Design in London, Mrs. Parry worked for two years at the Birmingham Museum and Art Gallery. For the past six years she has been employed in the Department of Textiles and Dress at the Victoria and Albert Museum in London. She has contributed an article to the magazine *Apollo* on the subject of the tapestries of Burne-Jones.

Riitta Pylkkänen (Finland)

Until her retirement in 1975, Professor Pylkkänen was Director of the National Museum of Finland in Helsinki. Her major publications include books on Finnish renaissance and baroque costume and *The Use and Traditions of Mediaeval Rugs and Coverlets in Finland*, which appeared in 1974. She serves on the Costume Committee of the International Council of Museums.

Rosa Martín í Ros (Spain)

Dr. Martín í Ros, who graduated from the Central University of Barcelona in 1973 with an M.A. degree in the History of Art, is an editor of the history of art and costume section of the *Gran Enciclopedia Catalana*. She has worked for the publishers, Salvat, since 1974 and contributed to the periodicals *Destino* and *Estudios Pro Arte*; between 1975–6 she made a series of radio programs about Catalan artists of the nineteenth and twentieth centuries. A member of the International Council of Museums, Dr. Martín í Ros has been curator of the Textile Museum of Barcelona since 1976.

Monique Toury-King (France)

Assistant curator at the *Direction des Musées de France*, the *Musée des Beaux-Arts* in Grenoble and the *Musée des Thermes et de l'Hôtel de Cluny* in Paris from 1944 to 1960, Monique Toury-King has also been a *Conservateur des Musées de France* since 1970.

In collaboration with her husband, Donald King, Keeper of the Department of Textiles and Dress at the Victoria and Albert Museum, she translated *French Tapestry* by R. A. Weigert (1962) and wrote about a fifteenth-century tapestry depicting the story of Ahab in Fenway Court, Isabella Stewart Gardner Museum (1975). A catalogue of the textile collection of Waddesdon Manor, Buckinghamshire, England, is in the course of preparation. Mrs. King has also in the course of publication a chapter on the textile traditions of France which will be included in Vol. III of *Textile Collections of the World* (ed. Cecil Lubell).

Patricia Wardle (The Netherlands, Belgium)

Miss Wardle worked for ten years at the Victoria and Albert Museum in London, for much of that time as a research assistant in the Textiles and Dress Department where she specialized in embroidery and lace. In addition to numerous articles on embroidery and lace, her publications include a revised version of A. F. Kendrick's *English Needlework* (1967), *Victorian Lace* (1968) and the Victoria and Albert Museum *Guide to English Embroidery* (1970). She is now living in The Netherlands where she works as a translator in the field of art history.

Index

It has been impossible to index all the comments on every embroidery stitch described. We have indexed each stitch when it first appears and when it is illustrated. An entry "stitches" refers the reader to general comments on embroidery stitches. The glossary also defines each stitch and gives cross-references for stitches with several names.

Page numbers in *italics* indicate black-and-white illustrations. Plate references indicate color illustrations.